TRAIL GUIDE TO LEARNING

TO LEARNING

Paths of Exploration

- Volume One -

DEBBIE STRAYER & LINDA FOWLER

Trail Guide to Learning: Paths of Exploration - Volume 1

by Debbie Strayer and Linda Fowler

Published by Geography Matters, Inc.

2 Volume Set ISBN: 978-1-931397-61-2

Printed in the United States of America

Geography Matters, Inc.
800.426.4650
www.geomatters.com

Dedication

We dedicate this book to all those who have bravely chosen to follow the path that the Lord laid before them, in spite of the time, sacrifice and faith it took to do so. ~Debbie Strayer

This book is dedicated to all those who inspired it . . . and made it happen . . . but most especially to every mom who picks it up and breathes a sigh of relief. May it be a blessing to your family!   ~Linda Fowler

Acknowledgements

Debbie~

To my dear husband Greg, who has always put the Lord's plan for our family first in his life, and by doing so, liberated all of us to be obedient to the call of God and to be blessed for doing so. Thank you so much for being such an incredible example of devotion to the Lord. You are my sweet.

My amazing children Nate, Ashley and son-in-law Alex; Each of you has inspired me by your boldness to do what you felt the Lord has given you to do, and kept me going so many times during the journey with your love and faithfulness. Each of you has been given so many gifts and talents and you freely share them with others. No mother is more blessed than I.

My dear co-author Linda; what can I say. You are a gift to me from the Lord. Your wit, intelligence, insight, devotion and determination have kept me afloat so many times. God has blessed us with an amazing friendship, and for that, I am now and will always be truly grateful.

My publishers and newly added family, Josh and Cindy Wiggers; some relationships are born out of only common wishes or dreams. Ours was born out of divine direction, and came with the blessing of common hearts and common dreams. Thank you for making this dream come true for me, and I look forward to all the future holds for us together.

My dear mentor and friend, Dr. Ruth Beechick; though I have known you for many years, I always feel as though there is so much yet to learn from you. You have freely given of your heart and knowledge to me and I am truly grateful. I pray that I may carry on your gift to me in the years to come in a way that will be a blessing to you.

Linda~

Thank you, thank you, thank you to my amazing husband, Coke, for your unfailing support of this great adventure – evidenced daily by your uncanny ability to offer just the right encouragement and, maybe more importantly, to eat take-out with a smile.

Shout-outs also to my unique and quirky kids, both those birthed and those grafted (through marriage) -- Caleb, Cathryn, Betsy, Matt, Tracy, and Travis -- for being so wonderfully individual and creative, and for giving me a measure of understanding;

to the Wiggers clan – Cindy, Josh, Alex, and Ashley -- for attaching wings to this project and allowing it to fly far beyond our hopes, for hours and hours of oiling the "engine," and for literally keeping us out of the ditch;

and to my dear friend and cohort, Debbie, one of the most genuine and gifted people I know. Thank you, Deb, for rescuing me from the aimlessness of my empty nest, for having confidence in me, and for being the creative spark-plug that you just naturally are!

May the Lord bless and protect you all as you come and go, may He give you peace, and lavish His grace on all your efforts!

Table of Contents

Jamestown Unit

Pilgrim Unit

Appendix A

Lesson at a Glance

Skills and Topics Charts

Game Answer Keys

Appendix B

Columbus Games

Jamestown Games

Pilgrim Games

Preface

Why did we write the *Trail Guide to Learning Series*?

We wanted to create curriculum that was easy to use, yet able to lead students in developing higher thinking skills.

We wanted the things learned to come from real books, discussion, and a variety of activities so that students would enjoy the process.

We wanted information from different subject areas taught together in relationship to geography, as it occurs in real life.

We wanted students to become better communicators by learning and practicing language skills along with what they were learning, instead of through separate drill and practice. That way their drawing, writing, and speaking would be a natural response to their thinking and learning.

We wanted this book itself to be more than just a teacher's guide. We wrote it as a source of information for your student and a teacher's education course for you, giving you bite-sized and timely explanations of what we suggest you do, and why.

Lastly, we wanted to provide a way to strengthen a Biblical worldview.

It has taken years of labor and a team of workers, but we are excited to have met these goals in this first of the series, *Paths of Exploration*.

It is important for you to know who worked on it, because that helps explain why it is different from other curricula, and why you can have confidence when using it. The team of people who designed, wrote, read, edited, and supported this effort is impressive. It includes veteran home educators Greg and Debbie Strayer, Coke and Linda Fowler, Josh and Cindy Wiggers; young adults who were home educated Ashley (Strayer) Wiggers and her husband Alex Wiggers, and renowned home education author Dr. Ruth Beechick. We also highly valued the input of our "test driver" families, who used the curriculum with their children and gave us helpful feedback.

Why does all this matter? As we say in our Steps for Thinking,

> "The key to understanding the actions of
> others is to understand their thoughts."

If you know what our goals were, you will have a good starting point to use this curriculum to fit your own objectives for your students. When you look at the parts of the book you will see how easy it is to make your goals a reality.

Instructions

Paths of Exploration is divided into six units. The first three are found in Volume 1, and the second three in Volume 2:

- **Columbus**
- **Jamestown**
- **Pilgrims**
- **Daniel Boone**
- **Lewis and Clark**
- **Trails West**

Every unit contains six lessons with five parts. Each lesson is designed to take about a week—but you retain the freedom to make the curriculum's schedule fit the needs of your students. Because of this, even though one part can take one day, this curriculum is your servant, not your master.

Flexibility is built in, since every Lesson 6 completes the assignments for the unit and provides a time of review and assessment.

In addition, large parts of the lessons in Unit 6, Trails West, are devoted to review of the other units studied throughout the year.

Grade Levels

This curriculum targets grades 3, 4, and 5, but can be easily adapted for 2nd grade abilities by reducing reading assignments and substituting oral responses for written work. Likewise, 6th graders can be accommodated and challenged through increased reading and writing, and through the provided Enrichment Activities. In most assignments, the recommended activity levels are noted with icons: ᵞᵞ for the lowest, 👆 for higher, and 🐾 for highest. **If there is no icon (or trail marker) present, the activity is intended for all levels.**

Before beginning a lesson, look at the Materials List in Part 1 to be sure you have what you will need to complete the regular activities. In addition, every Part 5 contains additional resources for Enrichment Activities. Enrichment Activities are available for your older students (6th grade and up) who are completing the curriculum with you. Younger students who complete the lessons quickly, or who just enjoy learning on a more in-depth level, can use the Enrichment Activities as well.

Steps for Thinking

A typical lesson begins by introducing the Steps for Thinking. These are the big ideas demonstrated through the reading, discussion, and other activities of the lesson. Explain each step to your child and talk with him about any questions or ideas he has about it. You will revisit the Steps for Thinking at the end of each lesson, so don't require your student to understand them thoroughly at the beginning. By the end of the lesson, your student will have more experience with the concepts and be able to discuss them more thoroughly.

Grade level markings for assignments throughout the curriculum represent:

ᵞᵞ 3rd grade
👆 4th grade
🐾 5th grade

Enrichment Activites:

- 6th grade and up
- advanced students
- all students wanting to learn more

Answers and Appendices

Answers to the questions asked in the text and the Student Notebook are located on the last page of each lesson. Each Volume has two Appendices. In Volume 1, Appendix A contains teacher aides that include an At-A-Glance guide for each lesson in that volume, charts and references helpful to the lessons, instructions for various games assigned in the text, and answers for those games. Appendix B contains the games themselves and the Reading Log. In Volume 2, Appendices C and D correspond to the same descriptions.

Lesson Contents

Here is an in-depth description of each section in a typical lesson, and how to use it. After you read this and begin using the curriculum, there are many margin notes in the text to remind you of the important points contained here.

A. Copywork/Dictation

Copywork and dictation provides a consistent method for students to see, hear, and write language correctly. It is the first step in learning language skills. Start your student with copying the passage. It may take more than one day for your student to complete copying or dictation assignments, which is perfectly appropriate. This means that you will be using only two passages per week until, and for awhile after, he begins to experience success. When he is comfortable with the shorter assignments, gradually increase the length of his copywork or dictation, being careful to safeguard his sense of achievement. Meeting your child's individual need to successfully complete the assignment is more important than for him to rush to keep up with a suggested schedule. After copying, he should match what he has written word for word to the text, and correct anything that is not the same. This level is appropriate for many second and third graders throughout the year. It may also be appropriate for older students, and needs to continue for as long as your student seems sufficiently challenged. From time to time, you may want to attempt a bit of dictation by asking your child to choose a sentence himself to write from dictation. Allow him to choose a sentence or passage that he has already worked with, to build confidence. Don't worry, this isn't cheating. Your goal is to build the ability to read and write language, and teaching means providing the support needed to be successful. Assessment should come later.

If your student is a fourth or fifth grader, evaluate his level when he has copied the passages a few times and decide whether this activity seems too easy for him. If so, try dictating, or speaking, the first few words of the sentence slowly, and ask your student to write down what he hears. If he can write down at least a portion of the words correctly, then he is ready for dictation. The ability to write from dictation is a skill that must learned. It may be difficult at first, so give your student the help he needs. Allow him to become familiar with the sentence, or sentences, you dictate at first. You may even want to let him choose the sentence. After he is very successful at writing from dictation using this method, gradually start adding a few words of your choice. Remember that success is your goal, not quickly moving to more difficult dictation passages. Going through the process too quickly without allowing your student the time to become successful and confident may create resistance towards this type of language learning.

Another common problem, especially for younger students, is the struggle with handwriting. Before beginning the copywork and dictation process, your student needs to know how to form each letter. If handwriting is very frustrating and difficult for him, try different writing tools and surfaces. If he continues to experience difficulty, it is perfectly acceptable to allow your child to type the passages. This is also a good approach for the older student who prefers typing to handwriting. The goal is for your student to see the words, hear the words, and write the words. Remember that it is more important for him to learn the spelling mechanics and reading skills that result from dictation and copying than it is to handwrite the passage.

B. Reader

The natural method of learning continues in this section with the Reader assignments. These assignments occur in real literature, and there are several reasons why this is important. Real literature is more interesting. The language used is more natural. A willingness to read is built as your students experience the success of reading a real book.

Younger students are instructed to read their assignments aloud. The purpose for this is to build reading fluency. Fluency, or the ability to read something effortlessly, is also an important part of comprehension. If a student can read a passage aloud with expression, correct phrasing, and attention to punctuation, it is much more likely that he will also understand the meaning of the passage. To practice fluency at all levels, use passages that students can read without constant decoding. In other words, start with a few sentences that seem easy to read. Often, you can have them choose the passages for fluency practice, and sometimes you can select them in order to gauge their growth. To do this, find a passage that is a sentence or two longer than the last one they read, or one that contains structures requiring attention to punctuation, such as dialogue. Real books are perfect for this fluency practice. Artificial fluency practice is unnecessary when literature provides such an abundant source of reading materials.

Each Reader is coordinated with the unit, and provides a ready-made history lesson. The lives of real people become linked to places and events. In turn, this connection brings character and convictions to light, as well as great adventures and drama. From the wellspring of literature, examples of mechanics and word usage come, as well as phonics principles, spelling patterns, and vocabulary.

Every student is to read or listen to **both** literature selections for the unit. Reading or hearing the two perspectives adds richness to the stories and depth to the understanding of the events and circumstances of the times. Critical thinking skills build as the two related stories allow students to compare and contrast to find similarities and differences. An artist's illustrations contribute to learning about context clues, and the divisions of chapters and paragraphs help students recognize important main ideas and details that support the bigger ideas. All of these lessons come naturally from real books.

C. Read-Aloud, Discussion, Narration, and Reflective Writing

Most parents agree that it is good to read aloud to young children to develop pre-reading skills. However, the benefits don't stop there. Reading aloud to children of all ages is one of the easiest, most enjoyable, and effective ways to share ideas and begin thoughtful conversations. Since students do not have to worry about decoding during read-aloud time, they can focus totally on the meaning of what they are hearing. This allows them the opportunity to think about the ideas and information being presented, and to formulate their own thoughts. It prepares them to respond to what they have heard through discussion, retelling, or reflective writing. These skills form a natural way for teachers to see what their students have understood from passages read aloud.

Read-Aloud. As you read aloud, you also model fluency, expression, and comprehension. When your voice reflects punctuation, students can see its purpose and the way it makes the passage more understandable. As they listen and sometimes follow along with their eyes, students see the language and hear it read correctly, which provides an excellent example for their own reading. Because of this, Read-Aloud assignments are an important part of each lesson.

Discussion and Narration. Read-Aloud assignments also provide the basis for student responses. As they listen, it is natural for them to respond by speaking, which is a good first step toward meaningful discussion. In the give-and-take of discussion, you can listen to your student's understanding of the passage, ask questions, and share your thoughts. All of these combine to expand their thinking on the topic. It also lends itself to the natural memory practice of narration, or retelling. As students become familiar with the process of retelling, their ability to recall main ideas and details develops.

Reflective Writing. The last step in the process of response is that of writing. Reflective writing involves having students respond to a passage they have heard by writing their thoughts about it. This is the most complex way for students to respond to what they have heard, yet it is a very concrete way to begin using writing to answer questions. The answers that students give are correct because they come from their thoughts and understanding of what they have heard.

D. Word Study

The Word Study section exists to equip students with strategies to gain meaning from unknown or unfamiliar words. This information must be connected to other learning in order to remain with children on a long term basis. So the best time to teach them about phonics, word usage, mechanics, vocabulary, spelling, and grammar is when they read a word or hear it used in a story. Study of a sound or word form is natural and makes sense to students when they see a need to read, understand, and use that word. Word Study activities occur in every lesson, taking advantage of the opportunities presented in the literature to connect meaning and structure for your students.

Vocabulary is a focus of this curriculum as students make and collect cards with words and meanings listed. The purpose of this activity is not memorization or dictionary skills, but understanding. By building an awareness of new or unusual words, you are teaching your students an important strategy for understanding what they have read or heard. New vocabulary words appear in the context of a lesson or story, which helps students recognize the connection between the way a word is used and its meaning. This is an important reading strategy called using context clues. As children complete the vocabulary activities in this curriculum, they see the importance of learning and using new words as they read, write, discuss, and retell.

Spelling is a skill that has several components, such as perceptual ability and memory. Some of us are naturally good at spelling, and some are not. The goal of the spelling assignments is to improve your students' ability to spell by helping them make connections to meaning, phonics, and word patterns. Memorizing a list is not as valuable to students as increasing their ability to comfortably write words that express their understanding and opinions. The goal then, is to increase their ability to recognize and spell more words correctly—not just to be able to spell a new word correctly for a week or two and then forget it.

E. Geography, Science, and History

Making connections are an important part of this curriculum. The studies of Geography, Science, and History are connected. The knowledge of one area contributes to knowledge in the other areas. By considering the linkage of subjects in real life, connections occur naturally for the students. This helps them add to what they know when they encounter new information. It also helps students remember what they have learned.

Geography is the umbrella from which the other studies connect. Geography includes the study of places. If you learn about places, you learn about the impact those places have on people. If you learn about people, you learn about cultures and worldviews, and the impact those people have on places. So in the study of geography, you naturally learn about people, places, and all the ways they affect each other. All culture, history, and science connect to concepts of geography, so we study Science and History in the light of their connection to the people and places encountered by the explorers and their paths.

Science is naturally enjoyable to children through the study of nature. Following the practices of Charlotte Mason, we help the student gain skills that allow access to more information about nature and its connection to people and places. Observing, recording through drawing and describing, discussing, evaluating, and connecting new information to previously learned concepts are the core of the Science instruction. This curriculum also uses reading as a means of obtaining more information that is useful to your student, since reading about topics is just as valuable in learning science as doing activities.

History is a daily part of the curriculum through literature readings, discussions and activities. The study of history that focuses on dates and facts alone can be dry and hard to remember. When events in history are associated through the literature, the geography, and the relevant science concepts, it connects the learning and is much more likely to be retained. Great stories and biographies help students connect to the struggles and triumphs of the times. Literature provides a basis for discussion and evaluation of the decisions made and the results that occurred. Books read by the student, and read aloud by the teacher, provide the thread that ties the events, discoveries, and decisions of the explorers together. Learning history could not be more natural.

F. Writing, Drawing, Art, and Doing

Learning new things should inspire a response. Since we are not limited to conventional school-type methods, we can employ an array of effective and enjoyable ways of gaining and responding to information.

Writing is an integrated part of this curriculum. It is not a separate subject, but rather a set of skills with which to become familiar. Writing ability improves with practice and time, both of which come in the context of literature, history, science, and geography learning. Writing is best when it is a response to content learned, new ideas, or as a result of an activity or experience. Since writing begins with thinking, once your student engages in assigned thinking activities, the way is naturally prepared. As you use this approach, your student will begin to see himself as a writer, which is the first and most important step to becoming a writer.

Drawing was used by scientists for many years to record new information. It was also a tool used by explorers to communicate what they encountered with others. As your students develop the important skill of drawing, they will naturally build their power to observe and notice detail. This, in turn, equips them to communicate what they learn more effectively. Combining what your students see with what they know builds powerful thinking skills. Use of the *North American Wildlife Guide* also develops the ability to research and compare what they notice to what others have seen. Not to mention the fact that drawing is fun! Experts like Barry Stebbing and Sharon Jeffus help your child develop needed skills to observe and draw successfully.

Doing something is a powerful teacher. Students gain the ability to sequence and organize what they do, and think through the activities that are included in this curriculum. The *Handbook of Nature Study* and the *1911 Boy Scouts Handbook* offer time-tested, effective, and enjoyable ways to gain skills and information through activities. Motivation is a key component of successful learning, and our Doing activities certainly help keep motivation strong. Since connecting learning to doing is an important part of this curriculum, these activities illustrate that important connection and provide the basis for authentic writing activities.

G. Independent Reading

This is an important part of each student's daily schedule. It provides regular practice for word study and reading skills, as well as time for practice of thinking skills. Quiet time to consider ideas and tie new information with old is essential in building new understandings. Though you may be tempted to skip this activity to save time, please don't! Completing the reading log each day also gives your students a sense of accomplishment, as well as some time to work independently.

Student Notebook

The Student Notebook is not only a vital part of the curriculum, but it also provides a **portfolio** of your student's work. Maps, charts, and other activities assigned in the textbook are included in an easy, ready-to-use format for the student. In lower level notebooks, copywork passages are located directly next to the space for writing, for ease of copying and checking.

Having the Student Notebook on CD allows you to print all the pages for your child's level either before you begin a unit, or lesson by lesson. We suggest that students keep their notebooks in a three-ring binder, which allows them to add or remove pages as needed. For example, if students complete an art project on construction paper it can easily be dated, 3-hole punched, and inserted in the notebook at the appropriate place. If they would rather complete their copywork assignment on different paper, or remove the pages provided to make writing easier, they can do so. Unit games can be cut out of the book and laminated or printed separately on cardstock for greater durability. Unit games printed on cardstock are also available as a separate item for your convenience. (See Resources) All in all, you and your students have the flexibility to adapt the notebook to your individual needs.

How can you begin to transfer the responsibility for completing assignments from yourself to your student? Daily checklists are included in the Student Notebook to ease this process. Students have a ready-made task list to guide and direct their efforts, and the teacher can tell at a glance what needs to be done. This checklist system encourages students to take responsibility for their daily work, and allows them to be easily accountable for assignments.

A portfolio is often the best possible written measure of student achievement. Completion of the Student Notebook creates an excellent, consecutive record of student work in reading, writing, geography, history, science, and art. The Student Notebook gives teacher, student, and evaluator a clear picture of sequential progress in each subject area, samples of student work, and examples of creative projects. It includes dates assignments were completed, assisting with the documentation process. This helps teachers to see time spent on each unit, as well as giving students a sense of accomplishment as they look over the finished product.

Print the Student Notebook pages directly from the CD-ROM that came with this book. Or if you prefer, printed notebooks are also available separately. (See Resources)

Supportive Resources

Assessments

For those who prefer not to use the portfolio method of evaluation, or who want to supplement their child's portfolio, **assessments** for each level of the first five units are available on a separate CD. These, coupled with your daily observations and interactive discussions and games, provide ample material upon which to base an accurate evaluation. There is no assessment for Unit 6, Trails West, since this unit is largely devoted to review of the previous five. The review activities serve as evaluation tools themselves, and can be assigned point values if you choose.

Light for the Trail **Bible Curriculum**

This optional Bible curriculum helps your students make the most important connection of all - the one between their faith and their view of the world around them. This easy-to-use guide provides daily assignments which include memory verses for the week, discussion topics, writing assignments and longer-term memory projects. These elements blend with Prayer Times, Worship Times and Blazing the Trail (teacher sharing) to enable students to make real-life connections between the content of the curriculum and the lessons of scripture.

Required Resource List

The following materials are required for use with *Paths of Exploration*. For ordering information see Resources at the back of the book.

Volume 1

Meet Christopher Columbus by James T. de Kay
Christopher Columbus by Bennie Rhodes
Stories of the Pilgrims by Margaret Pumphrey (2nd Edition, Christian Liberty Press)
Stories of the Pilgrims Answer Key
Squanto, Friend to the Pilgrims by Clyde Robert Bulla
A Lion to Guard Us by Clyde Robert Bulla
Surviving Jamestown: The Adventures of Young Sam Collier by Gail Karwoski
*Profiles from History by Ashley Strayer Wiggers
*Handbook of Nature Study by Anna Comstock
*North American Wildlife Guide published by Reader's Digest
*Eat Your Way Around the World by Jamie Aramini
*Intermediate World Atlas published by Rand Mc Nally
RealEarth® GlobeMap™
*Large-Scale U.S. and World Outline Maps
Student Notebook pages (printed from CD-ROM included or available separately)

Volume 2

Daniel Boone, Frontiersman by Janet and Geoff Benge
Daniel Boone, Young Hunter & Tracker by Augusta Stevenson
Munford Meets Lewis and Clark by Jamie Aramini
Seaman: The Dog Who Explored the West with Lewis and Clark by Gail Karwoski
Trouble for Lucy by Carla Stevens
Johnny Appleseed by David Collins
1911 Boy Scout Handbook
United States History Atlas
Lewis & Clark Hands On by Sharon Jeffus (©2009, Geography Matters)
Going West!: Journey on a Wagon Train to Settle a Frontier Town, a Kaleidoscope Kids book
Student Notebook pages (printed from CD-ROM included or available separately)

*Used with both Volume 1 and 2

Optional Supportive Resources - available on CD ROM

The following materials are valuable aids, but not required to complete the curriculum.

Paths of Exploration Assessments
Light for the Trail Bible Supplement

Lesson 1, Part 1

> ### ❧ Steps for Thinking ❧
>
> 1. Journeys are made for a reason.
>
> 2. Knowing the reason for a journey helps you understand the decisions people make along the way.
>
> 3. Planning ahead and making preparations are essential for a successful journey.

The **Steps for Thinking** section gives you the main ideas about the topics presented. Understanding these helps you to have productive discussions with your children so they, too, understand the bigger ideas. This forms more permanent learning, contrary to just learning facts, which tends to be temporary. These steps are useful prior to instruction, and they are also useful for review at the end of the week.

❧ Materials ❧

- *Meet Christopher Columbus*
- *Christopher Columbus*
- *Intermediate World Atlas*
- *Eat Your Way Around the World*
- Student Notebook
- Globe
- Crayons or Colored Pencils
- Paste
- Thesaurus
- Dictionary
- Birthday Pictures
- Yellow Highlighter or Crayon
- Index Cards or Paper
- Graph Paper
- Magazines, Newspapers, etc.
- Large world outline map

Additional resources for Enrichment Activities are found in Part 5.

𝒜. Copywork/Dictation   *Language Skills*

Look at the first stanza from the poem "A Journey of Adventure." Silently read the passage and point out any words that you don't know. Now, read the passage aloud to your teacher, or ask her to read it to you. This is a poem about the experiences of exploring.

A Journey of Adventure

The walls of the mightiest fortress,
The wake of a ship on the sea,
Charts lead to the busiest seaports,
Trails light up the paths of the free.

🐾 Copy the first stanza of "A Journey of Adventure" into your Student Notebook. When you are finished, compare your copy to the model (word by word) and make any needed corrections.

🐾 Listen as your teacher dictates the passage above, and write it in your Student Notebook. When you are finished, compare your copy to the model and make any needed corrections.

🐾 Carefully read and then copy, or write as your teacher dictates, paragraph 4 (starting with "Walking home…") on page 4 of Rhodes' *Christopher Columbus*. When you are finished, compare your copy to the text and make any needed corrections.

𝒜. Copywork and dictation assignments go from an easier level (designated by 🐾) to harder levels (designated by 🐾 and 🐾). Take two days for the copywork if that is more comfortable for your child. Please adapt instructions to your child's individual needs. Your child should be **consistently successful** at one level before progressing to the next, **regardless of grade**.

ℬ. Reader   *Language Skills, Thinking Skills, History*

In your book, *Meet Christopher Columbus,* read pages 1 and 2 aloud.

🐾 Read one or two paragraphs in your read-aloud book, *Christopher Columbus.*

🐾 Read one or two pages from today's read-aloud assignment in *Christopher Columbus.*

C. Discussion is very important in developing your child's ability to organize his thoughts. This in turn builds the ability to think and write. The goal of the discussion questions is not just to find the answer to a particular question, but also to create a situation where thoughts about the question and its answer are shared and considered in a detailed way. Do not rush this activity, but encourage your student to share his or her ideas relating to the topic, and any additional ideas that may come to mind. You can also share your thoughts and questions as an example for your students.

C. **Read-Aloud and Discussion**   *Language Skills, Thinking Skills, Writing*

In *Christopher Columbus*, listen as your teacher reads pages 1–6 aloud.

Listen to your teacher read the story and the following discussion question. Think about what you know from the story, and answer in your own words. Give any examples you can think of that help show your answer.

Discussion Question: What do you think Christopher Columbus' dream was when he was a young boy?

D. **Word Study**   *Spelling, Phonics, Vocabulary*

Three words in the poem spell the long *i* sound with the letters *igh*. These three letters say the long *i* sound. On the list in your Student Notebook, use a red crayon or marker to underline the letters *igh* in each of the words, then read the words for your teacher.

sigh	high	thigh
night	light	might
bright	fright	flight
fight	right	sight

You can use these words as your spelling words for this lesson. Practice by spelling them aloud to your teacher or writing them on a chalkboard or dry erase board.

See how many of your spelling words you can fit into one long, silly sentence. Write your sentence.

The prefix *un* means not. The word in your read-aloud passage (paragraph 4, page 4 in *Christopher Columbus*) that has the prefix *un* is "uncharted." This means not charted. Think of a list of six other words that start with the prefix *un* and tell what each word means. Write your words in your Student Notebook.

Find Genoa, Italy, on the map. Genoa is a port city. Find Venice, Italy, and Palermo, Italy, on the map. They are also port cities.

Write what you think a port is in your Student Notebook. Now read the definition of the word "port" in a dictionary. Did your definition include the important parts of the meaning?

Do you know of any port cities near you? Can you think of any port cities in the United States?[1]

E. Geography

Science

A **compass** is a device that tells us where north is, no matter where we are. The picture below is a **compass rose.** It is found on the face of a compass.

There are four major directions. They are north, south, east, and west. Directions are very important when you travel because they tell you which way to go. Without directions, it would be impossible to find places on a map or to use roads that are new to you.

Directions always stay the same. When you go north, you are always going toward the North Pole. Find the North Pole on your globe. (It is at the very top.)

When you travel south, you are always going toward the South Pole. Find the South Pole on your globe. (You will find it at the bottom.)

The sun always rises in the east, and always sets in the west.

With the help of your parent or teacher, find out where the sun rises when you are in your house or at school. That direction is generally east. The farther north from the equator you live, the more to the southeast it actually is, but for now you can call it east.

After you find east, you will be able to find north. Follow these directions:

Stand facing east (where the sun came up.) Hold your left arm straight out to your side. Your left arm is pointing to the north.

D. The small superscript numbers that appear after some of the questions in this unit refer to answers found in the answer key, located immediately after Part 5.

E. Each word in bold letters is considered a vocabulary word. It is a word that may or may not be new to your child. You can write these vocabulary words on index cards and use them for occasional review, but not for memorizing. Give the child the meaning of the words if he doesn't remember. Try to use the new vocabulary words during conversation, and encourage your students to do the same.

Each time your student makes a vocabulary card for this unit, have him write a "C" (for Columbus) in the upper left corner. This will make it possible to review vocabulary by unit at the end of the year.

Write the word "North" on a card or piece of paper. Put it on the wall that is on the north side of your house or room.

Fill in the compass rose in your Student Notebook with the main directions of north, south, east, and west. The north compass point is the one pointing up. The south compass point is pointing down. The east compass point is pointing to the right, or this way ➜, and the west compass point is pointing to the left, or this way ⬅ .

Add the intermediate directions.

Northeast (the point between north and east)
Northwest (the point between north and west)
Southeast (the point between south and east)
Southwest (the point between south and west)

Notice the words north or south come at the beginning of each intermediate direction.

F. Writing   *Thinking Skills*

Listen carefully as your teacher rereads pages 5 and 6 in *Christopher Columbus,* focusing on the part that tells about Christopher's birthday.

In your Student Notebook list the things that happened on his birthday.[2]

Together with your teacher, make a list of words or phrases that tell what happened on your birthday. You may want to look at pictures from your birthday so you can remember.

Reread the list of things in our story that happened on Christopher's birthday. Tell what things were the same as your birthday. What things were different?

Fill in the two lists in your Student Notebook telling about Christopher's birthday and your birthday. Fill in the third list with the things that are the same in the two lists. Use words or phrases.

On the Venn diagram in your Student Notebook, fill in the two lists telling about Christopher's birthday and your birthday. Now fill in the third list, in the middle, with the things that are the same in both lists.

G. Independent Reading

Choose something to read that you will enjoy. Find a quiet, comfortable place and read for the following length of time:

20 minutes

G. Reading fluency is developed through having frequent silent reading opportunities that continue for the length of time suggested here. Since a primary focus of this activity is to nurture your child's enjoyment of reading, help him to choose reading material that interests him and is at a level that allows him to read with understanding by himself. You can incorporate this activity into your school day whenever it is most convenient.

If the suggested length of time is too long for your child to continue reading by himself, start with an amount of time he can accomplish successfully and make the suggested time a goal.

🐾 25 minutes

🐾 30 minutes

Over time, it's fun to see how much you have read. Be sure to write down what you read today on the Reading Log in your Student Notebook.

⁂

Lesson 1, Part 2

A. **Copywork/Dictation**   *Language Skills, Thinking Skills*
Silently read the second stanza of the poem "A Journey of Adventure." Show your teacher any words that you don't know, and practice reading them aloud. Now, read this stanza aloud to your teacher, or ask her to read it to you.

A Journey of Adventure

To the east or the west where the compass rose points,
A bazaar of strange foods we shall see.
To the north or the south as the map shows the signs,
We'll follow the road's decree.

🐾🐾 Copy the lines from the second stanza into your Student Notebook When you are finished, compare your copy to the model (word by word) and make any needed corrections.

🐾 Listen as your teacher dictates the passage above, and write it in your Student Notebook. When you are finished, compare your copy to the model and make any needed corrections.

🐾 Carefully read and then copy, or write as your teacher dictates, paragraph 2 on page 8 of Rhodes' *Christopher Columbus*. When you are finished, compare your copy to the text and make needed corrections.

B. **Reader**   *Language Skills*
Read pages 3 and 4 in *Meet Christopher Columbus* aloud.

🐾 Read one or two paragraphs in your read-aloud book, *Christopher Columbus*.

🐾 Read one or two pages from today's read-aloud assignment in *Christopher Columbus*.

A. The dictation method enables your child to hear language and correctly write down what he hears. It involves building two different skills. First, the ability to listen and understand what is heard, and second, the ability to transfer what is heard into written language. This process takes time and practice, so begin as gradually as needed for successfully reaching the goal of getting the words the child hears on the paper correctly. 1) Read the whole passage, then reread one sentence at a time, giving your child time to write what he hears. 2) After he has finished, reread the passage again, allowing him to double check what he has written. 3) Then proceed to the step of comparing his writing to the model. As his skill builds, you can move more quickly through the steps, maintaining your child's level of success.

C. The skill of narration is gained over time. If your child has never retold a story, start with the assignment for the lower level, no matter what grade he is in. Work up from there, being careful to allow him to stay at the level of success for a while before going to a longer section.

C. Read-Aloud and Narration

Language Skills, Thinking Skills

Listen carefully as your teacher reads pages 6–10 aloud from Rhodes' *Christopher Columbus.*

To **narrate** means to retell. In your own words, tell what happened in your assigned passage below. Try to remember as many details as possible. Listen carefully as your teacher reads (or rereads) the part you are to retell.

Last paragraph on page 4 and top of page 5 in read-aloud book.

Paragraph 3 on page 5, and paragraph 1 on page 6 in read-aloud.

Paragraph 2 on page 6 and paragraph 3 on page 7 in read-aloud.

D. Word Study

Spelling, Phonics

Reread your list of spelling words and see if you can spell them without looking.

sigh	high	thigh
fight	light	night
right	sight	might
bright	fright	flight

Find the spelling words that fit these clues and write them in your Student Notebook.[3]

I am dark and come after daytime. Who am I?

I am not down low. I am up. Who am I?

I am not a good thing for you to do with someone else. Who am I?

I am not on your left side, I am on the other side. Who am I?

I am what the sun brings each day. Who am I?

I am a trip on an airplane. Who am I?

After you find the spelling words that fit the above clues, you will have six words left over. Make up your own clues for three of those words, and write them in your Student Notebook.

Usually to make a word tell us that something has already happened, we add *ed* to the end, like these words:

talk — talked

play — played

Sometimes the entire word changes to show that something has already happened, like:

take — took

see — saw

Find the words in today's read-aloud (page 8 of *Christopher Columbus*) that tell us the following things already happened, and write them in your Student Notebook.

kneel _____　　come _____

sit _____　　know _____

The word *strange* is used in the poem and in the first paragraph on page 4 of *Meet Christopher Columbus*. What two things were described as strange?[4] Tell what you think strange means. Look in a thesaurus to find a synonym, or word that means the same thing, for *strange*. Write it in your Student Notebook.

🐾 Look at the end of page 3 through page 4 in *Meet Christopher Columbus*. Make a list in your Student Notebook of the countries Columbus visited bordering the Mediterranean Sea.[5] Then tell where he went outside of the Mediterranean.[6] Look at the map of the Mediterranean Sea on the Europe Political Map in the *Intermediate World Atlas*. Trace with your finger and tell the route he would have to take to get to England.[7]

E. Geography

Thinking Skills

A **bazaar** is a market held in an open area. The word refers especially to marketplaces found in Middle Eastern countries like Egypt, Israel, Turkey, and Iraq. Many explorers wanted to visit bazaars so they could bring new things back to sell in their own countries. Bazaars had many colorful items for sale such as food, spices, cloth, jewelry, and sometimes animals. Does a bazaar sound like a strange kind of place to you?

A bazaar may sound a little like a flea market. Have you ever been to a flea market? Was it like a bazaar?

Where is your favorite place to go shopping? What do you think people would notice if they went to your favorite store for the first time?

Think about a trip to your favorite store. Imagine seeing at least two things, hearing at least two things, and touching at least two things. Try to describe what you saw, heard, and touched while you were shopping. Write about your imaginary trip to the store in your Student Notebook or tell your teacher about it and ask her to write it down for you.

F. Art

Many things in a bazaar or a market are made by hand. Items sold in each market reflect what the people who live in that area like to make. In North Africa, beautiful cloth and rugs are made by the people. The pictures on the next page show examples of rugs from

D. When using the Europe Political Map in the *Intermediate World Atlas*, England may be a little difficult for your child to identify. Be sure to point out that England is part of the United Kingdom.

E. If your child is a reluctant writer, he can dictate his answer to you and then copy the answer that you have written down. If your child gets upset about making a mistake in his writing, have him write his answer on a sheet of scratch paper. You can check to make sure it is correct and then he can copy his answer into his notebook.

F. The pictures of North African rugs are shown courtesy of Sharon Jeffus and Jamie Aramini from their book *Geography through Art.*

North Africa. Look at them carefully, and then design your own rugs on the graph paper found in your Student Notebook. Notice how important lines and designs are in the rugs. You can also add color to your designs. Try making some other things that might be found in a bazaar or market, such as hand-made clothing, pottery, jewelry, or special foods. There are recipes from Egypt and Morocco in the cookbook *Eat Your Way Around the World* by Jamie Aramini.

G. See Independent Reading note in Part 1.

G. Independent Reading
Choose something to read that you will enjoy. Find a quiet, comfortable place and read for the following length of time:

🐾 20 minutes

🐾 25 minutes

🐾 30 minutes

Be sure to write down what you read today on the Reading Log in your Student Notebook.

Lesson 1, Part 3

A. **Copywork/Dictation**   *Language Skills*
Silently read the third stanza from the poem, "A Journey of Adventure." Point out any words you don't know and practice them with your teacher. Now, read the poem aloud, or ask your teacher to read it to you. Practice reading the verse aloud.

A. See Copywork/Dictation note in Part 1.

A Journey of Adventure

A journal they write gives us faraway sight;
The fame of their travels leads on.
From Cathay to Venice to points on the way,
The steps of the Polos are drawn.

Copy the third stanza into your Student Notebook. When you are finished, compare your copy to the model (word by word) and make any needed corrections.

Listen as your teacher dictates the passage above, and write it in your Student Notebook. When you are finished, compare your copy to the model and make any needed corrections.

Carefully read and then copy, or write as your teacher dictates, paragraph 2 on page 12 of *Christopher Columbus*. When you are finished, compare your copy to the model and make any needed corrections.

B. **Reader**   *Language Skills*
Read pages 5–7 in *Meet Christopher Columbus* aloud.

Read one or two paragraphs in your read-aloud book, *Christopher Columbus*.

Read one or two pages from today's read-aloud assignment in *Christopher Columbus*.

C. **Read-Aloud and Discussion**   *Language Skills*
Listen carefully as your teacher reads pages 11–15 from *Christopher Columbus* aloud.

C. See Discussion note in Part 1.

Discussion: Bartholomew and Christopher were caught in a storm. Describe the storm and how it affected the boat they were in. What effect do you think the storm had on the brothers?

D. **Word Study**   *Spelling, Phonics, Vocabulary*
Syllables are the parts of a word. Words can be made up of one syllable or many syllables. A syllable is a part of a word that we read or hear when we say the word. Read these examples, or listen as your teacher reads them aloud:

One syllable—dog, hat, on, big, the

Two syllables—into, before, after, happy, sister

Three syllables—afternoon, basketball, grandmother

Sometimes it is helpful to find syllables by clapping each time you hear a new sound when you say a word. For instance, if you use this method with the word *before*, you'll say *be* (clap) *fore* (clap.) Or try putting the back of your hand under your chin so that your fingers are lightly touching it, and say a word slowly. Notice how many times your chin slightly moves your hand. Practice by saying the above words.

Find at least three words from the poem that have one syllable.
Find at least two words that have two syllables.
Find one word that has three syllables.

Write all of these words in your Student Notebook under the correct heading.

Practice the words in your word study list from Part 1.

The prefix *re* means to do something again. In the read-aloud, Christopher loses his footing and has to regain it. *Regain* means to gain his footing again. Make a list of at least six words that start with the prefix *re* and write them in your Student Notebook. To help you, think of things you can do again, like *review*.

There are several words in the passage you copied today that tell us just how hard the situation was for Christopher and his brother. Good writers don't add words that are not needed. They just choose words that make the meaning clear. Make a list of words or phrases from the passage that tell what it was like.[8] The first word could be *afraid*.

E. Geography   *History, Thinking Skills*

As a young boy, Christopher Columbus heard about the travels of an explorer named Marco Polo. Marco Polo had traveled from Italy to China and written about it in a book. His journey took him a long time. He traveled through the countries of Europe to China. He brought back many wonderful things from China such as spices, silk, and gold. The people in Europe liked these things very much and wanted more of them. There were many obstacles to going over land like Marco Polo traveled, so people tried to think of another way to get there.

Christopher Columbus thought that he had the answer to this problem. He studied several books, including the Bible, and felt that the answer was to cross the Ocean Sea, which we now know as the Atlantic Ocean, to get to China. When he looked at the **globe** that was used at that time, this seemed like a very good idea. A globe is used to show what the earth looks like. It is a model of the earth. The globe that Christopher Columbus used was very different from globes today, because at that time the Europeans did not know about all the land that is on the earth. The only land they knew about was where their explorers had already been, and had written about so others would know.

A globe is a **sphere,** or ball, that shows us what the earth looks like. You can see what part is land and what part is water. The land on a globe is usually green, brown, orange, or other colors. The water on a globe is almost always blue. If you look at a picture of a globe, it looks like a circle. If you see or hold a globe, you can tell that it is a sphere, not a circle. Here are some other things that are spheres: baseballs, marbles, and basketballs. You may be able to find more spheres around your house. Remember, spheres are round, so a football would not be a sphere.

Look at your globe. If you are using the RealEarth®GlobeMap™ that came with these lessons, you will notice that it is not actually a sphere, because it is not round. Instead, it is a shape with 24 sides. This is because it has to be folded up. But it is still a map of the earth's surface and you can use it like a globe. Set your globe on the table with the white part called Antarctica on the bottom. Look at the top part of your globe. In that section is an area called Europe. In Europe, you will find an orange drawing (only if using the GlobeMap™) of a country called Spain. This is where Christopher Columbus lived. Turn your globe until you find a large yellow country called China. This is where Columbus wanted to go. Take your finger and show a path to get from Spain to China over land. It only took you a few seconds to do this, but it took travelers years to make that journey in Columbus' time.

E. Political boundaries and the names of countries in various parts of the world can change suddenly. This fact makes it difficult for maps and globes to guarantee accuracy beyond their publication date. For this reason, you may find some inaccuracies in mapping and labeling on the RealEarth® GlobeMap™. These are relatively minor and do not affect globe study in this unit.

Turn your globe back to Spain. Take your finger and go out into the blue water of the Atlantic Ocean and keep going until you get to China. Did you cross over land? Now do it again, but this time only trace your finger over the blue parts, or the water. Remember, explorers at that time used ships to travel long distances. Did you find a path to China? Did it seem longer than the path to get to China over the land?

Christopher Columbus had a problem. His goal was to get to China by sailing his ships across the Ocean Sea. He did not know that there was so much land on the other side of the Ocean Sea that was not China. What do you think was going to happen to Columbus when he sailed west?

Spend some time looking at your globe. See if any of the names on the globe sound familiar. Which do you think there is more of on earth—land or water?

F. Writing

Famous explorers often wrote in journals to remember all that happened on their journeys and to tell people about what they saw. Journal entries don't have to be long or written by famous people. Read this journal entry, or listen as it is read to you. Follow the words with your eyes. Notice that it starts with a date.

October 1, 2006 – Ashley and I got up early. We packed our suitcases and went downstairs to eat breakfast. It was a beautiful morning, even though it was chilly outside. After eating, I checked out of the hotel and Ashley put our things in the car. By 7:30 A.M. we were leaving Cheyenne, Wyoming, driving east towards St. Louis, Missouri. The leaves on the trees were bright red, yellow, and orange.

Use a yellow highlighter or crayon to mark each capital letter in the journal entry. Write each of these capitalized words in one of the following categories in your Student Notebook:[9]

Five capitalized words that are names of places;

One capitalized word that is the name of a person in a sentence;

Six capitalized words that begin sentences;

Two capitalized letters that are an abbreviation.

Create a journal entry to tell about your day. Remember, a journal entry does not have to be exciting; it can merely tell someone else what happened from your point of view. Try to include at least three things that happened today.

From your journal entry, choose one event and think about how it made you feel. Now, write at least two sentences that will explain your feeling to someone else.

G. See Independent Reading note in Part 1.

G. Independent Reading

Choose something to read that you will enjoy. Find a quiet, comfortable place and read for the following length of time:

20 minutes

25 minutes

30 minutes

Be sure to write down what you read today on the Reading Log in your Student Notebook.

Lesson 1, Part 4

A. **Copywork/Dictation**   *Language Skills, Thinking Skills*
Silently read the fourth stanza of the poem "A Journey of Adventure." Show your teacher any words you don't know, and practice reading them aloud. Now, read the stanza aloud to your teacher, or ask her to read it to you. Practice reading it until you feel comfortable with all the words.

A. See Copywork/Dictation note in Part 1.

A Journey of Adventure

Come join the explorers and travel the globe.
You can add to the maps that they make
Of the stars, or the towns, or the new sights you see,
With the bright thoughts your travels awake.

Copy the fourth stanza into your Student Notebook. When you are finished, compare your copy to the model (word by word) and make any needed corrections.

Listen as your teacher dictates the passage above, and write it in your Student Notebook. When you are finished, compare your copy to the model and make any needed corrections.

Carefully read and then copy, or write as your teacher dictates, paragraph 3 on page 20 (starting with "All night…") in *Christopher Columbus.* When you are finished, compare your copy to the text and make any needed corrections.

B. **Reader**   *Language Skills*
Read pages 8–10 in *Meet Christopher Columbus* aloud.

Read one or two paragraphs in your read-aloud book, *Christopher Columbus.*

Read one or two pages from today's read-aloud assignment in *Christopher Columbus.*

C. **Read-Aloud and Narration**   *Language Skills, Thinking Skills*
Listen carefully as your teacher reads pages 16–22 aloud from *Christopher Columbus.*

C. See Narration note in Part 2.

To *narrate* means to retell. In your own words, tell what happened in your assigned passage below. Try to remember as many details as possible. Listen carefully as your teacher reads, or rereads, the part you are to retell.

Paragraph 5 on page 18 of *Christopher Columbus.*

Paragraphs 4 and 5 on page 19.

🐾 Paragraph 6 on page 18 to the end of page 20. Retell what happened to Christopher when his ship was attacked.

D. Word Study   *Spelling, Phonics, Vocabulary*

Look on pages 8 and 9 of *Meet Christopher Columbus.* Find all the words you can that have three syllables. Remember, a syllable is a part of a word that you hear when you say it. Try to find all ten words.

Make a list of the three syllable words you found.[10]

See if you can spell the words on this lesson's word study list from Part 1 without looking.

🐾🐾 Look at pages 5–7 in *Meet Christopher Columbus,* and make a list of at least 5 things that happened to Columbus and his ship. Put the items in the order that they happened and write them in your Student Notebook.[11]

🐾 Look at pages 5–7 in *Meet Christopher Columbus,* and the end of page 18 through page 22 in *Christopher Columbus* and tell about the mighty battle that Christopher's ship was a part of. After listening to the story and reading both accounts, make a list of the events that took place. Write the list in your Student Notebook.[12] Did the additional details help you get a better picture of what happened?

E. Geography   *Art, Thinking Skills*

A **map** is a diagram that shows what a place, or part of a place, looks like. Maps are usually flat and are drawn as though looking down on the place from above. There are maps of towns, cities, states, and countries. There are even maps of stars and planets. A map can be drawn to show where things are, no matter how big or small or how far away. Maps help us learn about something by comparing that thing to the other things that are around it. You can make a map of places you know. You don't even have to write it down. You can make a map that is a picture of a place in your mind.

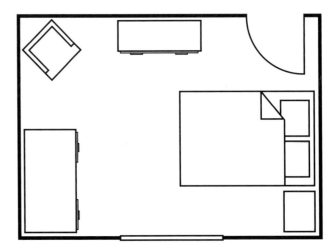

Close your eyes. Think about your bedroom. Picture the door, your bed, your clothes, and maybe your toys. Picture where things are.

Think about a map you could draw to show where things are in your room. Remember, when you make a map of something, imagine that you are standing above it. If you are drawing a room, pretend that you are looking down on the room from the ceiling. When you look at a globe, you are looking at the earth from out in space.

Look at the shapes. Practice drawing these shapes in your Student Notebook. Rectangles often show the shape of a bed, dresser, or shelves. Circles can show things like lamps. Ovals might show rugs, and squares are used for chairs.

Drawing was an important skill for explorers to have. Often they had to draw maps or pictures of the things they saw. This was an important part of sharing what they learned with others. Remember, most people have to practice drawing in order to be as good as they would like it to be. This is just the start of your drawing practice.

🐾🐾 Think about your kitchen. Using the shapes you practiced above, make a map showing where tables and chairs, the sink, stove, and refrigerator are located.

🐾 Think about the area outside your home. Using the shapes you practiced above, make a map showing things around your home. For example, use circles for trees and bushes, rectangles for cars, sheds, or garages, and so forth.

F. **Writing**   *Thinking Skills, Art, Language Skills*

A **trip** is a short journey. When you take a trip it is because you want to go to a certain place. Think of a trip you have taken recently. Draw a picture of where you went and tell your teacher about it.

Where did you go? Why did you go? Discuss your answers to these questions with your teacher. Use phrases, which are a few words that go together (complete sentences are not necessary.) Now think of a place that you would like to visit. Draw a picture of where you would like to go and tell your teacher about it.

Write the name of the place. Why do you want to go there? In your Student Notebook, answer this question with a complete sentence starting with "I want to go to _____ because _____." If you want, add more sentences to tell about where you want to go.

🐾 Look in magazines and newspapers and find places you would like to visit. With your teacher's permission, cut out the pictures and paste them in your Student Notebook.

🐾 Do you have pictures from a trip you've taken recently? With your teacher's permission, choose at least three pictures and put them in the order they happened.

Write at least two sentences that tell what is happening in each picture.

G. See Independent Reading note in Part 1.

G. Independent Reading

Choose something to read that you will enjoy. Find a quiet, comfortable place and read for the following length of time:

🐾 20 minutes

🐾 25 minutes

🐾 30 minutes

Be sure to write down what you read today on the Reading Log in your Student Notebook.

Lesson 1, Part 5

This part is set aside for completion of any work left undone from the lesson, and review of concepts and content. It is also a time to expand the work in the lesson by doing art, timeline activities, or games.

• Review the Steps for Thinking from the beginning of this lesson.

Most of the labeling has already been completed in the Student Notebook during this lesson. Instruct students to use the maps in their Student Notebooks as a reference. When they label the larger map, students will see the "big picture" and gain a broader understanding of their lessons.

• On the large outline map of the world label: Italy; China; Spain; Genoa, Italy; and several places where Marco Polo traveled. For Marco Polo information, use the library, an encyclopedia, or, with your parent's permission, the Internet. The following site has a nice map with Marco Polo's comments about each place: http://www.susqu.edu/history/medtrav/marcopolo/travel.htm

• Review the spelling words for this lesson. In your Student Notebook, write a sentence using each word that tells how it is related to the unit. Do your best to write the spelling words correctly. After you have finished, check your sentences against the list in your Student Notebook and see how many spelling words you spelled correctly. (Don't count off for other words that are misspelled.) Remember your goal is to improve, not necessarily to get them all right immediately.

Teachers can find a copy of this game in Appendix B. Instructions and answer keys for all games are located in Appendix A.

• Complete the Columbus Word Search located in your Student Notebook.

- Explorers made drawings to show other people what they had seen. Drawing is still an important skill, especially if a person wants to show others his ideas about what he has observed. Read the Nature art lesson included in Appendix A. Then draw flowers or bugs on the page provided in your Student Notebook.

Enrichment Activities

1. Read about the country of Spain. Prepare a presentation for others, telling them what you have learned.

2. Learn more about Queen Isabella and King Ferdinand. Tell when they were the rulers of Spain and what happened in Spain during their rule. See if you can find pictures that show how they looked.

3. Look in the cookbook *Eat Your Way Around the World* and find dishes from Spain to prepare. Share them with others. This activity can be combined with #1.

4. Plan a trip for you and your family. It could be a real trip you will take or an imaginary trip on a long vacation. Make a list of the things you would need, how you would travel, what your schedule would be, and how much you think it would cost. You may want to share this with your family for future consideration!

Additional Resources

I, Columbus – Edited by Peter and Connie Roop

Videos about Columbus

Books listed in the bibliography of *Christopher Columbus* by Bennie Rhodes

Eat Your Way Around the World by Jamie Aramini

Internet listings

Tour guide books (available from AAA) or travel information

How Great Thou Art has a full line of art supplies and curriculum written by Barry Stebbing. We are extremely grateful to Mr. Stebbing for the Nature art lesson found in your Student Notebook. This is a sample of the many materials he has created for teaching art to homeschoolers. Please visit this website to see all of his resources: www.howgreatthouart.com.

Use one or more of the Enrichment Activities if your child completes his assigned work and has the time or desire to learn more. These activities are flexible, so choose the one(s) that seem most interesting to your student. Allow him to work at a level that is appropriate for him, and remember that the learning process is more important than the product.

It is suggested that parents preview all videos.

Answers

1. Possible answers: Boston, Jacksonville, Houston, New Orleans, Los Angeles, New York, Seattle, Tampa, Savannah, Port Canaveral

2. Christopher's birthday: Christopher received a gift; Christopher celebrated his birthday on the feast day of St. Christopher; Christopher and his family went to church.

3. night, high, fight, right, light, flight

4. Two strange things: bazaars; cities. Synonym: out of the ordinary; peculiar

5. France, Africa, Greece

6. England, past Spain, Portugal, France

7. He would sail from Genoa into the Mediterranean Sea, past France and Spain to the Strait of Gibraltar, then upwards past Portugal, Spain and France to England.

8. Possible answers: grimaced, strained heavily, pitched forward, throwing to our knees, crashed, reeling

9. Places: Cheyenne, Wyoming; St. Louis, Missouri; Person: Ashley; Begin the sentence: Ashley, We, It, After, By, The; Abbreviation: A. M.

10. Christopher, Columbus, Portugal, Diego, Africa, Germany, cinnamon, anything, everyone, decided

11. Cannon balls smashed into the side of his ship; Cannon balls tore the ropes and sails; Cannon balls knocked down the masts; Other sailors on the ship were hit by cannon balls; The ship was sunk; Columbus jumped into the sea; He finally made it to shore in Portugal.

12. Events: A French frigate had rammed their ship; French privateers came on board their ship and attacked the sailors; Columbus fought a sword fight with a Frenchman; Two pirates tried to choke him, then he was stabbed with a sword; Columbus was badly injured but swam towards shore.

Lesson 2, Part 1

```
❧ Steps for Thinking ❧

1. The best way to learn something new is to start
   with what you already know about the subject.

2. When you learn something new, think about ways
   to apply it to your life.

3. The key to understanding the actions of others is
   to understand their thoughts.
```

The **Steps for Thinking** section gives you the main ideas about the topics presented. Understanding these helps you to have productive discussions with your children so they, too, understand the bigger ideas. This forms more permanent learning, contrary to just learning facts, which tends to be temporary. These steps are useful prior to instruction, and they are also useful for review at the end of the week.

A. **Copywork/Dictation**   *Language Skills*

Read the fifth stanza of the poem "A Journey of Adventure." Read it silently and show your teacher any words you don't know. Practice reading them aloud. Now read the poem aloud, or ask your teacher to read it to you.

A Journey of Adventure

The vagabonds join you to share all the joys,
That seeking and finding can be.
Just open your atlas and unlock the door,
With the ease of geography's key.

Can you say the stanzas without looking at the words? At the end of today's lessons you will prepare to share this poem with your family or class.

🐾 Copy the fifth stanza into your Student Notebook. When you are finished, compare your copy to the model (word by word) and make any needed corrections.

🖐 Listen as your teacher dictates the passage above, and write it in your Student Notebook. When you are finished, compare your copy to the model and make any needed corrections.

🐾 Carefully read and then copy, or write as your teacher dictates, paragraph 3 (starting with "Lisbon…") on page 24 of *Christopher Columbus*. When you are finished, compare your copy to the text and make any needed corrections.

◈─ *Materials* ─◈

• *Meet Christopher Columbus*
• *Christopher Columbus*
• *Intermediate World Atlas*
• *Handbook of Nature Study*
• *Profiles from History*
• Student Notebook
• Watch or Timing Device
• Spices (at least 4)
• Dictionary
• Highlighter
• Index Cards/Marker
• Globe
• Crayons or Colored Pencils
• Napkin or Paper Towel
• Access to Library or Internet
• Supplies for Experiment: cup, saucer, small square of paper, salt, water, hand lens
• Large world outline map

Additional resources for Enrichment Activities are found in Part 5.

A. Copywork and dictation assignments go from an easier level (designated by 🐾) to harder levels (designated by 🖐 and 🐾). Take two days for the copywork if that is more comfortable for your child. Please adapt instructions to your child's individual needs. Your child should be **consistently successful** at one level before progressing to the next, **regardless of grade**.

B. Reader   *Language Skills*

Read pages 11 and 12 in *Meet Christopher Columbus* aloud.

Read one or two paragraphs in your read-aloud book, *Christopher Columbus.*

Read one or two pages from today's read-aloud assignment in *Christopher Columbus.*

C. Read-Aloud and Discussion   *Language Skills, Thinking Skills*

Listen carefully as your teacher reads pages 23–28 aloud from *Christopher Columbus.*

Discussion: It was during this time in Columbus' life that he came up with the idea of finding China and Japan by sailing west across the ocean. Tell about some of the people, places, or things that you think helped Columbus come to this new thought.

D. Word Study   *Spelling, Phonics, Vocabulary*

Rhyming words have the same ending sounds, and are often used in poems like "A Journey of Adventure." Reread all five stanzas of the poem, or listen as your teacher reads them aloud. Do you hear the rhyming words?

Each stanza has two words that rhyme. You can find these words at the end of the second and fourth lines. In your Student Notebook, color or highlight the rhyming words in each stanza. Read the words you marked to your teacher. Are they always spelled the same?

Can you think of more rhyming words for each pair? Write them in your Student Notebook.

A **vagabond** means a person who wanders from place to place to see interesting sights and meet new people. A vagabond usually doesn't have a home, but lives his life traveling around. When you look at maps, atlases, or books you can visit places without ever leaving home.

Look at your globe. If you could be a pretend vagabond, where on the globe would you want to go? (Remember, you don't really have to go there, so use your imagination!) Complete the following sentence in your Student Notebook:

"If I were a vagabond, I would go to _____ because _____." Give at least three reasons why you would go there.

Find Lisbon, Portugal, on the Europe Political Map in the *Intermediate World Atlas.* What do you think the difference is between a seaport and a harbor? Write down your guess on a piece of scratch paper, then look up each word in the dictionary. Was your idea close? Write down the difference between the two words.

C. Discussion is very important in developing your child's ability to organize his thoughts. This in turn builds the ability to think and write. The goal of the discussion questions is not just to find the answer to a particular question, but also to create a situation where thoughts about the question and its answer are shared and considered in a detailed way. Do not rush this activity, but encourage your student to share his or her ideas relating to the topic, and any additional ideas that may come to mind. You can also share your thoughts and questions as an example for your students.

D. The complete text of the poem "A Journey of Adventure" is located in Appendix A.

Each word in bold letters is considered a vocabulary word. It is a word that may or may not be new to your child. You can write these vocabulary words on index cards and use them for occasional review, but not for memorizing. Give the child the meaning of the words if he doesn't remember. Try to use the new vocabulary words during conversation, and encourage your students to do the same.

Each time your student makes a vocabulary card for this unit, have him write a "C" (for Columbus) in the upper left corner. This will make it possible to review vocabulary by unit at the end of the year.

What do you think the difference is between a map and a **chart?** Write down your guess and then check the words in a dictionary. Write down the difference between the two words.[1]

E. Geography

Thinking Skills, Art

Do you remember the lesson about making a map, or picture, in your mind? That kind of map is called a "mental map." Think about the mental map you made of your room.

Using the shapes you practiced during the last lesson, draw a map of your room in the rectangle in your Student Notebook.

On your map, use your finger to trace your steps around your room as you:

- Come in the door and go to bed;
- Get up from your bed and look out the window (or go to the door;)
- Come in the door and get your coat;

Make a mental map of your neighborhood.

Who lives next to you on each side? Who lives in front of you, or behind you? What road do you live on? After making a mental picture of your house and what is closest to you, draw your map in your notebook. It doesn't have to be perfectly drawn, just a sketch will do.

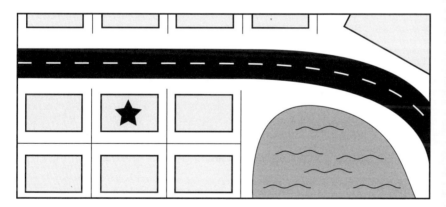

Pay attention the next time you go to church or the store from your house. First, try to time it to see how long it takes you. Ask your parent if the time it took was normal, longer, or shorter due to traffic. Try to see the names of one or two streets that you travel on and write them down. Each time you make this trip for a while, try to record the name of another street you drive on or the direction you turn for each street. Here is an example:

> To go to the store:
> Turn left out of my driveway.
> Turn right on Mayberry Street.
> Turn left onto Main Street.

D. The small superscript numbers that appear after some of the questions in this unit refer to answers found in the answer key, located immediately after Part 5.

Go down Main Street for a long time.
Turn right into the Main Street Grocery parking lot.

Instead of using the terms left or right on your instructions, determine what compass direction you are going at each step or turn.

F. Speaking/Presentation Skills   *Language Skills, Thinking Skills*

Today you have finished reading the poem "A Journey of Adventure." Now you will prepare to present the poem to an audience. This audience could be your brothers and sisters, mom and dad, or others in your family or neighborhood. Go through the following steps to prepare your presentation:

1. Practice reading the poem aloud until you feel comfortable with the words. Remember to use a clear, strong voice and read with expression, pausing where there is a comma and lowering your voice when you come to the end of a stanza.

2. Make sure you stand up straight, with your arms and hands still. Think about whether or not you would like to show your audience something during your presentation, such as rug designs you made in Lesson 1, Part 3, or something new, such as a picture. If you decide to show something, have another person hold the item or picture so that your hands are free to hold the poem.

3. Consider memorizing the poem, but remember that it is not necessary. It is more important to read smoothly and with expression than it is to memorize it.

4. Choose a time to make your presentation, and invite the people you would like to have in the audience. If you want to make a fancy occasion out of it, you could serve refreshments to your audience as well.

5. Make your presentation. Now that you have completed the poem, enjoy the responses of others to your efforts.

G. Independent Reading

Choose something to read that you will enjoy. Find a quiet, comfortable place and read for the following length of time:

🐾 20 minutes

🐾 25 minutes

🐾 30 minutes

Over time, it's fun to see how much you have read. Be sure to write down what you read today on the Reading Log in your Student Notebook.

G. Reading fluency is developed through having frequent silent reading opportunities that continue for the length of time suggested here. Since a primary focus of this activity is to nurture your child's enjoyment of reading, help him to choose reading material that interests him and is at a level that allows him to read with understanding by himself. You can incorporate this activity into your school day whenever it is most convenient.

If the suggested length of time is too long for your child to continue reading by himself, start with an amount of time he can accomplish successfully and make the suggested time a goal.

—❦—

Lesson 2, Part 2

A. **Copywork/Dictation**   *Language Skills, Thinking Skills*

Look carefully at your assigned passage, either below or in the read-aloud book, and read it silently. Show your teacher any words you don't know, and practice saying them aloud. Now read the passage aloud, or ask your teacher to read it to you.

> Christopher Columbus was born to be an explorer. He grew up in an exciting port city. There were always ships coming and going with interesting cargo.

🐾 Copy the above lines into your Student Notebook. When you are finished, compare your copy to the model (word by word) and make any needed corrections.

🐾 Listen as your teacher dictates the passage above, and write it in your Student Notebook. When you are finished, compare your copy to the model and make any needed corrections.

🐾 Copy, or write as your teacher dictates, paragraph 4 (beginning with "Prince Henry,") on page 24 of *Christopher Columbus*. When you are finished, compare your copy to the text and make any needed corrections.

B. **Reader**   *Language Skills, Thinking Skills*

Read pages 13 and 14 in *Meet Christopher Columbus* aloud.

🐾 Read one or two paragraphs in your read-aloud book, *Christopher Columbus*.

🐾 Read one or two pages from today's read-aloud assignment in *Christopher Columbus*.

C. **Read-Aloud and Narration**   *Language Skills, Thinking Skills*

Listen carefully as your teacher reads pages 29–33 in *Christopher Columbus*.

To *narrate* means to retell. In your own words, tell what happened in your assigned passage below. Try to remember as many details as possible. Listen carefully as your teacher reads, or rereads, the part you are to retell.

🐾 Paragraph 9 on page 24 starting with "I sailed…." Tell what happened in this passage.

🐾 Paragraph 4 on page 23 through paragraph 2 on page 24. Tell about Christopher's time with his brother.

A. See Copywork/Dictation note in Part 1.

C. The skill of narration is gained over time. If your child has never retold a story, start with the assignment for the lower level, no matter what grade he is in. Work up from there, being careful to allow him to stay at the level of success for a while before going to a longer section.

🐾 Paragraph 9 on page 25 through paragraph 3 on page 27. Tell about the things Columbus learned during this time.

D. **Word Study**   *Spelling, Phonics, Vocabulary*

🐾🐾 Look at the words *explorer* and *exciting* in today's copywork passage. Both words start with the sound *x*. How is the sound of *x* spelled?[2] Highlight the letters that spell the *x* sound on your copy of the passage.

🐾 Write the words *explorer* and *exciting* in your Student Notebook. How is the sound of *x* spelled in these words? Highlight the letters that spell the *x* sound.

🐾🐾🐾 Look at the following list of words. In your Student Notebook, highlight the two letters that spell the *x* sound in each word.

exit	expand	exam
except	exist	expect
exalt	excited	

You can use these words as your spelling words for this lesson. Practice by spelling them aloud to your teacher, or writing them on a chalkboard or dry erase board.

🐾🐾 When *ing* is added to the end of a word it changes the meaning of the word. Make a list of the words from your dictation passage that end with *ing*.[3] The **root**, or spelling of a word before anything else is added, of the words with *ing* are *excite, come, go,* and *interest*. What was done to each word to add *ing*?[4] Find at least eight other words that end with *ing* in one of your books. Make a list of those words in your Student Notebook. Can you tell what each root word, or beginning word, was before *ing* was added? Write what you think it was next to each *ing* word.

Make up a rule you can follow when you want to add *ing* to a word that ends with an *e*. Write the rule in your Student Notebook. Do you think your rule will work for adding other endings to a word that ends in *e*? Try adding *ed* to your list of words. Did your rule still apply?[5]

🐾 Prince Henry was known for his interest in exploration. During this time in Portugal's history, explorers and exploration were very popular. Prince Henry the Navigator started a school. Using the Internet or other resource materials, look up the answers to the following questions. Write your answers in your Student Notebook.

What was the purpose of Prince Henry's school?
Who went there?
What do you think was the result of his school?

To **navigate** means to steer or direct. What two words in the passage you copied today come from the word *navigate*?[6]

ℰ. History   *Thinking Skills*

You have heard some of the story of Christopher Columbus. He was a very famous explorer. Think about the qualities that a person might need in order to be an explorer. Write a list in your Student Notebook. Don't worry if you don't know too many qualities yet, because you can add to this list later. Tell your teacher the answers to these questions about what you think an explorer is like:[7]

Is he afraid of new things?

Does he work hard to learn new things?

Is he very determined to go and do things?

Do other people always understand why he wants to go somewhere or do something?

Does he believe his plans will work?

Explorers all through history have had these qualities. That is what makes them want to be explorers. Do you know any people like this? They do not have to be explorers! Who are the people you know? Tell your teacher about them, and why you think they are like explorers.

Sometimes there are other reasons for explorers to explore, such as:

• To tell people about their religion;

• To become famous;

• To bring honor to their home countries;

• To go somewhere new.

Each explorer had different reasons for exploring. Keep these reasons in mind as you continue to learn about Columbus.

Tell how you think the above reasons for exploration applied to Columbus.

ℱ. Drawing   *Science, Art*

Drawing is a skill that is built over time. Continue to build your skills of observing and drawing by following these directions:

Go outside. It can be into your yard, on your porch or to a park. Choose a spot that has a tree or bushes, and sit a short distance away from them. Sit for at least three minutes and **observe**, or quietly watch and listen to what goes on near you. Ask your teacher to time you, or time yourself. Then make a list in your Student Notebook of what you see and hear, or tell your teacher and ask her to make the list. Then you can copy it into your Student Notebook.

Repeat the process for another three minutes. What time of the day did you come? Do you think you would observe more if you came at another time?

Choose at least one thing that you saw during your observation times and draw it. It can be something small like a leaf or flower, or big like a tree. Don't worry about how well your drawing turns out. This is practice. Most explorers made drawings and wrote about what they saw, so that they could show others.

G. See Independent Reading note in Part 1.

G. Independent Reading

Choose something to read that you will enjoy. Find a quiet, comfortable place and read for the following length of time:

- 20 minutes
- 25 minutes
- 30 minutes

Be sure to write down what you read today on the Reading Log in your Student Notebook.

Lesson 2, Part 3

A. See Copywork/Dictation note in Part 1.

A. Copywork/Dictation
Language Skills

Silently read the passage below, and show your teacher any words you don't know. Practice reading them aloud. Now, read the lines aloud to your teacher, or ask her to read them to you.

> Coming and going were all he could think about.
> He helped his family with the weaving they did
> but he longed to be out on the sea.

- Copy the above lines into your Student Notebook. When you are finished, compare your copy to the model (word by word) and make any needed corrections.

- Listen as your teacher dictates the passage above, and write it in your Student Notebook. When you are finished, compare your copy to the model and make any needed corrections.

- Copy, or write as your teacher dictates, the last paragraph on page 25 through to the end of the third sentence in paragraph 1 on page 27 in *Christopher Columbus*. When you are finished, compare your copy to the text and make needed corrections.

B. Reader　　　　　　　　　　　　　　　　　*Language Skills*

Read pages 15–17 in *Meet Christopher Columbus* aloud.

🐾 Read one or two paragraphs in your read-aloud book, *Christopher Columbus.*

🐾 Read one or two pages from today's read-aloud assignment in *Christopher Columbus.*

C. Read-Aloud and Discussion　　*Language Skills, Thinking Skills*

Listen carefully as your teacher reads pages 34–38 in *Christopher Columbus.*

Discussion: Columbus ran into some hard times. Things happened that made him sad. He went to see King John of Portugal several times about his idea to sail west. Felipa became very sick and died. What did these two situations cause Columbus to do?

C. See Discussion note in Part 1.

D. Word Study　　　　　　　　　　　　　　　*Spelling, Phonics*

Look at your list of spelling words. Practice reading them aloud.

exit	expand	exam
except	exist	expect
exalt	excited	

Find the spelling words that fit these clues and write them in your Student Notebook.[8]

I make something that is small get bigger. Who am I?

I am a test you can take. Who am I?

I am how you feel when you know something is going to happen. Who am I?

I describe what you do for someone who is worthy of praise. Who am I?

I am something you feel when you are about to open a present or get on a fun ride. Who am I?

I am a word that describes being left out. Who am I?

After you find the spelling words that fit the above clues, you will have two words left over. Make up your own clues for those words, and write them in your Student Notebook.

Today's copywork passage for 🐾 and 🐾 says that Christopher longed to be out on the sea. What do you thing *longed* means? Write what you think it means in your Student Notebook. Then look this word up in the dictionary. Is your meaning close to the dictionary meaning?

Have you ever longed to do something? Write a couple of sentences and tell about it. Make sure to use the word *longed* in one of your sentences.

🐾 In your Student Notebook, make a list of the *ing* words in today's dictation passage. Write what you think the root, or beginning, word is next to them.[9] Also make a list of words that end with *ed*. Write the root words next to them.[10]

🐾 Make a list of the different languages that Christopher and his brother were learning to read and speak. Write them in your Student Notebook.[11] Why do you think it was helpful in the mapmaking business to speak more than one language?[12] Do you know any words or phrases in another language?

The printing press had recently been invented. Books were now available to common men, not just wealthy people. Why do you think the book-selling business appealed to Columbus so much?[13]

E. Science

Explorers used all of their senses to observe. Your "senses" are seeing (with your eyes), hearing (with your ears), tasting (with your mouth), smelling (with your nose), and touching (mostly with your hands). That means that explorers looked, listened, smelled, touched, and when it was safe, tasted. This is called "using your senses."

Look at, or think about, your favorite food. Draw a picture of it in your Student Notebook and use words to describe what it looks like, tastes like, feels like, and if it has a sound, what it sounds like. Write those words under your picture.

🐾🐾 One of the main reasons Columbus wanted to explore and find a way to China and the Far East was to bring spices back to Spain to sell. Everyone wanted their food to taste better, and spices were the answer.

With your parent's permission, look at the spices in your kitchen at home. Ask permission to smell some of them, but be careful. Spices can taste and smell very strong.

Choose four spices. Pour a small amount of each spice onto a napkin or paper towel. Observe the spices, then draw each one in your Student Notebook. Under the drawing, tell what it smells like and, if your teacher says it is safe, what it tastes like. Which spice do you like the best? Which don't you like? Ask your teacher what spices she uses the most. Do you like those spices?

🐾 Choose one additional spice in your cabinet and look up information about it in library books or on the Internet. Tell what the spice looks like, tastes like (with permission), and where the spice comes from. Draw a picture of the spice in your Student Notebook.

F. **Geography**   *Thinking Skills*

A **worldview** is the way a person thinks about what happens around him. Everyone has a worldview. You are learning about the world and building your own worldview. Most children learn much of their worldview from their parents, teachers, and family members. It is also built by things you learn about your faith. Most people's families help them build their faith. Your faith is also shaped by the way people around you think.

Who or what do you think has taught you the most about what is right and wrong? Those people or things have shaped your worldview.

Christopher Columbus had a certain worldview that came from the same three places as many of us: his family, his faith, and those who lived in his country. From the story you are listening to about the time and place that Columbus lived in, give at least three reasons why you think Columbus wanted to explore.

Write these reasons in your Student Notebook or tell them to your teacher and ask her to write them down. Later you can copy them into your notebook.

🐾 Talk with your parent and choose a topic of interest to you. Come up with a question you can ask several people about. After you find out their opinions, talk with your parent about whether each person's worldview might be the same or different from yours. Remember, if someone has a different opinion about something, it does not necessarily mean that their whole worldview is different from yours. Try to find out what part of their worldview is different from yours.

🐾 With your parent's permission, talk with someone from another country about how people in his homeland might view things such as education, family life, or possessions. You may think of other things you would like to discuss with him as well. When this person talks to you about how people in his country view things, he is talking about a part of their worldview. When you are finished, find out how the people in your family view the same things. Do you think there are any differences between the worldviews of people in your country and the other person's country?

G. See Independent Reading note in Part 1.

G. Independent Reading

Choose something to read that you will enjoy. Find a quiet, comfortable place and read for the following length of time:

- 20 minutes
- 25 minutes
- 30 minutes

Be sure to write down what you read today on the Reading Log in your Student Notebook.

Lesson 2, Part 4

A. See Copywork/Dictation note in Part 1.

A. Copywork/Dictation

Language Skills

Silently read the passage below, and show your teacher any words you don't know. Practice reading them aloud. Now, read the lines aloud to your teacher, or ask her to read them to you.

> Columbus was in luck. When he was fourteen years old, he got to take short trips for his father's trade. He finally made it to the deck of a ship.

- Copy the above lines into your Student Notebook. When you are finished, compare your copy to the model (word by word) and make any needed corrections.

- Listen as your teacher dictates the passage above, and write it in your Student Notebook. When you are finished, compare your copy to the model and make any needed corrections.

- Copy, or write as your teacher dictates, paragraph 2 on page 27 of *Christopher Columbus.* When you are finished, compare your copy to the text and make any needed corrections.

B. Reader

Language Skills

Read pages 18–20 in *Meet Christopher Columbus* aloud.

- Read one or two paragraphs in your read-aloud book, *Christopher Columbus.*

- Read one or two pages from today's read-aloud assignment in *Christopher Columbus.*

C. Read-Aloud and Narration   *Language Skills, Thinking Skills*   C. See Narration note in Part 2.

Listen carefully as your teacher reads pages 39–44 in *Christopher Columbus.*

To *narrate* means to retell. In your own words, tell what happened in your assigned passage below. Try to remember as many details as possible. Listen carefully as your teacher reads, or rereads, the part you are to retell.

ᕼᕼ Listen to the last paragraph on page 44. Things had not gone well for Christopher. Retell what this paragraph tells you about how he felt.

ᕼ Reread the last paragraph on page 42 to paragraph 7 on page 43. Tell what Christopher shared with Queen Isabella and how she reacted.

ᕼ Reread pages 43 and 44. Describe what happened to Christopher with Queen Isabella and King John. Did he give up on his dreams?

D. Word Study   *Spelling, Phonics, Vocabulary*

Columbus longed to be on a ship. The passage you copied today tells that he was finally able to take short trips when he was fourteen. The word *finally* is a good word to use when you write because it is very clear. If you say that you finally got to do something, everyone knows that you have had to wait to do it. Yesterday, you wrote a couple of sentences about something you longed to do. Did you get to do the thing you longed for yet? If you did, write one or two sentences about it in your Student Notebook. Include the word *finally* in your sentences.

If you have not gotten to do the thing you longed to do yet, make up a sentence or two telling what you think it will be like when you finally get to do that special thing.

Combining yesterday's writing and today's, you should have three or four sentences, which means you finally have a paragraph written about the thing you longed to do. Paragraphs are easy to make when you put sentences together over several days that are about the same ideas. Read your paragraph to your teacher from beginning to end.

ᕼᕼ One way to find the main idea of a paragraph is to decide what big question the paragraph answers.

Look at paragraph 2 on page 19 in *Meet Christopher Columbus.* What question does this paragraph answer?[14]

ᕼ Sometimes another person's thoughts can greatly affect your thinking. This was true about Columbus and the thoughts of Marco Polo. Columbus was very interested in his book and read it many times.

What do you think interested Columbus the most?

Why do you think Columbus was so determined to visit new lands? Read paragraph 3 on page 27 in *Christopher Columbus.* Is the reason given here the reason you thought of?

E. This experiment can be finished in Part 5 if necessary.

E. Science   *Geography*

Look at your globe. It shows both water and land. The water is probably blue, and there is much more of it than there is land. The largest areas of water on Earth are called **oceans.** Oceans are made up of salt water.

Have you ever seen an ocean either in person or on television? What did it look like to you?

Read Lesson 212 beginning on page 753 in the *Handbook of Nature Study* aloud or have your teacher read it to you. Do the experiment described in Method. In your Student Notebook, answer questions 1–4 in Observations. Why do you think the ocean is salty?

When the experiment is completed, look at the salt crystals with your hand lens.

 Read paragraphs 3–5 on page 753 in the *Handbook of Nature Study.* Discuss the answers to questions 5–7 on page 754.

F. Geography

The five largest oceans on earth are called:

> Atlantic Ocean
> Pacific Ocean
> Indian Ocean
> Arctic Ocean
> Southern Ocean (Antarctic Ocean)

Find each of these oceans on your globe. Put a check mark by each name listed in your Student Notebook after you find it.

Look at the list of ocean names in your Student Notebook. Use a yellow highlighter or crayon to mark each capital letter. Each ocean name tells about a particular place on earth. That is why the names start with capital letters.

Look at Map C-1 of the oceans. Find where each ocean is located and write its name on the unlabeled map in your Student Notebook. Remember to start each part of the name with a capital letter.

Color all the oceans light blue.

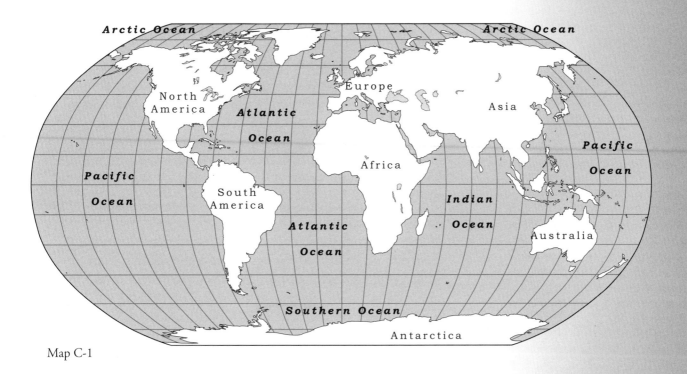

Map C-1

🐾 Look at the chart in the front of the *Intermediate World Atlas* that tells the sizes of the oceans. On the ocean map in your Student Notebook, put a number 1, 2, 3, 4, or 5 in front of the name of each ocean to tell its size. (Write a 1 in front of the largest and a 5 in front of the smallest.)

🐾 Which ocean is nearest to where you live? Look for information about that ocean and write five things in your Student Notebook that you learned about it.

G. **Independent Reading**

Choose something to read that you will enjoy. Find a quiet, comfortable place and read for the following length of time:

G. See Independent Reading note in Part I.

🌵🌵 20 minutes

🐾 25 minutes

🐾 30 minutes

Be sure to write down what you read today on the Reading Log in your Student Notebook.

Lesson 2, Part 5

This part is set aside for completion of any work left undone from the lesson, and review of concepts and content. It is also a time to expand the work in the lesson by doing art, timeline activities, or games.

Most of the labeling has already been completed in the Student Notebook during this lesson. Instruct students to use the maps in their Student Notebooks as a reference. When they label the larger map, students will see the "big picture" and gain a broader understanding of their lessons.

• Review the Steps for Thinking from the beginning of this lesson.

• On the large outline map of the world label: Portugal, Spain, and the five oceans.

• Review the spelling words for this lesson. In your Student Notebook, write a sentence using each word that tells how it is related to the unit. Do your best to write the spelling words correctly. After you have finished, check your sentences against the list in your Student Notebook and see how many spelling words you spelled correctly. (Don't count off for other words that are misspelled.) Remember your goal is to improve, not necessarily to get them all right immediately.

Teachers can find a copy of this game in Appendix B. Instructions and answer keys for all games are located in Appendix A.

• Complete the Columbus Word Scramble located in your Student Notebook.

• Listen to or read the story about Marco Polo in *Profiles from History.* Complete the timeline activities and any other activities you would like to do.

Enrichment Activities

Use one or more of the Enrichment Activities if your child completes his assigned work and has the time or desire to learn more. These activities are flexible, so choose the one(s) that seem most interesting to your student. Allow him to work at a level that is appropriate for him, and remember that the learning process is more important than the product.

1. Look for poetry about maps, travel, or specific countries or places. Present the poems to your family by memorizing them or just reading them aloud. You can also illustrate the poetry with drawings or photos.

2. Read about the country of Portugal. Tell others what you have learned. Take what you know about Spain and compare it to what you have learned about Portugal. How are Portugal and Spain similar? How are they different?

3. Have you ever been on a boat or a ship? Draw a picture or write about the boat or ship that you were on. You could also make up a story about a boat or ship you would *like* to go on. Make sure and include what you think makes travel on the water different from other ways to travel.

Additional Resources

Books, pictures, or videos about boats and ships

Resources containing poetry

Answers

1. A map is usually used to show formations on land and a chart is used to give information—in this case, about waterways.

2. ex

3. exciting, coming, going, interesting

4. excite – dropped e, added *ing;* come – dropped e, added *ing;* go – added *ing;* interest – added *ing*

5. Possible answer: When you add *ing* to a word that ends with e, take the e off before adding the ending.

6. navigator, navigation

7. no; yes; yes; no; yes

8. expand; exam; expect; exalt; excited; except

9. coming – come; going – go; weaving – weave

10. helped – help; longed – long

11. Portuguese, Spanish, Latin

12. Possible answer: sailors from many different countries would have come to them for maps, so it would be helpful to be able to speak to them.

13. Possible answer: book selling may have appealed to Columbus because he was unable to learn to read as a child and reading became very important to him as an adult.

14. What prizes did Columbus want if he found the Indies?

Lesson 3, Part 1

> ### ❧ Steps for Thinking ❧
>
> 1. When you learn about people, it helps you learn about things.
>
> 2. Observation is a key skill needed for learning about things in our world. It is the basis for success in science.
>
> 3. The goal of reading is to gain understanding. Hopefully it is also a source of enjoyment.

The **Steps for Thinking** section gives you the main ideas about the topics presented. Understanding these helps you to have productive discussions with your children so they, too, understand the bigger ideas. This forms more permanent learning, contrary to just learning facts, which tends to be temporary. These steps are useful prior to instruction, and they are also useful for review at the end of the week.

✒ Materials ✒

- *Meet Christopher Columbus*
- *Christopher Columbus*
- *Handbook of Nature Study*
- *U.S. History Atlas*
- Crayons or Colored Pencils
- Dictionary
- Student Notebook
- Index Cards/Marker
- Library or Internet access
- RealEarth® GlobeMap™ or globe
- Large world outline map

Additional resources for Enrichment Activities are found in Part 5.

A. Copywork/Dictation *Language Skills, Thinking Skills*

Look carefully at your assigned passage, either below or in the read-aloud book, and read it silently. Show your teacher any words you don't know, and practice saying them aloud. Now read the passage aloud, or ask your teacher to read it to you.

> Short trips became long trips for him as a young sailor. He would visit places far from his home. His adventures on the seas had just begun.

🐾 Copy the above lines into your Student Notebook. When you are finished, compare your copy to the model (word by word) and make any needed corrections.

🐾 Listen as your teacher dictates the passage above, and write it in your Student Notebook. When you are finished, compare your copy to the model and make any needed corrections.

🐾 Copy, or write as your teacher dictates, paragraph 4 on page 45 of *Christopher Columbus*. When you are finished, compare your copy to the text and make any needed corrections.

A. Copywork and dictation assignments go from an easier level (designated by 🐾) to harder levels (designated by 🐾 and 🐾). Take two days for the copywork if that is more comfortable for your child. Please adapt instructions to your child's individual needs. Your child should be **consistently successful** at one level before progressing to the next, **regardless of grade**.

B. Reader *Language Skills, Thinking Skills*

Read pages 27 and 28 in *Meet Christopher Columbus* aloud.

🐾 Read one or two paragraphs in your read-aloud book, *Christopher Columbus*.

🐾 Read one or two pages from today's read-aloud assignment in *Christopher Columbus*.

C. Discussion is very important in developing your child's ability to organize his thoughts. This in turn builds the ability to think and write. The goal of the discussion questions is not just to find the answer to a particular question, but also to create a situation where thoughts about the question and its answer are shared and considered in a detailed way. Do not rush this activity, but encourage your student to share his or her ideas relating to the topic, and any additional ideas that may come to mind. You can also share your thoughts and questions as an example for your students.

D. The small superscript numbers that appear after some of the questions in this unit refer to answers found in the answer key, located immediately after Part 5.

E. Each word in bold letters is considered a vocabulary word. It is a word that may or may not be new to your child. You can write these vocabulary words on index cards and use them for occasional review, but not for memorizing. Give the child the meaning of the words if he doesn't remember. Try to use the new vocabulary words during conversation, and encourage your students to do the same.

Each time your student makes a vocabulary card for this unit, have him write a "C" (for Columbus) in the upper left corner. This will make it possible to review vocabulary by unit at the end of the year.

C. **Read-Aloud and Discussion**   *Language Skills, Thinking Skills*

Listen carefully as your teacher reads pages 45–50 in *Christopher Columbus.*

Discussion: It had been six years since the first time Columbus went to see King Ferdinand and Queen Isabella about his plan to sail west. It looked like all was lost when the answer was again "no." What do you think changed the king and queen's minds about the trip? How would you have felt after waiting so long to get permission to make this trip?

D. **Word Study**   *Spelling, Phonics, Vocabulary*

Words that have opposite meanings are called **antonyms.** Two words in your copywork passage that are antonyms are *short* and *long.* Here are some other words from your passage. See if you can think of an antonym for each of them.[1]

     young _____   begun _____

     far _____   him _____

Antonyms are helpful when you want to show how different two things can be. Read the saying below and tell what you think it means:

"My brothers are as different as night and day."

Does the use of antonyms in this saying help make it clear how different the two brothers are? For example, if one brother likes to run and play outside, what might the other brother like to do? If one brother is very tall, what might the other brother be? Make up your own list of at least five antonyms.

Can you think of two people who are as different as night and day? If you can't think of anyone, you can make them up. Draw a picture in your Student Notebook to show the people you thought of and their differences. Make a list of words to describe each person under his or her picture. Make sure the words you use to describe each person are antonyms.

E. **Geography**

In times past, other than horses or horse drawn wagons, ships were the main source of transportation over long distances. The great exploring nations of Spain and Portugal had many ships and were always trying to improve the design of the ships and how they could be used. Great explorers at that time needed a good knowledge of ships and **navigation,** or how to direct the ships from one place to another.

Look at the diagram on pages 24 and 25 of *Meet Christopher Columbus.* Look for as many details of the ship as you can in the picture.

Look at the ship in sections to understand what the parts do. Anything with the word "sail" in it refers to the **sails**, which were very important. Sails were made of strong fabric and were usually in the shape of a triangle, rectangle, or square. The purpose of the sail was to catch the wind and move the ship forward. The different names of the sails refer to the position of the sail. A *mizzen* is a sail that is found on a *mizzenmast,* or the third **mast** of a ship. Point out the four sails to your teacher.

The *masts* were also of great importance to the ships. A mast is a pole that is very large and strong. Ships were often described by the number of masts that they had. Find the three masts on the ship in the picture. Which mast was largest?[2] Why do you think that mast was in the middle of the ship?[3] Which sail is attached to the main, or middle, mast?[4] At the top of the mast is a place shaped like a basket where a man could stand. This is called the *crow's nest.* Why do you think it is called that?[5] What do you think the purpose of the crow's nest was?[6]

Now look at the ship's *deck.* There are several types of decks on the diagram. A deck is a floor or level part of a boat that can be walked on. There are many sayings that relate to the deck, such as "Come up on deck," or "All hands on deck," or "Get below deck." Sayings like these direct people to specific places on the ship. Find the four types of decks on this ship and show them to your teacher.

The last section of the ship is the part that is below the deck. This is the part you can't see from the surface of the water. Find at least six places on the diagram that would be considered below deck.

🐾 Ships have been very important throughout the history of exploration. There is a special vocabulary that is used to understand sailing on a ship and the parts of a ship. Read the following terms and try to decide what you think they mean. Then look the words up in a dictionary and see what you need to add or change about your understanding. Tell others what these terms mean. Add any other words you learn about ships.

rigging	**bow**	**stern**
knots (speed)	**fore**	**aft**

🐾 Columbus chose this type of ship for his flagship because it was larger than the *Niña* and the *Pinta.* It was not any longer than the other ships but it could carry more men and more weight because it was rounder and had a larger area below deck. A **flagship** is the ship that carries the admiral or commander of a group, or **fleet**, of ships.

The *Santa Maria* was the type of ship called a *nao*. The *Niña* and the *Pinta* were called caravels. Look in the library or on the Internet and find out about caravels. In your Student Notebook, give at least two reasons why the caravel was so important to explorers.[7]

F. Art   *Writing*

Draw or trace the ship found on pages 24 and 25 of *Meet Christopher Columbus.* Include as many parts as you can and label them. This is called a **diagram.** A diagram is a simple drawing that makes something easier for you to understand.

G. Independent Reading

Choose something to read that you will enjoy. Find a quiet, comfortable place and read for the following length of time:

🐾 20 minutes

🖐 25 minutes

🐾 30 minutes

Be sure to write down what you read today on the Reading Log in your Student Notebook.

G. Reading fluency is developed through having frequent silent reading opportunities that continue for the length of time suggested here. Since a primary focus of this activity is to nurture your child's enjoyment of reading, help him to choose reading material that interests him and is at a level that allows him to read with understanding by himself. You can incorporate this activity into your school day whenever it is most convenient.

If the suggested length of time is too long for your child to continue reading by himself, start with an amount of time he can accomplish successfully and make the suggested time a goal.

Lesson 3, Part 2

A. Copywork/Dictation   *Language Skills, Thinking Skills*

Look carefully at your assigned passage, either below or in the read-aloud book, and read it silently. Show your teacher any words you don't know, and practice saying them aloud. Now read the passage aloud, or ask your teacher to read it to you.

> One time his ship was sunk by pirates. Columbus had to swim a long way to survive. He was hurt but his brother took care of him.

🐾 Copy the above lines into your Student Notebook. When you are finished, compare your copy to the model (word by word) and make any needed corrections.

🖐 Listen as your teacher dictates the passage above, and write it in your Student Notebook. When you are finished, compare your copy to the model and make any needed corrections.

A. The dictation method enables your child to hear language and correctly write down what he hears. It involves building two different skills. First, the ability to listen and understand what is heard, and second, the ability to transfer what is heard into written language. This process takes time and practice, so begin as gradually as needed for successfully reaching the goal of getting the words the child hears on the paper correctly. 1) Read the whole passage, then reread one sentence at a time, giving your child time to write what he hears. 2) After he has finished, reread the passage again, allowing him to double check what he has written. 3) Then proceed to the step of comparing his writing to the model. As his skill builds, you can move more quickly through the steps, maintaining your child's level of success.

🐾 Copy, or write as your teacher dictates, paragraph 7 on page 51 of *Christopher Columbus*. When you are finished, compare your copy to the text and make any needed corrections.

B. Reader　　　　　　　　　　　　　　　*Language Skills, Thinking Skills*
Read pages 29–31 in *Meet Christopher Columbus* aloud.

🐾 Read one or two paragraphs in your read-aloud book, *Christopher Columbus*.

🐾 Read one or two pages from today's read-aloud assignment in *Christopher Columbus*.

C. Read-Aloud and Narration　　　　　　*Language Skills, Thinking Skills*
Listen carefully as your teacher reads pages 51–55 in *Christopher Columbus*.

To *narrate* means to retell. In your own words, tell what happened in your assigned passage below. Try to remember as many details as possible. Listen carefully as your teacher reads, or rereads, the part you are to retell.

🐾🐾 Paragraph 4 on page 53 of the read-aloud book (starting with "Friday, August 3….") Tell your teacher what happened that morning.

🐾 Paragraph 6 on page 53 through the end of the page. Tell what special thing happened for Columbus.

🐾 Paragraph 7 on page 54 through the end of page 55. Tell what Columbus was feeling as his voyage began.

C. The skill of narration is gained over time. If your child has never retold a story, start with the assignment for the lower level, no matter what grade he is in. Work up from there, being careful to allow him to stay at the level of success for a while before going to a longer section.

D. Word Study
Sometimes words that tell us what has already happened are unusual. These words are not made by adding *ed* like most words. Instead, their spelling is changed. Here are some examples:

go — went

sleep — slept

fight — fought

In the passage you copied today, look for the word that tells that these things have already happened, and write them in your Student Notebook:[8]

sink _____　　has _____

is _____　　take _____

Look at yesterday's copywork passage and find the words that show something has already happened, and write them in your Student Notebook:[9]

become _____ begin _____

Look on pages 29 and 30 in *Meet Christopher Columbus*. See if you can find the words that tell that these things already happened, and write them in your Student Notebook:[10]

blow _____   make _____

hold _____   write _____

🐾 Look at pages 26 through 28 in *Meet Christopher Columbus*. Find as many words as you can that tell something has already happened, either by having *ed* added to the end of the word, or by showing a new form of the root word, like sing and sang. Make a list of all the words you find.[11] You do not need to list any word more than once.

🐾 Look at page 47 of *Christopher Columbus*. Find all the words you can on this page that tell that something has already happened. Make a list of all the words you find.[12] You do not need to list any word more than once. Divide the list into words that are made the regular way, by adding *ed*, and words that are made by changing the root words, which arc called *irregular*.

E. Geography

Look at Map C-2 below that shows what Columbus thought the world looked like. You can see Spain, from where he would sail, and you can see where he thought China (Cathay) and Japan would be. If he had been right, it would have been easy to get to the Far East by sea. But this map was not correct.

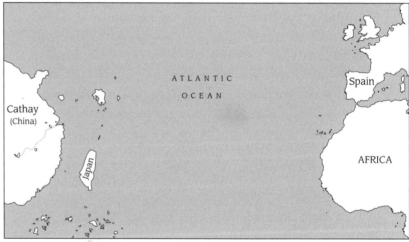

Map C-2

Look at your globe. Trace your finger from Spain, across the Atlantic Ocean to America. Now find China on your globe. Are they even close?

Now look at Map C-3. This shows the part of the world where Columbus traveled. On Map C-3 in your notebook find the Atlantic

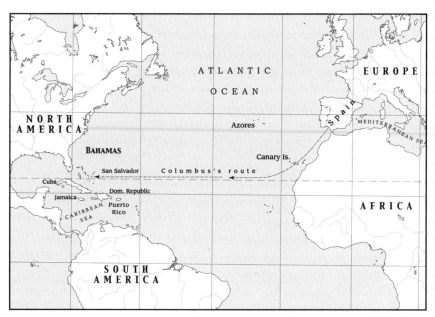

Map C-3

Ocean and put a dot by its name. Now find these continents and put a dot by each of their names:

- Europe
- Africa
- North America
- South America

A **continent** is a large mass of land. There are seven continents. Most of the dry land on earth is made up of these continents. Continents are made up of countries. Find the country of Spain and put a dot by its name. It is part of the continent of Europe.

Also on your map are some important islands. An **island** is a piece of land that is completely surrounded by water. Put a dot by these islands:

- Canary Island
- Cuba
- Jamaica
- San Salvador
- Azores
- Dominican Republic
- Bahamas
- Puerto Rico
- Color the Atlantic Ocean blue. Color the continents and the islands green.
- Find the Mediterranean Sea and the Caribbean Sea. Put a dot by each one. **Seas** are large bodies of salt water that cover a large part of the earth. Seas can also be surrounded by land. A sea is usually smaller than an ocean.

🐾 Label Map C-4 in your Student Notebook with the Atlantic Ocean, the continents, and the seas.

🐾 Label Map C-4 in your Student Notebook with the oceans, continents, seas, and islands.

F. Writing

Vocabulary

Look at the list of islands in Section E above. Choose one of the islands and find some information about it. You can look in an encyclopedia, at the library or, with your parent's permission on the Internet. Tell where the island is located. Use the map activity above if you need help describing where it is.

Find a picture of the island you chose. Use the space in your Student Notebook to draw what you see in the picture, and then describe it to your teacher.

What kinds of plants and animals are there on this island? What do the people who live there eat as their main foods? What is the weather like on this island? What do you think Columbus and his men could have found on this island to help them? Add these things to your drawing if they are not already there.

A **brochure** is a pamphlet that gives information about a topic. It is usually folded in thirds or halves.

Make a travel brochure for the island you chose. Use any type of paper you want, and include information on each side of the paper to make your brochure as interesting as possible.

Find information about the island and then create a picture and descriptions that would make someone want to visit there. Remember to build up all the good points about the island. If the weather is usually good, that would be a good selling point for the island. If there are beaches and many fruits that grow there, those are good points that you can include.

G. See Independent Reading note in Part 1.

G. Independent Reading

Choose something to read that you will enjoy. Find a quiet, comfortable place and read for the following length of time:

20 minutes

25 minutes

30 minutes

Over time, it's fun to see how much you have read. Be sure to write down what you read today on the Reading Log in your Student Notebook.

Lesson 3, Part 3

𝒜. **Copywork/Dictation**   *Language Skills*

Look carefully at your assigned passage, either below or in the read-aloud book, and read it silently. Show your teacher any words you don't know, and practice saying them aloud. Now read the passage aloud, or ask your teacher to read it to you.

𝒜. See Copywork/Dictation note in Part 1.

> His brother made maps for sailors. Columbus wanted to know more, so he learned how to read and write. He read the Bible and books about exploring.

ᵞᵞ Copy the above lines into your Student Notebook. When you are finished, compare your copy to the model (word by word) and make any needed corrections.

ᵚ Listen as your teacher dictates the passage above, and write it in your Student Notebook. When you are finished, compare your copy to the model and make any needed corrections.

ᵚ Copy, or write as your teacher dictates, paragraph 1 on page 57 of *Christopher Columbus*. When you are finished, compare your copy to the text and make any needed corrections.

ℬ. **Reader**   *Language Skills, Thinking Skills*

Read pages 32–34 in *Meet Christopher Columbus* aloud.

ᵚ Read one or two paragraphs in your read-aloud book, *Christopher Columbus*.

ᵚ Read one or two pages from today's read-aloud assignment in *Christopher Columbus*.

𝒞. **Read-Aloud and Discussion**   *Language Skills, Thinking Skills*

Listen carefully as your teacher reads pages 56–61 in *Christopher Columbus*.

𝒞. See Discussion note in Part 1.

Discussion: What happened to the *Pinta* just three days after they had left Spain? Do you think Columbus was upset about this problem? Explorers should expect to have some hard times during their trips. What do you think their attitude should be when they have a problem?

𝒟. **Word Study**   *Spelling, Phonics, Vocabulary*

Look at the words you wrote when you labeled the parts of the ship like the *Santa Maria*. Practice reading them aloud.

Find the label from the word bank in your Student Notebook that fits these clues:[13]

I am the biggest sail. Who am I?

I am the main place where things are carried. Who am I?

I am the small piece that steers the ship. Who am I?

I point to show which direction the ship is going in. Who am I?

I am the sail on the back of the ship. Who am I?

I am the place where most things happen on deck. Who am I?

I am able to carry you from the ship to the shore. Who am I?

After you have found the label that answers each of the "Who Am I" clues above, make up your own clues for at least three of the remaining labels.

Make a game with index cards by putting the name of each label on one card and the meaning on another card. Mix the cards up and place them face down to play a "Concentration" type matching game. If you want want, draw a picture on the card that has the meaning on it so anyone can play.

E. Science   *Geography*

Wind is a flow of air. Some winds are soft and light, and others are strong and hard. Storms have strong winds, but not all winds are part of storms. Some winds help us.

Go outside and see if you can feel any wind blowing. How does the wind feel to you? Is it hot or cold, hard or soft? Can you look around and see any effects of the wind blowing?

Winds are caused by several things. The turning of the earth is one thing that helps create wind. The sun heating up the earth also helps make winds blow. Some winds are a part of bad weather. One kind of wind that helps people is called the **trade wind.** It is called that because sailing ships used to carry goods from one country to another so they could be traded. The trade winds filled the sails of the ships and helped them move more quickly to their destinations.

Trade winds are winds that blow towards the **equator** from the north or from the south. The equator is an imaginary line that runs around the middle of the earth.

Look at your globe and find the line that runs around the middle. Find the word equator.

The equator divides the globe into two parts. The top part, or the part above the equator, is called the Northern Hemisphere. A **hemisphere** is half of a sphere.

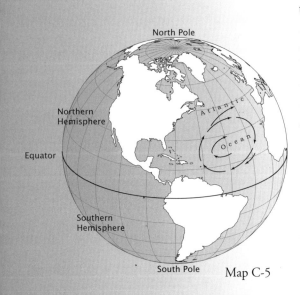

Map C-5

Show your teacher the Northern Hemisphere on your globe.

The bottom part, or part below the equator, is called the Southern Hemisphere. Why do you think they are called the Northern and Southern Hemispheres?[14]

Look at Map C-6 of the trade winds around the Atlantic Ocean. With your finger, trace the path Columbus took across the ocean. Do you think the trade winds helped him?

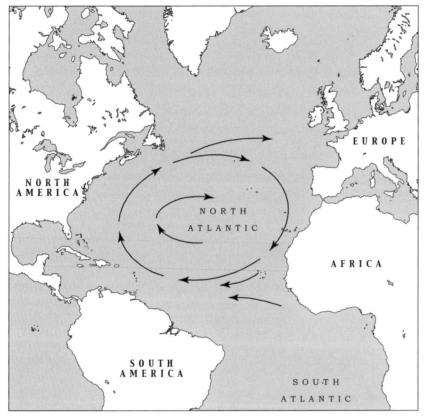

Map C-6

For years after Columbus' voyage to the New World, sailors used the same route he had taken. He had found what our *Handbook of Nature Study* calls the rivers of air (trade winds) and rivers under the ocean (currents). These rivers of air and water moved ships more quickly to the New World and back to Europe. Do you think the discovery of these two types of rivers (air and under the ocean) helped direct the way things happened in history?

🐾 Label the equator, the Northern Hemisphere and the Southern Hemisphere on Map C-7 in your Student Notebook.

🐾 Look at the chart of earth's prevailing winds on page 792 in the *Handbook of Nature Study*. Show your teacher the trade winds on the chart. Draw the trade winds on Map C-8 in your Student Notebook. Add North Pole and South Pole labels to Map C-7.

F. Art

This activity may take several days to complete.

1. Go outside during the time of the day when it is the windiest. In your Student Notebook, draw what the clouds look like to you. If you make a blue background, use white or gray crayons, pastels, or colored pencils to show the clouds. Choose one spot and look up at the clouds from that position.

2. Repeat this process at least twice more from the same spot, but at different times of the day. Try to choose times when the level of the winds is different. Put the date and time on each drawing. If there are no clouds on the days you are drawing, draw the bushes or trees around you to show the movement of the wind. Remember that explorers also included drawings of the weather in an area to help others understand what the area was like.

Tell or write what you think the difference is between the following words. Then look up their definitions in a dictionary. Put them in order from most gentle to strongest.[15]

wind   breeze   gale

The most destructive type of storm experienced in the Caribbean is called a hurricane. As Columbus traveled in this area, it was always possible to run into a hurricane. Use reference materials, the library, or, with your parent's permission, the Internet to find out more about this type of storm. Tell or write what makes a storm a hurricane. What effect do you think a hurricane would have had on Columbus' ships?

G. See Independent Reading note in Part 1.

G. Independent Reading

Choose something to read that you will enjoy. Find a quiet, comfortable place and read for the following length of time:

20 minutes

25 minutes

30 minutes

Be sure to write down what you read today on the Reading Log in your Student Notebook.

Lesson 3, Part 4

A. **Copywork/Dictation**   *Language Skills, Thinking Skills*

Look carefully at your assigned passage, either below or in the read-aloud book, and read it silently. Show your teacher any words you don't know, and practice saying them aloud. Now read the passage aloud, or ask your teacher to read it to you.

> Exploring was part of his wife's life as well. Her father had been governor on an island. His old charts and maps helped Columbus learn more about the ocean.

🐾 Copy the above lines into your Student Notebook. When you are finished, compare your copy to the model (word by word) and make any needed corrections.

🐾 Listen as your teacher dictates the passage above, and write it in your Student Notebook. When you are finished, compare your copy to the model and make any needed corrections.

🐾 Copy, or write as your teacher dictates, paragraph 5 on page 65 of *Christopher Columbus*. When you are finished, compare your copy to the text and make any needed corrections.

B. **Reader**   *Language Skills, Thinking Skills*

Read pages 35–37 in *Meet Christopher Columbus* aloud.

🐾 Read one or two paragraphs in your read-aloud book, *Christopher Columbus*.

🐾 Read one or two pages from today's read-aloud assignment in *Christopher Columbus*.

C. **Read-Aloud and Narration**   *Language Skills, Thinking Skills*

Listen carefully as your teacher reads pages 62–69 in *Christopher Columbus*.

To *narrate* means to retell. In your own words, tell what happened in your assigned passage below. Try to remember as many details as possible. Listen carefully as your teacher reads, or rereads, the part you are to retell.

🐾 Paragraph 4 on page 69.

🐾 Paragraph 4 on page 63 through paragraph 4 on page 64. What was Pedro worried about? How did Columbus comfort him?

A. See Copywork/Dictation note in Part 1.

C. See Narration note in Part 2.

🐾 Paragraph 4 on page 61 through to the end of page 62. Tell what you have learned about Pedro de Salcedo. Are there any ways that you and Pedro are the same?

D. Word Study   *Spelling, Phonics, Vocabulary*

A **compound** word is a word made up of at least two smaller words that have recognizable meanings. Compound words are very common when we speak, read, and write. Here are some examples of compound words:

> dog + house = doghouse   basket + ball = basketball
>
> book + shelf = bookshelf   back + pack = backpack

Look at the chart on pages 24 and 25 of *Meet Christopher Columbus.* See how many words you can find that look like two words put together. Make a list of the words you think are compound words.

In a dictionary, look up the words on your list. If the two words are separated by a space, it is not a compound word. If it is connected by a dot or a dash and the two parts are words you recognize as separate words, it is a compound word. You do not need to write the meaning down, just put a check by the word if it is really a compound word. For the words that are, draw a line between the two parts of the word.[16]

🖐 Look in the dictionary for compound words that begin with the word *main.* In your Student Notebook, make a list of the words you find.

Do the same thing with the beginning word *ship.* Circle the words that you write down that relate to sailing a ship.

🐾 Look in the dictionary for compound words that begin with the word *quarter.* Make a list of the words you find. Try the same procedure with the beginning word *sea.* Circle the words you write down that relate to sailing a ship.

E. Geography   *Science*

Dead reckoning was a method of **navigation,** or steering and figuring paths for ships, that was used by Columbus. Listen as your teacher rereads paragraph 7 on page 62 in *Christopher Columbus.*

This method of navigation was very important for explorers. Often the weather would not allow them to use the stars to navigate at night, and using instruments to tell where they were depended on good weather. Dead reckoning was a way of telling their location when they did not know it. Here is a description of the method used:

A floating object would be dropped next to the front of the ship.

The navigator would then time it to see how long it took for the object to get to the back of the ship.

By knowing how long the ship was, the navigator could tell how far the ship traveled in a specific amount of time.

By starting with their last position and the time they began to travel, they could figure out how far the ship had traveled.

Can you think of any problems with this system?[17] Can you think of any benefits of using this system?[18] What would keep a navigator from being able to use this system?[19]

Much of the skill that Columbus had as a navigator came from his many observations. Thinking about the stories you have heard or the pages that you have read, make a list of some of the things that Columbus observed on a regular basis. How do you think these observations helped him?[20]

❦ Think about your reading and your read-aloud story and tell some of the things that Columbus observed to help him know they were nearing land.

From your books, try to find other specific examples of things that Columbus observed that were encouragements to him and his men that land was near. Make a list of the things that they saw.

❦ Dead reckoning was just one method of navigation during Columbus' time. Other methods of navigation included the use of instruments like the sextant and the astrolabe. Using the library or the Internet, find out how these instruments worked. Draw a picture of at least one of them and write what it did. Which method of navigation do you think was best for Columbus or other explorers of the time to use?

F. Writing   *Art*
Look at the pictures of the *Niña, Pinta,* and *Santa Maria* on pages 66 and 67 of *Christopher Columbus.* See how many parts of the ships you can identify using the labels of ship parts you learned on pages 24 and 25 of *Meet Christopher Columbus.* Also, look for extra parts, such as the crow's nest.

❦ Looking at a picture such as this tells us about what was happening at the time. Look at this picture like a detective. How many clues can you find that tell about the weather, the time of day, their nearness to land? Write the clues you see in your Student Notebook. Write them as phrases, or a few words, not as complete sentences. What do you think the moods, or feelings, of the sailors were at this time on the ship?

Trace or draw one or all of the ships in this picture. Add color to your picture with colored pencils or crayons to help show what the day may have looked like. Underneath the pictures, write some words that you think describe your picture. Put each word in one of these categories:

ship   sky   sea

Include words that help others know what the ocean may have looked like, sounded like, smelled like, felt like, or tasted like. It is good to use all your senses when you describe something for someone.

G. See Independent Reading note in Part 1.

G. Independent Reading

Choose something to read that you will enjoy. Find a quiet, comfortable place and read for the following length of time:

20 minutes

25 minutes

30 minutes

Be sure to write down what you read today on the Reading Log in your Student Notebook.

Lesson 3, Part 5

This part is set aside for completion of any work left undone from the lesson, and review of concepts and content. It is also a time to expand the work in the lesson by doing art, timeline activities, or games.

• Review the Steps for Thinking from the beginning of this lesson.

Most of the labeling has already been completed in the Student Notebook during this lesson. Instruct students to use the maps in their Student Notebooks as a reference. When they label the larger map, students will see the "big picture" and gain a broader understanding of their lessons.

• On the large outline map of the world label: the seven continents, Japan, the seas from this lesson, and mark the route Columbus traveled in orange.

• Review the spelling words for this lesson. In your Student Notebook, write a sentence using each word that tells how it is related to the unit. Do your best to write the spelling words correctly. After you have finished, check your sentences against the list in your Student Notebook and see how many spelling words you spelled correctly. (Don't count off for other words that are misspelled.) Remember your goal is to improve, not necessarily to get them all right immediately. OR----

- Choose five words that have antonyms, that you used in the Word Study section during this lesson. Act each one out for your family until someone guesses the correct word. See if anyone can guess its antonym.

- Play Ocean and Continent Concentration with the cards found on your Student Resources CD. If you made a card game this week with the names of the parts of the ship and a description of the parts, you may want to play that game again as well.

- Complete the Simple Nature Studies and Color Chart art lesson by Barry Stebbing found in your Student Notebook.

Teachers can find a copy of this game in Appendix B. Instructions and answer keys for all games are located in Appendix A.

Enrichment Activities

Use one or more of the Enrichment Activities if your child completes his assigned work and has the time or desire to learn more. These activities are flexible, so choose the one(s) that seem most interesting to your student. Allow him to work at a level that is appropriate for him, and remember that the learning process is more important than the product.

1. Read the book *Carry On, Mr. Bowditch* by Jean Lee Latham. This book is the story of Nathaniel Bowditch, yet it contains much information about the navigation of ships. Make a list of some of the things you learn about navigation and share them with your family. This activity may take more than one week.

2. One of the islands where Columbus landed was Jamaica. The climate in this area is tropical. Think about all the things that you would see, hear, feel, and taste on a tropical island. With your parent's permission, create a meal with foods that come from this island. (Recipes can be found in *Eat Your Way Around the World* by Jamie Aramini.) Encourage your family to dress for a tropical environment when they come to your meal. You may want to find music that would be played on this island to play in the background.

3. Contact your local weatherman, or visit the Weather Channel's website for information on hurricanes and a hurricane tracking chart. When hurricane season begins, track as many storms as you can. Since each storm that becomes a hurricane is named, you may want to keep a journal that lists each storm and what became of it. Learn the steps to be prepared for a hurricane if you live in a hurricane prone area.

Additional Resources

Carry On, Mr. Bowditch by Jean Lee Latham

Resources on tropical islands, or the islands of the West Indies

Information on hurricanes

Eat Your Way Around the World by Jamie Aramini

Answers

1. Possible answers: young-old; begun-ended; far-close; him-her

2. middle

3. Having the largest mast in the middle kept the ship balanced.

4. mainsail

5. It was up high, like a bird's nest, and sailors could sit in it.

6. It was a place to look out around the ship.

7. Possible answers: Caravels were faster than other ships for exploring, and they were easier to steer.

8. sink-sunk; has-had; is-was; take-took

9. become-became; begin-began

10 blow-blew; make-made; hold-held; write-wrote

11. headed, were, belonged, planned, sailed, started, tossed, rolled, smashed, saw, was, fixed, snapped, began, struggled, decided, did, went, seemed, said, had, seen, told, found, made

12. adding *ed*: insulted, degraded, kicked, muttered, guided, traveled, called, turned, asked; irregular: had, been, led, heard, kept

13. mainsail; hold; rudder; compass; mizzen; maindeck; longboat

14. The Northern Hemisphere is the half of the globe near the North Pole. The Southern Hemisphere is the half of the globe near the South Pole.

15. breeze-wind-gale

16. quarter/deck, helms/man, main/sail, fore/sail, spent/sail, fore/castle, long/boat, cabin

17 Possible answer: currents and winds could change, affecting speed

18. Possible answer: did not depend on clear skies

19. Possible answer: bad weather could keep a navigator from using this system.

20. Possible observations: birds, objects, or wood floating in the water, seaweed, certain fish or mammals

Lesson 4, Part 1

> ### ❧ Steps for Thinking ❧
>
> 1. Look for relationships between things you are studying. This will help you understand how new things fit into what you already know. For instance, there is a relationship between climate and what you choose to wear or do. Now you can understand why knowing about climate is important when you travel.
>
> 2. The purpose of writing is to communicate. When someone else understands what you know or think that means you are writing clearly.

The **Steps for Thinking** section gives you the main ideas about the topics presented. Understanding these helps you to have productive discussions with your children so they, too, understand the bigger ideas. This forms more permanent learning, contrary to just learning facts, which tends to be temporary. These steps are useful prior to instruction, and they are also useful for review at the end of the week.

A. Copywork/Dictation *Language Skills, Thinking Skills, History*

Look carefully at your assigned passage, either below or in the read-aloud book, and read it silently. Show your teacher any words you don't know, and practice saying them aloud. Now read the passage aloud, or ask your teacher to read it to you.

> The old maps gave Columbus a new idea. People wanted to get to the Far East. He believed they could get there by sailing across the Ocean Sea.

🐾 Copy the above lines into your Student Notebook. When you are finished, compare your copy to the model (word by word) and make any needed corrections.

✋ Listen as your teacher dictates the passage above, and write it in your Student Notebook. When you are finished, compare your copy to the model and make any needed corrections.

🐾 Copy, or write as your teacher dictates, paragraph 2 on page 72 of *Christopher Columbus*. When you are finished, compare your copy to the text and make any needed corrections.

B. Reader *Language Skills, Thinking Skills, History*

Read pages 38 and 39 in *Meet Christopher Columbus* aloud.

✋ Read one or two paragraphs in your read-aloud book, *Christopher Columbus*.

🐾 Read one or two pages from today's read-aloud assignment in *Christopher Columbus*.

❧ Materials ❧

- *Meet Christopher Columbus*
- *Christopher Columbus*
- *Profiles from History*
- *Intermediate World Atlas*
- Student Notebook
- Dictionary
- *Handbook of Nature Study*
- Highlighter
- Television, Newspaper, or Internet Access
- Dark Construction Paper
- Common Household Items (pen, key, spoon, etc.)
- Crayons or Colored Pencils
- City Map
- Almanac (🐾)
- Large world and U.S. outline maps

Additional resources for Enrichment Activities are found in Part 5.

A. Copywork and dictation assignments go from an easier level (designated by 🐾) to harder levels (designated by ✋ and 🐾). Take two days for the copywork if that is more comfortable for your child. Please adapt instructions to your child's individual needs. Your child should be **consistently successful** at one level before progressing to the next, **regardless of grade**.

C. Discussion is very important in developing your child's ability to organize his thoughts. This in turn builds the ability to think and write. The goal of the discussion questions is not just to find the answer to a particular question, but also to create a situation where thoughts about the question and its answer are shared and considered in a detailed way. Do not rush this activity, but encourage your student to share his or her ideas relating to the topic, and any additional ideas that may come to mind. You can also share your thoughts and questions as an example for your students.

D. The small superscript numbers that appear after some of the questions in this unit refer to answers found in the answer key, located immediately after Part 5.

C. **Read-Aloud and Discussion**   *Language Skills, Thinking Skills, History*

Listen carefully as your teacher reads pages 70–75 in *Christopher Columbus.*

Discussion: Columbus realizes his dream of reaching land during this chapter. The first five paragraphs on page 74 describe the reaction of his crew upon claiming the New World for Spain. Listen as your teacher rereads these paragraphs then tell why you think the crew asked forgiveness from Columbus. How do you think this made Columbus feel?

Do you think this event helped make up for all the times people doubted Columbus and his plan?

D. **Word Study**   *Spelling, Phonics, Vocabulary*

Silent letters may not say anything when we pronounce a word, but they help us know how to say the letters around them. When *k* and *n* stand together, the letter whose sound we hear is the *n.*

Find the word on page 37 of *Meet Christopher Columbus* that has the letters *kn* together, that is pronounced with an *n* sound. Now look on page 38 and find the *kn* word on that page. [1]

Read these *kn* words for your teacher or listen as she reads them to you. In your Student Notebook highlight the letters in each word that make the *n* sound.

knit	knack	knot
knight	knob	knock
know	knuckle	

Discuss the meaning of each word with your teacher. Look up any words in the dictionary you would like to know more about. See if you can write one long silly sentence using all the words.

🖐 Look in the dictionary under *kn.* See how long a list of words you can make (try for at least 10) that are spelled with *kn* as the first two letters. The only rule for adding a word to your list is that you be able to tell your teacher what it is, so try to look for words that you have heard of before.

🐾 Look in the dictionary under *kn.* Find at least ten words that you have never heard of before and write them down, along with their definition. Be prepared to tell others what the words are and what they mean. Try to use your new words in conversation.

E. Science

Writing

The **sun** is the head of our solar system family. Our solar system is made up of the sun and planets and everything else that is held in orbit around our sun by gravity. The sun is by far the largest star near us, even though it is only a medium-sized star. In early times, people thought the earth was at the center of the solar system and that the sun revolved around us. Copernicus was a scientist who did not believe that. He believed the sun was the center of the solar system. Once people got this fact straight, they could learn a lot of other things about our sun.

The sun is a star made up of hot gases. The temperature at the center of the sun, which is called the **core,** is millions of degrees. The outer layers of the sun are hotter than anything you can imagine. The sun is made up mostly of a gas called hydrogen, and another gas called helium. These gases are the fuel that the sun burns. The sun has two important jobs in our solar system. The first is to keep us warm.

The other job the sun does for us is to provide light. In fact, the sun does its job so well that you cannot look directly at it without hurting your eyes very badly — so please don't ever do that! When the sun's light is shining on you, it is daytime. When the place where you are on earth turns away from the sun, it is nighttime. It takes about 24 hours for the earth to turn completely around, and usually about half of that time is daytime, and half is nighttime.

Watch the weather report for your area to find out what times the sun will rise and set where you are. You can also find this information in an almanac, in the newspaper, or on the Internet.

With your teacher's help, figure out how much daylight you will have today. Write what you find out in your Student Notebook.

🖐 Make a list of at least three things you know about the sun. Write them in your Student Notebook.

🐾 Read Lesson 231 (page 852) in your *Handbook of Nature Study.* Answer questions #1–8 orally or in writing. Use an almanac to answer the length of days questions. Do #9 and #13 and record your observations to put in your Student Notebook. Share what you observe with others.

F. Art

You are learning about the effects of the sun. Now you will learn how to show the effects of sunlight on things you draw. Use Art Lesson: Shading found in Appendix A. This lesson is from the book *Master Drawing* by Sharon Jeffus, who teaches art to homeschoolers.

E. Each word in bold letters is considered a vocabulary word. It is a word that may or may not be new to your child. You can write these vocabulary words on index cards and use them for occasional review, but not for memorizing. Give the child the meaning of the words if he doesn't remember. Try to use the new vocabulary words during conversation, and encourage your students to do the same.

Each time your student makes a vocabulary card for this unit, have him write a "C" (for Columbus) in the upper left corner. This will make it possible to review vocabulary by unit at the end of the year.

E. Background information for Lesson 231 begins on page 851.

F. You can learn more about products by Sharon Jeffus for teaching art to homeschoolers at her website www.visualmanna.com.

G. Reading fluency is developed through having frequent silent reading opportunities that continue for the length of time suggested here. Since a primary focus of this activity is to nurture your child's enjoyment of reading, help him to choose reading material that interests him and is at a level that allows him to read with understanding by himself. You can incorporate this activity into your school day whenever it is most convenient.

If the suggested length of time is too long for your child to continue reading by himself, start with an amount of time he can accomplish successfully and make the suggested time a goal.

A. See Copywork/Dictation note in Part 1.

G. **Independent Reading**
Choose something to read that you will enjoy. Find a quiet, comfortable place and read for the following length of time:

ᔥ 20 minutes

ᔥ 25 minutes

ᔥ 30 minutes

Over time, it's fun to see how much you have read. Be sure to write down what you read today on the Reading Log in your Student Notebook.

Lesson 4, Part 2

A. **Copywork/Dictation**   *Language Skills, Thinking Skills*
Look carefully at your assigned passage, either below or in the read-aloud book, and read it silently. Show your teacher any words you don't know, and practice saying them aloud. Now read the passage aloud, or ask your teacher to read it to you.

> Columbus got his chance to cross the ocean. He kept a log to tell his story, but sadly, it was lost. Others told his story too.

ᔥ Copy the above lines into your Student Notebook. When you are finished, compare your copy to the model (word by word) and make any needed corrections.

ᔥ Listen as your teacher dictates the passage above, and write it in your Student Notebook. When you are finished, compare your copy to the model and make any needed corrections.

ᔥ Copy, or write as your teacher dictates, paragraph 2 on page 79 of *Christopher Columbus*. When you are finished, compare your copy to the text and make any needed corrections.

B. **Reader**   *Language Skills, Thinking Skills*
Read pages 40–42 in *Meet Christopher Columbus* aloud.

ᔥ Read one or two paragraphs in your read-aloud book, *Christopher Columbus*.

ᔥ Read one or two pages from today's read-aloud assignment in *Christopher Columbus*.

C. Read-Aloud and Narration
Language Skills, Thinking Skills

Listen carefully as your teacher reads pages 76–81 in *Christopher Columbus*.

To *narrate* means to retell. In your own words, tell what happened in your assigned passage below. Try to remember as many details as possible. Listen carefully as your teacher reads, or rereads, the part you are to retell.

🌵 Paragraph 5 on page 77.

🐾 Paragraph 7 on page 77 to the end of paragraph 1 on page 78.

🐾 Paragraph 5 on page 79 through the end of the chapter on page 81.

D. Word Study
Spelling, Phonics, Vocabulary

Review your list of *kn* words from yesterday. Listen as someone reads the list of words to you. Write each word as you hear it. When you are finished, check your words by looking at your list. Put a check by all the words that are spelled correctly. Put a dot by any words that are spelled incorrectly. Don't forget to include the words *knee* and *knives* from the story.

Find the word *island* on pages 37 and 39 of *Meet Christopher Columbus*. This word has a silent letter. Can you tell what it is? Highlight the silent letter in this word in your Student Notebook. What do you think an island is? Write what you think it is. Then look up the definition in a dictionary. Write down anything you need to add to your definition.

Look at the word *isle* in your Student Notebook. Highlight the letter that you think is silent. The word *isle* is similar to the word *island*. What do you think an isle is? Look up the definition and tell how it is different from an island.

🐾 Look on pages 38 and 39 of *Meet Christopher Columbus*. Find two words that have *gh* as silent letters.[2] Make a list of at least two other words that rhyme with each of these words. Highlight the silent *gh* in each word.

🐾 Look in the dictionary. What words can you find that start with the letters *gh?* What sound does *gh* make when it is at the beginning of a word? Make a list of at least five words that begin with *gh*. Write what you think they mean in your Student Notebook. Look the words up in a dictionary and add any important information you left out.

E. Science
Geography, Writing

Listen as your teacher reads pages 780 and 781 to you from the *Handbook of Nature Study*. As the story about the **weather** and **climate** tells you, they are two different things. Weather is what is

C. The skill of narration is gained over time. If your child has never retold a story, start with the assignment for the lower level, no matter what grade he is in. Work up from there, being careful to allow him to stay at the level of success for a while before going to a longer section.

happening around us right now. Some weather conditions include rain, sunshine, cloudiness, windiness, cold, hot, etc. Climate tells about what the weather is usually like in a place over a period of years. Weather can be determined for a day, but climate takes years to identify. What is the weather like where you are today?

Maps can show us what the climate is like in a particular part of the country or the world. Turn to the United States thematic maps in the *Intermediate World Atlas,* and look at the Climate Map. With your teacher's help, find where you live. Tell what the climate or the weather is usually like in the place you live. Is the weather where you are in keeping with the climate for your area? Are the weather and the climate shown on the map the same?

Find the climate for these three places in the United States:

• New York City, New York

• Denver, Colorado

• Los Angeles, California

Use the words from the climate map to tell what the climate is in each place.

The climate in Cuba and Jamaica, where Columbus visited, is the same. Tell what the climate is like in these places.[3] The answer can be found on the Climate Map, in the North America thematic maps section in your *Intermediate World Atlas.*

The climate is the same in Portugal and Spain, where Columbus was from. Tell what the climate is like in these places.[4] Is the climate where Columbus lived similar to the places he discovered while exploring?[5] Do you think this would make it easier or harder while exploring? Tell why or why not.

Look on the climate map and find at least three other places in the country that have the same climate as the place where you live. Find at least three places that have a different climate from where you live.

Have you ever visited a place that had a different climate from the place where you live, or moved from one climate to another? Tell about some of the things that were different. If you have not visited a different place, choose a place with a different climate on your climate map. Tell what would be different about visiting that place. Here is an example:

I grew up in South Florida where the summer climate is warm and humid with mild winters. I moved to North Florida where the summer climate is the same but the winter climate is very different. It is much colder and rainier. I had a very difficult time adjusting to the longer and colder winters.

F. Writing   *Thinking Skills, Science, Language Skills, Art*

When you travel, it is always important to think about the weather. The time of year when you are traveling is also important. Below are two very different places for a vacation. Think about the places and times of year. Make a list of things you would need to bring along for a fun vacation at each place.

A Florida beach in the summer:

_____   _____
_____   _____
_____   _____

A Colorado snow-ski lodge in the winter:

_____   _____
_____   _____
_____   _____

What kinds of things would you want to do at each of these places?

Florida Beach in summer: Colorado ski lodge in winter:

_____   _____
_____   _____
_____   _____

What would happen if your plans got mixed up and the suitcase for your Florida trip ended up with you on a trip to Colorado? What problems would you have?[6] Tell, draw, or write about what might happen.

Use this word bank to help you complete the above activities:

warm	cold	hot
freezing	bathing suit	shorts
coat	hat	snow skis
swimming	skiing	sand
snow	hot chocolate	ice cream
towel	beach	blanket
snowball	snowman	

G. Independent Reading

Choose something to read that you will enjoy. Find a quiet, comfortable place and read for the following length of time:

🐾🐾 20 minutes

🐾 25 minutes

🐾 30 minutes

Be sure to write down what you read today on the Reading Log in your Student Notebook.

G. See Independent Reading note in Part 1.

Lesson 4, Part 3

A. See Copywork/Dictation note in Part 1.

A. Copywork/Dictation
Language Skills, Thinking Skills

Look carefully at your assigned passage, either below or in the read-aloud book, and read it silently. Show your teacher any words you don't know, and practice saying them aloud. Now read the passage aloud, or ask your teacher to read it to you.

> Everyone tells the story his own way, but many agree on what happened. Columbus told the King and Queen of Spain about his great ideas.

Copy the above lines into your Student Notebook. When you are finished, compare your copy to the model (word by word) and make any needed corrections.

Listen as your teacher dictates the passage above, and write it in your Student Notebook. When you are finished, compare your copy to the model and make any needed corrections.

Copy, or write as your teacher dictates, paragraph 9 on page 83 (starting with "The men were…") in *Christopher Columbus.* When you are finished, compare your copy to the text and make any needed corrections.

B. Reader
Language Skills, Thinking Skills

Read pages 43–46 in *Meet Christopher Columbus* aloud.

Read one or two paragraphs in your read-aloud book, *Christopher Columbus.*

Read one or two pages from today's read-aloud assignment in *Christopher Columbus.*

C. See Discussion note in Part 1.

C. Read-Aloud and Discussion
Language Skills, Thinking Skills

Listen carefully as your teacher reads pages 82–86 in *Christopher Columbus.*

Discussion: Pedro and the crew had been worried about how they would get back to Spain. Once the *Niña* and the *Pinta* started the trip back home, how did Pedro feel then? What was helping the ships go back towards Spain? How did the crew show their happiness?

D. Word Study

Spelling, Phonics, Vocabulary

Words start with capital letters for different reasons. Sentences start with capital letters. The names of particular places, people, and things also start with capital letters. Turn to pages 44–46 in *Meet Christopher Columbus* and look for all the words that start with capital letters that are not at the beginning of a sentence. Put each of the words you find into one of these categories, but write each word only one time:[7]

> Particular Place
> Particular Person
> Particular Thing

After you finish making your lists, choose one word from each category. Use each word that you selected in a sentence; write the sentences in your Student Notebook.

Add at least three words to each category above.

E. Science

Language Skills, Geography

Earlier in this lesson you learned about the sun as the head of our solar system family. Now you will learn about some of the **planet**s and their places in the solar system. A planet is one type of object that orbits a star. None of the planets of our solar system or their moons make light for themselves. They all shine by reflecting the light of the sun. Because of this, you see the planets the same way you see stars at night, only their light often looks a little different.

Listen while your teacher reads the first five stanzas of the poem "A Happy Family" on page 837 of the *Handbook of Nature Study.*

The first four planets are called the Inner Planets because they are nearest the sun. Listen as your teacher reads about each Inner Planet (paragraph 4 on page 835 through paragraph 2 on page 836.) As your teacher reads about each planet, fill in the name of the planet on the chart in your Student Notebook, starting with the planet nearest to the sun.

In your Student Notebook, write one fact you learned about each planet.

🐾 Write two facts you learned about each planet in your Student Notebook.

🐾 Use the *Handbook of Nature Study* to fill out the chart of information about the sun and the first four planets in your Student Notebook.

F. Art

Choose several pieces of dark-colored construction paper. Find several common household objects, such as a pen, key, or a spoon and place them on the construction paper in direct sunlight. Leave the objects on the paper for as long as possible in daylight. You may want to leave them for more than one day.

Take the objects off the paper. Do you see the outline of the objects on the construction paper? What do you think caused the outline to be visible on the paper?[8]

Try it again with different objects and with different amounts of sunlight. What makes the best outline on the paper? Are there any colors of construction paper that work better?

🐾 The change in the paper is caused by the color fading. The sunlight is what causes the paper to fade, or lose color. What other things do you think the sunlight might cause to fade?[9]

🐾 The sun's rays are very powerful. This is one example of its effects on you here on earth. What are some other effects you might feel from the sun's rays?[10]

G. See Independent Reading note in Part 1.

G. Independent Reading

Choose something to read that you will enjoy. Find a quiet, comfortable place and read for the following length of time:

🐾🐾 20 minutes

🐾 25 minutes

🐾 30 minutes

Over time, it's fun to see how much you have read. Be sure to write down what you read today on the Reading Log in your Student Notebook.

Lesson 4, Part 4

A. **Copywork/Dictation**   *Language Skills, Thinking Skills*

Look carefully at your assigned passage, either below or in the read-aloud book, and read it silently. Show your teacher any words you don't know, and practice saying them aloud. Now read the passage aloud, or ask your teacher to read it to you.

> Columbus wanted to find a way to sail to the Far
> East and tell people about his faith in God. It
> took money to buy ships and food.

Copy the above lines into your Student Notebook. When you are finished, compare your copy to the model (word by word) and make any needed corrections.

Listen as your teacher dictates the passage above, and write it in your Student Notebook. When you are finished, compare your copy to the model and make any needed corrections.

Copy, or write as your teacher dictates, paragraph 5 on page 91 of *Christopher Columbus*. When you are finished, compare your copy to the text and make any needed corrections.

B. **Reader**   *Language Skills, Thinking Skills*

Read pages 47–49 in *Meet Christopher Columbus* aloud.

Read one or two paragraphs in your read-aloud book, *Christopher Columbus*.

Read one or two pages from today's read-aloud assignment in *Christopher Columbus*.

C. **Read-Aloud and Narration**   *Language Skills, Thinking Skills*

Listen carefully as your teacher reads pages 86–91 in *Christopher Columbus*.

To *narrate* means to retell. In your own words, tell what happened in your assigned passage below. Try to remember as many details as possible. Listen carefully as your teacher reads, or rereads, the part you are to retell.

Paragraph 6 on page 86.

Paragraph 9 on page 85 through paragraph 4 on page 86.

Paragraph 6 on page 88 through paragraph 5 on page 89.

A. See Copywork/Dictation note in Part 1.

C. See Narration note in Part 2.

D. Word Study
Spelling, Phonics, Vocabulary

One way to know more about something is to compare it to something else. This is what antonyms, or opposites, do. They help us understand the differences between things.

Look at this group of words. Find the pairs of antonyms in your Student Notebook and circle each word in the pair with the same color. Use six different colored pencils or crayons to mark the pairs:

east	angry	morning
leave	long	filled
short	empty	west
glad	evening	stay

Seven of the words in the antonym pairs above are in your reading assignment. Look for the words that are in *Meet Christopher Columbus* from pages 47 through 49. Underline the words in the list that you find in your reader.[11]

Look at the passage you wrote from dictation. Choose at least three words from the passage that you can think of antonyms for and write the antonym pairs in your Student Notebook.

Choose at least five words from your copywork passage and think of an antonym for each word. Write the words you chose and the antonyms in your Student Notebook.

E. Geography
Thinking Skills

There are many different ways to tell about where you are. Each direction you add makes it easier for someone to find you. It also narrows down the number of people who might be at the same place you are. It is not hard to figure out your complete address.

First you can tell what planet you are on. Then you can tell what continent you are on. Then you can tell your country. If you live in the United States, you can tell your state (or province in Canada.) Next name your city and then finally your street address. If you don't know the answer to any of these questions, ask your teacher to tell you what it is and fill out your address in your student book.

Now take all the steps you just used to write your address and use them to find your home on a map. Start with a map of the world, and then move to a map of your country. These types of maps are found in a world atlas. Next, find the state or province in which you live. If you live in a large city it may be in the world atlas. If you do not, you will have to have a map of your state to find your city.

The most detailed local map you can find yourself on is a map of your city. If your teacher has a city map, find the street you live on.

If not, you can use a computer and the Internet to find your address. With your teacher's help, use programs such as Mapquest or Google Earth to find your home. Practice finding where another family member lives and write his or her address in your Student Notebook.

Look at the population chart in Appendix A. Find the number of people who live on your continent. Then find the number of people who live in your country. (If your country is not included, you can find the population of your country on the Internet. Go to the website of your country's government for information.) Then locate the number of people who live in your state. Write this information in your Student Notebook.

After finding the population of your continent, country, and state, continue by finding the population of your city. You can usually find this information on your city's website or at your library. Ask your librarian for help finding the correct reference source. How does the size of your city compare to the capital of your state? If you live in the capital city of your state, compare your capital city to that of a nearby state. Write this information in your Student Notebook. After looking at all these numbers, are you surprised at the number of people who live in your city or state? Can you find another state with about the same size population?

F. Art   *Thinking Skills, Writing*

Look at the picture on page 87 of *Christopher Columbus.* Draw or trace the ship in the picture. You may want to include the ocean in the picture as well. Give your picture a title. Titles are important because they help us know what a picture or story is telling about. Write your title above the picture on the line.

Think about what you see in the picture and how you would describe it. Think particularly about how you would describe the ocean, the ship, and the weather.

Now look back at the pictures of the ships on pages 66 and 67 of *Christopher Columbus* and the picture you drew of the ships in the last lesson. Compare, or look at those pictures and then look at the picture on page 87. What looks different to you?[12] What looks the same?

Read the words in the word bank below, or listen as your teacher reads them to you. Do you notice anything about the pairs of words?[13] Choose the words in each pair that belong with each picture. In your Student Notebook, write the words from each pair under the title for the picture you think the words fit.

smooth — rough	calm — stormy
peaceful — violent	gliding — tossed

| sailing — bobbing | waves — ripples |
| sails up — sails unfurled | people on deck — no one on deck |

Write at least two sentences about the picture you have drawn today. Include words or phrases from your word bank as your write your sentences.

Write three sentences telling what you see in your picture. Include words or phrases from your word bank. These are details about your picture. After you write these three sentences, go back and write a sentence that tells about the most attention-getting part of the picture, which is the storm. Since it is the main thing you notice in this picture, it becomes the main idea of your group of sentences, or paragraph. The main idea tells you the information you need in order to understand the paragraph. Underline the main idea of your paragraph.

G. See Independent Reading note in Part 1.

G. Independent Reading

Choose something to read that you will enjoy. Find a quiet, comfortable place and read for the following length of time:

20 minutes

25 minutes

30 minutes

Be sure to write down what you read today on the Reading Log in your Student Notebook.

Lesson 4, Part 5

This part is set aside for completion of any work left undone from the lesson, and review of concepts and content. It is also a time to expand the work in the lesson by doing art, timeline activities, or games.

• Review the Steps for Thinking from the beginning of this lesson.

• On the large outline map of the world label: Cuba, Jamaica, the country where you live, and Florida. On the large outline map of the U.S. label Florida and the state where you live.

Most of the labeling has already been completed in the Student Notebook during this lesson. Instruct students to use the maps in their Student Notebooks as a reference. When they label the larger map, students will see the "big picture" and gain a broader understanding of their lessons.

• Review the spelling words for this lesson. In your Student Notebook, write a sentence using each word that tells how it is related to the unit. Do your best to write the spelling words correctly. After you have finished, check your sentences against the list in your Student Notebook and see how many spelling words you spelled correctly. (Don't count off for other words that are misspelled.) Remember your goal is to improve, not necessarily to get them all right immediately.

- Play Columbus Bingo found on your Student Resources CD. You may also want to play Ocean and Continent Concentration also located on the Student Resources CD.

- Read the story about Gutenberg in your book *Profiles from History.* Complete the timeline activities and any other activities you would like to do.

Enrichment Activities

1. Sign language is a way of communicating without speaking or writing. Read about sign language and learn how to say a few phrases. Practice speaking to others in your family using sign language. This language was created to enable deaf people to communicate with other people.

2. Look at the list of climates on a climate map. Think about what you would wear if you visited several different climates. For instance, what clothes would you take with you to a tropical island, or to the North Pole? You may draw clothes that fit each climate or with your parent's permission, cut out clothes from magazines or catalogs that fit each climate.

3. Activities also vary with climate. Come up with a list of sports that can be played in different climates. You may want to make a chart of this information that includes pictures of the various sports being played, or equipment needed for the sport. For example, in cold, snowy climates the sports that could be played would be skiing, snowboarding, ice skating, etc.

Additional Resources

Information on Sign Language

Sporting goods catalogs

Magazines

Use one or more of the Enrichment Activities if your child completes his assigned work and has the time or desire to learn more. These activities are flexible, so choose the one(s) that seem most interesting to your student. Allow him to work at a level that is appropriate for him, and remember that the learning process is more important than the product.

Answers

1. page 37, knees; page 38, knives

2. bright and thought

3. tropical, with seasonal rain, which means very hot and humid

4. moderate, with dry summers, which means not extreme in temperature

5. Answers will vary. However, although the climates are somewhat different, they were not an extreme change for Columbus and his men.

6. Possible answers: You would not have the right clothes for the climate; you would have lightweight, summer clothes when you actually need heavy winter clothes, or just the opposite.

7. Particular Place: Babeque, Hispaniola, Cibao, Cipango, La Navidad; Particular Person: Columbus, Indians; Particular Thing: Niña, Santa Maria, Christmas, Spanish

8. Sunlight caused the paper not covered by the objects to fade.

9. Possible answers: cloth, paint, paper, carpet, etc.

10. Possible answers: sunburn, warmth, glare or bright sunshine, heat stroke, exhaustion or dehydration

11. east, angry, morning, leave, long, filled, glad

12. Possible answers: the ocean, the ship, the weather, etc.

13. They are antonyms, or opposites.

Lesson 5, Part 1

❦ Steps for Thinking ❦

1. Knowing how to get information and use it is one of the most important skills children can gain. Learning to look for information is as important as finding an answer because it develops the ability to think.

2. Children develop the skills to learn at an individual rate. It is more important to successfully use each learning skill (reading, writing, discussing, narrating, drawing) to gain understanding than to merely memorize unrelated pieces of information.

The **Steps for Thinking** section gives you the main ideas about the topics presented. Understanding these helps you to have productive discussions with your children so they, too, understand the bigger ideas. This forms more permanent learning, contrary to just learning facts, which tends to be temporary. These steps are useful prior to instruction, and they are also useful for review at the end of the week.

A. **Copywork/Dictation** *Language Skills, Thinking Skills, History*

Look carefully at your assigned passage, either below or in the read-aloud book, and read it silently. Show your teacher any words you don't know, and practice saying them aloud. Now read the passage aloud, or ask your teacher to read it to you.

> After a long wait, the king and queen gave him the money he needed. The trip started with three ships. Sometimes it was very hard.

🐾 Copy the above lines into your Student Notebook. When you are finished, compare your copy to the model (word by word) and make any needed corrections.

🐾 Listen as your teacher dictates the passage above, and write it in your Student Notebook. When you are finished, compare your copy to the model and make any needed corrections.

🐾 Copy, or write as your teacher dictates, paragraph 4 on page 96 in *Christopher Columbus*. When you are finished, compare your copy to the text and make any needed corrections.

B. **Reader** *Language Skills, Thinking Skills, History*

Read pages 50–52 in *Meet Christopher Columbus* aloud.

🐾 Read one or two paragraphs in your read-aloud book, *Christopher Columbus*.

❧Materials❧

- *Meet Christopher Columbus*
- *Christopher Columbus*
- *North American Wildlife Guide*
- *Handbook of Nature Study*
- Student Notebook
- Dictionary
- Index Cards/Marker
- Black Construction Paper
- White Crayon or Pencil
- Crayons or Colored Pencils
- Library or Internet Access
- Large world outline map

Additional resources for Enrichment Activities are found in Part 5.

A. Copywork and dictation assignments go from an easier level (designated by 🐾) to harder levels (designated by 🐾 and 🐾). Take two days for the copywork if that is more comfortable for your child. Please adapt instructions to your child's individual needs. Your child should be **consistently successful** at one level before progressing to the next, **regardless of grade**.

Read one or two pages from today's read-aloud assignment in *Christopher Columbus*.

C. **Read-Aloud and Discussion**　　*Language Skills, Thinking Skills, History*
Listen carefully as your teacher reads pages 92–97 in *Christopher Columbus*.

Discussion: Look at the title of Chapter 9 in *Christopher Columbus*. Predict what you think the trouble will be in the New World. Tell what is different about the beginning of this voyage from the last voyage Columbus made, such as the number of men and ships, and the extra people who were going. Why do you think things are so different?

D. **Word Study**
In this lesson you will look at many different words that have the letter *g* in them, and learn about the different sounds that *g* can make.

Find all the words in today's reading assignment that have the letter *g* in them. Put each of them in the category that tells what sound the letter *g* makes.[1] You do not have to write a word more than once.

> *g* that is silent
> *g* that says *g* like goat
> *ng*

Find the word *gale* in your reading passage. Write what you think it means. Now look it up in the dictionary and write down anything you did not include in your definition.

Look at pages 92 and 93 in *Christopher Columbus* and find all the *g* words. Put each of them in the category that tells what sound the letter *g* makes.[2] You do not have to write a word more than once.

> *g* that says *g* like goat
> *g* that says *j*
> *ng*

In your Student Notebook, write down what you think the word *gawk* means. Now look it up in the dictionary and write down anything you did not include in your definition.

E. **Geography**　　　　　　　　　　　　　　*Vocabulary*
A **map** is a picture of a place. It is drawn as if you were looking down on it from the sky. Look at Map C-9 of Haiti. Start by noticing the largest things on a map first. What looks the biggest to you?[3] The following bodies of water go from largest to smallest. An **ocean** is the largest body of saltwater on the earth. A **sea** is another salty body of water that covers a large part of earth, just not as large as an ocean. A **gulf** is a part of a sea that has land around it on several sides. Find

---

C. Discussion is very important in developing your child's ability to organize his thoughts. This in turn builds the ability to think and write. The goal of the discussion questions is not just to find the answer to a particular question, but also to create a situation where thoughts about the question and its answer are shared and considered in a detailed way. Do not rush this activity, but encourage your student to share his or her ideas relating to the topic, and any additional ideas that may come to mind. You can also share your thoughts and questions as an example for your students.

D. The small superscript numbers that appear after some of the questions in this unit refer to answers found in the answer key, located immediately after Part 5.

E. Each word in bold letters is considered a vocabulary word. It is a word that may or may not be new to your child. You can write these vocabulary words on index cards and use them for occasional review, but not for memorization. The meaning of the word should be given to the child if he doesn't remember. Try to use the new vocabulary words during conversation, and encourage your students to do the same.

Each time your student makes a vocabulary card for this unit, have him write a "C" in the upper left corner. This will make it possible to review vocabulary by unit at the end of the year.

these three bodies of water on Map C-9 and write them on the map in your Student Notebook:

Atlantic Ocean   Caribbean Sea   Gulf of Gonâve

Color the water around the island light blue so that you can still see the names of the bodies of water.

Just as a key unlocks a door, you have to look at a **key** to understand a map. A key to a map helps you understand the meaning of the symbols and writing on the map.

Look at the key for the map of Haiti. Both the star and the circle in the key stand for cities on this map. The star represents Haiti's capital city of Port-au-Prince. Write that name next to the star on Map C-10 in your Student Notebook. The circle stands for another important city called Cap-Hatien. Write that name next to the circle on the map in your Student Notebook. Cap-Hatien is near where Columbus established the fort La Navidad on Christmas week of 1492.

Color the country of Haiti yellow. Be careful to stop at the dotted line which is the border of Haiti and the country next to it, which is the Dominican Republic. This dotted line is in your key.

 Add the following features to your map:

Look at the key for the word *river*. Notice what a river looks like on the map of Haiti, and find the Antibonite River. Label this river on your map, and then trace it in dark blue.

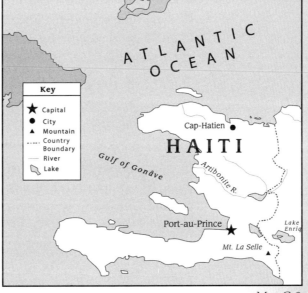

Map C-9

Look at the key for the symbol that represents a mountain. Near the Caribbean Sea in Haiti there is a mountain called Mount la Selle. Label this mountain on your map, and then color the triangle that shows where it is brown.

 On your map trace over the boundary between Haiti and the Dominican Republic with red. This dotted line shows the division between two separate countries. When Columbus came to this island ,he named it Hispaniola. The Spanish settlers who later came to live on Hispaniola tried to make the native Indians who lived there work on their **plantations**, or large farms. This didn't work, so some years later, black slaves from Africa were brought to work on the plantations. Haiti became an independent country in 1804, more than 300 years after Columbus first came to the island.

What happened while Columbus returned to Spain for supplies that was the beginning of problems for the native Indians and the Spanish settlers?[4]

Look in your library or on the Internet to find information on the country of Haiti. Make a list of at least five facts that you learn about Haiti and share them with your teacher. Are the people of Haiti free to live as they wish now?[5]

F. Drawing

Look at page 30 in *Meet Christopher Columbus.* It shows a picture of Christopher Columbus. On that page, it tells that he wrote about everything he saw on his journey. It says he wrote about the weather and the stars and wind. It also says that he wrote about the fish and birds that came around the ship. Why do you think he did this?

Columbus was the first person from the continent of Europe to see all these things. He felt a great responsibility to the king and queen to give a good accounting of his trip by making drawings and writing descriptions.

Some of the things he saw on the trip were flying fish. Look at them on page 213 in the *North American Wildlife Guide.* In your Student Notebook, write down the name of the fish, its size, and where it lives. Also tell what it eats.[6] What was so unusual about this fish?[7]

In your Student Notebook there is space provided for a picture of a flying fish. You can trace it onto plain white paper and then cut it out and glue it in your notebook, or you can draw it in the box.

Another type of wildlife that Columbus and his men saw at sea were birds such as the Brown Pelican.

Look up the Brown Pelican on page 82 of the *North American Wildlife Guide.* In your Student Notebook write down the name of the bird and tell its size, where it lives, and what it eats.[8] Is there anything unusual about this bird?[9]

Trace or draw a picture of the Brown Pelican in the box.

Another account of Columbus' journey tells about the men seeing dolphins swimming next to the ship.

Look up Bottle-nosed Dolphin in the *North American Wildlife Guide* on page 72. In your Student Notebook tell its size and where it lives.[10] Trace or draw a picture of a Bottle-nosed Dolphin in the box.

G. Independent Reading

Choose something to read that you will enjoy. Find a quiet, comfortable place and read for the following length of time:

❧❧ 20 minutes

❧ 25 minutes

❧ 30 minutes

Over time, it's fun to see how much you have read. Be sure to write down what you read today on the Reading Log in your Student Notebook.

G. Reading fluency is developed through having frequent silent reading opportunities that continue for the length of time suggested here. Since a primary focus of this activity is to nurture your child's enjoyment of reading, help him to choose reading material that interests him and is at a level that allows him to read with understanding by himself. You can incorporate this activity into your school day whenever it is most convenient.

If the suggested length of time is too long for your child to continue reading by himself, start with an amount of time he can accomplish successfully and make the suggested time a goal.

Lesson 5, Part 2

A. Copywork/Dictation   *Language Skills, Thinking Skills, History*

Look carefully at your assigned passage, either below or in the read-aloud book, and read it silently. Show your teacher any words you don't know, and practice saying them aloud. Now read the passage aloud, or ask your teacher to read it to you.

> When the sea was rough the sailors were afraid.
> When they saw strange things, they were afraid
> too. Columbus had to tell them to have faith.

❧❧ Copy the above lines into your Student Notebook. When you are finished, compare your copy to the model (word by word) and make any needed corrections.

❧ Listen as your teacher dictates the passage above, and write it in your Student Notebook. When you are finished, compare your copy to the model and make any needed corrections.

❧ Copy, or write as your teacher dictates, paragraph 8 on page 98 of *Christopher Columbus*. When you are finished, compare your copy to the text and make any needed corrections.

B. Reader   *Language Skills, Thinking Skills, History*

Read pages 53–55 in *Meet Christopher Columbus* aloud.

❧ Read one or two paragraphs in your read-aloud book, *Christopher Columbus*.

❧ Read one or two pages from today's read-aloud assignment in *Christopher Columbus*.

A. The dictation method enables your child to hear language and correctly write down what he hears. It involves building two different skills. First, the ability to listen and understand what is heard, and second, the ability to transfer what is heard into written language. This process takes time and practice, so begin as gradually as needed for successfully reaching the goal of getting the words the child hears on the paper correctly. 1) Read the whole passage, then reread one sentence at a time, giving your child time to write what he hears. 2) After he has finished, reread the passage again, allowing him to double check what he has written. 3) Then proceed to the step of comparing his writing to the model. As his skill builds, you can move more quickly through the steps, maintaining your child's level of success.

C. The skill of narration is gained over time. If your child has never retold a story, start with the assignment for the lower level, no matter what grade he is in. Work up from there, being careful to allow him to stay at the level of success for a while before going to a longer section.

C. **Read-Aloud and Narration**   *Language Skills, Thinking Skills, History*

Listen carefully as your teacher reads pages 98–102 in *Christopher Columbus*.

To *narrate* means to retell. In your own words, tell what happened in your assigned passage below. Try to remember as many details as possible. Listen carefully as your teacher reads, or rereads, the part you are to retell.

Paragraph 1 on page 98.

Paragraph 9 on page 101 through paragraph 3 on page 102.

Paragraph 5 on page 100 through paragraph 7 on page 101.

D. **Word Study**

Today you will continue looking at the different sounds the letter *g* makes.

Find all the *g* words on page 55 of *Meet Christopher Columbus* and write each one in the correct category.[11]

> *gh* that says *f*
> *g* that says *g* like goat
> *g* that says *j*
> *ng*

Look at the word *rage*. What sound does the letter *g* make? What do you have to do to add *ing* to the end of *rage?* In your Student Notebook, write the word rage with *ing* added to the end. Now scan page 55 in Meet Christopher Columbus and see if you can find the word you wrote. Did you add *ing* to the word rage correctly?

Find all the *g* words on page 99 in *Christopher Columbus* and put them in the correct category.[12]

> *g* that says *g* like goat
> *g* that says *j*
> *ng*

Write down what you think the word *gaiety* means. Now look it up in the dictionary and write down anything you did not include in your definition.

E. Read "The Story of the Stars" on pages 815–817 in the *Handbook of Nature Study* for background information on the sun and stars.

E. **Science**   *History*

For explorers, many things changed from day to day. The surroundings, the weather, and even the people might be constantly new. One thing that was always the same was the sky. This brought comfort to explorers and it also brought help. The stars could be used to find directions. What were the explorers looking at in the night sky? Mainly, they were seeing two things—planets and stars. You have already read about the planets. They stay in almost the same orbit around the sun year after year.

Stars are very different from planets. A **star** is a mass of gases that gives off light and heat as a result of the reactions taking place in its center, or core. Stars do not really change their positions enough that most people would notice. Our sun is actually a star. Here is a diagram of the sun:

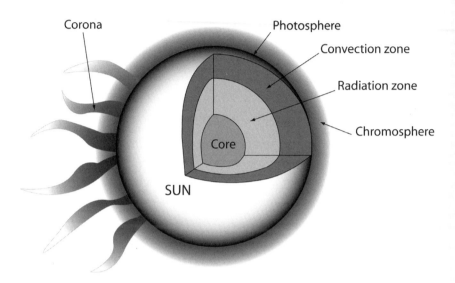

Label the parts on the chart of the sun in your Student Notebook.

Stars are usually very large and very far away. Our sun is the closest to us, and it is approximately 93,000,000 miles away. All the rest of the stars you see in the sky are much farther away than that. Our sun is a medium sized star. There are some stars that are much bigger and some that are smaller. The reason the big stars don't look so big to us is because they are so far away. The next closest star to earth is called Sirius. It is more than eight times farther away than our sun, yet it is the brightest of all the stars you can see in the sky.

Look at the sky tonight and tell your parent what you see. Look for the brightest stars, groups of stars, or stars that look different. Try to look at the stars away from bright lights. Observe them for at least three to five minutes.

 Stars are graded by how bright they are. This measurement is called **magnitude.** The magnitude scale was created by an ancient Greek astronomer. The lower the number is, the brighter the light. For instance, if a star is a first magnitude star it is very bright. If it is a fifth magnitude, it is faint, or hard to see. The scale now includes negative numbers to show greater levels of brightness and higher numbers because we can see more through telescopes. The sun and moon are very great negative magnitudes. Sirius is −1 magnitude and the planet Saturn is a +1. The stars of the Big Dipper are +2. Knowing a star's magnitude will help you find it in the night sky.

Look on the star map on page 824 of the *Handbook of Nature Study* and find these stars:

- Polaris (or the Polestar)
- Rigel (pronounced RYE´-gel)
- Betelgeuse (pronounced BEEtle-juice)
- Orion's Belt (pronounced or-I-on's)

Put a check by the name of each star you see on this list of stars in your Student Notebook. Write a few words describing each star you find in the sky.

Stars are different colors. You can read a very basic explanation of this on page 816 in your *Handbook of Nature Study.*

Find out why stars are considered red, yellow, blue, or white. Look this up at the library or, with your parent's permission, on the Internet. Do they change colors? If so, tell why.

F. Writing

Constellations are groups of stars on star maps. These groups were named long ago. The stories that go along with the names are ancient and today we call them **myths**, or legends.

Read aloud, or listen as your teacher reads about the Big Bear and Little Bear constellation myths on the bottom of pages 819 and 820 in your *Handbook of Nature Study.*

Looking up at the sky at night, the stars can look like shiny dots. Draw the stars you see on a piece of black construction paper with a white crayon or pencil. Look at the dots you have drawn for stars. Connect the dots to make a pattern, and see if you can imagine an animal or object in the dots. Come up with whatever picture you can.

Now make up a myth about the pattern you see. Tell your teacher the story or write it in your Student Notebook along with your star-dots picture.

G. See Independent Reading note in Part 1.

G. Independent Reading

Choose something to read that you will enjoy. Find a quiet, comfortable place and read for the following length of time:

20 minutes

25 minutes

30 minutes

Be sure to write down what you read today on the Reading Log in your Student Notebook.

Lesson 5, Part 3

A. **Copywork/Dictation**   *Language Skills, Thinking Skills, History*
Look carefully at your assigned passage, either below or in the read-aloud book, and read it silently. Show your teacher any words you don't know, and practice saying them aloud. Now read the passage aloud, or ask your teacher to read it to you.

> Columbus believed they would find land soon. They saw signs such as birds, and wood floating in the water. Everyone wanted to be the first to see land.

🐾 Copy the above lines into your Student Notebook. When you are finished, compare your copy to the model (word by word) and make any needed corrections.

🐾 Listen as your teacher dictates the passage above, and write it in your Student Notebook. When you are finished, compare your copy to the model and make any needed corrections.

🐾 Copy, or write as your teacher dictates, paragraph 3 on page 104 through the top of page 105 in *Christopher Columbus*. When you are finished, compare your copy to the text and make any needed corrections.

B. **Reader**   *Language Skills, Thinking Skills, History*
Read pages 56–59 in *Meet Christopher Columbus* aloud.

🐾 Read one or two paragraphs in your read-aloud book, *Christopher Columbus*.

🐾 Read one or two pages from today's read-aloud assignment in *Christopher Columbus*.

C. **Read-Aloud and Discussion**   *Language Skills, Thinking Skills, History*
Listen carefully as your teacher reads pages 103–107 in *Christopher Columbus*.

Discussion: Read the title for Chapter 10. Do you know what mainland they are searching for?

In this chapter, you hear that Columbus is somewhat discouraged. He feels he should have reached his goal by now. What troubles does Columbus have in this part of the chapter?[13] Do you think these are common problems for all explorers?[14]

A. See Copywork/Dictation note in Part 1.

C. See Discussion note in Part 1.

D. Word Study

Today you will continue looking at the different sounds the letter *g* makes.

Find all the *g* words on pages 56–59 of *Meet Christopher Columbus* and write each one in the correct category:[15]

> *g* that is silent
>
> *g* that says *g* like goat
>
> *ng*

Look at the word *belong.* What sound does the *g* make? Now look at *belonged.* What ending was added to *belong?*

What do you think happens to the sound of the letter *g* when it is next to the letter *h* in the words on these pages?[16]

Find all the *g* words on the bottom of page 104 through page 105 in *Christopher Columbus* and write each of them in the proper category.[17]

> *g* is silent
>
> *g* that says *g* like goat
>
> *g* that says *j*
>
> *ng*

Write what you think the word *kedging* means. Now look it up in the dictionary and write down anything you did not include in your definition.

What sound do you think the letters *d* and *g* make when they are next to each other as in the word *kedging?*[18] Can you think of any other words with the letters *d* and *g* making the same sound as *kedging?*

E. Geography
Thinking Skills

You learned in this lesson that a **map** is a picture of a place. It is drawn as if you were looking down on it from the sky. Look at the map of the Dominican Republic. Start by noticing the largest things on a map first. What looks the biggest to you?[19] The following bodies of water go from largest to smallest. An **ocean** is the largest body of saltwater on the earth. A **sea** is another saltwater body of water that covers a large part of earth, just not as large as an ocean.

Find these bodies of water on the map and write them on the map in your Student Notebook:

Atlantic Ocean　　　　　Caribbean Sea

Color the water around the island light blue so that you can still see the names of the bodies of water.

Map C-10

Remember that just as a key unlocks a door, you have to look at a **key** to understand a map. A key to a map helps you understand the meaning of the symbols and writing on the map.

Look at the key for the map of the Dominican Republic. Find a star and a circle. Both of these mean cities on this map. The star stands for the capital city of Santo Domingo. Write that name next to the star on your map. The circle stands for the name of a regular city called Puerto Plata. Write that name next to the circle in your Student Notebook.

Color the country of the Dominican Republic orange. Be careful to stop at the dotted line which is the border of the Dominican Republic and the country next to it, which is Haiti. This dotted line is in your key.

 Add the following features to the map in your Student Notebook.

Look at Map C-10 of the Dominican Republic. Find the word *river* in the map's key, and notice what the symbol for a river looks like. A river is a large natural stream of water that flows toward a larger body of water. Now locate the Ozama River and add it to your map by tracing the river's course in dark blue and writing its name right above the line. Do the same for the Yuna River.

Near the Caribbean Sea is a mountain. Look at the key for the mountain symbol. It is called Mount Tina (also Duarte Peak.) Label Mount Tina on your map, then trace and color the mountain triangle brown.

🐾 Add two more types of bodies of water to your map. A **bay** is an area of water from an ocean, sea, or gulf that extends into the land. It usually has a curved coastline. Find these three bays and write them on your map:

Ocoa Bay   Escocesa Bay   Samana Bay

A **lake** is a body of water that is surrounded by land. Lake Enriquillo is located near the border of Haiti and the Dominican Republic. Look at the key to see what a lake looks like on this map. Then write Lake Enriquillo's name on your map next to its symbol, and color it blue.

This lake is special because it is home to a beautiful bird — the Flamingo. Look for information about Flamingoes at the library or, with your parent's permission, on the Internet. List at least five facts you learn about Flamingoes and either trace or draw a picture of a Flamingo in your Student Notebook. Share what you learn with others.

F. **Writing**   *Art, Thinking Skills*

Columbus wrote in his journal about the wildlife he encountered along the way. An explorer wants to give detailed descriptions and drawings or pictures of what he finds so that others will recognize what they see.

Paragraph 3 on page 105 of *Christopher Columbus* tells about a way of fishing used by the native Indians. Reread this paragraph or listen as your teacher reads it.

Find the Remora fish in the *North American Wildlife Guide* on page 221. Draw or trace a picture of the remora in your Student Notebook. In a couple of sentences, tell about how the Indians fished using remora.

🐾🐾 Columbus and his men often saw birds flying overhead during their voyage and considered them a sign that they were near land. As they neared the West Indies and Florida, a common bird they would have seen was the Laughing Gull.

Look on page 103 in the *North American Wildlife Guide.* Trace or draw a picture of an adult Laughing Gull in your Student Notebook.

Write three things you learned from the description of the Laughing Gull.

🐾 Loggerhead Turtles are commonly seen around the Gulf Stream.

Look on page 165 of the *North American Wildlife Guide.* Trace or draw a picture of a Loggerhead Turtle in your Student Notebook.

Write at least three sentences telling what you learned about Loggerhead Turtles from its description.

After reading about Loggerhead Turtles and thinking about the ocean they live in, tell what you think makes the Loggerhead Turtle a threatened species.

G. **Independent Reading**
Choose something to read that you will enjoy. Find a quiet, comfortable place and read for the following length of time:

✸ 20 minutes

✸ 25 minutes

✸ 30 minutes

Be sure to write down what you read today on the Reading Log in your Student Notebook.

G. See Independent Reading note in Part 1.

Lesson 5, Part 4

A. **Copywork/Dictation**   *Language Skills, Thinking Skills, History*
Look carefully at your assigned passage, either below or in the read-aloud book, and read it silently. Show your teacher any words you don't know, and practice saying them aloud. Now read the passage aloud, or ask your teacher to read it to you.

A. See Copywork/Dictation note in Part 1.

> After some mistakes by excited sailors, they finally saw land. Columbus and his men went to the shore. They thanked God for leading them.

✸ Copy the above lines into your Student Notebook. When you are finished, compare your copy to the model (word by word) and make any needed corrections.

✸ Listen as your teacher dictates the passage above, and write it in your Student Notebook. When you are finished, compare your copy to the model and make any needed corrections.

✸ Copy, or write as your teacher dictates, paragraph 3 on page 109 in *Christopher Columbus.* When you are finished, compare your copy to the text and make any needed corrections.

B. **Reader**   *Language Skills, Thinking Skills, History*
Read pages 60–62 in *Meet Christopher Columbus* aloud.

✸ Read one or two paragraphs in your read-aloud book, *Christopher Columbus.*

C. See Narration note in Part 2

🐾 Read one or two pages from today's read-aloud assignment in *Christopher Columbus.*

C. **Read-Aloud and Narration**   *Language Skills, Thinking Skills, History*
Listen carefully as your teacher reads pages 108–113 in *Christopher Columbus.*

To narrate means to retell. In your own words, tell what happened in your assigned passage below. Try to remember as many details as possible. Listen carefully as your teacher reads, or rereads, the part you are to retell.

🐾🐾 Paragraphs 4 and 5 on page 109.

🐾 Paragraph 2 through paragraph 9 on page 111.

🐾 Paragraph 4 on page 112 to the end of page 113.

D. **Word Study**
Today you will continue looking at the different sounds the letter *g* makes.

🐾🐾🐾 Find all the *g* words on pages 60–62 in *Meet Christopher Columbus.* Write each of them in the correct category: [20]

> *g* is silent
> *g* that says *g* like goat
> *g* that says *j*
> *ng*

🐾 Write down what you think the word *glory* means. Now look it up in the dictionary and write down anything you did not include in your definition.

🐾 Find all the *g* words on pages 109–111 in *Christopher Columbus* and write each of them in the correct category.[21]

> *g* is silent
> *g* that says *g* like goat
> *g* that says *j*

Write down what you think the word *thriving* means. Now look it up in the dictionary and write down anything you did not include in your definition.

E. **Science**
The stars were very important to explorers. On a clear night they were always there to show which direction was north. If the explorer could find north, he could find east, west, and south as well. (Remember the activity to find north in Lesson 1, Part 1.)

The way explorers could be sure of their direction was by finding a star called the Polestar. This star is very important. It also has several other names such as the North Star and Polaris. If you live in the Northern Hemisphere (countries in the part of the earth above the equator), then you can see the North Star. To find it, you must first find the Big Dipper. The Big Dipper is a **constellation.** A constellation is a group of stars that people long ago thought looked like a certain shape.

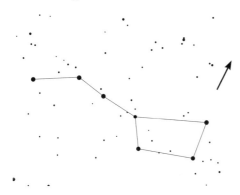

Look at the drawing on page 820 in your *Handbook of Nature Study.* This drawing shows the Big Dipper, Little Dipper, and the Polestar. Go outside at night with your parent and find the Big Dipper. Draw a picture of the Big Dipper in your Student Notebook.

If you can find the constellation called the Big Dipper, you can find the Polestar. Two of the stars in the "bowl" point towards the Polestar. See if you can find the Polestar in the sky. Add it to your night sky drawing.

The Polestar is the last star in the handle of the Little Dipper. See if you can find the Little Dipper in the sky. Then draw the Little Dipper into your night sky drawing.

🐾 After observing the Big and Little Dippers and finding the Polestar, answer questions 1–7 on page 820 in the *Handbook of Nature Study.* The answers can be found in the information on pages 818 and 819.

🐾 Answer questions 8–12 on page 820 in the *Handbook of Nature Study.* The answers can be found in the information on pages 818 and 819.

F. **Writing**

Poetry can be written by anyone. The main thing needed in order to write a poem is a subject that interests you. You have been learning about the oceans, wildlife, sun, planets, and stars. Now you are going to write some poetry about them.

A **cinquain** is a type of poem that has five lines. There are a certain number of words in each line. Here is a form to follow:

> Line 1: One word (the subject or title of the poem)
>
> Line 2: Two words (two words that describe the subject)
>
> Line 3: Three words (three words that tell what the subject of the poem can do)

Line 4: Four words (four words that tell about a feeling or thought about the subject)

Line 5: One word (a synonym or word that means the same as the subject)

Here is an example:

Ocean
big, salty
flowing, deep, mysterious
a highway for explorers
sea

Talk with your teacher about the topics you have read or discussed. As you choose a topic, see if you can come up with ideas to fill in the lines before you write.

Try to write at least one cinquain about your unit so far.

Try to write at least two cinquains about topics you have learned about such as Columbus, the ocean, wildlife, the stars, or anything else you have studied.

Try to write at least three cinquains relating to the topics covered.

G. See Independent Reading note in Part 1.

G. Independent Reading

Choose something to read that you will enjoy. Find a quiet, comfortable place and read for the following length of time:

20 minutes

25 minutes

30 minutes

Be sure to write down what you read today on the Reading Log in your Student Notebook.

⸺◦◦◦⸺

Lesson 5, Part 5

This part is set aside for completion of any work left undone from the lesson, and review of concepts and content. It is also a time to expand the work in the lesson by doing art, timeline activities, or games.

• Review the Steps for Thinking from the beginning of this lesson.

- On the large outline map of the world label: Dominican Republic, Haiti, Caribbean Sea, and Santo Domingo.

- Choose two words that make each *g* sound that you studied in this lesson. Write a sentence using each word. After you have finished, check your sentences against the words in your Student Notebook and see how many words you spelled correctly. (Don't count off for other words that are misspelled.) Remember your goal is to improve, not necessarily to get them all right immediately.

- Review the clues you used to play Columbus Bingo. Now use those clues to find the words that fit in the Columbus crossword puzzle in your Student Notebook.

- The ships that Columbus sailed to the New World had masts and sails, like all large sailing ships of his time. With your parent's help, make a model of a sailing ship by following the directions in your Student Notebook.

Enrichment Activities

1. Choose a country in which you are interested. Find information on that country in as many sources as possible. Some sources are almanacs, atlases, the Internet, travel agencies, and the library. Pick out the most interesting information to you and plan a way to teach your family about the country. You could make posters, word searches, puzzles, or presentations to teach what you know. This activity may take more than one week.

2. Dolphins are fascinating creatures to learn about. Have you ever had a chance to see a dolphin? If so, tell about your experience. Look for information on dolphins and the places you can go to see them, such as Seaworld. What are the qualities that you think make dolphins so special to people?

Additional Resources

Almanacs, atlases, travel information, etc.

Videos about dolphins

Movies including dolphins such as *Flipper*

Most of the labeling has already been completed in the Student Notebook during this lesson. Instruct students to use the maps in their Student Notebooks as a reference. When they label the larger map, students will see the "big picture" and gain a broader understanding of their lessons.

Teachers can find a copy of this game in Appendix B. Instructions and answer keys for all games are located in Appendix A.

We are thankful to Sharon Jeffus of Visual Manna for allowing us to use the model sailing ship lesson from her book *Teaching Science Through Art.*

Use one or more of the Enrichment Activities if your child completes his assigned work and has the time or desire to learn more. These activities are flexible, so choose the one(s) that seem most interesting to your student. Allow him to work at a level that is appropriate for him, and remember that the learning process is more important than the product.

It is suggested that parents preview all videos.

Answers

1. *g* that is silent: night; *g* that says *g* like goat: gale, great, God, got, go, gave; *ng*: morning, giving, going, King

2. *g* that says *g* like goat: good, aggravated, magnificent, girdle, God, gawked, long, begin; *g* that says *j*: voyage, strange, cages; *ng*: making, king, following, nothing, long

3. the bodies of water

4. When Columbus returned on his second voyage to the New World, no one was left at La Navidad. The fort had been destroyed and the men killed because of their cruel treatment of the native Indians.

5. yes

6. flying fish - size: 6-12 inches; lives: near the shore in tropical and subtropical areas, near the surface in the open sea; eats: smaller fish

7. It is able to "fly," or glide, for a short distance above the water.

8. brown pelican - size: 3½-4½ feet tall, 7 ft. wingspan; lives: near the ocean or brackish water; eats: fish

9. no

10. bottle-nosed dolphin - size: 6-9 ft. long; lives: along the Atlantic and Pacific coasts

11. *gh* that says *f*: rough; *g* that says *g* like goat: Portugal; *g* that says *j*: strange, voyage, huge; *ng*: morning, raging

12. *g* that says *g* like goat: Gromera, gaiety, began, go; *g* that says *j*: voyage; *ng*: young, anything, going, shortening, morning, along

13. He becomes sick; his ships need repairs; he didn't find what he was looking for; and the people of the settlements didn't follow instructions.

14. yes

15. *g* that is silent: fight, through, signs, night; *g* that says *g* like goat: go, gold, give, gave, given, great, Portugal, flags, guns, grew; *ng*: King, angry, belonged, fingers, leaving

16. It is silent.

17. *g* that is silent: thought, bright, eighty; *g* that says *g* like goat: mahogany, flamingo; *g* that says *j*: giant, strange, larger, kedging; *ng*: sailing, mingo, alongside, kedging

18. *D* and *g* together make the *j* sound.

19. the bodies of water

20. *g* is silent: through, bright; *g* says *g* like goat: gold, glory, gave, great; *g* says *j*: cages; *ng*: leading, king, nothing

21. *g* is silent: brought; *g* says *g* like goat: Gold, good, go, God, get, again, Margarito, Aguado, given, govern; *g* says *j*: giant; *ng*: building, bringing, king, thinking

Lesson 6, Part 1

A. **Copywork/Dictation**   *Language Skills, Thinking Skills, History*
Look carefully at your assigned passage, either below or in the read-aloud book, and read it silently. Show your teacher any words you don't know, and practice saying them aloud. Now read the passage aloud, or ask your teacher to read it to you.

> Columbus then claimed the land for the king and queen. Friendly Indians came to meet them. The New World was now open for many who would follow.

Copy the above lines into your Student Notebook. When you are finished, compare your copy to the model (word by word) and make any needed corrections.

Listen as your teacher dictates the passage above, and write it in your Student Notebook. When you are finished, compare your copy to the model and make any needed corrections.

Copy, or write as your teacher dictates, paragraph 4 on page 116 in *Christopher Columbus* (starting with "I was sure that…") When you are finished, compare your copy to the text and make any needed corrections.

B. **Reader**   *Language Skills, Thinking Skills, History*
Read pages 63 and 64 in *Meet Christopher Columbus* aloud.

Read one or two paragraphs in your read-aloud book, *Christopher Columbus*.

Read one or two pages from today's read-aloud assignment in *Christopher Columbus*.

C. **Read-Aloud and Discussion**   *Language Skills, Thinking Skills, History*
Listen carefully as your teacher reads pages 114–118 in *Christopher Columbus*.

Discussion: Discovering a new land must have been very exciting for Columbus. Right after this, when he returned to Santo Domingo, he had to deal with many problems. Talk about what happened with the men left at the settlement. Why do you think all the problems took place? Do you think Columbus did a good job of trying to restore peace to the island?

⟶Materials⟵

- Meet Christopher Columbus
- *Christopher Columbus*
- *Handbook of Nature Study*
- *Profiles from History*
- *Intermediate World Atlas/Globe*
- Student Notebook
- Optional: 4×6 Index Card
- Vocabulary Cards
- Crayons or colored pencils

Additional resources for Enrichment Activities are found in Part 5.

A. Copywork and dictation assignments are meant to go from an easier level (designated by 🐾) to harder levels (designated by 🐾 and 🐾). Copywork can be accomplished over two days if that is more comfortable for your child. Please adapt instructions to your child's individual needs. Your child should be **consistently successful** at one level before progressing to the next, **regardless of grade**.

C. Discussion is very important in developing your child's ability to organize his thoughts. This in turn builds the ability to think and write. The goal of the discussion questions is not just to find the answer to a particular question, but also to create a situation where thoughts about the question and its answer are shared and considered in a detailed way. Do not rush this activity, but encourage your student to share his or her ideas relating to the topic, and any additional ideas that may come to mind. You can also share your thoughts and questions as an example for your students.

D. The purpose of many of the activities during the final week of this unit will be to review and solidify what has been learned. Understanding the ideas taught is of greater importance than merely remembering names and dates. Review activities will be completed by everyone, so remember, where no level is indicated, an activity is to be completed by all students.

E. Read the section entitled "The Moon" on pages 855 and 856 in the *Handbook of Nature Study* for background information on the moon.

F. Each word in bold letters is considered a vocabulary word. It is a word that may or may not be new to your child. You can write these vocabulary words on index cards and use them for occasional review, but not for memorization. The meaning of the word should be given to the child if he doesn't remember. Try to use the new vocabulary words during conversation, and encourage your students to do the same.

Each time your student makes a vocabulary card for this unit, have him write a "C" in the upper left corner. This will make it possible to review vocabulary by unit at the end of the year.

D. Word Study

Gather together all the vocabulary cards you have made for this unit. Practice reading the words and telling what you think they mean.

Make a stack of the words you remember, and another stack of words you need to review.

From the stack of words you remember, tell your teacher how you think each word relates to our study of Columbus.

E. Science

The next body in space that you will learn about is the earth's moon. The moon is much smaller than the earth, and has no **atmosphere.** Atmosphere is the mixture of gases that surround a planet or other body in space. There is also no known life on the moon. The **climate** is either very cold or very hot, depending on where you go on the moon's surface.

With your parent's permission, go outside at night and observe the moon. Follow the same procedure you have used for observations of nature before. Sit in one spot for several minutes and then draw what you see in your Student Notebook.

Read the section entitled "A Visit to the Moon" on pages 856 and 857 in your *Handbook of Nature Study.* This passage was written long ago and many new things have been learned about the moon through space exploration, as well as from the men who have explored the moon's surface. Make a list of anything you feel is no longer accurate information.

F. Art   *Science, Thinking Skills, Writing*

The appearance of the moon changes gradually every day as the moon **orbits,** or goes around, the earth. When the part of the moon we see is getting smaller, we say the moon is **waning.** When the part of the moon we see is getting larger, we say the moon is **waxing.**

You will find eight circles in your Student Notebook. With your parent's permission, go outside and observe the moon every three or four days. Draw what you see in the circles.

Look at the diagram of the moon's phases. On the diagram in your Student Notebook write the name of the phase that looks the closest to what you drew in each circle.

Write at least two sentences describing how things look outside when the moon is in the *new moon* phase, or when there is no moonlight. You can also complete this assignment on a cloudy night when there is no moonlight.

Phases of the Moon

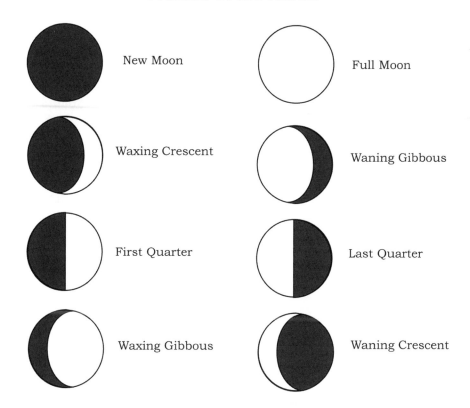

🐾 Write at least three sentences describing how things look outside when the moon is *full*. Tell how you think moonlight makes things look. If it is not near this phase of the moon you can do this assignment from memory, or wait until there is a full moon.

𝒢. Independent Reading

Choose something to read that you will enjoy. Find a quiet, comfortable place and read for the following length of time:

🐾 20 minutes

🐾 25 minutes

🐾 30 minutes

Over time, it's fun to see how much you have read. Be sure to write down what you read today on the Reading Log in your Student Notebook.

𝒢. Reading fluency is developed through having frequent silent reading opportunities that continue for the length of time suggested here. Since a primary focus of this activity is to nurture your child's enjoyment of reading, help him to choose reading material that interests him and is at a level that allows him to read with understanding by himself. You can incorporate this activity into your school day whenever it is most convenient.

If the suggested length of time is too long for your child to continue reading by himself, start with an amount of time he can accomplish successfully and make the suggested time a goal.

Lesson 6, Part 2

A. See Copywork/Dictation note in Part 1.

The islands that Columbus named are now known by different names. What he named Juana is now Cuba. Cathay was the name for China in those days.

A. **Copywork/Dictation** *Language Skills, Thinking Skills, History*

Listen to your teacher read Part 1 of this letter. Then listen as she reads it again and follow along as she reads each word.

Summary of the Letter Columbus Wrote to King Ferdinand
PART I

> You will be pleased to hear of the success of my journeys, so I write now to tell you. On the thirty-third day after I sailed I came to the Indian Sea where I found many inhabited islands. We flew your flag and made loud announcements that we take possession for you. No one objected.
>
> I named the first island San Salvadore to honor our Savior who helped me reach these islands. Then I named Santa Maria, Fernandina, and Isabella. Then I followed along a coast for so much distance that I thought I had found the mainland of Cathay. But there were no towns and cities, just some villages and rude farms with inhabitants who ran away in fright. I finally decided it was an island, and named it Juana.

A. The small superscript numbers that appear after some of the questions in this unit refer to answers found in the answer key, located immediately after Part 5.

❦ Fill in the blanks in your Student Notebook with the correct words.[1] You may want to use a highlighter to mark off each word on the original copy as you read it, and then copy the words in the spaces. When you are finished, compare your copy to the model (word by word) and make any needed corrections.

❦ Fill in the blanks in your Student Notebook with the correct words.[1] When you are finished, compare your copy to the model and make any needed corrections.

❦ Copy, or write as your teacher dictates, Part 1 of the letter Columbus wrote to King Ferdinand. When you are finished, compare your copy to the text and make any needed corrections.

B. **Reader** *Language Skills, Thinking Skills, History*

Read pages 65–67 in *Meet Christopher Columbus* aloud.

❦ Read one or two paragraphs in your read-aloud book, *Christopher Columbus.*

❦ Read one or two pages from today's read-aloud assignment in *Christopher Columbus.*

C. Read-Aloud and Narration   *Language Skills, Thinking Skills, History*

Listen carefully as your teacher reads pages 120–124 in *Christopher Columbus.*

To *narrate* means to retell. In your own words, tell what happened in your assigned passage below. Try to remember as many details as possible. Listen carefully as your teacher reads, or rereads, the part you are to retell.

🌵 Paragraph 9 on page 121 (starts with "We spent the day…").

🐾 Paragraph 10 on page 123 through the end of page 124.

🐾 Begin with the last two lines on page 121 through the first two lines on page 123.

D. Word Study   *Vocabulary*

Gather together all the vocabulary cards you have made for this unit. Practice reading the words and telling what you think they mean.

Make a stack of the words you remember, and another stack of words you need to review.

From the stack of words you remember, tell your teacher how you think each word relates to our study of Columbus.

E. Geography   *Thinking Skills, Language Skills*

You have been introduced to many places on the map since the beginning of this unit. Use your globe or map to point out to your teacher all the places you have learned about, as well as things on the map or globe, such as the compass rose or a key. Tell your teacher what you remember about each place or thing.

You may want to play a game where one person picks a place and the other person tries to tell what it is and how it relates to the Columbus Unit. (Players should only choose places covered in the unit.) Or you can choose a place off the list below and find it.

If you forget, here are some hints for you:

Oceans: Atlantic, Pacific, Indian, Arctic, Antarctic (or Southern)

Seas: Mediterranean Sea, Caribbean Sea

Continents: North America, South America, Africa, Asia, Europe

Countries: Spain, Portugal, England, Italy, Cuba, Dominican Republic, Jamaica, Puerto Rico, Haiti

Map Markers: Equator, Northern Hemisphere, Southern Hemisphere, North Pole, South Pole

You may want to add any other country or place that you have studied. Look at all the places you have learned about!

C. The skill of narration is gained over time. If your child has never retold a story, start with the assignment for the lower level, no matter what grade he is in. Work up from there, being careful to allow him to stay at the level of success for a while before going to a longer section.

D. Remember, the goal of this activity is for the meaning of the words to be understood, not for the words and definitions to be memorized.

F. Writing   *History, Thinking Skills*

Think about what you have learned about Christopher Columbus. Look at the Explorer page in your Student Notebook. Read over the questions and discuss your answers with your teacher. When you feel you know how to best answer each question, write your answers in the spaces provided.

Plan to share what you have learned about Columbus with your family at the end of this lesson. You may want to use these questions as a guide for your Unit Presentation. Make sure you include your answers in your presentation.

G. See Independent Reading note in Part 1.

G. Independent Reading

Choose something to read that you will enjoy. Find a quiet, comfortable place and read for the following length of time:

- 20 minutes
- 25 minutes
- 30 minutes

Be sure to write down what you read today on the Reading Log in your Student Notebook.

Lesson 6, Part 3

A. See Copywork/Dictation note in Part 1.

A. Copywork/Dictation   *Language Skills, Thinking Skills, History*

Listen to your teacher read Part 2 of this letter. Then listen as she reads it again and follow along as she reads each word.

PART 2

This island has the best harbors I have seen. We anchored in one bay and I sent two men ashore to see if this land had a king. They traveled three days and found people and small houses, but seemingly no government. There are health-giving rivers and high mountains. There are seven or eight kinds of palm trees, far taller than ours and more beautiful. The nightingales and other birds were singing in November.

On the island of Hispania there are spices and
gold. The people here do not dress as we do. After
they learned not to fear us, they traded valuable
things for small trifles like dishes and glass or keys
and shoestraps. They thought they were getting
the most beautiful jewels in the world, but I
forbade the men to trade small things of no value.

Fill in the blanks in your Student Notebook with the correct words.[2]
You may want to use a highlighter to mark off each word on the
original copy as you read it, and then copy the words in the spaces.
When you are finished, compare your copy to the model (word by
word) and make any needed corrections.

Fill in the blanks in your Student Notebook with the correct words.[2]
When you are finished, compare your copy to the model and make
any needed corrections.

Copy, or write as your teacher dictates, Part 2 of the letter Columbus
wrote to King Ferdinand. When you are finished, compare your
copy to the text and make any needed corrections.

B. Reader
Language Skills, Thinking Skills, History
Read pages 68–69 in *Meet Christopher Columbus* aloud.

Read one or two paragraphs in your read-aloud book, *Christopher
Columbus.*

Read one or two pages from today's read-aloud assignment in
Christopher Columbus.

C. Read-Aloud and Discussion
Language Skills, Thinking Skills, History

C. See Discussion note in Part 1.

Listen carefully as your teacher reads pages 125–130 in *Christopher
Columbus.*

Discussion: Do you agree with Columbus' decision to go to Santo
Domingo to look for another ship even though the queen had asked
him to stay away from there? What happened as a result of his decision to go to Santo Domingo?

D. Word Study
The poem "A Happy Family" by Nancy L. Moorefield tells about the
solar system as a family, with the sun as the father. Look at the poem
on pages 837 and 838 of the *Handbook of Nature Study*. Listen as
your teacher reads it the first time. As your teacher reads it a second
time, listen as she reads a sentence, then repeat it after her. Try to say
the words and sentence the same way your teacher does. Speak with
the same tone and enthusiasm she uses.

Choose at least two words from the poem that you are not familiar with. Write them in your Student Notebook and then write what you think the words mean. Look them up in the dictionary and write down anything that you did not include in your definition.

Prepare to read this poem as part of your Unit Presentation at the end of this week. You may want to do what you practiced with your parent and read each sentence after her, or you may want to read it independently. A third way to prepare the poem for presentation is to memorize it. Prepare to present this poem in whatever way you and your teacher agree best suits you.

E. Science   *Language Skills*

You have learned about various aspects of science that relate to your study of Christopher Columbus and his explorations. One thing you have read and thought about is the solar system. Look through your Student Notebook, and tell your teacher what you have learned.

Here are some hints if you need them:

- the arrangement of the solar system
- all the individual planets
- the sun and stars
- the moon

Tell how these parts of the solar system relate to Christopher Columbus, his voyage and his explorations. Make a list of at least two things that connect what you have learned about space and the solar system to what you have learned about Christopher Columbus.

F. Art   *Language Skills, Thinking Skills*

Tomorrow you will complete your read-aloud book, *Christopher Columbus*. In preparation for the end of this unit, review the chapter titles of this book and look at the pictures in each chapter. Discuss the main events that occurred in each chapter. Choose one event from the story that you think was the most interesting and draw a picture of it to go in your Student Notebook. Underneath the picture, tell what event you chose and why.

G. Independent Reading

G. See Independent Reading note in Part 1.

Choose something to read that you will enjoy. Find a quiet, comfortable place and read for the following length of time:

- 20 minutes
- 25 minutes
- 30 minutes

Be sure to write down what you read today on the Reading Log in your Student Notebook.

Lesson 6, Part 4

A. Copywork/Dictation   *Language Skills, Thinking Skills, History*

Listen to your teacher read Part 3 of this letter. Then listen as she reads it again and follow along as she reads each word.

A. See Copywork/Dictation note in Part 1.

> PART 3
>
> The same kinds of people are on all these <u>islands</u> and all seem to have the same <u>language</u>. That is an important fact for converting them to the holy religion of Christ, which I suppose is the desire of our most illustrious king. As far as I can see, they are ready for it.
>
> No one claims to have seen these islands before, and what we heard about them seemed like fables. So now let the king and queen and their most fortunate kingdom, and all other countries of Christendom, give thanks to our Lord and Savior Jesus Christ who has bestowed upon us so great a gift.
>
> I have briefly told the things I have done. Farewell. From Lisbon on March 14, 1493.
>
> Christopher Columbus, Admiral of the Ocean Fleet

Fill in the blanks in your Student Notebook with the correct words.[3] You may want to use a highlighter to mark off each word on the original copy as you read it, and then copy the words in the spaces. When you are finished, compare your copy to the model (word by word) and make any needed corrections.

Fill in the blanks in your Student Notebook with the correct words.[3] When you are finished, compare your copy to the model and make any needed corrections.

Copy, or write as your teacher dictates, Part 3 of the letter Columbus wrote to King Ferdinand. When you are finished, compare your copy to the text and make any needed corrections.

B. Reader   *Language Skills, Thinking Skills, History*

Read pages 70–72 in *Meet Christopher Columbus* aloud.

Read one or two paragraphs in your read-aloud book, *Christopher Columbus.*

C. See Narration note in Part 2.

D. Before your child begins to write his thoughts or opinions, discuss words he would like to use to express himself. Make a word bank by listing the words he suggests with their proper spelling. Saying a word, seeing a word, and correctly using a word are effective ways to build spelling skills and encourage your child to write on a level that reflects his thoughts in an interesting way.

Teachers can find a copy of this game in Appendix B. Instructions and answer keys for all games are located in Appendix A.

🐾 Read one or two pages from today's read-aloud assignment in *Christopher Columbus.*

C. **Read-Aloud and Narration**   *Language Skills, Thinking Skills, History*
Listen carefully as your teacher reads pages 131–137 in *Christopher Columbus.*

To *narrate* means to retell. In your own words, tell what happened in your assigned passage below. Try to remember as many details as possible. Listen carefully as your teacher reads, or rereads, the part you are to retell.

🌵 Page 137.

🐾 Paragraphs 4–9 on page 136.

🐾 Paragraph 6 on page 132 through paragraph 9 on page 133.

D. **Word Study**   *Language Skills, Thinking Skills, History*
As you review the Columbus Unit, you will retell important events from literature and history. Play Columbus Charades to review those main events. Before you begin each charade, tell whether Columbus was a boy (gesture to show the height of a small child), a young man (make a muscle with each arm to show a young, strong man), or an explorer (hold hand up to forehead as if you are looking out to sea.)

Find the cards with the Columbus Charades on your Student Resources CD, and cut them out. Act out the event listed on the card until someone guesses what it is.

- (Boy) Columbus helps card (comb) wool as a boy in his father's shop.

- (Young man) Pirates attack his ship and he fights with them and is wounded by a sword.

- (Explorer) Columbus is put into shackles (chains on his hands and feet) by the new leaders of Hispaniola.

- (Boy) Columbus watches ships in the port and dreams of sailing on ships.

- (Explorer) Columbus claims the New World for the King and Queen of Spain.

- (Young man) Columbus becomes a bookseller and mapmaker.

- (Explorer) While Columbus sleeps, the *Santa Maria* hits the rocks and is shipwrecked.

- (Explorer) Columbus goes to see the King and Queen as the hero of the New World.

Think of other events from the stories about Columbus to retell with charades. Consider playing this game as part of your Unit Presentation at the end of the Columbus Unit.

E. Science   *Science, Thinking Skills*

Nicholas Copernicus was a man who lived at the same time as Christopher Columbus. He believed that the earth revolved around the sun. Up until then, people had believed that the sun revolved around the earth. Copernicus is considered the father of a part of science called **astronomy,** or the study of the things in the universe and what they do. Since you have learned about the solar system, do you agree with Copernicus?

Also around the same time that Columbus made his first voyage to the New World, a great artist was begining his career in Italy. His name was Michelangelo.

Listen to or read Michelangelo's profile in *Profiles from History.* Complete the activities at the end of the chapter. Talk about the discussion questions with your teacher; be sure to give any examples you can think of in your answers.

F. Writing   *Language Skills, Thinking Skills*

Now that you have completed your reader and the read-aloud book, make a book review card. The purpose of a book review card is to give a brief description of what you read or heard, and then to tell what you thought of the book. It should not include as much information as a book report. The goal is to give someone who has not read the book enough information to decide whether or not they might like to read it. In a sense, it is like an advertisement for a book. Give enough information to let someone know the good points about the book, while not retelling the story.

How to Create a Book Review Card:

Your book review can be written on a large index card or on the page provided in your Student Notebook. Include the following information on your card:

- name of the book

- author of the book (person who wrote the book)

- illustrator of the book (person who drew the pictures)

- name of the company who published the book

- date the book was published

Most of this information can be found on the title page of the book.

Rehearse, or practice telling, what you will say about the story and how you liked it. Once you have discussed your thoughts enough to know what you want to write, you can begin. If you don't know how to spell some of the words you want to use, ask your teacher to make a word bank for you.

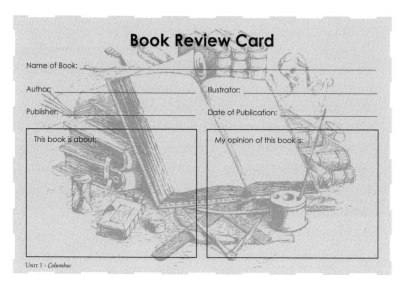

Next, write a few sentences to tell what the story was about. Since you only have a few sentences, you will have to choose the most important facts to tell.

Then write a few sentences to tell what you thought about the story. Tell whether or not you liked the book, and then give some examples of what you did or did not like about it.

Create a book review card on the reader *Meet Christopher Columbus.*

Create a book review card on either the reader *Meet Christopher Columbus* or the read-aloud *Christopher Columbus.*

Create a book review card on the read-aloud book *Christopher Columbus.*

G. See Independent Reading note in Part I.

G. Independent Reading

Choose something to read that you will enjoy. Find a quiet, comfortable place and read for the following length of time:

20 minutes

25 minutes

30 minutes

Congratulations on completing six lessons of independent reading! Today's entry in your reading log will be the last one for this unit. Make sure you have included all the information needed on your log such as book titles, authors, and dates read.

Look over all that you have accomplished during your independent reading time. If you would like, share your reading log with others during your Unit Presentation in Part 5.

Lesson 6, Part 5

This part is set aside for completion of any work left undone from the lesson, and review of concepts and content. It is also a time to expand the work in the lesson by doing art, timeline activities, or games.

• Listen as your teacher reviews the Steps for Thinking from the Columbus Unit that you have just completed. Discuss how you see the Steps for Thinking applying to what you have learned.

• Make a Unit Presentation to your family telling about what you have learned in the unit you have just completed on Christopher Columbus and his exploration of the New World. Share your Student Notebook and display things you may have made during this unit such as your milk carton ship or your salt crystals. Choose something that you wrote to read for your audience. You may also choose to recite poetry you have memorized, or read it aloud.

Use your Explorer page as a guideline for what to tell about. Don't forget to speak clearly and stand still while speaking. Pass examples around for your audience to see and don't forget to ask if they have any questions.

• Play Columbus Bingo or Ocean and Continent Concentration.

Teachers can find a copy of these games in Appendix B. Instructions and answer keys for all games are located in Appendix A.

Additional Resources

Information about lunar travel

Destination Moon by James Irwin

Videos on lunar travel

Survival training information

My Side of the Mountain by Jean Craighead George

Congratulations on completing Unit 1 of the *Paths of Exploration!*

Answers

1. Blanks for Student Notebook: pleased, journeys, sailed, Sea, islands, flag named, honor, islands, coast, mainland, cities, villages, island

2. Blanks for Student Notebook: harbors, bay, ashore, houses, rivers, mountains, trees, birds, island, gold, dress, traded, trifles, jewels, value

3. Blanks for Student Notebook: islands, language, Christ, king, ready, islands, fables, queen, kingdom, thanks, Lord, gift, Farewell, Columbus, Ocean

Lesson 1, Part 1

> ### ❧ Steps for Thinking ☙
>
> 1. If you know about a person's background, it's easier to understand what they say and do.
>
> 2. People are influenced by the customs and beliefs of their country.
>
> 3. All people want to be treated with respect.

The **Steps for Thinking** section gives you the main ideas about the topics presented. Understanding these helps you to have productive discussions with your children so they, too, understand the bigger ideas. This forms more permanent learning, contrary to just learning facts, which tends to be temporary. These steps are useful prior to instruction, and they are also useful for review at the end of the week.

❧ Materials ☙

- *A Lion to Guard Us*
- *Surviving Jamestown*
- *Intermediate World Atlas*
- *Profiles from History*
- Globe
- Index cards/marker
- Newspaper or Internet access
- Student Notebook
- Access to folk tales
- Tracing paper
- Glue
- Tape
- Scissors
- Crayons or colored pencils
- Large U.S. outline map

Additional resources for Enrichment Activities are found in Part 5.

A. Copywork and dictation assignments go from an easier level (designated by 🐾) to harder levels (designated by 🐾 and 🐾). Take two days for the copywork if that is more comfortable for your child. Please adapt instructions to your child's individual needs. Your child should be **consistently successful** at one level before progressing to the next, **regardless of grade**.

A. **Copywork/Dictation**   *Language Skills*

Look carefully at the following passage, and read it silently. Show your teacher any words you don't know, and practice saying them aloud. Now read the passage aloud, or ask your teacher to read it to you.

> Times were hard for many people in England. There weren't enough good jobs. There weren't enough places to live. If you were not born into a rich family, life was hard in England in 1607.

🐾 Copy the above lines into your Student Notebook. When you are finished, compare your copy to the model (word by word) and make any needed corrections.

🐾 Listen as your teacher dictates the above lines, and write them in your Student Notebook. When you are finished, compare your copy to the model and make any needed corrections.

🐾 Copy, or write as your teacher dictates, paragraph 7 on page 2 through the top of page 4 in *Surviving Jamestown.* When you are finished, compare your copy to the text and make any needed corrections.

B. **Reader**   *Language Skills, Thinking Skills, History*

In your book, *A Lion to Guard Us,* read Chapter 1 aloud.

🐾 Read one or two paragraphs in your read-aloud book, *Surviving Jamestown.*

🐾 Read one or two pages from today's read-aloud assignment in *Surviving Jamestown.*

C. The skill of narration is gained over time. If your child has never retold a story, start with the assignment for the lower level, no matter what grade he is in. Work up from there, being careful to allow him to stay at the level of success for a while before going to a longer section.

D. Each word in bold letters is considered a vocabulary word. It is a word that may or may not be new to your child. You can write these vocabulary words on index cards and use them for occasional review, but not for memorizing. Give the child the meaning of the words if he doesn't remember. Try to use the new vocabulary words during conversation, and encourage your students to do the same

Each time your student makes a vocabulary card for this unit, have him write a "J" (for Jamestown) in the upper left corner. This will make it possible to review vocabulary by unit at the end of the year.

The small superscript numbers that appear after some of the questions in this unit refer to answers in the answer key, located immediately after Part 5.

C. **Read-Aloud and Narration**   *Language Skills, Thinking Skills*

In *Surviving Jamestown,* listen as your teacher reads the Preface through paragraph 1 on page 7 aloud.

To *narrate* means to retell. In your own words, tell what happened in your assigned passage below. Try to remember as many details as possible. Listen carefully as your teacher reads (or rereads) the part you are to retell.

ᵛᵞ Paragraph 1 on page 2.

ᵂ Paragraph 4 on page 4.

ᵂ Paragraphs 2 through 6 on page 5.

D. **Word Study**   *Spelling, Phonics, Vocabulary*

An **apostrophe** (') is a mark that is used to show that letters have been removed from a word, or to show that something belongs to someone.

Look at page 2 in *A Lion to Guard Us* and make a list of all the words that have an apostrophe in them.[1]

An apostrophe is used in a **contraction**, which can be a single word, but is most often made when two words are joined together. The apostrophe shows that some letters have been left out.

Look at the list of words with apostrophes that you made. Now read page 2 in *A Lion to Guard Us* again, only this time replace each contraction with the two words it takes the place of. Does the story still make sense?

she's = she is	there's = there is
shouldn't = should not	can't = can not
you're = you are	I'm = I am

Freebold's = *Not* a contraction — read the next part!

In the word *Freebold's,* the apostrophe does not make a contraction, or show that letters have been left out. *Freebold's* has an apostrophe s, ('s) added to the end to show that something belongs to Freebold.

Look back at *Freebold's* on page 2. What word comes right after it? The thing that belonged to James Freebold in the story was his girl, or daughter, Amanda.

ᵂ See if you can figure out how to make the following pairs of words into contractions.[2] Write down your guess. *Hint: Look at the contractions at the beginning of this section.*

he is	where is
would not	could not
they are	we are

🐾 Make two lists of words with apostrophes from page 6 in *Surviving Jamestown*.[3] In your Student Notebook, list each word you find under either "contractions" or "words that show belonging," or that something belongs to someone. The word *somebody's* is tricky because the same spelling can make it either a contraction or a word that shows belonging. From reading page 6, which list do you think it should be written in this time?

E. Geography

Those who made the journey to Jamestown started out in England. England is part of the United Kingdom. Look at the Europe Political Map in the *Intermediate World Atlas*. A **political map** shows country borders that have been established by governments.

With your teacher's help, find the area labeled United Kingdom, which is orange on this map, and trace its outline onto another sheet of paper. If you wish you may use the larger Map J-1 on this page instead of the one in your atlas. Place a plain piece of paper over the map and hold it in place with a small piece of tape. Trace around the edges of the United Kingdom with a pencil. Remember to just do your best.

E. The United Kingdom consists of England, Scotland, Wales, and Northern Ireland.

Map J-1

Include the (red) boundary lines that divide England, Wales, Scotland, and Northern Ireland. Write the name of each country on or next to it. Add the city of London and mark it with a star and circle. Also write in the Atlantic Ocean, the North Sea, and the English Channel. A **channel** is a body of water that connects two larger bodies of water.

Add the country of Ireland to your map, as well as St. George's Channel, the Irish Sea, and the Thames River.

England is part of the continent of Europe. All the countries in color on the Europe Political Map are also part of that continent. Point out three or four more countries in Europe to your teacher.

Add these capital cities to your map:

> Scotland – Edinburgh
>
> Northern Ireland – Belfast
>
> Wales – Cardiff
>
> Ireland – Dublin

Also add the Strait of Dover to your map. A **strait** is a narrow waterway linking two bodies of water.

F. Writing   *Thinking Skills*

A **tale** can have three different meanings. Tales can be stories you tell about true things that happened. If you tell the story of how you hurt your finger, you are telling that kind of tale. A tale can also be a made up story, such as a fairy tale. The third kind of tale is telling bad things, or things that are not true. This is the kind of tale your parents tell you not to tell. As we read the word *tale,* think about the different kinds of tales there are.

In the reader, *A Lion to Guard Us,* read what the sailor told Amanda about her father. Their conversation starts on the top of page 3 and goes to the bottom. What kind of tale has the sailor told?[4]

Tell your teacher a tale about something true that has happened to you. Think of sentences that tell how your tale begins and how it ends. Then think of something that happened in the middle.

Write a couple of sentences about your tale in each box in your Student Notebook.

Think of a tale about something that has happened to you. Above each box in your Student Notebook, write a few words that tell what happened, such as "went to circus," "saw elephants," or "ate cotton candy." Now, write a couple of sentences in the beginning and ending boxes telling more about what you did. Then go back and write about something interesting that happened in the middle box.

G. Independent Reading

Choose something to read that you will enjoy. Find a quiet, comfortable place and read for the following length of time:

🐾 20 minutes

🐾 25 minutes

🐾 30 minutes

Over time, it's fun to see how much you have read. Be sure to write down what you read today on the Reading Log in your Student Notebook.

G. Reading fluency is developed through having frequent silent reading opportunities that continue for the length of time suggested here. Since a primary focus of this activity is to nurture your child's enjoyment of reading, help him to choose reading material that interests him and is at a level that allows him to read with understanding by himself. You can incorporate this activity into your school day whenever it is most convenient.

If the suggested length of time is too long for your child to continue reading by himself, start with an amount of time he can accomplish successfully and make the suggested time a goal.

Lesson 1, Part 2

A. Copywork/Dictation   *Language Skills*

Look carefully at the following passage, and read it silently. Show your teacher any words you don't know, and practice saying them aloud. Now read the passage aloud, or ask your teacher to read it to you.

> What could make men leave their homes in 1607? The hope of a better life for their families made them risk everything. Hope for them lay across the ocean.

🐾 Copy the above lines into your Student Notebook. When you are finished, compare your copy to the model (word by word) and make any needed corrections.

🐾 Listen as your teacher dictates the above lines, and write them in your Student Notebook. When you are finished, compare your copy to the model and make any needed corrections.

🐾 Copy, or write as your teacher dictates, paragraph 3 on page 12 in *Surviving Jamestown.* When you are finished, compare your copy to the text and make any needed corrections.

A. The dictation method enables your child to hear language and correctly write down what he hears. It involves building two different skills. First, the ability to listen and understand what is heard, and second, the ability to transfer what is heard into written language. This process takes time and practice, so begin as gradually as needed for successfully reaching the goal of getting the words the child hears on the paper correctly. 1) Read the whole passage, then reread one sentence at a time, giving your child time to write what he hears. 2) After he has finished, reread the passage again, allowing him to double check what he has written. 3) Then proceed to the step of comparing his writing to the model. As his skill builds, you can move more quickly through the steps, maintaining your child's level of success.

B. Reader   *Language Skills, Thinking Skills, History*

In your book, *A Lion to Guard Us,* read Chapter 2 aloud.

🐾 Read one or two paragraphs in your read-aloud book, *Surviving Jamestown.*

C. Discussion is very important in developing your child's ability to organize his thoughts. This in turn builds the ability to think and write. The goal of the discussion questions is not just to find the answer to a particular question, but also to create a situation where thoughts about the question and its answer are shared and considered in a detailed way. Do not rush this activity, but encourage your student to share his or her ideas relating to the topic, and any additional ideas that may come to mind. You can also share your thoughts and questions as an example for your students.

❧ Read one or two pages from today's read-aloud assignment in *Surviving Jamestown.*

C. Read-Aloud and Discussion   *Language Skills, Thinking Skills*

Listen carefully as your teacher reads paragraph 3 on page 7 through the end of page 14 aloud from *Surviving Jamestown.*

Listen as your teacher rereads paragraph 4 on page 8 and the following discussion question. Think about what you know from the story, and answer in your own words. Give any examples you can think of that help show your answer.

Discussion Question: Why was the Virginia Company sending these ships to America? How was their mission the same as Christopher Columbus'?

D. Word Study   *Spelling, Phonics, Vocabulary*

Create a Jamestown Word Bank to help when you write during this unit. The first words you will put into your Word Bank are the names of the places mentioned in your stories. The first three columns in your Jamestown Word Bank are "America," "England," and "Other Places."

Find the names of places in Chapters 1 and 2 of *A Lion to Guard Us.* List these places under the correct heading.[5]

❧❧ One of the sounds of the letter *g* is *j*. One of the ways to spell this sound is with the letters *dge.* Look at the word *bridge.* Write this word on a piece of scrap paper and underline the letters that say *j.* Here are some other words that have the same sound: *badge, judge, ledge, widget.* Read them to your teacher.

❧ Look at Chapter 1 in *Surviving Jamestown.* Find the places that are named in the chapter, and write them in your Student Notebook under the category where you think they belong.[6]

E. Science   *Geography, Thinking Skills*

The **climate** in England is moderate. Climate is the way the weather usually is in a place. The climate of a place includes what the temperature usually is, how much it rains, and how much moisture is usually in the air.

Turn to the Europe thematic maps in the *Intermediate World Atlas.* Find England on the Climate Map. It is dark green, which means the climate is moderate. **Moderate** means without extremes. It usually does not get very hot or very cold, even though it could occasionally. Look at the key of the climate map. What does it say about summer weather for the climate in England?[7]

The climate of a place is affected by three things: how close the place is to an ocean; how close it is to mountains; and how close it is to the Equator. When the answers to these three things are similar, then the climates of different places are similar. Understanding the geography of a place tells you much about the climate and weather there. Think about how these three factors apply to England:

1. England is close to the ocean. Ocean water holds warmth better than land. The closer a place is to an ocean, the warmer its climate will be in the winter, and cooler breezes will blow over it in the summer. In the summer the oceans **absorb,** or soak up, heat, and in the winter oceans help warm the land around them.

In your Student Notebook, cut out the "Ocean" symbol square and glue it in the first box on the climate page. A **symbol** is something that stands for something else.

Ocean symbol

2. There are no mountains in England to block warm air from the ocean from coming onshore. When there are no mountains, the air from the ocean comes ashore. When mountains are there to block the air, winters will be warmer on the side by the ocean and cooler on the other side. In the summer it is just the opposite—cooler on the side by the ocean and warmer on the other side.

In your Student Notebook, cut out the "Mountain" symbol square and glue it in the second box on the climate page.

Mountain symbol

You can locate mountains on a **physical map.** A physical map shows you what the land and water on earth are like. It shows you things like how high or low land is, compared to the level where the ocean meets the land. This is called **sea level.**

Look at England on the Europe Physical Map in your *Intermediate World Atlas.* Most of England is dark green on this map. When you look at the key in the box on the left side of the page, you see that dark green means the **elevation**, or height of the land, goes from exactly level with the sea up to 650 feet, about the height of the Empire State Building.

3. England is about halfway between the Equator and the North Pole. Look at your globe and find the Equator and the North Pole. Now find England on your globe. The closer you get to the North Pole or South Pole, the colder it gets. Other places that are about the same distance from the equator will have similar climates. Imaginary lines on a globe or map that measure the distance north or south from the Equator are called lines of **latitude.**

In your Student Notebook, cut out the "Latitude" symbol square and glue it into the third box on the climate page.

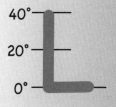

Latitude symbol

🐾 The climate of England is similar to that of Seattle, Washington, in the United States. In the newspaper or on the Internet, find and write down the high and low temperatures for London, England, and Seattle, Washington, for five days in a row. Are they similar?

🐾 Look in your *Intermediate World Atlas* and compare the maps for London, England, and Seattle, Washington. Make a list of at least two ways that they are similar.[8] Can you make a list of at least two ways they are different?[9]

F. Drawing

In Part 1 you told a tale about something that happened to you.

Use the three boxes in your Student Notebook to draw illustrations that show the beginning, middle, and end of your tale. You can **illustrate,** or draw pictures, for the tale you already wrote or you can make up a new tale.

🐾 After you draw your illustrations, list the names of the characters shown under their pictures.

🐾 After you have drawn your illustrations, write a **caption** for each picture. A caption is a short comment that explains what is shown in a picture or illustration.

G. See Independent Reading note in Part 1.

G. Independent Reading

Choose something to read that you will enjoy. Find a quiet, comfortable place and read for the following length of time:

🐾 20 minutes

🐾 25 minutes

🐾 30 minutes

Over time, it's fun to see how much you have read. Be sure to write down what you read today on the Reading Log in your Student Notebook.

Lesson 1, Part 3

A. See Copywork/Dictation note in Part 1.

A. Copywork/Dictation   *Language Skills*

Look carefully at the following passage, and read it silently. Show your teacher any words you don't know, and practice saying them aloud. Now read the passage aloud, or ask your teacher to read it to you.

The Virginia Company sent men and ships across the ocean. They sailed from England to America. People came who thought they had nowhere else to turn. The desire for money made some people come to America.

🐾 Copy the above lines into your Student Notebook. When you are finished, compare your copy to the model (word by word) and make any needed corrections.

🐾 Listen as your teacher dictates the above lines, and write them in your Student Notebook. When you are finished, compare your copy to the model and make any needed corrections.

🐾 Copy, or write as your teacher dictates, paragraph 1 on page 15 in *Surviving Jamestown*. When you are finished, compare your copy to the text and make any needed corrections.

B. **Reader**   *Language Skills, Thinking Skills, History*
In your book, *A Lion to Guard Us*, read Chapter 3 aloud.

🐾 Read one or two paragraphs in your read-aloud book, *Surviving Jamestown.*

🐾 Read one or two pages from today's read-aloud assignment in *Surviving Jamestown.*

C. **Read-Aloud and Narration**   *Language Skills, Thinking Skills*
In *Surviving Jamestown*, listen as your teacher reads page 15 through the end of paragraph 3 on page 21 aloud.

To *narrate* means to retell. In your own words, tell what happened in your assigned passage below. Try to remember as many details as possible. Listen carefully as your teacher reads (or rereads) the part you are to retell.

🐾 Paragraph 2 on page 15.

🐾 Paragraph 3 on page 15.

🐾 Paragraphs 1 through 6 on page 16.

C. See Narration note in Part 1.

D. **Word Study**   *Spelling, Phonics, Vocabulary*
🐾 Remember that an apostrophe is used to show that letters have been left out in a contraction, or to show that something belongs to someone. Look at Chapter 3 in *A Lion to Guard Us* and list the words with apostrophes in your Student Notebook under the correct category.[10]

🐾 Look at page 12 of *Surviving Jamestown*. Find the words with apostrophes and write them in the correct category in your Student Notebook.[11]

Decide what two words you think have been put together to make each contraction. Then reread the sentences and use those two words instead of the contractions to make sure they sound right. Next to each contraction you wrote in your Student Notebook, write the two words it replaces.[12]

E. Geography

Those who got aboard the *Susan Constant, Godspeed,* and *Discovery* in England were headed for Virginia, on the coast of America. With your teacher's help, find the state of Virginia on the map of the United States Political Map in your *Intermediate World Atlas.*

Trace the outline of Virginia. Place a plain piece of paper over the map and hold it in place with a small piece of tape. Trace around the edges of Virginia with a pencil. (Virginia is a yellow state on the map in your atlas.) Remember to just do your best. If you wish you may use the larger Map J-2 below instead of the one in your atlas. When you are finished, cut out your map and glue or tape it into your Student Notebook.

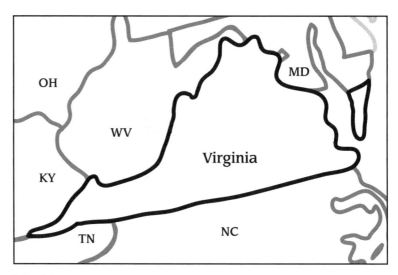

Map J-2

This map shows Virginia as it is now. Include a star with a circle around it for the capital city of Richmond. Put a larger star and circle right next to Virginia to show our nation's capital, Washington, D.C. Write in the Atlantic Ocean.

 Add the Chesapeake Bay to your map. Also add the James River, which is the river that runs right by Richmond.

Virginia is part of the United States, which is part of the continent of North America. Look at the North America Political Map in your *Intermediate World Atlas.* Other countries that are a part of North America are in color. Point out three or four other countries on this continent to your teacher.

Add the states that share a border with Virginia to your map. Those states would be Maryland, West Virginia, Kentucky, Tennessee, and North Carolina.

Add these capital cities to your map (mark them with a star with a circle around it):

Maryland – Annapolis	West Virginia – Charleston
Kentucky – Frankfort	Tennessee – Nashville
North Carolina – Raleigh	

Add the Roanoke River to your map as well. At the library or, with your parent's permission, on the Internet find out what person or people the Roanoke River and the city of Raleigh were named after.[13]

F. Writing   *Thinking Skills*

Another kind of tale is a made up story. Fairy tales and folk tales are this kind of tale. For hundreds of years people all over the world have made up these kinds of tales. Sometimes they begin with phrases like "Once upon a time."

Talk with your teacher and see if you can think of some fairy tales or folk tales that you know. (Hints: *Cinderella, Sleeping Beauty, Paul Bunyan, Grimm's Fairy Tales*, etc.)

Retell as much of the story as you can remember.

With your parent's help, choose a fairy tale, folk tale, or tall tale to read or listen to. There are many to choose from. If you do not have one at home, your library is sure to have a good selection. Tell your teacher about it after you have read or listened to it.

Read a fairy tale, folk tale, or tall tale and then tell your teacher about it. In your Student Notebook, make a list of fun or interesting events from the story that could not happen in real life. These events are called **fiction**, or made up parts of a story.

G. Independent Reading

Choose something to read that you will enjoy. Find a quiet, comfortable place and read for the following length of time:

20 minutes

25 minutes

30 minutes

Be sure to write down what you read today on the Reading Log in your Student Notebook.

F. As with any type of literature, please preview the content of imaginary stories for appropriateness.

G. See Independent Reading note in Part 1.

Lesson 1, Part 4

A. See Copywork/Dictation note in Part 1.

A. **Copywork/Dictation** *Language Skills*

Look carefully at the following passage, and read it silently. Show your teacher any words you don't know, and practice saying them aloud. Now read the passage aloud, or ask your teacher to read it to you.

> The English people did not like change. Many stayed in England even though they were unhappy. A few people found the strength to make a brave choice.

Copy the above lines into your Student Notebook. When you are finished, compare your copy to the model (word by word) and make any needed corrections.

Listen as your teacher dictates the above lines, and write them in your Student Notebook. When you are finished, compare your copy to the model and make any needed corrections.

Copy, or write as your teacher dictates, paragraph 5 on page 21 in *Surviving Jamestown.* When you are finished, compare your copy to the text and make any needed corrections.

B. **Reader** *Language Skills, Thinking Skills, History*

In your book, *A Lion to Guard Us,* read Chapter 4 aloud.

Read one or two paragraphs in your read-aloud book, *Surviving Jamestown.*

Read one or two pages from today's read-aloud assignment in *Surviving Jamestown.*

C. See Discussion note in Part 2.

C. **Read-Aloud and Discussion** *Language Skills, Thinking Skills*

Listen carefully as your teacher reads paragraph 4 on page 21 through the end of page 27 aloud from *Surviving Jamestown.*

Listen as your teacher reads the story and the following discussion question. Think about what you know from the story, and answer in your own words. Give any examples you can think of that help show your answer.

Discussion Question: A **mutiny** is openly disobeying the person in charge of a ship, and encouraging others to join in. It is a very serious crime on a ship. Do you think John Smith was part of a mutiny? Why do you think he was charged with mutiny?

D. Word Study   *Spelling, Phonics, Vocabulary*

Today you will add to the Jamestown Word Bank you are making for this unit.

Look for the names of people on pages 1 and 2 in *A Lion to Guard Us* and put them in a list under the heading "People."[14] These names start with capital letters. Don't write a name more than once.

Look for the names of people from page 1 through the middle of page 8 in *Surviving Jamestown* and put them in a list under the heading "People."[15] These names start with capital letters. Don't write a name more than once.

E. Science   *Geography*

Climate is the way weather usually is in a place. The climate in Virginia is moderate.

Turn to the United States thematic maps in your *Intermediate World Atlas* and look at the climate map for the United States. The area of the map that includes Virginia is green. What does this say about Virginia's climate?[16] Remember to look at the key for the answer. **Humid** means damp or moist heat. Do you remember what moderate means?[17]

In your Student Notebook, look at the first symbol square that you glued to the climate page. Is Virginia near the ocean? If so, which one?[18] If you can, tell how being near the ocean affects climate. If you can't remember, review the information in Lesson 1, Part 2, Section E.

Look at the second symbol square glued to the climate page in your Student Notebook. Answer this question about Virginia: Is Virginia near mountains?[19] Look at the United States Physical Map in your *Intermediate World Atlas*. Are there mountains in Virginia?[19] Where are they?[20] Would the mountains block the breezes from the ocean?[21] Look at the key and the color of most of the state of Virginia. What level is the land?[22]

Look at the third symbol square on the climate page in your Student Notebook. Look at your globe and find the Equator and the North Pole. Now find Virginia on your globe. Virginia is a little less than halfway between the Equator and the North Pole. What happens to climate the farther you get away from the Equator?

With your teacher's help, look in a newspaper or on the Internet. Find the high and low temperatures for Richmond, Virginia, and write them down each day for five days. Do the same thing for London, England. Also write down the amount of rainfall each city gets for the same five days. At the end of the five days, look at your numbers for both cities. Are they similar? What does this tell you about the climate in each city at this time of the year?[23]

🐾 Look in your *Intermediate World Atlas* and compare the climate, population, economy, and environment maps for London, England, and the place where Richmond, Virginia, is found. With your teacher's help, tell how they are the same and how they are different.[24] Though they are not exactly the same, do you think their differences are very great?[25]

F. Drawing

In Part 3 you remembered, read, or listened to a fairy tale, folk tale, or tall tale. Use the three boxes in your Student Notebook to draw illustrations that show the beginning, middle, and end of that tale. Illustrations are especially important for stories that are fiction, or not true. They help the person who reads the story get the best idea of what the writer was telling about.

🐾 After you draw your illustrations, list the names of the characters you drew under their pictures.

🐾 After you have drawn your illustrations, write a caption for each picture. Remember, a caption is a short comment that explains what is shown in a picture or illustration.

G. See Independent Reading note in Part 1.

G. Independent Reading

Choose something to read that you will enjoy. Find a quiet, comfortable place and read for the following length of time:

🐾 20 minutes

🐾 25 minutes

🐾 30 minutes

Over time, it's fun to see how much you have read. Be sure to write down what you read today on the Reading Log in your Student Notebook.

Lesson 1, Part 5

This part is set aside for completion of any work left undone from the lesson, and review of concepts and content. It is also a time to expand the work in the lesson by doing art, timeline activities, or games.

• Review the Steps for Thinking from the beginning of this lesson.

- On the large outline map of the U.S. label: the states and capitals covered during this lesson; Washington, D.C.; and Chesapeake Bay.

- Look at the Jamestown Word Bank you began during this lesson, and choose at least eight words. Then write a sentence for each one in your Student Notebook, telling how that word is related to the unit. Do your best to spell the word correctly. When you are finished, check your sentences against the list in your Word Bank. Don't count off for other words that are misspelled. Remember that your goal is to improve, not necessarily to get them all right immediately.

- Listen to or read the story about John Smith in *Profiles from History.* Complete the timeline activities and any other activities you would like to do.

- Drawing was a very important skill for an explorer to have so that he could show other people what he had seen. Drawing is also a needed skill for someone to have who is going to make observations and then show other people what he has seen. Complete the art lesson in your Student Notebook.

Enrichment Activities

1. Learn about Queen Elizabeth I. She was the Queen of England around the year 1600. She ruled England for quite a while. Learn about her and her effect on England. Why do you think she had such a big impact on the people of England?

2. Sir Walter Raleigh was another Englishman with a love for adventure and exploration. Read about him and tell others what you learn. What happened to him in the end? How was he like Columbus? How was he different? What was the Lost Colony?

3. What was London, England like in 1600? Make a poster or brochure showing what the city looked like. Be sure to include famous sights such as Big Ben and London Bridge, and what the people looked like. How many people lived in London at that time?

Additional Resources

John Smith of Virginia, by Robert Syme

James Towne, by Marcus Sewell

Most of the labeling has already been completed in the Student Notebook during this lesson. Instruct students to use the maps in their Student Notebooks as a reference. When they label the larger map, students will see the "big picture" and gain a broader understanding of their lessons.

We are extremely grateful to Barry Stebbing for today's art lesson, which is a sample of the many materials he has created for teaching art to homeschoolers. How Great Thou Art has a full line of art supplies and curriculum written by Barry Stebbing. Please visit this website to see all of the resources he has created: www.howgreatthouart.com.

Use one or more of the Enrichment Activities if your child completes his assigned work and has the time or desire to learn more. These activities are flexible, so choose the one(s) that seem most interesting to your student. Allow him to work at a level that is appropriate for him, and remember that the learning process is more important than the product.

Answers

1. she's, can't, there's, you're, shouldn't, Freebold's, I'm

2. he's, where's, wouldn't, couldn't, they're, we're

3. contractions: don't, It's, We'll, Somebody's, It's, you're, there's; Words that show belonging: Sam's stomach, father's farm, Sam's eyes, man's action

4. the story of what had happened to her father.

5. England: London Bridge, Fish Street, London; America: Jamestown, Virginia, New World

6. England: Lincolnshire, Blackwall Port, Thames River, London, English Channel; America: Virginia, Roanoke Island; Other Places: Atlantic Ocean, Canary Islands, Africa, Newfoundland, Transylvania, Orient

7. Summers are rainy.

8. climate - moderate with rainy summers; environment - urban

9. population - over 500 people per sq. mi. for London and 100–500 people per sq. mi. for Seattle; economies - manufacturing and commerce for London and forestry and agriculture for Seattle

10. contractions: I'm, it's, I'll, don't, can't, he's, ma'am, that's, wouldn't, I'd, needn't, we're; words that show belonging: cook's face, Mother's place

11. contractions: you're, it's, don't, that's, I'm, it's, won't, what's, didn't; words that show belonging: captain's words, captain's mood, Virginia Company's first venture

12. you're – you are; it's – it is; don't – do not; that's – that is; I'm – I am; won't – will not; what's – what is; didn't – did not

13. Roanoke - for Algonquian people (possibly Algonquian word for shell money); Raleigh - Sir Walter Raleigh

14. Mistress Freebold, Mistress Trippet, Annie, Amanda, James Freebold, Jemmy, Cook, Father, Meg, Meggie, Dr. Crider

15. John Smith, Nathaniel Peacock, Master Smith, Nate Peacock, Sam Collier, James Brumfield, Master Cathorp, James Thomas, and Anne Collier

16. Virginia's climate is moderate with humid summers.

17. moderate: without extremes, does not get very hot or cold.

18. Atlantic Ocean

19. yes

20. far inland

21. no

22. between 0, or sea level, and 656 feet

23. It gets colder.

24. There are no ways they are the same. They are different in all 4 ways.

25. No. Both climates are moderate with humid or rainy summers. Both economies have business or commerce with nearby agriculture or farming. Populations are different because Richmond is smaller and the environment is different. Richmond is in a swamp area and London is in an urban, or city, area.

Lesson 2, Part 1

❧ Steps for Thinking ☙

1. It is important to communicate clearly and truthfully.

2. You must learn to tell if what you hear is the truth.

3. People are influenced by what they hear.

The **Steps for Thinking** section gives you the main ideas about the topics presented. Understanding these helps you to have productive discussions with your children so they, too, understand the bigger ideas. This forms more permanent learning, contrary to just learning facts, which tends to be temporary. These steps are useful prior to instruction, and they are also useful or review at the end of the week.

❧ Materials ☙

- *A Lion to Guard Us*
- *Surviving Jamestown*
- *Intermediate World Atlas*
- *North American Wildlife Guide*
- *Eat Your Way Around the World*
- Student Notebook
- Globe
- Plain or tracing paper
- Watch or timing device
- Newspaper, library, or Internet access
- Index cards/marker
- Ingredients for English tea time recipes
- Crayons or colored pencils
- Construction paper
- Dictionary
- Large world outline map

A. **Copywork/Dictation**   *Language Skills*

Look carefully at the following passage, and read it silently. Show your teacher any words you don't know, and practice saying them aloud. Now read the passage aloud, or ask your teacher to read it to you.

> The choice to go to America was not always easy. There were many tales of danger told about the ocean. There were different tales told about the Indians. Some said they were kind and some said they were warlike.

🐾 Copy the above lines into your Student Notebook. When you are finished, compare your copy to the model (word by word) and make any needed corrections.

🐾 Listen as your teacher dictates the above lines, and write them in your Student Notebook. When you are finished, compare your copy to the model and make any needed corrections.

🐾 Copy, or write as your teacher dictates, paragraph 2 on page 28 (beginning with "When Sam heard the call…") in *Surviving Jamestown*. When you are finished, compare your copy to the text and make any needed corrections.

B. **Reader**   *Language Skills, Thinking Skills, History*

In your book, *A Lion to Guard Us,* read Chapter 5 aloud.

🐾 Read one or two paragraphs in your read-aloud book, *Surviving Jamestown.*

🐾 Read one or two pages from today's read-aloud assignment in *Surviving Jamestown.*

A. Copywork and dictation assignments go from an easier level (designated by 🐾) to harder levels (designated by 🐾 and 🐾). Take two days for the copywork if that is more comfortable for your child. Please adapt instructions to your child's individual needs. Your child should be **consistently successful** at one level before progressing to the next, **regardless of grade**.

C. The skill of narration is gained over time. If your child has never retold a story, start with the assignment for the lower level, no matter what grade he is in. Work up from there, being careful to allow him to stay at the level of success for a while before going to a longer section.

C. **Read-aloud and Narration**   *Language Skills, Thinking Skills*

In *Surviving Jamestown*, listen as your teacher reads page 28 through the end of paragraph 1 on page 34 aloud.

To *narrate* means to retell. In your own words, tell what happened in your assigned passage below. Try to remember as many details as possible. Listen carefully as your teacher reads (or rereads) the part you are to retell.

Paragraph 3 on page 29.

Paragraph 7 on page 32 through paragraph 2 on page 33.

Paragraph 2 on page 30 through the end of paragraph 1 on page 31.

D. **Word Study**   *Spelling, Phonics, Vocabulary*

The letter *c* has no sound of its own. It usually makes a *k* sound, such as in the word *cup*. But it can also sound like another letter. When *c* comes before the letters *e* or *i*, it makes the *s* sound. Look at the following words and read them aloud, or listen to your teacher read them:

c that says *s*		*c* that says *k* like *cup*	
cent	circle	captain	cuff
certain	cinder	carve	curve
citizen	celebrate	Cathay	curtain
city		cause	code
		count	cousin
		cough	custom

Choose at least four words in each category above to learn how to spell. If you know how to spell all the words, look in a dictionary and find four more words for each category. Add them to the lists, and learn how to spell them.

Choose at least five words in each category above to learn how to spell. If you know how to spell all or most of the words, look in a dictionary and find five more words for each category. Add them to the lists, and learn how to spell them.

D. The small superscript numbers that appear after some of the questions in this unit refer to answers in the answer key, located immediately after Part 5.

When *c* is next to another consonant like *h, l,* or *r,* the *c* sound blends with the letter next to it. Look at page 29 in *Surviving Jamestown*. Find the words with *c* in them and put them in the correct category in your Student Notebook.[1] Look carefully, because many of these *c* sounds are not at the beginning of the word.

Choose at least ten words from those you just found in *Surviving Jamestown*, and learn how to spell them. If you know how to spell all these words, look at pages 28-33 in your book and follow the directions above to find ten words you do not know how to spell. Learn how to spell them.

E. Geography   *Language Skills, Science*

A **river** is a large, natural stream of water that flows towards a larger body of water, bringing fresh water to lakes or oceans. This is important because ocean water is always in the process of **evaporating,** or heating and turning into water vapor. This vapor becomes clouds, which eventually fall to the earth again as rain. This process is called the **water cycle**, and you will learn more about it later this year. The water cycle is important because all living things need water. If rivers did not do the important job of bringing water back to the oceans, before long there would be a great problem with the world's water supply.

Look at the Europe Political Map in the *Intermediate World Atlas.* Find the United Kingdom, then England. Now find the capital city of London. Put your finger on the small blue line that goes into London. That is the River Thames.

Notice that the blue line begins out in the English countryside. The place where a river begins is called its **source.** A river's source could be a spring that bubbles up out of the ground, or snow that melts in the mountains. The beginning of a river can be large or small. The beginning of the Thames River is just a small stream or brook in the Cotswold Hills of England. From there it flows gently through the countryside, with other waterways joining it. These waterways are called **tributaries.** Tributaries feed the Thames more water and rain adds water to the flow, so the Thames grows larger and stronger. It also becomes wider and able to carry larger boats. The Thames flows into the North Sea. It is 260 miles long.

Find the following rivers on their continents. They are the four longest rivers in the world. You can find them on a globe or the World Physical Map in your *Intermediate World Atlas.* Remember, on a map a river is a blue line:

River	Continent
Nile	Africa
Amazon	South America
Yangtze	Asia
Mississippi	North America

Look at the World Political Map in the *Intermediate World Atlas.* Tell at least one country that each of these rivers flows through.[2] If you can see more than one country, add it:

E. Each word in bold letters is considered a vocabulary word. It is a word that may or may not be new to your child. You can write these vocabulary words on index cards and use them for occasional review, but not for memorizing. Give the child the meaning of the words if he doesn't remember. Try to use the new vocabulary words during conversation, and encourage your students to do the same.

Each time your student makes a vocabulary card for this unit, have him write a "J" (for Jamestown) in the upper left corner. This will make it possible to review vocabulary by unit at the end of the year.

Nile_____Amazon_____

Yangtze_____Mississippi_____

For a closer view, look at the political maps for each continent.

F. Writing   *Thinking Skills*

In each of your stories, there are very colorful characters. A character is *colorful* when he has many qualities that you notice, or that stand out. Sometimes characters stand out because of good qualities, and sometimes because of bad qualities.

Think about these two characters from *A Lion to Guard Us:* Amanda and Mrs. Trippett. Look back through the book to see pictures of the characters and reread descriptions of them given in the story.

Now tell your teacher what you know about each character. Tell as much as you know about each one, so that someone else might know them if they were to meet. Start with what the character looks like and what kind of person they seem to be. Then tell at least two things that the character did in the story. Lastly, tell whether or not you like the character. Tell why you do or do not like them. Remember to use your Jamestown Word Bank to help you.

Your teacher can make notes of your answers for you, or you can write down your thoughts about each character. You can use phrases, not complete sentences. This is "thinking writing."

Write down your answers to these questions. You can use phrases, not complete sentences, since this is "thinking writing."

Think about what you have read or heard so far about the characters of Sam Collier, Nate Peacock, and John Smith from *Surviving Jamestown*. Complete the Character Portrait in your Student Notebook for each one.

G. Independent Reading

Choose something to read that you will enjoy. Find a quiet, comfortable place and read for the following length of time:

20 minutes

25 minutes

30 minutes

Over time, it's fun to see how much you have read. Be sure to write down what you read today on the Reading Log in your Student Notebook.

G. Reading fluency is developed through having frequent silent reading opportunities that continue for the length of time suggested here. Since a primary focus of this activity is to nurture your child's enjoyment of reading, help him to choose reading material that interests him and is at a level that allows him to read with understanding by himself. You can incorporate this activity into your school day whenever it is most convenient.

If the suggested length of time is too long for your child to continue reading by himself, start with an amount of time he can accomplish successfully and make the suggested time a goal.

Lesson 2, Part 2

A. **Copywork/Dictation**   *Language Skills*

Look carefully at the following passage, and read it silently. Show your teacher any words you don't know, and practice saying them aloud. Now read the passage aloud, or ask your teacher to read it to you.

> Even if people were afraid of Indians, they could make changes when things became too hard to keep going. Men, women, and even children started boarding ships for America, looking for a happier life.

Copy the above lines into your Student Notebook. When you are finished, compare your copy to the model (word by word) and make any needed corrections.

Listen as your teacher dictates the above lines, and write them in your Student Notebook. When you are finished, compare your copy to the model and make any needed corrections.

Copy, or write as your teacher dictates, paragraph 3 on page 37 of *Surviving Jamestown.* When you are finished, compare your copy to the text and make any needed corrections.

B. **Reader**   *Language Skills, Thinking Skills, History*

In your book, *A Lion to Guard Us,* read Chapter 6 aloud.

Read one or two paragraphs in your read-aloud book, *Surviving Jamestown.*

Read one or two pages from today's read-aloud assignment in *Surviving Jamestown.*

C. **Read-Aloud and Discussion**   *Listening Skills, Thinking Skills*

Listen carefully as your teacher reads paragraph 2 on page 34 through the end of page 41 aloud from *Surviving Jamestown.*

Listen as your teacher rereads paragraphs 1–3 on page 37 and the following discussion question. Think about what you know from the story, and answer in your own words. Give any examples you can think of that help show your answer.

Discussion Question: In Reverend Hunt's mind, what do you think the difference is between the English and "savages."

A. See Copywork/Dictation note in Part 1.

C. Discussion is very important in developing your child's ability to organize his thoughts. This in turn builds the ability to think and write. The goal of the discussion questions is not just to find the answer to a particular question, but also to create a situation where thoughts about the question and its answer are shared and considered in a detailed way. Do not rush this activity, but encourage your student to share his or her ideas relating to the topic, and any additional ideas that may come to mind. You can also share your thoughts and questions as an example for your students.

D. Remember, vowels are *a, e, i, o, u,* and sometimes *y;* consonants are all the remaining letters of the alphabet.

D. Word Study   *Spelling, Phonics, Vocabulary*

Look at the word *happier* in the copywork passage printed in Section A above. This word means to be more happy than before. You can add *er* to the end of a word that tells what something or someone was like before. There are several ways to do this.

If a word ends with a consonant, just add *er,* like this: *rich — richer.*

If a word ends with *e,* just add an *r,* like this: *true — truer.*

If a word ends with *y,* change the *y* to *i* first and then add *er,* like this: *funny — funnier.* When the word *happy* was changed to *happier,* the *y* was changed to an *i* first. Then the letters *er* were added to the end.

Tell how you think you would add *er* to the end of these words:[3]

hard	rich
sorry	risky
white	brave

Look at these words from Chapter 5 of *A Lion to Guard Us.* Apply the rules above to make the words that mean more than before:[4]

late	wild
busy	strange

Read these words that describe the colonists' lives before they came to Virginia. In your Student Notebook, add *er* to each word and then write "yes" or "no" after it to tell whether or not it is true.[5]

easy	quiet	rich
hard	bold	brave
risky	calm	

E. Science   *Thinking Skills, Art*

Along the riverbank of the Thames, before it becomes a very large river, there is an abundance of life. Long ago, as the river attracted people to live near it, it also drew certain creatures. This is true of most rivers where the water has not been greatly polluted. When water, air, or soil is called **polluted,** that means it has become very dirty.

The first group of animals from the riverbank that you will learn about are called **mammals.** Mammals are warm-blooded animals that have backbones. Their babies are born alive and the mother mammal feeds her baby mammal by providing milk. **Warm-blooded** means that something's blood is constantly warmed from the inside.

The river otter is just such a creature. Though this animal is found in England, it also lives in North America. Read, or listen to your teacher read, about it on page 61 in the *North American Wildlife Guide*. Draw or trace the river otter into your Student Notebook. Tell where it lives, what it eats, and what it looks like.[6]

Birds make up the second group of living things you can see along the riverbank. **Birds** have backbones and are warm-blooded. They give birth to their young by laying eggs. Birds have two legs, wings, and are covered with feathers. Read, or listen to your teacher read, about the mute swan on page 88 in the *North American Wildlife Guide*.

Draw or trace the mute swan into your Student Notebook. Tell where it lives, what it eats, and what it looks like.[7]

In the river itself you can find the group of living things called **fish**. A fish lives in the water, has a backbone, and breathes air through gills instead of lungs. Fish are usually covered with scales, have fins, and are cold-blooded. When something is **cold-blooded**, the temperature of its blood varies depending on its surroundings.

Look at the stickleback on page 215 in the *North American Wildlife Guide*. This fish is often found in rivers. Draw or trace the stickleback into your Student Notebook. Then tell where it lives, what it eats, and what it looks like.[8]

Another fish found in rivers is the minnow. Look at the mudminnow on page 208 in the *North American Wildlife Guide*. Draw or trace the mudminnow in your Student Notebook. Then tell where it lives, what it eats, and what it looks like.[9]

F. **Drawing**   *Thinking Skills, Language Skills*

Have you ever been to a river, pond, stream, or lake? If you can go near any water, with your parent's permission, take your drawing paper and colored pencils or crayons. Sit for three to five minutes and observe the scene around you. Look at the color of the water, the types of plants nearby, and any wildlife. (Remember, even birds and insects are wildlife!)

After observing for several minutes, choose one part of the scene to draw. Your goal is to show others what you see, not to make a perfect drawing. Only take a few minutes to draw. This is just a **sketch,** or a quick, roughly done drawing, and is not meant to be a finished product.

Observe for another three to five minutes and make another sketch. If you would like to add to your drawings later, make notes on the side telling colors to use or things to add.

🐾 Add a description to your sketch of the water and the surroundings. Tell what it looked like, the weather (temperature, cloud cover, time of day, etc.), the atmosphere, or what it was like near the water. As you continue to observe, you may find that you are noticing different aspects of the same scene.

G. See Independent Reading note in Part 1.

G. Independent Reading
Choose something to read that you will enjoy. Find a quiet, comfortable place and read for the following length of time:

🐾 20 minutes

🐾 25 minutes

🐾 30 minutes

Over time, it's fun to see how much you have read. Be sure to write down what you read today on the Reading Log in your Student Notebook.

Lesson 2, Part 3

A. See Copywork/Dictation note in Part 1.

A. Copywork/Dictation   *Language Skills*
Look carefully at the following passage, and read it silently. Show your teacher any words you don't know, and practice saying them aloud. Now read the passage aloud, or ask your teacher to read it to you.

> When the first settlers came to America, most people looked forward to living in freedom. Many settlers were willing to work hard, but some who came wanted to bring old ways. They thought they wouldn't have to help if they were from a rich family.

🐾 Copy the above lines into your Student Notebook. When you are finished, compare your copy to the model (word by word) and make any needed corrections.

🐾 Listen as your teacher dictates the above lines, and write them in your Student Notebook. When you are finished, compare your copy to the model and make any needed corrections.

🐾 Copy, or write as your teacher dictates, paragraph 4 on page 44 of *Surviving Jamestown.* When you are finished, compare your copy to the text and make any needed corrections.

B. Reader   *Language Skills, Thinking Skills, History*
In your book, *A Lion to Guard Us,* read Chapter 7 aloud.

🐾 Read one or two paragraphs in your read-aloud book, *Surviving Jamestown.*

🐾 Read one or two pages from today's read-aloud assignment in *Surviving Jamestown.*

C. Read-Aloud and Narration   *Language Skills, Thinking Skills*
In *Surviving Jamestown,* listen as your teacher reads pages 42 through 47 aloud.

C. See Narration note in Part 1.

To *narrate* means to retell. In your own words, tell what happened in your assigned passage below. Try to remember as many details as possible. Listen carefully as your teacher reads (or rereads) the part you are to retell.

🐾🐾 Paragraph 3 on page 42.

🐾 Paragraph 3 on page 42 through the end of paragraph 1 on page 43.

🐾 Paragraph 7 on page 44 through paragraph 6 on page 46.

D. Word Study   *Spelling, Phonics, Vocabulary*
Review the words you didn't know from Part 1's Word Study lists. See if you can spell these words without looking. Continue to practice spelling them if necessary.

🐾🐾🐾 Tell your teacher how each of the words below is spelled when you add *er* to the end:[10]

> bold
>
> sorry
>
> pale

🐾 Read this word or listen to your teacher read it: *Indian*

It has three syllables, or sounds. When *ian* is put at the end of a word, it often describes a person. Read this list of words for your teacher:

> *guardian* (a person who guards another person)
>
> *Virginian* (a person from Virginia)
>
> *Christian* (a person who follows Christ)

See if you can spell the four words above. If not, practice them. Try to think of at least two more words that end with *ian.*

E. Science

History, Language Skills

In Part 1 you learned about the Thames River. This river starts out small and grows to be a large and wide river. It is also an important part of the history of London. The city of London began right after the time that Christ lived on earth. The Romans were in charge of "Londinium," which is the name London was called at that time. The River Thames was very important because it provided a way to carry people and goods to and from faraway ports.

London grew and around a thousand years later a ruler came to power called William the Conqueror. He started building things in London out of stone, not wood like before. The Tower of London and London Bridge were built with stone, which made them much stronger. The Thames River was more important than ever as people wanted to live by it. They wanted to have water nearby, but they also wanted to have a place to throw their waste and garbage. The people didn't know that this would **pollute** the water, or make it dirty. The dirty water in the Thames River was part of the reason people in London got sick in later years.

Pollution is when the water, air, or soil is made dirty. In years past, people often did not understand that what they were doing could cause problems later. That is how it was in London. Scientists had not yet learned about the connection between eating or drinking things that were not clean and becoming sick.

Talk with your family to find out what they do to make sure that your food and water are clean.

☙ Keeping your food and water supply clean is an important part of staying healthy. What are some ways you and your family help keep the environment clean in your town?[11]

☙ Look in your local newspaper, in your library, or on the Internet to find out if there are any problems with pollution in the town where you live. Tell your teacher about the problem and how the community is trying to correct it.

F. Writing

History

Large cities grew up around large rivers because the rivers did so much for the people. The river provided a source of water, food and transportation. Many people came to live in London. Around the time of the Jamestown expedition, London had about 75,000 residents! That was a very large city for those times. Because so many people wanted to live there, it became very crowded. Over time, only those who were the richest people could afford to own homes in London. Many other people became the servants of others, or lived on the streets as homeless people.

It may be difficult to imagine what life would have been like as a servant or homeless person in London hundreds of years ago. Life was harder for everyone back then, and especially for those who did not have anything of their own. Even though you may not be rich, you can still be very grateful for the life you have.

Write down a list of people, places, and things you are grateful for. Make a thank you card for someone who takes care of you by folding a piece of construction paper in half. Now choose at least three things from your list, and write about each thing in a sentence. Tell what it is you're grateful for, and tell why. Write your sentences in your card and give it to someone who takes care of you. Here are some examples:

I am grateful for my family because they love me.

Thank you for my room because I have a place to sleep and play.

Decorate the front of your card any way you want.

🐾 Choose at least three things from your list that you are grateful for. In your card, write at least two sentences telling about each thing and why you are grateful. Give your card to someone who takes care of you.

🐾 On your card, write at least two paragraphs that tell about things you are grateful for. Since a paragraph is a group of sentences about one topic, write several sentences that focus on each thing you are grateful for, such as your home or your family. Give several details about each thing so that those who read what you write will know how much you appreciate what you have. Give your card to someone who takes care of you.

G. **Independent Reading**
Choose something to read that you will enjoy. Find a quiet, comfortable place and read for the following length of time:

🐾🐾 20 minutes

🐾 25 minutes

🐾 30 minutes

Be sure to write down what you read today on the Reading Log in your Student Notebook.

G. See Independent Reading note in Part 1.

Lesson 2, Part 4

A. See Copywork/Dictation note in Part 1.

A. **Copywork/Dictation** *Language Skills*

Look carefully at the following passage, and read it silently. Show your teacher any words you don't know, and practice saying them aloud. Now read the passage aloud, or ask your teacher to read it to you.

> Everyone had to help to build a new colony and a new country. It would take some time for people to change the way they thought. When trouble came, it made everyone work together.

Copy the above lines into your Student Notebook. When you are finished, compare your copy to the model (word by word) and make any needed corrections.

Listen as your teacher dictates the above lines, and write them in your Student Notebook. When you are finished, compare your copy to the model and make any needed corrections.

Copy, or write as your teacher dictates, paragraph 2 on page 50 in *Surviving Jamestown*. When you are finished, compare your copy to the text and make any needed corrections.

B. **Reader** *Language Skills, Thinking Skills, History*

In your book, *A Lion to Guard Us*, read Chapter 8 aloud.

Read one or two paragraphs in your read-aloud book, *Surviving Jamestown*.

Read one or two pages from today's read-aloud assignment in *Surviving Jamestown*.

C. See Discussion note in Part 2.

C. **Read-Aloud and Discussion** *Language Skills, Thinking Skills*

Listen carefully as your teacher reads pages 48 through 54 aloud from *Surviving Jamestown*.

Listen as your teacher reads the story and the following discussion question. Think about what you know from the story, and answer in your own words. Give any examples you can think of that help show your answer.

Discussion Question: Many people seemed to object to John Smith being appointed to the group of leaders of the colony. Why do you think so many people objected?

D. Word Study

Spelling, Phonics, Vocabulary

When the letters *wr* are together at the beginning of a word, they make the *r* sound like the beginning of the word *red*. Look at page 43 in *A Lion to Guard Us*. Find three different words on that page that begin with the letters *wr*.[12]

Play Word Study Charades. With your eyes closed choose a slip of paper. Read the word on it. If you do not know what it means, you can look it up in the dictionary. You may want to tell everyone that the word you are acting out starts with the letters *wr*. They may use a dictionary to figure out your word.

wrap	wrist	writes
wrong	wrestler	wreck

Choose at least three more words from the dictionary that start with *wr* to act out.

D. Word Study Charades: Write each of the charade words on a separate slip of paper. Let students draw one and act it out.

E. Geography

History

Look at Map J-3 of the city of London. On this map are several **landmarks,** or famous places. Also on this map is the River Thames. Notice how this river runs right through the heart of London.

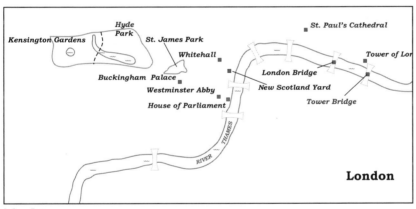

London

Map J-3

Using the map in your notebook, color the river blue. Find these landmarks and color them green:

Kensington Gardens
Hyde Park
St. James Park

The rest of the landmarks on this map are marked with squares. Read about each landmark and then highlight its name on your map:

Westminster Abbey: A church in London where the Kings and Queens of England have been crowned for almost 1000 years.

Houses of Parliament: The government of Great Britain, made up of the House of Lords (those who have held titles in England for generations) and the House of Commons (those who are elected to hold office).

Buckingham Palace: Traditional home of the King and Queen.

Whitehall: The place of government offices.

New Scotland Yard: Headquarters of the London police.

St. Paul's Cathedral: A church in London rebuilt by Christopher Wren, who designed many buildings in London.

Tower of London: Old prison where the Crown Jewels are kept.

London Bridge: Original site of the London Bridge.

Tower Bridge: Bridge by the Tower of London.

This map shows only a few places on the banks of the River Thames. What landmarks are in your town? With your teacher's help, make a list of those places near you that are famous. Tell why each is famous.

There are great stories to go with each of the landmarks in London described above. You may want to read more about them on the Internet or at your library.

F. Drawing
Writing, History

Look at the pictures of landmarks in London in Appendix A.

Draw or trace at least two of them into your Student Notebook. After you draw them, describe them to your teacher. Tell how they look and where they are located in London.

Draw or trace at least three of them into your Student Notebook. After you draw them, describe them to your teacher. Tell how they look and where they are located in London.

G. See Independent Reading note in Part 1.

G. Independent Reading

Choose something to read that you will enjoy. Find a quiet, comfortable place and read for the following length of time:

20 minutes

25 minutes

30 minutes

Over time, it's fun to see how much you have read. Be sure to write down what you read today on the Reading Log in your Student Notebook.

Lesson 2, Part 5

This part is set aside for completion of any work left undone from the lesson, and review of concepts and content. It is also a time to expand the work in the lesson by doing art, timeline activities, or games.

- Review the Steps for Thinking from the beginning of this lesson.

- On the large outline map of the world label: England; London, England; and the four longest rivers in the world. You may use the *Intermediate World Atlas* to help you.

Most of the labeling has already been completed in the Student Notebook during this lesson. Instruct students to use the maps in their Student Notebooks as a reference. When they label the larger map, students will see the "big picture" and gain a broader understanding of their lessons.

- Review the spelling words for this lesson. In your Student Notebook, write a sentence using each word. Do your best to write the spelling words correctly. After you have finished, check your sentences against the list in your Student Notebook and see how many spelling words you spelled correctly. (Don't count off for other words that are misspelled.) Remember your goal is to improve, not necessarily to get them all right immediately.

- On your Student Resources CD, find the cards to play the Old World/New World Opposites game. One set of cards tells about something that would happen in the Old World. Match the Old World fact with its opposite New World fact.

Teachers can find a copy of this game in Appendix B. Instructions and answer keys for all games are located in Appendix A.

- When the colonists came to the New World from England, they brought many customs with them. One of the most important was the way that they cooked. In the book, *Eat Your Way Around the World* by Jamie Aramini, turn to the section on Great Britain and read about the tradition of tea time. To learn more about English customs, have a tea time with your family. For your tea time you may want to make traditional British dishes such as Scones, Cucumber Sandwiches, or Mushroom Turnovers from the recipes found in *Eat Your Way Around the World*.

Enrichment Activities

1. Learn about the history of London. Make a timeline showing the major events in London since its founding around 43 A.D. You may want to add the story of any of London's famous landmarks to your timeline.

2. Learn about archery, or shooting an arrow from a bow. It is a very popular sport. Tell what you learn and show how bows and arrows have changed over the years, either with pictures or drawings.

Use one or more of the Enrichment Activities if your child completes his assigned work and has the time or desire to learn more. These activities are flexible, so choose the one(s) that seem most interesting to your student. Allow him to work at a level that is appropriate for him, and remember that the learning process is more important than the product.

Answers

1. *c* that says *sh:* ocean; *sc:* scouring, scrubbed, scoops, schools; *ch:* reached, beach, approached, searching, chuckled; *cl:* clothes, clear, clean; *ck:* stuck, kicking, chuckled, rocked; *c* that says *c* like *cup:* colorful, Calthrop, come

2. (Answers may vary.) Nile: Egypt, Sudan; Amazon: Brazil, Bolivia; Yangtze: China; Mississippi: United States

3. harder, richer, sorrier, riskier, whiter, braver

4. later, wilder, busier, stranger

5. easier (no), quieter (no), richer (no), harder (yes), bolder (yes), braver (yes), riskier (yes), calmer (no)

6. river otter: lives in rivers, streams, lakes; eats fish, frogs, crayfish, and other small animals; has dark brown fur, short arms and legs, thick long tail, long body

7. mute swan lives in lakes, ponds, marshes; eats aquatic plants and insects; is large, white, 4–5 feet long, neck held in a s-curve, orange bill

8. stickleback: lives in cool, shallow water; is small, 2–3 inches in length; green with spiky-looking dorsal fins

9. minnow: lives in small lakes, ponds, streams; eats aquatic plants and small fish; is small, 3–8 inches long, brown with a rounded tail and short snout

10. bolder, sorrier, paler

11. Answers will vary: recycling, taking batteries to special collection sites, etc.

12. wrong, write, writing

Lesson 3, Part 1

> ### ⸱ Steps for Thinking ⸱
>
> 1. When in a new situation, be alert for new ideas and ways of doing things.
>
> 2. A wise person learns from the experiences of others.
>
> 3. Remember to follow what you believe is true. Circumstances shouldn't change your beliefs.

The **Steps for Thinking** section gives you the main ideas about the topics presented. Understanding these helps you to have productive discussions with your children so they, too, understand the bigger ideas. This forms more permanent learning, contrary to just learning facts, which tends to be temporary. These steps are useful prior to instruction, and they are also useful for review at the end of the week.

⸰Materials⸰

- *A Lion to Guard Us*
- *Surviving Jamestown*
- *North American Wildlife Guide*
- *Profiles from History*
- *Intermediate World Atlas*
- Student Notebook
- Crayons or colored pencils
- Index cards/marker
- Plain or tracing paper
- Large world outline map

A. **Copywork/Dictation**   *Language Skills*

Look carefully at the following passage, and read it silently. Show your teacher any words you don't know, and practice saying them aloud. Now read the passage aloud, or ask your teacher to read it to you.

> The voyage across the ocean had good moments and bad. Soon the passengers found out about life at sea. Many were sick at first, but the sound and movement of the ship was bound to feel more normal after awhile.

A. Copywork and dictation assignments go from an easier level (designated by 🐾) to harder levels (designated by 🐾 and 🐾). Take two days for the copywork if that is more comfortable for your child. Please adapt instructions to your child's individual needs. Your child should be **consistently successful** at one level before progressing to the next, **regardless of grade**.

🐾 Copy the above lines into your Student Notebook. When you are finished, compare your copy to the model (word by word) and make any needed corrections.

🐾 Listen as your teacher dictates the above lines, and write them in your Student Notebook. When you are finished, compare your copy to the model and make any needed corrections.

🐾 Copy, or write as your teacher dictates, paragraph 2 on page 54 (from the colon in sentence 3 through the end of the paragraph) in *Surviving Jamestown.* When you are finished, compare your copy to the text and make any needed corrections.

B. **Reader**   *Language Skills, Thinking Skills, History*

In your book, *A Lion to Guard Us,* read chapter 9 aloud.

🐾 Read one or two paragraphs in your read-aloud book, *Surviving Jamestown.*

🐾 Read one or two pages from today's read-aloud assignment in *Surviving Jamestown.*

C. Discussion is very important in developing your child's ability to organize his thoughts. This in turn builds the ability to think and write. The goal of the discussion questions is not just to find the answer to a particular question, but also to create a situation where thoughts about the question and its answer are shared and considered in a detailed way. Do not rush this activity, but encourage your student to share his or her ideas relating to the topic, and any additional ideas that may come to mind. You can also share your thoughts and questions as an example for your students.

D. The small superscript numbers that appear after some of the questions in this unit refer to answers in the answer key, located immediately after Part 5.

C. **Read-Aloud and Discussion**   *Language Skills, Thinking Skills*

In *Surviving Jamestown,* listen as your teacher reads page 55 through the bottom of page 62 aloud.

Listen as your teacher reads the story and the following discussion question. Think about what you know from the story, and answer in your own words. Give any examples you can think of that help show your answer.

Discussion Question: John Smith told Sam Collier to pay close attention to every detail of the Indians' language and behavior. He felt it was very important to learn all they could. He thought it might be the difference between living and dying some day. Do you think John Smith was right? How could paying attention to the Indians' ways help the colonists?

D. **Word Study**   *Spelling, Phonics, Vocabulary*

The letters *ou* make different sounds depending on what letters they are next to. When consonant letters like *nd, t, s,* or *d* are next to *ou,* it usually says *ow.*

Read this list of words to your teacher, or listen to her read them:

    out

    ground

    mouse

Find the five words in your copywork passage printed in Section A that have the sound *ow* spelled with the letters *ou,* and write them in your Student Notebook.[1]

🐾 Look in Chapter 9 of *A Lion to Guard Us* and find all the words with the sound *ow* spelled with the letters *ou.* Make a list of these words in your Student Notebook.[2]

🐾 Look on pages 57–59 of *Surviving Jamestown* and find all the words that have the sound *ow* spelled with the letters *ou.* Make a list of these words in your Student Notebook.[3]

E. **Science**   *Geography, History*

When the Jamestown explorers first came to America, they arrived in the area of Chesapeake Bay. Look at the United States Political Map in your *Intermediate World Atlas.* Virginia is mid-way up the coast of the Atlantic Ocean. Find Chesapeake Bay on Virginia's coastline. Remember, a bay is an area of water from an ocean, sea, or gulf that extends into the land.

The area around Chesapeake Bay is called a Tidal Marsh. On page 36 in the *North American Wildlife Guide,* look at the picture and read, or listen to your teacher read, the description of a Tidal Marsh. Marshes are unique because they are areas where saltwater from the ocean meets fresh water from rivers. The wildlife there is perfectly suited for this mix of environments.

Look at the shore crab on page 283 in the *North American Wildlife Guide*. This is the kind of crab that the colonists saw along the shore and looked for as food to eat. Draw or trace this crab into your Student Notebook. Then write down where it lives and what it looks like?[4]

Another source of food for the colonists was oysters. Oysters are part of a group of living things called **mollusks.** Mollusks are a large group of animals that have soft bodies covered with a hard shell. They are **invertebrates,** or animals that have their skeletons on the outside. Examples of mollusks are snails, oysters, and clams. Look at the eastern oyster on page 255 in the *North American Wildlife Guide*. Draw or trace it into your Student Notebook. Then write down where it lives and what it looks like.[5]

Look at the Atlantic surf clam on page 257 of the *North American Wildlife Guide,* and draw or trace it into your Student Notebook. Write down what it looks like and where it lives.[6]

Look at the blue crab on page 283 of the *North American Wildlife Guide*, and draw or trace it into your Student Notebook. This swimming crab is highly sought after for eating. Write down what it looks like and where it lives.[7]

F. Art   *Thinking Skills*

Look at the title page of *A Lion to Guard Us.* On the opposite page is a picture of the brass door knocker that Jemmy got from his father. Trace or draw this door knocker into your Student Notebook. Tell why you think the "knock-knock," as Jemmy called it, was so important to them. Remember to explain everything so that other people can understand your answer.

Trace the map of the Chesapeake Bay area from the front of *Surviving Jamestown* and put it into your Student Notebook. Label all the bodies of water, Jamestown, and Virginia.

E. Each word in bold letters is considered a vocabulary word. It is a word that may or may not be new to your child. You can write these vocabulary words on index cards and use them for occasional review, but not for memorizing. Give the child the meaning of the words if he doesn't remember. Try to use the new vocabulary words during conversation, and encourage your students to do the same.

Each time your student makes a vocabulary card for this unit, have him write a "J" (for Jamestown) in the upper left corner. This will make it possible to review vocabulary by unit at the end of the year.

G. Reading fluency is developed through having frequent silent reading opportunities that continue for the length of time suggested here. Since a primary focus of this activity is to nurture your child's enjoyment of reading, help him to choose reading material that interests him and is at a level that allows him to read with understanding by himself. You can incorporate this activity into your school day whenever it is most convenient.

If the suggested length of time is too long for your child to continue reading by himself, start with an amount of time he can accomplish successfully and make the suggested time a goal.

A. The dictation method enables your child to hear language and correctly write down what he hears. It involves building two different skills. First, the ability to listen and understand what is heard, and second, the ability to transfer what is heard into written language. This process takes time and practice, so begin as gradually as needed for successfully reaching the goal of getting the words the child hears on the paper correctly. 1) Read the whole passage, then reread one sentence at a time, giving your child time to write what he hears. 2) After he has finished, reread the passage again, allowing him to double check what he has written. 3) Then proceed to the step of comparing his writing to the model. As his skill builds, you can move more quickly through the steps, maintaining your child's level of success.

G. Independent Reading

Choose something to read that you will enjoy. Find a quiet, comfortable place and read for the following length of time:

- 20 minutes
- 25 minutes
- 30 minutes

Over time, it's fun to see how much you have read. Be sure to write down what you read today on the Reading Log in your Student Notebook.

Lesson 3, Part 2

A. Copywork/Dictation   *Language Skills*

Look carefully at the following passage, and read it silently. Show your teacher any words you don't know, and practice saying them aloud. Now read the passage aloud, or ask your teacher to read it to you.

> The push of the trade winds brought the ships to the Canary Islands. The passengers thought the sand and warm breezes were very welcome. The sailors sought, or looked for, wood, food, and fresh water.

- Copy the above lines into your Student Notebook. When you are finished, compare your copy to the model (word by word) and make any needed corrections.

- Listen as your teacher dictates the above lines, and write them in your Student Notebook. When you are finished, compare your copy to the model and make any needed corrections.

- Copy, or write as your teacher dictates, paragraphs 5 and 6 on page 66 in *Surviving Jamestown*. When you are finished, compare your copy to the text and make any needed corrections.

B. Reader   *Language Skills, Thinking Skills, History*

In your book, *A Lion to Guard Us,* read Chapter 10 aloud.

- Read one or two paragraphs in your read-aloud book, *Surviving Jamestown.*

🐾 Read one or two pages from today's read-aloud assignment in *Surviving Jamestown*.

C. **Read-Aloud and Narration**   *Language Skills, Thinking Skills*

Listen carefully as your teacher reads from the top of page 63 through page 70 aloud from *Surviving Jamestown*.

To *narrate* means to retell. In your own words, tell what happened in your assigned passage below. Try to remember as many details as possible. Listen carefully as your teacher reads (or rereads) the part you are to retell.

🌵🌵 Retell what Dr. Crider did for Amanda, Jemmy, and Meg in Chapter 10 of *A Lion to Guard Us*.

🐾 Listen as your teacher reads paragraphs 4 and 5 on page 66 of *Surviving Jamestown*. Retell what happened.

🐾 Reread paragraph 6 on page 64 to the end of page 65. Retell what happened.

D. **Word Study**   *Spelling, Phonics, Vocabulary*

In Part 1 you learned that *ou* sometimes says *ow*. Another sound that *ou* sometimes says is in the word *ought*. Look at the copywork passage printed in Section A and find three words with the letters *ou* that sound as in *ought*.[8] The letters *ght* come after *ou* to make the word *ought*.

🌵🌵 Practice spelling the words you found yesterday in your passage.

🐾 There are several *ou* words in Chapter 10 of *A Lion to Guard Us* in which the *ou* sounds like *ow*. Can you find them?[9] There is one tricky word that looks like it should say *ow*, but it doesn't. It is the name of the town they sailed from, Plymouth.

Practice spelling the words you found yesterday in the passage and Chapter 9.

🐾 Look on page 69 of *Surviving Jamestown* and find the words where *ou* says *ow*.

Read the copywork passage printed in Section A above, and find the words that rhyme with the word *ought*.[11] Look on page 68 in *Surviving Jamestown* and find words that rhyme with *ought*.[12]

E. **Geography**   *History*

The James River plays a key role in our history since it was chosen by the colonists for the first permanent English settlement in America. Before the English came, this river was known as the Powhatan River. It was named for the chief of the Algonquin tribes that lived in the area.

C. The skill of narration is gained over time. If your child has never retold a story, start with the assignment for the lower level, no matter what grade he is in. Work up from there, being careful to allow him to stay at the level of success for a while before going to a longer section.

The source, or beginning, of the James River is in the Allegheny Mountains, which are part of the Appalachian Mountain Range. The James River is 340 miles long, longer than the Thames River, and it flows across the entire state of Virginia. It is a tributary that flows into the Chesapeake Bay. Almost all the land around this river is covered by **forest,** or trees and smaller bushes.

Look at the United States Physical Map in the *Intermediate World Atlas.* Find Virginia, then find the James River. With your finger, trace its blue line from the Chesapeake Bay into the Appalachian Mountains. This shows you the source of the river.

Next, find the city of Richmond on the map. That is close to where the Jamestown settlement was located.

Look at the map of Virginia found in the front of *Surviving Jamestown.* Find the location of the Jamestown settlement. It is marked by a triangle. In your Student Notebook make a list of all the bodies of water shown on this map.[13]

Tell your teacher what you know about rivers. List as many details as you can think of.

F. Writing　　　　　　　　　　　　　　　　　*Thinking Skills*

In both stories, the children were offered help and protection. In *A Lion to Guard Us,* Dr. Crider came to the aid of the Freebold children. In *Surviving Jamestown,* John Smith looked after young Sam Collier.

Talk with your teacher about how you feel when someone takes care of you or helps you do something hard.

Think of ways that Dr. Crider took care of the Freebold children. In your Student Notebook, make a list of the things he did for them. How do you think the children, especially Amanda, felt after he started to help them? Remember to use your Jamestown Word Bank to help you.

In your Student Notebook, make a list of the things your parents do to take care of you that you appreciate.

Think of ways that John Smith took care of Sam Collier. In your Student Notebook, make a list of things he did for Sam. How do you think Sam felt about the guidance and protection John Smith gave him? Remember to use your Jamestown Word Bank to help you.

G. Independent Reading

Choose something to read that you will enjoy. Find a quiet, comfortable place and read for the following length of time:

🌵🌵 20 minutes

🐾 25 minutes

🐾 30 minutes

Over time, it's fun to see how much you have read. Be sure to write down what you read today on the Reading Log in your Student Notebook.

G. See Independent Reading note in Part 1.

Lesson 3, Part 3

A. Copywork/Dictation   *Language Skills*

Look carefully at the following passage, and read it silently. Show your teacher any words you don't know, and practice saying them aloud. Now read the passage aloud, or ask your teacher to read it to you.

> John Smith never left the job of soldier, for he was always on the lookout for danger. Even on a warm, inviting island, his thoughts turned to weapons and being prepared for unseen trouble.

A. See Copywork/Dictation note in Part 1.

🌵🌵 Copy the above lines into your Student Notebook. When you are finished, compare your copy to the model (word by word) and make any needed corrections.

🐾 Listen as your teacher dictates the above lines, and write them in your Student Notebook. When you are finished, compare your copy to the model and make any needed corrections.

🐾 Copy, or write as your teacher dictates, paragraph 7 on page 75 in *Surviving Jamestown*. When you are finished, compare your copy to the text and make any needed corrections.

B. Reader   *Language Skills, Thinking Skills, History*

In your book, *A Lion to Guard Us*, read Chapter 11 aloud.

🐾 Read one or two paragraphs in your read-aloud book, *Surviving Jamestown*.

🐾 Read one or two pages from today's read-aloud assignment in *Surviving Jamestown*.

C. See Discussion note in Part 1.

C. **Read-aloud and Discussion**   *Language Skills, Thinking Skills*

In *Surviving Jamestown,* listen as your teacher reads page 71 through paragraph 5 on page 77 aloud.

Listen as your teacher reads the story and the following discussion question. Think about what you know from the story, and answer in your own words. Give any examples you can think of that help show your answer.

Discussion Question: After Sam Collier heard that James Brumfield had been killed, his mind was filled with many thoughts. Tell what memories Sam had about James. How do you think he felt about him? Do you think Sam wanted to do anything differently?

D. If you want your student to solve the clues without the Word Bank, you can cover it with a card or a piece of paper.

D. **Word Study**   *Spelling, Phonics, Vocabulary*

🐾🐾🐾 Use the Word Bank below to find an *ou* word that answers each of the following clues:[14]

brought	found	about
sound	thought	sought
bound	out	

Something you hear with your ears is a _____.

It used to be lost, now it is _____.

The opposite of in is _____.

The ships were going to Jamestown. They were _____ for Jamestown.

Something you think is a _____.

If it is in your backpack, you _____ it with you.

When my pet was lost, I _____ (or looked for) it.

Since you have read the book, please tell me what it is _____.

🐾 Make up clues for at least six of the *ou* words you found in your passages yesterday.

E. **Geography**   *Science*

About a month after leaving the Canary Islands, the *Susan Constant, Discovery,* and *Godspeed* arrived in the West Indies.

Look at the map of the West Indies found immediately after the Acknowledgements in *Surviving Jamestown.* The journey from the

Canary Islands to the West Indies followed the route of the trade winds and the ocean currents. Tell why you think it was helpful for the ships to stop in the Canary Islands and the West Indies.[15]

On the map, show your teacher the four continents you can see.[16] Find the name of the ocean shown.[17]

The West Indies were called the "Indies" by Columbus when he first arrived because he thought that he had reached the islands off the coast of India. Later, people who spoke English added the word "West" because these islands were on the far west side of the ocean. Many islands are included in the term West Indies, such as Guadeloupe, Dominica, and Martinique. Find these islands on the map.

While on the island of Nevis, the sailors hunted for animals that could be used for food. One **reptile** they hunted was the alligator. A reptile is a cold-blooded animal with a back-bone, that crawls on its belly or creeps on short, stubby legs. Look on page 160 in your *North American Wildlife Guide.* Draw or trace the alligator into your Student Notebook. Tell what it looks like, where it lives, and what it eats.[18]

 Another reptile they hunted was the loggerhead turtle. Read about the loggerhead turtle on page 165 of the *North American Wildlife Guide.* Trace or draw the turtle and tell what it looks like, where it lives, and what special problems it has.[19]

F. Drawing   *Thinking Skills*

The colonists had now spent time on several islands. Nowadays when we think of islands, we tend to think of vacations and relaxing. But the colonists spent their time on shore making repairs, restocking, and recovering.

Try to imagine what it would have been like for you if you had been one of the colonists. Draw a picture of life on an island. If you need help knowing what to draw, look at pages 28–42 in *Surviving Jamestown* and reread some of the descriptions of their time on the islands.

G. See Independent Reading note in Part 1.

G. Independent Reading

Choose something to read that you will enjoy. Find a quiet, comfortable place and read for the following length of time:

✹ 20 minutes

✹ 25 minutes

✹ 30 minutes

Over time, it's fun to see how much you have read. Be sure to write down what you read today on the Reading Log in your Student Notebook.

Lesson 3, Part 4

A. See Copywork/Dictation note in Part 1.

A. Copywork/Dictation   *Language Skills*

Look carefully at the following passage, and read it silently. Show your teacher any words you don't know, and practice saying them aloud. Now read the passage aloud, or ask your teacher to read it to you.

> A month later, the ships arrived at an island called Martinique. The chance to get fresh supplies and walk on dry land was a great relief to the colonists. This time, however, they were not alone on the island.

✹ Copy the above lines into your Student Notebook. When you are finished, compare your copy to the model (word by word) and make any needed corrections.

✹ Listen as your teacher dictates the above lines, and write them in your Student Notebook. When you are finished, compare your copy to the model and make any needed corrections.

✹ Copy, or write as your teacher dictates, paragraph 5 on page 78 in *Surviving Jamestown.* When you are finished, compare your copy to the text and make any needed corrections.

B. Reader   *Language Skills, Thinking Skills, History*

In your book, *A Lion to Guard Us,* read Chapter 12 aloud.

✹ Read one or two paragraphs in your read-aloud book, *Surviving Jamestown.*

🐾 Read one or two pages from today's read-aloud assignment in *Surviving Jamestown*.

C. Read-Aloud and Narration   *Language Skills, Thinking Skills*

Listen carefully as your teacher reads paragraph 6 on page 77 through page 84 aloud from *Surviving Jamestown*.

To *narrate* means to retell. In your own words, tell what happened in your assigned passage below. Try to remember as many details as possible. Listen carefully as your teacher reads (or rereads) the part you are to retell.

🐾 Retell what happens in Chapter 12 of *A Lion to Guard Us* that is very sad for the children.

🐾 Retell the events of paragraph 4 to the end of page 80 in *Surviving Jamestown*.

🐾 Reread paragraph 5 on page 78 and paragraphs 1–3 on page 79 in *Surviving Jamestown*. Tell what happened in connection with John Smith.

D. Word Study   *Spelling, Phonics, Vocabulary*

🐾 Look in Chapter 12 of *A Lion to Guard Us*. In your Student Notebook, make a list of all the names of particular people, places, or things.[20] Write each name only once. Remember that all the names start with capital letters. Be sure to include all of these words in the Jamestown Word Bank you began in Part 1, if they are not already listed.

🐾 Look in Chapter 11 of *A Lion to Guard Us*. In your Student Notebook, make a list of all the names of particular people, places, or things.[21] Remember that all the names start with capital letters. Be sure to include all of these words in the Jamestown Word Bank you began in Part 1, if they are not already listed.

🐾 Look at paragraph 5 on page 78 through paragraph 4 on page 79 in *Surviving Jamestown*. Make a list of all the names of particular people, places, or things.[22] Remember that all the names start with capital letters. Write the names you find in your Student Notebook under the correct heading, either "People," "Places," or "Things." Be sure to include all of these words in the Jamestown Word Bank you began in Part 1, if they are not already listed.

E. Science   *Thinking Skills*

So far in this curriculum you have learned about the following categories of animals:

reptiles   mammals   birds
fish   invertebrates

C. See Narration note in Part 2.

E. Each time your student makes an Animal I.D. card for this unit, have him write a "J" (for Jamestown) in the upper left corner. This will make it possible to review the animals studied by unit at the end of the year.

Review the qualities of each of the categories above. Then look at the list of animals below. You may have learned about some of them already, but if you haven't they can all be found in the *North American Wildlife Guide*. Follow the directions below and make two Animal I.D. cards for each one so that you can use them to play a game in another lesson.

To make an Animal I.D. card, begin by writing the name of one of the animals at the top of an index card. Under that, write down any important or interesting information you have learned about it. If you want, you may include a drawing of the animal. Finally, write the category of the animal at the bottom. All of these animals can be found in the *North American Wildlife Guide*.

bottle-nosed dolphin	oysters
river otter	clams
brown pelican	mute swan
laughing gull	flying fish
alligator	loggerhead turtle
mudminnow	stickleback

F. Writing

Thinking Skills

In Part 3 you drew a picture showing what life was like for the colonists on the islands. Now create a Word Bank in your Student Notebook to describe the islands. Think of as many words as you can to describe the word in bold print at the top of each column. There are two words in each list to get you started.

beach	water	trees	flowers/ fruit	weather	animals/ birds
sandy	salty	green	beautiful	sunny	chirping
bright	splashing	shady	tasty	warm	colorful

G. See Independent Reading note in Part I.

G. Independent Reading

Choose something to read that you will enjoy. Find a quiet, comfortable place and read for the following length of time:

🌿 20 minutes

🐾 25 minutes

🐾 30 minutes

Over time, it's fun to see how much you have read. Be sure to write down what you read today on the Reading Log in your Student Notebook.

Lesson 3, Part 5

This part is set aside for completion of any work left undone from the lesson, and review of concepts and content. It is also a time to expand the work in the lesson by doing art, timeline activities, or games.

- Review the Steps for Thinking from the beginning of this lesson.

- On the large outline map of the world label the Canary Islands and the island of Martinique.

- Review the spelling words for this lesson. In your Student Notebook, write a sentence using each word that tells how it is related to the unit. Do your best to write the spelling words correctly. After you have finished, check your sentences against the list in your Student Notebook and see how many spelling words you spelled correctly. (Don't count off for other words that are misspelled.) Remember your goal is to improve, not necessarily to get them all right immediately.

- Complete the Jamestown Word Search located in your Student Notebook.

- Listen to or read the story about Leonardo da Vinci in *Profiles from History*. Complete the timeline activities and any other activities you would like to do.

Most of the labeling has already been completed in the Student Notebook during this lesson. Instruct students to use the maps in their Student Notebooks as a reference. When they label the larger map, students will see the "big picture" and gain a broader understanding of their lessons.

Teachers can find a copy of this game in Appendix B. Instructions and answer keys for all games are located in Appendix A.

Enrichment Activities

1. If possible, visit an aquarium or zoo. Take a clipboard or notebook with the following categories listed: Mammals, Birds, Fish, Invertebrates, Reptiles. As you look at the animals, try to find at least three that will fit each category and record their names.

2. Learn more about Leonardo da Vinci and his many inventions. Look at designs da Vinci created for modern devices such as the helicopter and figure out how long it was from his lifetime until the date of the actual invention. How close was da Vinci's idea to the actual invention?

Use one or more of the Enrichment Activities if your child completes his assigned work and has the time or desire to learn more. These activities are flexible, so choose the one(s) that seem most interesting to your student. Allow him to work at a level that is appropriate for him, and remember that the learning process is more important than the product.

Answers

1. found, out, about, sound, bound

2. out, round, about, house, outside

3. found, about, counted, around, sound, ground, rounded

4. shore crab: lives in tidal marshes and on beaches; is 1–4 inches wide, brown-grayish color, 8 walking legs and two claws—one may be much larger than the other

5. mollusks: usually 2–6 inches long, gray to white with layers of shell; lives in bays, offshore areas

6. Atlantic surf clam: 4–9 inches long, creamy to yellowish white, thick shell; lives in sand near shore

7. blue crab: 3–9 inches wide; oval shell; blue, red, and green on the shell and legs; lives in bays and offshore

8. brought, thought, sought

9. southwest, ours, out, our, bound, cloud

10. ground, ours, out, announce

11. brought, thought, sought

12. thought, sought

13. Atlantic Ocean, Chesapeake Bay, James River, Potomac River, Rappahannock River, Mattaponi River, Pamunkey River, Chickahominy River

14. sound, found, out, bound, thought, brought, sought, about

15. Answers may vary but should include: water, food, repairs.

16. continents: North America, South America, Europe, Africa

17. Ocean: Atlantic

18. alligator: between 6–15 feet long, gray-black with yellow crossbands; lives in marshes, swamps, rivers and bayous; eats fish, turtles, birds and small animals

19. loggerhead turtle: shell is 3–4 feet in length, reddish-brown shell with scales; lives in open seas, salt marshes, and bays. Special problem: their large size, large number of eggs, and predictable habits have worked against their survival, as has development in coastal areas where they lay their eggs.

20. Amanda, John Rolfe, Robert Waters, Chris Carter, Hopkins family, Master Stephen Hopkins, Anne, David, Jemmy, Meg, Virginia, New World, Dr. Crider, Master Rolfe

21. Jemmy, Amanda, Dr. Crider, Blessing, Catch, Lion, Virginia, Christopher Newport, Thomas Gates, Sir George Somers, Meg, Admiral

22. people-Captain Newport, Reverend Hunt, John Smith, Master Wingfield, Sam; places-England, Jamestown; things-Susan Constant, Godspeed, Discovery, Virginia Company

Lesson 4, Part 1

⸙ Steps for Thinking ⸙

1. Great accomplishments often require great effort. Don't overlook the value of something just because it's difficult.

2. Good leadership involves not only upright words, but upright actions as well. You can admire the actions of a good leader.

3. Determination was a major ingredient for success in Jamestown. Without determination, the best of intentions are often fruitless.

The **Steps for Thinking** section gives you the main ideas about the topics presented. Understanding these helps you to have productive discussions with your children so they, too, understand the bigger ideas. This forms more permanent learning, contrary to just learning facts, which tends to be temporary. These steps are useful prior to instruction, and they are also useful for review at the end of the week.

A. **Copywork/Dictation**   *Language Skills*

Look carefully at the following passage, and read it silently. Show your teacher any words you don't know, and practice saying them aloud. Now read the passage aloud, or ask your teacher to read it to you.

> Much to the colonists' relief, the Indians on the island were peaceful. In spite of their fears and the tales of grief they had heard, all was calm. Several days later the three ships left the West Indies behind and sailed towards Virginia.

ᵛᵞ Copy the above lines into your Student Notebook. When you are finished, compare your copy to the model (word by word) and make any needed corrections.

ᵛ Listen as your teacher dictates the above lines, and write them in your Student Notebook. When you are finished, compare your copy to the model and make any needed corrections.

ᵛ Copy, or write as your teacher dictates, paragraph 2 on page 86 in *Surviving Jamestown*. When you are finished, compare your copy to the text and make any needed corrections.

ᵛ—*Materials*—ᵛ

- *A Lion to Guard Us*
- *Surviving Jamestown*
- Student Notebook
- *Profiles from History*
- *North American Wildlife Guide*
- Stationery and envelope (if desired)
- Ingredients for a strawberry dish
- Dictionary
- Crayons or colored pencils
- Plain or tracing paper
- Ruler
- Large world and U.S. outline maps

A. Copywork and dictation assignments go from an easier level (designated by ᵛᵞ) to harder levels (designated by ᵛ and ᵛ). Take two days for the copywork if that is more comfortable for your child. Please adapt instructions to your child's individual needs. Your child should be **consistently successful** at one level before progressing to the next, **regardless of grade**.

B. The readers used in this unit describe events that could have taken place. Since this time in history included violent or difficult events, you may wish to prepare your children for certain realities of the times that seem harsh, or to edit the content that you read aloud or that your children read independently.

C. Discussion is very important in developing your child's ability to organize his thoughts. This in turn builds the ability to think and write. The goal of the discussion questions is not just to find the answer to a particular question, but also to create a situation where thoughts about the question and its answer are shared and considered in a detailed way. Do not rush this activity, but encourage your student to share his or her ideas relating to the topic, and any additional ideas that may come to mind. You can also share your thoughts and questions as an example for your students.

D. Each word in bold letters is considered a vocabulary word. It is a word that may or may not be new to your child. You can write these vocabulary words on index cards and use them for occasional review, but not for memorizing. Give the child the meaning of the words if he doesn't remember. Try to use the new vocabulary words during conversation, and encourage your students to do the same.

Each time your student makes a vocabulary card for this unit, have him write a "J" (for Jamestown) in the upper left corner. This will make it possible to review vocabulary by unit at the end of the year.

The small superscript numbers that appear after some of the questions in this unit refer to answers in the answer key, located immediately after Part 5.

B. **Reader**   *Language Skills, Thinking Skills, History*

In your book, *A Lion to Guard Us,* read Chapter 13 aloud.

☙ Read one or two paragraphs in your read-aloud book, *Surviving Jamestown.*

☙ Read one or two pages from today's read-aloud assignment in *Surviving Jamestown.*

C. **Read-aloud and Discussion**   *Language Skills, Thinking Skills*

Listen carefully as your teacher reads page 85 through paragraph 2 on page 91 aloud from *Surviving Jamestown.*

Listen as your teacher reads the story and the following discussion question. Think about what you know from the story, and answer in your own words. Give any examples you can think of that help show your answer.

Discussion Question: Almost everyone in the colony had gotten sick. Sam thought about the fact that neither group was safe from sickness. The gentlemen, raised with comfort and riches, got just as sick as the common workers. A lifetime of working hard hadn't protected the common workers against sickness either. Since everyone in the colony had been so conscious of a person's rank in society, what do you think Sam decided about these thoughts?

D. **Word Study**   *Spelling, Phonics, Vocabulary*

In the copywork passage printed in Section A above, find the word that means "full of peace." The word *peaceful* has the letters *ful* added to the end. This means that the word is "full" of that quality. Because it is added to the end of another word, you write *ful* with only one *l* instead of two.

Read this list for your teacher:

truthful	plentiful
fearful	beautiful
playful	flavorful

Tell your teacher what you think each word means.

☙ Think of a word or a group of words that mean the opposite of each of the above words that have the **suffix** *ful*. A suffix is a letter or group of letters added to the end of a word that change its meaning.

☙ Look at page 91 in *Surviving Jamestown.* Find the words with the suffixes *ful* and *ness.*[1] The suffix *ness* turns a describing word into a thing, like when *blind* becomes *blindness.*

In your Student Notebook, make a list of at least five words that have the suffix *ness*. Think of a word that describes something and then see if it sounds right to add *ness* to it. You can check your words in the dictionary to see if they are correct.

E. Science
Writing, Art

Many of the foods that the Jamestown colonists ate were things that lived and grew in the wilds of Virginia. They would pick and store as much as they could. The local Indians also used these foods in their diet.

Look at the red mulberry on page 301 in the *North American Wildlife Guide*. Trace or draw this berry into your Student Notebook. Tell what it looks like and where it grows. Also include at least one interesting fact.[2]

A second source of food that was found in the area around Jamestown was the wild strawberry. Look on page 385 in the *North American Wildlife Guide* and read about it. Draw or trace the wild strawberry into your Student Notebook. Tell what it looks like, where it grows, and whether or not a strawberry is actually a berry.[3]

Do you like strawberries? Tell about your favorite way to eat strawberries. With your teacher's permission, make a dish that includes strawberries.

F. Writing
Language Skills, History

In *Surviving Jamestown*, Sam Collier gave many letters to Captain Newport to take back to England. Letters like these were the main way people communicated in 1600. They brought precious news to family and friends. Letters were very important because not only did they communicate thoughts and feelings, but they also gave instructions to leaders and directed business and government affairs. It could take months to send and receive letters, so news was often very old by the time it was received. Today our mail system is much better. It only takes days to send and receive a letter, and now there are even faster ways to communicate.

Letter writing is still an important skill, so today you will learn how to write a friendly letter. This is the kind of letter you would send to a friend or family member.

Ask your parent if you or someone in your family have ever received a friendly letter. If possible, look at it. Think of someone you would like to send a friendly letter to. When you write this type of letter, it should include the following parts:

E. Have a 12-inch ruler available so that your students can see the approximate sizes of items described in science lessons. Also, be sure to remind your child not to eat anything without your permission.

F. Addressing envelopes will be taught in Part 3 of this lesson.

Heading: Your address and the date in the upper right hand corner;

Skip a line or two;

Greeting: Usually begins with "Dear" and the person's name followed by a comma;

Skip a line;

Body: Your thoughts and ideas written in paragraphs;

Skip a line;

Closing: Capitalize the first word of the closing and follow with a comma;

Signature: Sign your name under the closing; make sure and start it with a capital letter.

Here is an example:

(Heading)   25 Spring Street
                                         Jonesville, FL 05050
                                              April 1, 2007

(One or Two Spaces)

(Heading)   Dear Grandma,

(Space)

(Body)   How are you? I am fine, and so is everyone in the family.

                 Yesterday we all went to the beach. It was a lot of fun. It was sunny and hot. We found shells and saw fish in the water. We built sand castles and ate a picnic. It was a fun day.

                 How long will it be before you come to visit us? I am looking forward to you being here. I have some things for us to make together and some videos to watch.

                 Please write soon and let me know how you are doing. Could you send pictures of the flowers in your garden?

(Two Spaces)

(Closing)   Love,

(Signature)   Sally

Now choose someone to write a letter to. Write a **rough draft,** or first try, of your letter. After showing it to your parent, make any changes that the two of you agree on, and copy your letter onto a fresh sheet of paper. You may want to use stationery.

G. Independent Reading

Choose something to read that you will enjoy. Find a quiet, comfortable place and read for the following length of time:

🐾 20 minutes

🐾 25 minutes

🐾 30 minutes

Over time, it's fun to see how much you have read. Be sure to write down what you read today on the Reading Log in your Student Notebook.

G. Reading fluency is developed through having frequent silent reading opportunities that continue for the length of time suggested here. Since a primary focus of this activity is to nurture your child's enjoyment of reading, help him to choose reading material that interests him and is at a level that allows him to read with understanding by himself. You can incorporate this activity into your school day whenever it is most convenient.

If the suggested length of time is too long for your child to continue reading by himself, start with an amount of time he can accomplish successfully and make the suggested time a goal.

Lesson 4, Part 2

A. Copywork/Dictation   *Language Skills*

Look carefully at the following passage, and read it silently. Show your teacher any words you don't know, and practice saying them aloud. Now read the passage aloud, or ask your teacher to read it to you.

A. See Copywork/Dictation note in Part 1.

> The greeting from the Indians on the shores of Virginia was quite a different story. As always, John Smith was ready. He and a few other men fired their guns and the Indians ran back into the forest.

🐾 Copy the above lines into your Student Notebook. When you are finished, compare your copy to the model (word by word) and make any needed corrections.

🐾 Listen as your teacher dictates the above lines, and write them in your Student Notebook. When you are finished, compare your copy to the model and make any needed corrections.

🐾 Copy, or write as your teacher dictates, paragraphs 2–4 on page 97 in *Surviving Jamestown.* When you are finished, compare your copy to the text and make any needed corrections.

B. Reader   *Language Skills, Thinking Skills, History*

In your book, *A Lion to Guard Us,* read Chapter 14 aloud.

🐾 Read one or two paragraphs in your read-aloud book, *Surviving Jamestown.*

C. The skill of narration is gained over time. If your child has never retold a story, start with the assignment for the lower level, no matter what grade he is in. Work up from there, being careful to allow him to stay at the level of success for a while before going to a longer section.

🐾 Read one or two pages from today's read-aloud assignment in *Surviving Jamestown*.

C. **Read-Aloud and Narration**   *Language Skills, Thinking Skills*

In *Surviving Jamestown*, listen as your teacher reads paragraph 3 on page 91 through page 97 aloud.

To *narrate* means to retell. In your own words, tell what happened in your assigned passage below. Try to remember as many details as possible. Listen carefully as your teacher reads (or rereads) the part you are to retell.

🐾🐾 Chapter 14 in *A Lion to Guard Us*.

🐾 Paragraph 4 on pages 91 and 92 in *Surviving Jamestown*.

🐾 Paragraphs 3–6 on page 95 in *Surviving Jamestown*.

D. **Word Study**   *Spelling, Phonics, Vocabulary*

🐾🐾🐾 Read over the following words. Make sure each one is included in the Jamestown Word Bank you have already begun in Part 1. Add any new words under the correct category. See how many of them you can spell. Knowing these words will help you when you want to write about the stories.

Virginia	Amanda
Jemmy	Meg
Dr. Crider	door knocker
brass	lion

🐾 Read over the following words, and add each one to the correct category in your Jamestown Word Bank, if they are not already listed. Start with the group above and then move to the group below, and see how many you can spell. Do not work on more than these two lists in one lesson.

Powhattan	Jamestown
Susan Constant	New World
Godspeed	gentlemen
Discovery	

🐾 Read over the above words, and make sure each one is included in the Jamestown Word Bank you have already begun in Part 1. Add any new words under the correct category. Practice spelling the words in the Word Bank. If you can spell them all, then find six more words that you want to be able to spell when you write about Jamestown. Be sure to write your words in the correct column. You can choose words from the reader or read-aloud.

E. Geography

A grid is a series of lines that cross and make squares. Grid lines are used on maps and charts and help people find specific places by giving every square its own name. A grid names the squares in two steps. The first step is to assign a letter to each square on a map, from the top to the bottom. (See Grid Map A)

The second step is to label the squares from left to right with numbers. (See Grid Map A) When this is done, you can find any square on the map by using its letter and number as an "address." For example, look carefully at Grid Map A below. To find the address for the airplane, put your finger on the square where the plane is located. Then decide which letter is on the same row as the plane, and which number is above its square. The letter and number together, A2, name the location, or address, of the airplane.

Grid Map A

Give the address of each object. Remember to give the letter first, then the number:[4]

ball _____   snail _____

flower _____   bird _____

car _____   fish _____

Do the same thing with Grid Map B in the Student Notebook. Find the locations of these objects. Write the address for each object starting with the letter and then the number.[5]

sailboat _____   snowflake _____

book _____   ice cream cone _____

dog _____   baseball glove _____

bee _____

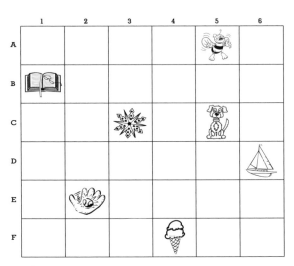

Grid Map B

🐾 Now that you know how to use a grid map, look at the cat in Grid Map C. Use the blank grid map in your Student Notebook to make your own drawing of the cat. Try to make each one of your grid boxes look like the grid boxes on the cat drawing.

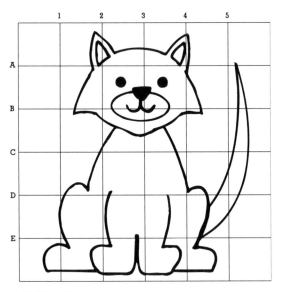

Grid Map C

🐾 Look at the United States Political Map in your *Intermediate World Atlas*. Find the letters and numbers, called grid markers, on the side and top.

Now locate the following places on the map. In your Student Notebook, write down all the parts of each place's address, using the letters and numbers found at the side and top of the map. For example:

New Mexico: D4, D5, E4, E5

Sante Fe, New Mexico: D4

Find all the locations of the these places:[6]

Florida: _____, _____, _____, _____

Ohio: _____, _____

California : _____, _____, _____, _____,
_____, _____, _____

Colorado: _____. _____, _____, _____

The state where you live:_____

Be sure to write the letter part of each address first, and then the number.

F. Art

Yesterday you wrote a friendly letter. Today make a picture to send with your letter.

Make a **sketch,** or rough drawing with a pencil, of your pet or favorite animal. When you have finished the sketch, color it with crayons or colored pencils. You may add some background if you want, but the most important thing in the drawing is the pet. Finish your drawing by writing your pet's name at the top. All artists should sign their work, so write your name and the date in the bottom right hand corner.

If you do not have a pet, or you feel it is too hard to draw, choose your favorite animal in the *North American Wildlife Guide* and follow the above directions.

G. Independent Reading

Choose something to read that you will enjoy. Find a quiet, comfortable place and read for the following length of time:

G. See Independent Reading note in Part 1.

❦❦ 20 minutes

❦ 25 minutes

❦ 30 minutes

Over time, it's fun to see how much you have read. Be sure to write down what you read today on the Reading Log in your Student Notebook.

Lesson 4, Part 3

A. See Copywork/Dictation note in Part 1.

A. Copywork/Dictation　　　　　*Language Skills*

Look carefully at the following passage, and read it silently. Show your teacher any words you don't know, and practice saying them aloud. Now read the passage aloud, or ask your teacher to read it to you.

> Now everyone was ready to stay alert for travel. The colonists started looking for a home along the river named for King James. A spot was chosen that seemed good, and work began. The Virginia Company wanted men to quickly explore for gold.

Copy the above lines into your Student Notebook. When you are finished, compare your copy to the model (word by word) and make any needed corrections.

Listen as your teacher dictates the above lines, and write them in your Student Notebook. When you are finished, compare your copy to the model and make any needed corrections.

Copy, or write as your teacher dictates, paragraph 2 on page 103 in *Surviving Jamestown.* When you are finished, compare your copy to the text and make any needed corrections.

B. Reader　　　　　*Language Skills, Thinking Skills, History*

In your book, *A Lion to Guard Us,* read Chapter 15 aloud.

Read one or two paragraphs in your read-aloud book, *Surviving Jamestown.*

Read one or two pages from today's read-aloud assignment in *Surviving Jamestown.*

C. See Discussion note in Part 1.

C. Read-Aloud and Discussion　　　　　*Language Skills, Thinking Skills*

In *Surviving Jamestown,* listen as your teacher reads pages 88 through 105 aloud.

Listen as your teacher reads the story and the following discussion question. Think about what you know from the story, and answer in your own words. Give any examples you can think of that help show your answer.

Discussion Question: Reverend Hunt reminded the colonists to thank God for saving them from certain death. He said that the difficult times had tested their faith. Talk with your parents about this idea.

D. Word Study   *Spelling, Phonics, Vocabulary*

Words that end with *ly* usually tell how something has been done. Look at the copywork passage printed in Section A above, and find the word that ends in *ly.*[7] The word *quickly* tells how the men explored for gold.

Read these sentences and look for the word that tells how something was done:

> The Indians came up peacefully.
> John Smith worked diligently.
> The trade winds blew strongly.
> The colonists fearfully watched the storm.
> Reverend Hunt faithfully cared for the people.

Look in a book you have at your house. Try to find at least five words that end in *ly.* List these words in your Student Notebook.

🐾 Look in a book you have at your house. Try to find at least three additional words that end in *ly.* Add them to the list in your Student Notebook.

🐾 Look in a book you have at your house. Try to find at least three additional words that end in *ly.* Add them to the list in your Student Notebook. Also tell what each *ly* word is talking about. Here are some examples:

The picture was painted beautifully.
ly word <u>beautifully</u> telling about <u>how it was painted</u>

We quickly cleaned up the house.
ly word <u>quickly</u> telling about <u>how we cleaned</u>

E. Science

Medicines were **scarce,** or rarely available, in a colony like Jamestown. Whenever possible, people used plants to help with various problems. Native Americans, or Indians, used many plants to create medicines.

Two of the plants commonly used in early colonies were sassafras and peppermint. Sassafras was collected and put in barrels. It was sent back to England for sale. Read, or listen to your teacher read, about sassafras on page 299 in the *North American Wildlife Guide.* Draw or trace the sassafras plant in your Student Notebook. Tell what it looks like and where it grows.[9]

Another plant commonly used for remedies was peppermint. Look at page 425 in the *North American Wildlife guide.* Read, or listen to your teacher read, the section about mints. Draw or trace pepper-

E. Have a 12-inch ruler available so that your students can see the approximate sizes of items described in science lessons. Also, be sure to remind your child not to eat anything without your permission.

mint, also called field mint, in your Student Notebook. Tell what it looks like and where it grows. Also tell what it was used for.[10]

Talk with your parent about other ways that peppermint and spearmint are used today.[11]

F. Writing

Since you wrote a friendly letter and made a sketch to go with it, today you will prepare the envelope for mailing.

Your name and address go in the upper left hand corner of the envelope. The name and address of the person you are sending it to goes in the middle. Make sure that all names and abbreviations are capitalized, and that you use your neatest handwriting. Here is an example:

Sally Parker   (Stamp goes here)
25 Spring St.
Jonesville, FL 05050

                        Mrs. Edith Parker
                        100 Sunny Dr.
                        Smithville, TN 10000

After your parent has **proofread,** or checked, your letter and envelope for mistakes, get ready to mail it. With your parent's help, place the correct postage stamp on the upper right hand corner of the envelope.

🐾 Write another friendly letter. Prepare an envelope for mailing. Allow your parent to proofread your letter and envelope. With their permission, mail it.

G. See Independent Reading note in Part 1.

G. Independent Reading

Choose something to read that you will enjoy. Find a quiet, comfortable place and read for the following length of time:

🐾🐾 20 minutes

🐾 25 minutes

🐾 30 minutes

Be sure to write down what you read today on the Reading Log in your Student Notebook.

Lesson 4, Part 4

A. **Copywork/Dictation**   *Language Skills*

Look carefully at the following passage, and read it silently. Show your teacher any words you don't know, and practice saying them aloud. Now read the passage aloud, or ask your teacher to read it to you.

> The explorers met more Indians. Most of these were friendly and curious about the English and their tools and weapons. John Smith was good at understanding what the Indians said. He watched them and listened carefully.

ᕼᕼ Copy the above lines into your Student Notebook. When you are finished, compare your copy to the model (word by word) and make any needed corrections.

ᕼ Listen as your teacher dictates the above lines, and write them in your Student Notebook. When you are finished, compare your copy to the model and make any needed corrections.

ᕼ Copy, or write as your teacher dictates, paragraph 4 on page 111 in *Surviving Jamestown*. When you are finished, compare your copy to the text and make any needed corrections.

B. **Reader**   *Language Skills, Thinking Skills, History*

In your book, *A Lion to Guard Us*, read Chapter 16 aloud.

ᕼ Read one or two paragraphs in your read-aloud book, *Surviving Jamestown*.

ᕼ Read one or two pages from today's read-aloud assignment in *Surviving Jamestown*.

C. **Read-Aloud and Narration**   *Language Skills, Thinking Skills*

Listen carefully as your teacher reads pages 106 through 114 aloud from *Surviving Jamestown*.

To *narrate* means to retell. In your own words, tell what happened in your assigned passage below. Try to remember as many details as possible. Listen carefully as your teacher reads (or rereads) the part you are to retell.

ᕼᕼ Chapter 16 in *A Lion to Guard Us*.

ᕼ Paragraph 5 on page 107 through paragraph 1 on the top of page 108 in *Surviving Jamestown*.

ᕼ Paragraph 4 to the end of page 110 in *Surviving Jamestown*.

A. See Copywork/Dictation note in Part 1.

C. See Narration note in Part 2.

D. Word Study

Spelling, Phonics, Vocabulary

There are two words in the copywork passage printed in Section A above that end with the letters *ly*. Find these two words.[12] What do these words refer to?[13] Practice spelling the *ly* words in the list you made yesterday.

Review the words in your Jamestown Word Bank. See if you can spell them without looking. Practice any words you do not know.

Add four more words to your Jamestown Word Bank from what you have read this week or that you would like to use when you write about the colonists.

E. Geography

History

A Lion to Guard Us is the fictional, or make-believe, story of the passengers aboard the ship *Sea Adventure,* bound from Plymouth, England, to Jamestown, Virginia. Some aspects of this story are true. A ship name the *Sea Adventure* (or *Sea Venture*) did sail from England and was shipwrecked on the shores of Bermuda's islands. The passengers were extremely fortunate to find a place to live. The captain and many of the leaders and passengers, such as John Rolfe, were really on board the ship. The children in the story are **fictional**, but they help readers understand what people went through to get to Jamestown.

Look at the map in the front of *Surviving Jamestown* that shows the West Indies. Find the islands of Bermuda on this map. You can see that Bermuda is fairly close to North America, but still many miles out into the ocean. Find out how many miles it is from Bermuda to the place where Jamestown was located.

To do this look at the Mexico and Middle America Physical Map in the *Intermediate World Atlas.* Find Bermuda in the Atlantic Ocean and the map key on the bottom left-hand corner of the map. Place your ruler on the map scale, with the first mark on the inch side of the ruler even with the 0 line on the scale. With your teacher's help, find out how many miles one inch on your ruler equals.[14] Now measure the distance from the island of Bermuda to the mouth of the James River (it is the first river directly above the North Carolina/Virginia state border.) The distance should be about three inches. You can find the mileage two ways, by adding or multiplying.

Bermuda to James River   = 3 inches
One inch   = 250 miles

Now add 250 three times: 250
                                 250
                             <u>+250</u>
                          750 miles

or you can multiply: 250
                          × 3
                          750 miles

Bermuda is approximately 750 miles from the mouth of the James River.

Now measure the distance in inches from Martinique (in the West Indies) to the mouth of the James River.[15] Since we know an inch equals approximately 250 miles on this map scale, either add 250 seven times or multiply 250×7.[16]

🐾 Choose two other places on this map and measure the distance between them. Write down the places, inches, and miles in your Student Notebook.

🐾 Choose at least four other places on this map and measure the distance between them. Write down the places, inches, and miles in your Student Notebook.

E. When beginning to use this approach, help your child choose the measurement that comes nearest to the inch mark on the ruler.

F. **Art**   *Geography, Science*

The passengers of the *Sea Venture* were very fortunate to land on the islands of Bermuda after they were shipwrecked. Bermuda was a very welcoming place after the hurricane they experienced. The islands were claimed for Britain by passengers on that ship, and became an English colony. It remains a territory of Great Britain to the present day.

Though most people cannot travel to Bermuda, you can look at pictures of many of the plants and birds found there. When you look at pictures of islands, you usually see lots of sand and water. Find the plants and birds named below in the *North American Wildlife Guide*. Page numbers where they can be found are provided for your convenience. After you have looked at them, choose several to include in a sketch of what you think Bermuda might look like. If you want to do research on Bermuda, you might find even more types of birds and plants to include in your drawing.

Birds

American white pelican, 82	green heron, 84
Leach's storm-petrel, 80	horned grebe, 81
greater shearwater, 80	roseate spoonbill, 86
American bittern, 85	

Plants

cedar tree (similar to Atlantic white cedar), 297
cabbage palmetto, 322
mangrove (like red mangrove), 316
saw-palmetto, 331

G. See Independent Reading note in Part 1.

G. **Independent Reading**

Choose something to read that you will enjoy. Find a quiet, comfortable place and read for the following length of time:

⁂ 20 minutes

✾ 25 minutes

✿ 30 minutes

Over time, it's fun to see how much you have read. Be sure to write down what you read today on the Reading Log in your Student Notebook.

Lesson 4, Part 5

This part is set aside for completion of any work left undone from the lesson, and review of concepts and content. It is also a time to expand the work in the lesson by doing art, timeline activities, or games.

• Review the Steps for Thinking from the beginning of this lesson.

• On the large outline map of the world label Bermuda. On the large outline map of the U.S. label Jamestown.

Most of the labeling has already been completed in the Student Notebook during this lesson. Instruct students to use the maps in their Student Notebooks as a reference. When they label the larger map, students will see the "big picture" and gain a broader understanding of their lessons.

• Review the words you practiced spelling in this lesson. In your Student Notebook, write a sentence using each word that tells how it is related to the unit. Do your best to write the spelling words correctly. After you have finished, check your sentences against the list in your Student Notebook and see how many spelling words you spelled correctly. (Don't count off for other words that are misspelled.) Remember your goal is to improve, not necessarily to get them all right immediately.

Teachers can find a copy of this game in Appendix B. Instructions and answer keys for all games are located in Appendix A.

• Play Jamestown Bingo found on your Student Resources CD.

• Listen to or read the story about Pocahontas in *Profiles from History*. Complete the timeline activities and any other activities you would like to do.

Enrichment Activities

1. At the library or, with your parent's permission, on the Internet research one or both of the following tribes: the Powhatan tribe, or the larger Algonquin tribe. Then fill out a Native American Profile sheet, from your Student Resources CD, for the tribe(s) you choose to find out more about. Add the profile sheet(s) to your Native American Notebook.

2. Together with your parent, visit a health food store and see what plants are available today for use in maintaining good health. Make a list of the ones that are most interesting to you and find out what benefits they provide as well as any dangers they may pose.

Use one or more of the Enrichment Activities if your child completes his assigned work and has the time or desire to learn more. These activities are flexible, so choose the one(s) that seem most interesting to your student. Allow him to work at a level that is appropriate for him, and remember that the learning process is more important than the product.

This year your child has many opportunities to research and learn about different Native American tribes as Enrichment Activities, and to make a Native American Notebook with the information he finds. Place the finished profiles in a separate binder or add them to your child's Student Notebook. Teachers can find a copy of this profile sheet in Appendix B.

Answers

1. careful, ladlefuls, sickness

2. red mulberry tree: a tree, 20–30 feet tall, leaves that are 3–5 inches long, dark red to purple fruit; grows in rich, moist soil

3. wild strawberry: 2–10 inches tall, yellow and white flowers, $\frac{1}{2}$–$\frac{3}{4}$ inches wide, red "berries"; grows in meadows and clearings, from April–July; not actually a berry

4. ball B6, snail C1, flower C4, bird D5, car E3, fish F6

5. sailboat D6, snowflake C3, book B1, ice cream cone F4, dog C5, baseball glove E2, bee A5

6. Florida-E8, E9, F8, F9; Ohio-C9, D9; California-C1, D1, D2, D3, E1, E2, E3; Colorado-C4, C5, D4, D5

7. quickly

8. peacefully, diligently, strongly, fearfully, faithfully

9. sassafras: looks like a tree, 30–40 feet tall, leaves that are 3–5 inches long and mitten-shaped, blue berry-like fruit; grows in fields and woods

10. peppermint: 6–36 inches tall, white to pale lavender flower clusters; grows in wet fields, shores, stream banks; used to repel insects

11. Answers will vary, but might include medicinal or flavoring uses.

12. friendly, carefully

13. friendly-the Indians; carefully-the way John Smith listened

14. One inch equals approximately 250 miles.

15. approximately 7 inches

16. 1,750 miles

Lesson 5, Part 1

> ### § Steps for Thinking ɛ
>
> 1. Having faith in your purpose is a key to remaining determined during difficulties. Without this faith, sacrifices don't seem worthwhile.
>
> 2. Explorers often show their creativity by the way they solve problems.

The **Steps for Thinking** section gives you the main ideas about the topics presented. Understanding these helps you to have productive discussions with your children so they, too, understand the bigger ideas. This forms more permanent learning, contrary to just learning facts, which tends to be temporary. These steps are useful prior to instruction, and they are also useful for review at the end of the week.

⟶ Materials ⟵

- *A Lion to Guard Us*
- *Surviving Jamestown*
- *North American Wildlife Guide*
- *Intermediate World Atlas*
- *Handbook of Nature Study*
- *Profiles from History*
- Student Notebook
- Index cards/marker
- Ruler
- Internet access (🐾)
- Plain or tracing paper
- Crayons or colored pencils
- Tape, glue, or stapler
- One or more of the following: dry erase board/markers, colored chalk, water-based paint, modeling clay
- Large world outline map

Additional resources for Enrichment Activities are found in Part 5.

A. **Copywork/Dictation**   *Language Skills*

Look carefully at the following passage, and read it silently. Show your teacher any words you don't know, and practice saying them aloud. Now read the passage aloud, or ask your teacher to read it to you.

> The colonists faced many challenges, or tests of their abilities and their faith. Even though all went well with their Indian neighbors at first, it would not always be so.

🐾 Copy the above lines into your Student Notebook. When you are finished, compare your copy to the model (word by word) and make any needed corrections.

🖐 Listen as your teacher dictates the above lines, and write them in your Student Notebook. When you are finished, compare your copy to the model and make any needed corrections.

🐾 Copy, or write as your teacher dictates, paragraphs 1–4 on page 119 in *Surviving Jamestown.* When you are finished, compare your copy to the text and make any needed corrections.

B. **Reader**   *Language Skills, Thinking Skills, History*

In your book, *A Lion to Guard Us,* read Chapter 17 aloud.

🖐 Read one or two paragraphs in your read-aloud book, *Surviving Jamestown.*

🐾 Read one or two pages from today's read-aloud assignment in *Surviving Jamestown.*

A. Copywork and dictation assignments go from an easier level (designated by 🐾) to harder levels (designated by 🖐 and 🐾). Take two days for the copywork if that is more comfortable for your child. Please adapt instructions to your child's individual needs. Your child should be **consistently successful** at one level before progressing to the next, **regardless of grade**.

B. Please note: Pages 120 and 121 of *Surviving Jamestown* have been excluded from these assignments due to the brutal events described. Please pre-read these pages before allowing your children to read or hear their content. The events are, unfortunately, historically accurate yet may be inappropriate for children.

C. Discussion is very important in developing your child's ability to organize his thoughts. This in turn builds the ability to think and write. The goal of the discussion questions is not just to find the answer to a particular question, but also to create a situation where thoughts about the question and its answer are shared and considered in a detailed way. Do not rush this activity, but encourage your student to share his or her ideas relating to the topic, and any additional ideas that may come to mind. You can also share your thoughts and questions as an example for your students.

D. The small superscript numbers that appear after some of the questions in this unit refer to answers in the answer key, located immediately after Part 5.

E. Each word in bold letters is considered a vocabulary word. It is a word that may or may not be new to your child. You can write these vocabulary words on index cards and use them for occasional review, but not for memorizing. Give the child the meaning of the words if he doesn't remember. Try to use the new vocabulary words during conversation, and encourage your students to do the same.

Each time your student makes a vocabulary card for this unit, have him write a "J" (for Jamestown) in the upper left corner. This will make it possible to review vocabulary by unit at the end of the year.

C. **Read-Aloud and Discussion** *Language Skills, Thinking Skills*

In *Surviving Jamestown,* listen as your teacher reads page 115 through the end of page 119, and pages 122 and 123 aloud.

Listen as your teacher reads the story and the following discussion question. Think about what you know from the story, and answer in your own words. Give any examples you can think of that help show your answer.

Discussion Question: John Smith took a trading party up the Chickahominy River. He gave the men and boys orders to stay on the boat and wait while he went ashore. The group disobeyed his orders with terrible results. One of the men was captured and killed. How important do you think it was for the men to obey their leader? Why was it so hard for them to obey?

D. **Word Study** *Spelling, Phonics, Vocabulary*

Certain letters can spell the long sound of *a*. The letters *ai* or *ay* together in a word, and the letter *a* with a silent *e* at the end both spell the long *a* sound. The letters *ei* and *ey* together also spell the long *a* sound.

Find the three words in the copywork passage printed in Section A above that have the long *a* sound.[1]

Here are some other examples of words with the long *a* sound. Read these words to your teacher, or listen as she reads them to you:

take	rain	vein
play	place	wait
reign	bay	

Look on page 84 of *A Lion to Guard Us.* Find the words with the long *a* sound spelled in the following ways. Write each word you find in the correct category in your Student Notebook.[2]

a with silent *e*   *ai*   *ay*   *ey*

Look on page 116 in *Surviving Jamestown.* Find all the words that have the long *a* sound and write them in the correct category in your Student Notebook.[3]

E. **Science**

This lesson you will continue learning about birds, plants, and insects that live along the water. The colonists commonly saw these creatures and plants. As you study the colony of Jamestown and the surrounding area, you are learning about the **environment,** or natural world, that they lived in.

One bird common to that area is the belted kingfisher, which is pictured on page 113 in the *North American Wildlife Guide.* Draw or trace both the male (boy) and female (girl) kingfishers into your Student Notebook. Read the description, or listen as your teacher reads it. Make a list of at least three facts you found out about it in your Student Notebook.

Another bird often seen around Chesapeake Bay is the Canada goose. This large bird is commonly seen on ponds and bays in Virginia during **migration,** which is when it is traveling from its winter home to its summer home. Since these birds are large, they were definitely hunted by the colonists for food. Look at The Canada goose on page 89 in the *North American Wildlife Guide.* Draw or trace this bird in your Student Notebook. Write at least three facts you learned about the Canada goose.

🐾 If you have access to the Internet at home or at a library, with your parent's permission go to the Cornell Lab of Ornithology website (www.birds.cornell.edu). Click on the section titled "All About Birds." From there, you can browse the site to learn about birds, conservation, and bird watching. To look up information about specific birds, click on the heading "Bird Guide."

Find more information about belted kingfishers and Canadian geese. Share what you learn with others.

ℱ. **Writing**   *Science, Language Skills*

Listen as your teacher reads "The Kingfisher (of England)" to you, or read it yourself. This poem is found on pages 99 and 100 in the *Handbook of Nature Study.* Listen as your teacher rereads each line of the poem, then read or repeat it after her. Try to speak the words with the same rhythm that she uses.

With your teacher's permission, take your *North American Wildlife Guide* and go out into your yard or a park. Look for a bird that you recognize or can identify using your wildlife guide. After observing this bird for as long as possible, make a sketch of the bird from memory or from the picture in the wildlife guide.

Below the picture, write a poem about your bird. Start by naming your poem after the kind of bird you were looking at. Then tell some things you observed about the bird's actions or appearance. Here is an example:

Cardinal

Darting, chirping,
this bird is bright red.

It's always with its mate,
hiding in the cedar tree;

Bright like a berry
in the winter trees.

G. Reading fluency is developed through having frequent silent reading opportunities that continue for the length of time suggested here. Since a primary focus of this activity is to nurture your child's enjoyment of reading, help him to choose reading material that interests him and is at a level that allows him to read with understanding by himself. You can incorporate this activity into your school day whenever it is most convenient.

If the suggested length of time is too long for your child to continue reading by himself, start with an amount of time he can accomplish successfully and make the suggested time a goal.

G. Independent Reading

Choose something to read that you will enjoy. Find a quiet, comfortable place and read for the following length of time:

🐾 20 minutes

🐾 25 minutes

🐾 30 minutes

Over time, it's fun to see how much you have read. Be sure to write down what you read today on the Reading Log in your Student Notebook.

Lesson 5, Part 2

A. The dictation method enables your child to hear language and correctly write down what he hears. It involves building two different skills. First, the ability to listen and understand what is heard, and second, the ability to transfer what is heard into written language. This process takes time and practice, so begin as gradually as needed for successfully reaching the goal of getting the words the child hears on the paper correctly. 1) Read the whole passage, then reread one sentence at a time, giving your child time to write what he hears. 2) After he has finished, reread the passage again, allowing him to double check what he has written. 3) Then proceed to the step of comparing his writing to the model. As his skill builds, you can move more quickly through the steps, maintaining your child's level of success.

A. Copywork/Dictation   *Language Skills*

Look carefully at the following passage, and read it silently. Show your teacher any words you don't know, and practice saying them aloud. Now read the passage aloud, or ask your teacher to read it to you.

From the beginning, most of the colonists
and Indians tried to be friends. Sometimes the
colonists didn't understand the Indians' ways
and trouble followed. It was hard for the Indian
leaders to understand the English.

🐾 Copy the above lines into your Student Notebook. When you are finished, compare your copy to the model (word by word) and make any needed corrections.

🐾 Listen as your teacher dictates the above lines, and write them in your Student Notebook. When you are finished, compare your copy to the model and make any needed corrections.

🐾 Copy, or write as your teacher dictates, paragraph 4 on page 130 in *Surviving Jamestown*. When you are finished, compare your copy to the text and make any needed corrections.

B. Reader   *Language Skills, Thinking Skills, History*

In your book, *A Lion to Guard Us,* read Chapter 18 aloud.

🐾 Read one or two paragraphs in your read-aloud book, *Surviving Jamestown*.

🐾 Read one or two pages from today's read-aloud assignment in *Surviving Jamestown*.

C. Read-Aloud and Narration   *Language Skills, Thinking Skills*

Listen carefully as your teacher reads page 124 through the end of paragraph 6 on page 130 aloud from *Surviving Jamestown*.

To *narrate* means to retell. In your own words, tell what happened in your assigned passage below. Try to remember as many details as possible. Listen carefully as your teacher reads (or rereads) the part you are to retell.

🐾🐾 Chapter 18 in *A Lion to Guard Us.*

🐾 Paragraph 3 through paragraph 9 on page 125 in *Surviving Jamestown*.

🐾 Last paragraph on page 128 through the end of page 129 in *Surviving Jamestown*.

D. Word Study   *Spelling, Phonics, Vocabulary*

In Part 1, you reviewed many ways to spell the long *a* sound. They included spelling it with the letters below. Read these words to your teacher, or listen as she reads them to you.

a with silent *e*	*ai*	*ei*	*ay*	*ey*
place	faith	neighbors	play	they
faced	wait	vein	bay	convey

Use the list above and the one you made yesterday and see how many words you can spell without looking. Practice any words that are hard for you to remember by looking at the words, spelling them aloud, and then looking at them again to check. You may also use a dry erase board and markers, a chalkboard or sidewalk and colored chalk, paint, or typing to practice your words.

C. The skill of narration is gained over time. If your child has never retold a story, start with the assignment for the lower level, no matter what grade he is in. Work up from there, being careful to allow him to stay at the level of success for a while before going to a longer section.

D. Now that your child has been working on spelling for awhile, it is good to vary the method used to practice. The multi-sensory approach suggested here provides variety and reinforcement on several levels of memory and comprehension.

🐾 Look in books at your house. Find at least six more words to add to the long *a* word list you began in Part 1.

🐾 Look in books at your house. Find at least ten more words to add to the long *a* word list you began in Part 1.

E. Geography

Geography

Since you completed the unit about Christopher Columbus and most of the unit on Jamestown, you have frequently looked at maps with oceans, continents, seas, and islands. Look at the World Political Map in the *Intermediate World Atlas*. Use your ruler and the map scale on the bottom left of the map to figure out how many miles equal one inch.[4]

Now use your ruler to measure the distances of some of the voyages you have read about. Put one end of your ruler on London and the other end at the Chesapeake Bay (just below Washington, D.C.) on the map. How many inches separate those two places?[5] Remember to add or multiply 1,500 three times. The approximate distance from London to the Chesapeake Bay is 4,500 miles if you sailed directly across the ocean. The route Columbus and the Jamestown ships took was farther because it followed the trade winds.

Measure the distance from London to the Canary Islands.[6] Add 1,500 (the distance one inch represents) and ½ of 1,500 (750—the distance ½ inch represents) together, or multiply 1,500 times 1.5.[7] This was the first leg of most journeys to the New World. Write this voyage's destination and distance in your Student Notebook.

Next measure from the Canary Islands to the West Indies (islands just below Puerto Rico on the map.) This distance is approximately two inches, or 1,500 miles plus 1,500 miles. Another way to figure out this distance is to multiply 1,500 times two. Write this voyage's destination and distance in your Student Notebook.[8]

Finally, measure from the West Indies to the Chesapeake Bay area. It is approximately one inch, which is equal to approximately 1,500 miles. Write this voyage's destination and distance in your Student Notebook.

Now add up all three legs of the journey from London to the Jamestown area.[9]

F. Art

Geography

You have spent several weeks learning to use the *Intermediate World Atlas*. Now it is time to have some fun with the shapes in the atlas. Look through the pages and choose a country from any political map. Remember, a political map is one with boundaries decided by people. Find a country or a state that has an interesting shape. Trace the country onto a piece of paper. Use the shape of the country as the beginning of your picture. Write the name of the country on the shape you started with.

As an example, Italy is shaped like a boot. Trace the shape of Italy and then add a leg and a person to the shape.

🐾 Try to find two countries or states to make pictures out of.

🐾 Try to find at least two countries to use together in the drawing of one picture.

G. Independent Reading

Choose something to read that you will enjoy. Find a quiet, comfortable place and read for the following length of time:

🐾 20 minutes

🐾 25 minutes

🐾 30 minutes

Over time, it's fun to see how much you have read. Be sure to write down what you read today on the Reading Log in your Student Notebook.

G. See Independent Reading note in Part 1.

———

Lesson 5, Part 3

A. Copywork/Dictation

Language Skills

Look carefully at the following passage, and read it silently. Show your teacher any words you don't know, and practice saying them aloud. Now read the passage aloud, or ask your teacher to read it to you.

> One leader the Indians understood was John Smith. He led groups of explorers into unknown places. He defended himself and others well. He did not show fear. This made the Indians respect him.

🐾 Copy the above lines into your Student Notebook. When you are finished, compare your copy to the model (word by word) and make any needed corrections.

A. See Copywork/Dictation note in Part 1.

🐾 Listen as your teacher dictates the above lines, and write them in your Student Notebook. When you are finished, compare your copy to the model and make any needed corrections.

🐾 Copy, or write as your teacher dictates, paragraph 4 on page 133 to the word "Pamunkeys" in *Surviving Jamestown*. When you are finished, compare your copy to the text and make any needed corrections.

B. **Reader**   *Language Skills, Thinking Skills, History*

In your book, *A Lion to Guard Us*, read Chapter 19 aloud.

🐾 Read one or two paragraphs in your read-aloud book, *Surviving Jamestown*.

🐾 Read one or two pages from today's read-aloud assignment in *Surviving Jamestown*.

C. See Discussion note in Part 1.

C. **Read-Aloud and Discussion**   *Language Skills, Thinking Skills*

In *Surviving Jamestown*, listen as your teacher reads paragraph 7 on page 130 through page 138 aloud.

Listen as your teacher reads the story and the following discussion question. Think about what you know from the story, and answer in your own words. Give any examples you can think of that help show your answer.

Discussion Question: The English seemed to have trouble understanding that the Indians who lived around them came from different tribes, and therefore had different attitudes towards the English and other Indians. John Smith tried to get them to understand that it was like being from different countries in Europe. Why do you think it was difficult for the English to see the Indians as separate groups?

D. **Word Study**   *Spelling, Phonics, Vocabulary*

You have been looking at the different ways to spell the sound of long *a*. Review your word lists for the past two days.

Use index cards to write your long *a* words. Put the category on the top half of the card (*a – e, ai, ay, ei, ey*). Write the long *a* word on the bottom half of the card. Now try to spell each word aloud. Practice the words you don't know. Try to practice your words by spelling them aloud, or using methods such as stamp letters, making letters with clay, or typing.

E. Science

In this lesson you will continue learning about life along a waterway. Read, or listen as your teacher reads, about the belted kingfisher on pages 97–99 in your *Handbook of Nature Study.* After reading or listening, discuss the answers to questions 1-7 on page 99 in the *Handbook of Nature Study* orally. In your Student Notebook, write what you know about how the kingfisher gets its food, what its nest is like, and how the male and female work together.[10]

🐾 After reading the section on the kingfisher or listening to your teacher read it, answer questions 1–7 on page 99 in the *Handbook of Nature Study.* Write these answers in your Student Notebook.

F. Writing

In Lesson 4 you learned how to write a friendly letter. Today, talk with your teacher and choose someone you would like to write to. Write that person a friendly letter and tell about the birds you have been studying. You may want to include a sketch of a bird you have drawn, and perhaps your poem.

In your letter, ask what birds he has seen in his yard. Maybe he will write you back and include a drawing or picture of birds he has seen and descriptions of the birds' activities. Place a copy of your letter and any response you get back in your Student Notebook.

G. Independent Reading

Choose something to read that you will enjoy. Find a quiet, comfortable place and read for the following length of time:

🐾🐾 20 minutes

🖐 25 minutes

🐾 30 minutes

Over time, it's fun to see how much you have read. Be sure to write down what you read today on the Reading Log in your Student Notebook.

E. Although questions 1-7 in the *Handbook of Nature Study* are based on personal observation, most can be answered from the reading assignment. If the answer is not in the text, and your child is unable to observe a Kingfisher, simply skip that question and go on to the next.

G. See Independent Reading note in Part I.

Lesson 5, Part 4

A. See Copywork/Dictation note in Part 1.

A. Copywork/Dictation *Language Skills*

Look carefully at the following passage, and read it silently. Show your teacher any words you don't know, and practice saying them aloud. Now read the passage aloud, or ask your teacher to read it to you.

> Respect from his fellow Englishmen was harder to win. Many still thought that only noblemen could lead. They soon found that John Smith's ways were more demanding but more helpful to the colony.

Copy the above lines into your Student Notebook. When you are finished, compare your copy to the model (word by word) and make any needed corrections.

Listen as your teacher dictates the above lines, and write them in your Student Notebook. When you are finished, compare your copy to the model and make any needed corrections.

Copy, or write as your teacher dictates, paragraph 3 on page 142 in *Surviving Jamestown*. When you are finished, compare your copy to the text and make any needed corrections.

B. Reader *Language Skills, Thinking Skills, History*

In your book, *A Lion to Guard Us,* read Chapter 20 aloud.

Read one or two paragraphs in your read-aloud book, *Surviving Jamestown*.

Read one or two pages from today's read-aloud assignment in *Surviving Jamestown*.

C. See Narration note in Part 2.

C. Read-Aloud and Narration *Language Skills, Thinking Skills*

Listen carefully as your teacher reads page 139 through paragraph 3 on page 149 aloud from *Surviving Jamestown*.

To *narrate* means to retell. In your own words, tell what happened in your assigned passage below. Try to remember as many details as possible. Listen carefully as your teacher reads (or rereads) the part you are to retell.

Chapter 20 in *A Lion to Guard Us.*

Paragraph 5 on page 145 through paragraph 3 on page 147 in *Surviving Jamestown*.

🐾 Paragraph 2 on page 148 through the end of page 149 in *Surviving Jamestown.*

D. Word Study   *Spelling, Phonics, Vocabulary*

Read through your long *a* word cards. Now practice spelling each word aloud. Put the words you can't spell into a stack and practice them by using dry erase markers, paint, colored chalk, or typing.

After you finish spelling practice, make a second set of cards exactly like the first set. Mix the cards up and deal five cards out to yourself and at least one other player. Put the rest in a pile face down. Now play a "Go Fish" type of game, where you ask the other person for a certain word. If he or she doesn't have it, draw a card. Your goal is to match word pairs. When you get a pair, put it down during your turn. When all the cards are gone, or someone matches all his cards, the game is over. The one with the most pairs wins.

E. Geography   *Art*

All who stood guard in Jamestown watched in several directions. They watched the forest for signs of Indian trouble, they watched the fort for signs of fire or struggle, and they watched the water for signs of a ship. When they saw a ship approaching, the first thing they looked for was her "colors," or the flag of the country the ship came from. The English flag brought joy, but the sight of the Spanish flag brought fear.

In your Student Notebook, color the flags from Great Britain and Spain. You can find the colors of the flags on the Internet or at the library.

F. Writing

🐾🐾🐾 You are almost finished with the stories you have been reading or listening to. Choose a character from *A Lion to Guard Us* and complete the Character Portrait in your Student Notebook for him or her. You may want to draw or trace a picture of the character you chose.

🐾 Choose at least two characters from *Surviving Jamestown.* Complete a Character Portrait in your Student Notebook for each one. You may want to draw or trace pictures of the characters your chose.

G. See Independent Reading note in Part 1.

G. **Independent Reading**

Choose something to read that you will enjoy. Find a quiet, comfortable place and read for the following length of time:

- 20 minutes
- 25 minutes
- 30 minutes

Over time, it's fun to see how much you have read. Be sure to write down what you read today on the Reading Log in your Student Notebook.

Lesson 5, Part 5

This part is set aside for completion of any work left undone from the lesson, and review of concepts and content. It is also a time to expand the work in the lesson by doing art, timeline activities, or games.

- Review the Steps for Thinking from the beginning of this lesson.

Most of the labeling has already been completed in the Student Notebook during this lesson. Instruct students to use the maps in their Student Notebooks as a reference. When they label the larger map, students will see the "big picture" and gain a broader understanding of their lessons.

- On the large outline map of the world label Great Britain, and mark the colonists' voyage from London to Jamestown in green.

- Review the spelling words for this lesson. Choose at least ten of your words and write a sentence for each one in your Student Notebook. Do your best to write the spelling words correctly. After you have finished, check your sentences against the list in your Student Notebook and see how many spelling words you spelled correctly. (Don't count off for other words that are misspelled.) Remember your goal is to improve, not necessarily to get them all right immediately.

Teachers can find a copy of this game in Appendix B. Instructions and answer keys for all games are located in Appendix A.

- Complete the Jamestown Crossword Puzzle in your Student Notebook.

- Jamestown was founded in 1607. The 400th anniversary was celebrated in 2007. With your parent's permission and supervision, look at several of the websites that tell about the celebrations and commemorations that took place. After looking at one or more websites, tell your teacher some of the new things you learned about Jamestown, or point out the things you already knew. What event do you think would have been the most appreciated by the people of the original Jamestown colony?

Enrichment Activities

1. Letters have been a very important tool of communication for thousands of years. Check the library or Internet to see if you can find letters written by famous people throughout history, such as George Washington or Thomas Jefferson. Documents such as the Bible also contain many important letters. Talk with your family and see if there are any letters from past generations that you can read. Out of all these choices, choose one letter and tell your parent why you like it, or write a letter in response.

2. There are tribes of Native American Indians throughout our country. At the library or, with your parent's permission, on the Internet research which tribes might live near you now, or might have lived in your area long ago. Then fill out a Native American Profile sheet, found on your Student Resources CD, for the tribes you choose to find out more about. Add the profile sheet(s) to your Native American Notebook.

Additional Resources

Historic letters

Letter writing materials

Videos, books, and community information on local American Indian tribes

Use one or more of the Enrichment Activities if your child completes his assigned work and has the time or desire to learn more. These activities are flexible, so choose the one(s) that seem most interesting to your student. Allow him to work at a level that is appropriate for him, and remember that the learning process is more important than the product.

This year your child has many opportunities to research and learn about different Native American tribes as Enrichment Activities, and to make a Native American Notebook with the information he finds. Place the finished profiles in a separate binder or add them to your child's student notebook. Teachers can find a copy of this profile sheet in Appendix B.

Answers

1. faced, faith, neighbors

2. *a* with silent *e:* gave, came, tales; *ai:* pailfull, pail, rainwater, sailor, Spain; *ay:* away; *ey:* they

3. *a* with silent *e:* caged, hates, same, case, Nate, aware, made; *ai*-waiting, wait, mainly; *ay:* day, say, stay; *ey:* they

4. approximately 1,500 miles

5. approximately three inches

6. approximately 1 ½ inches

7. 2,250 miles

8. 3,000 miles

9. approximately 6,750 miles

10. Answers will vary but may include some mention of the following: The kingfisher perches on a branch above the stream until it spots its prey, then it dives and captures the fish, or frog, or insect in its strong beak. Its nest is at the end of a burrow that the male digs horizontally into a bank, and it often appears to be lined with clean white fish bones. The male digs the burrow but the female helps make the nest; both parents help feed their young, but the male takes more responsibility in doing this.

Lesson 6, Part 1

A. **Copywork/Dictation**   *Language Skills*

Look carefully at the following passage, and read it silently. Show your teacher any words you don't know, and practice saying them aloud. Now read the passage aloud, or ask your teacher to read it to you.

The colony's survival became dependent on John Smith. He knew that to survive much hard work had to be done. Food had to be stored and houses built. He set the example by working harder than anyone else.

🐾 Copy the above lines into your Student Notebook. When you are finished, compare your copy to the model (word by word) and make any needed corrections.

🐾 Listen as your teacher dictates the above lines, and write them in your Student Notebook. When you are finished, compare your copy to the model and make any needed corrections.

🐾 Copy, or write as your teacher dictates, paragraph 7 on pages 150 and 151 in *Surviving Jamestown*. When you are finished, compare your copy to the text and make any needed corrections.

B. **Reader**   *Language Skills, Thinking Skills, History*

In your book, *A Lion to Guard Us*, read Chapter 21 aloud.

🐾 Read one or two paragraphs in your read-aloud book, *Surviving Jamestown*.

🐾 Read one or two pages from today's read-aloud assignment in *Surviving Jamestown*.

C. **Read-Aloud and Narration**   *Language Skills, Thinking Skills*

In *Surviving Jamestown*, listen as your teacher reads pages 150 to the beginning of paragraph 1 on page 156 aloud.

To *narrate* means to retell. In your own words, tell what happened in your assigned passage below. Try to remember as many details as possible. Listen carefully as your teacher reads (or rereads) the part you are to retell.

🐾 Chapter 21 in *A Lion to Guard Us*.

🐾 Paragraph 6 on page 151 to the end of page 152 in *Surviving Jamestown*.

⁓Materials⁓

- *A Lion to Guard Us*
- *Surviving Jamestown*
- *Intermediate World Atlas*
- Student Notebook
- *Profiles from History*
- Globe
- Paste
- Page Protector
- Long *a* cards
- Animal classification cards
- Index cards/marker
- Construction paper
- Scissors
- Vocabulary cards: Columbus Unit, Jamestown Unit
- One or two of the following: colored chalk, markers, clay, water-based paint, typewriter
- Large world outline map

A. Copywork and dictation assignments go from an easier level (designated by 🐾) to harder levels (designated by 🐾 and 🐾). Take two days for the copywork if that is more comfortable for your child. Please adapt instructions to your child's individual needs. Your child should be **consistently successful** at one level before progressing to the next, **regardless of grade**.

B. The readers used in this unit describe events that could have taken place. Since this time in history included violent or difficult events, you may wish to prepare your children for certain realities of the times that seem harsh, or to edit the content that you read-aloud or that your children read independently.

C. The skill of narration is gained over time. If your child has never retold a story, start with the assignment for the lower level, no matter what grade he is in. Work up from there, being careful to allow him to stay at the level of success for a while before going to a longer section.

❧ Paragraph 8 on page 153 to the end of page 154 in *Surviving Jamestown.*

D. The purpose of many of the activities during the final week of this unit is to review and solidify what has been learned. Understanding the ideas taught is of greater importance than merely remembering names and dates. Review activities will be completed by everyone, so remember, where no level is indicated, an activity is to be completed by all students.

E. Each time your student makes an Animal I.D. card for this unit, have him write a "J" (for Jamestown) in the upper left corner. This will make it possible to review the animals studied by unit at the end of the year.

D. **Word Study**   *Spelling, Phonics, Vocabulary*

Gather together all the vocabulary cards you have made for this unit. Practice reading the words and telling what you think they mean.

Make a stack of the words you remember, and another stack of words you need to review.

From the stack of words you remember, tell your teacher how you think each word relates to our study of Jamestown.

E. **Science**

In Lesson 3, Part 4 you reviewed the following categories of animals by making a set of cards with the name of each animal studied so far, as well as which category each animal fits into.

reptiles   mammals   birds   fish   invertebrates

Find the vocabulary card you made for each of the categories above, and review the qualities of each. Make sure you can tell your teacher what animals in each category are like. Now make cards for the belted kingfisher and the Canada goose that you learned about in Lesson 5, Part 1. Write the name of the animal on the top of the card. You may include a picture of the animal on the card and as well as important information. Then write the category of the animal on the bottom. Make two copies of each card so that you can use them to play a game later.

When you finish, you should have two cards for each of the following animals:

bottle-nosed dolphin	oysters
river otter	clams
brown pelican	mute swan
laughing gull	flying fish
alligator	loggerhead turtle
mudminnow	stickleback
belted kingfisher	Canada goose

Now you are ready to play the Animal I.D. game. Shuffle the cards and deal five cards face down to each player. Put the remainder of the cards in a stack, face down. There must be at least two players to play. This is a "Go Fish" type of game, which you begin by asking another player for an animal of your choice. If he or she doesn't have it, draw a card. Your goal is to match animal pairs. When you get a pair, put it down during your turn. When all the cards are gone, or someone matches all his cards, the game is over. The one with the most pairs wins.

F. Writing

History

Think about what you have learned about John Smith. Look at the Explorer page in your Student Notebook. Read over the questions and discuss your answers with your teacher. When you feel you know how to best answer each question, write your answers in the spaces provided. Remember to use your Jamestown Word Bank to help you.

You will be sharing what you have learned about Jamestown with your family at the end of this week. You may want to use these questions as a guide for part of your Unit Presentation. Make sure you include your answers in your presentation.

G. Independent Reading

Choose something to read that you will enjoy. Find a quiet, comfortable place and read for the following length of time:

- 20 minutes
- 25 minutes
- 30 minutes

Over time, it's fun to see how much you have read. Be sure to write down what you read today on the Reading Log in your Student Notebook.

G. Reading fluency is developed through having frequent silent reading opportunities that continue for the length of time suggested here. Since a primary focus of this activity is to nurture your child's enjoyment of reading, help him to choose reading material that interests him and is at a level that allows him to read with understanding by himself. You can incorporate this activity into your school day whenever it is most convenient.

If the suggested length of time is too long for your child to continue reading by himself, start with an amount of time he can accomplish successfully and make the suggested time a goal.

Lesson 6, Part 2

A. Copywork/Dictation

Language Skills

Look carefully at the following passage, and read it silently. Show your teacher any words you don't know, and practice saying them aloud. Now read the passage aloud, or ask your teacher to read it to you.

> Even hard work couldn't save all the colonists. Sickness took many lives. Conflict with the Indians cost the lives of some and, last of all, starvation almost wiped out Jamestown.

A. See Copywork/Dictation note in Part 1.

Copy the above lines into your Student Notebook. When you are finished, compare your copy to the model (word by word) and make any needed corrections.

🐾 Listen as your teacher dictates the above lines, and write them in your Student Notebook. When you are finished, compare your copy to the model and make any needed corrections.

🐾 Copy, or write as your teacher dictates, paragraph 1 on page 165 in *Surviving Jamestown*. When you are finished, compare your copy to the text and make any needed corrections.

B. **Reader**   *Language Skills, Thinking Skills, History*
In your book, *A Lion to Guard Us,* read Chapter 22 aloud.

🐾 Read one or two paragraphs in your read-aloud book, *Surviving Jamestown.*

🐾 Read one or two pages from today's read-aloud assignment in *Surviving Jamestown.*

C. **Read-Aloud and Discussion**   *Language Skills, Thinking Skills*
Listen carefully as your teacher reads paragraph 1 on page 156 through page 165 aloud from *Surviving Jamestown.*

Listen as your teacher reads the story and the following discussion question. Think about what you know from the story, and answer in your own words. Give any examples you can think of that help show your answer.

Discussion Question: Tell why you think John Smith did so well trading with the blue beads when Captain Newport gave them much more and received much less.

C. Discussion is very important in developing your child's ability to organize his thoughts. This in turn builds the ability to think and write. The goal of the discussion questions is not just to find the answer to a particular question, but also to create a situation where thoughts about the question and its answer are shared and considered in a detailed way. Do not rush this activity, but encourage your student to share his or her ideas relating to the topic, and any additional ideas that may come to mind. You can also share your thoughts and questions as an example for your students.

D. **Word Study**   *Spelling, Phonics, Vocabulary*
Read through the long *a* word cards that you made. Now practice spelling each word aloud. Put the words you can't spell into a stack and practice them by using dry erase markers, paint, colored chalk, or typing.

After you have finished spelling practice, mix the cards up and deal five cards out, face down, to yourself and at least one other player. Put the rest in a pile face down. Now play a "Go Fish" type of game, where you ask the other person for a certain word. If he or she doesn't have it, draw a card. Your goal is to match word pairs. When you get a pair, put it down during your turn. When all the cards are gone, or someone matches all his cards, the game is over. The one with the most pairs wins.

E. Geography

You have been introduced to many places on the map since the beginning of these units. Use your globe or a map to point out to your teacher all the places you have learned about, as well as other items on the map or globe, such as the compass rose or a key. Tell your teacher what you remember about each place or thing.

You may want to play a game where one person picks a place and the other person tries to tell what it is and how it relates to the Columbus or Jamestown unit. Players should only choose places covered in these units. If you forget some of the places that were covered, look at the list below for some hints.

> **Oceans:** Atlantic, Pacific, Indian, Arctic, Antarctic (or Southern)
>
> **Seas:** Mediterranean, Caribbean, North, Irish
>
> **Bays and Rivers:** Chesapeake Bay, James River, Thames River, English Channel
>
> **Continents:** North America, South America, Africa, Asia, Europe
>
> **Countries:** Spain, Portugal, England, Italy, Cuba, America, Dominican Republic, Jamaica, Puerto Rico
>
> **States:** Virginia
>
> **Islands:** Bermuda Islands, West Indies, Canary Islands
>
> **Map Markers:** Equator, Northern Hemisphere, Southern Hemisphere North Pole, South Pole, Latitude

You may want to add any other countries or things that you learned about. Look at all the places you have explored!

F. Art

Today take the poem you wrote in Lesson 5, Part 1 about a bird, and prepare it for display at your Unit Presentation. If necessary rewrite your poem either by typing or writing to make it look special. Choose a color of construction paper that goes well with the colors in your illustration, and attach both the illustration and poem to the construction paper. You may want to put the finished product in a page protector to keep it safe.

If you have created any other poetry, stories, or illustrations during this unit that you would like to share with your family, consider mounting them in the same way described above.

G. See Independent Reading note in Part 1.

G. Independent Reading

Choose something to read that you will enjoy. Find a quiet, comfortable place and read for the following length of time:

✸ 20 minutes

✸ 25 minutes

✸ 30 minutes

Over time, it's fun to see how much you have read. Be sure to write down what you read today on the Reading Log in your Student Notebook.

Lesson 6, Part 3

A. See Copywork/Dictation note in Part 1.

A. Copywork/Dictation   *Language Skills*

Look carefully at the following passage, and read it silently. Show your teacher any words you don't know, and practice saying them aloud. Now read the passage aloud, or ask your teacher to read it to you.

> Those who survived made it through what John Smith called "a seasoning." The challenges they faced built strong character in those who remained. The colonists were tested in every way, yet they endured.

✸ Copy the above lines into your Student Notebook. When you are finished, compare your copy to the model (word by word) and make any needed corrections.

✸ Listen as your teacher dictates the above lines, and write them in your Student Notebook. When you are finished, compare your copy to the model and make any needed corrections.

✸ Copy the first paragraph of Sam Collier's letter on page 170 in *Surviving Jamestown*. When you are finished, compare your copy to the text and make any needed corrections.

B. **Reader**   *Language Skills, Thinking Skills, History*
In your book, *A Lion to Guard Us,* read Chapter 23 aloud.

🐾 Read one or two paragraphs in your read-aloud book, *Surviving Jamestown.*

🐾 Read one or two pages from today's read-aloud assignment in *Surviving Jamestown.*

C. **Read-Aloud and Narration**   *Language Skills, Thinking Skills*   *C.* See Narration note in Part 1.
In *Surviving Jamestown,* listen as your teacher reads pages 166 through 176 aloud.

To *narrate* means to retell. In your own words, tell what happened in your assigned passage below. Try to remember as many details as possible. Listen carefully as your teacher reads (or rereads) the part you are to retell.

🐾🐾 Chapter 23 in *A Lion to Guard Us.*

🐾 Paragraph 1 on page 168 in *Surviving Jamestown.*

🐾 Paragraph 1 through paragraph 5 on page 173 in *Surviving Jamestown.*

D. **Word Study**   *Spelling, Phonics, Vocabulary*
Review the spelling words you worked on in Lessons 1 through 4 in the Jamestown Unit. Read over the lists of words and practice spelling them. When you feel ready, spell each word without looking. Ask your teacher to keep a list of all the words you spelled correctly. If you had trouble with any of the words, practice spelling them with colored chalk, markers, clay, or by typing them.

E. **Science**
You have learned about various aspects of science that relate to your study of the Jamestown colony. One thing you read and thought about is water. Look through your Student Notebook, and tell your teacher what you have learned about bodies of water and the life around them.

Here are some hints if you need them:

- rivers
- the water cycle
- pollution
- categories of animals
- plants and trees

Talk with your teacher about how the above topics relate to the Jamestown colony. Then, choose at least two things that connect them to Jamestown, and write those two in your Student Notebook.

F. Writing

Now that you have almost completed your reader and the read-aloud book, make a book review card. The purpose of a book review card is to give a brief description of what you read or heard, and then to tell what you thought of the book. It should not include as much information as a book report. The goal is to give someone who has not read the book enough information to decide whether or not they might like to read it. In a sense, it is like an advertisement for a book. Give enough information to let someone know the good points about the book, while not retelling the story.

How to Create a Book Review Card:

Your book review can be written on a large index card or on the page provided in your Student Notebook. Include the following information on your card:

- name of the book

- author of the book (person who wrote the book)

- illustrator of the book (person who drew the pictures)

- name of the company who published the book

- date the book was published

Most of this information can be found on the title page of the book.

Rehearse, or practice telling, what you will say about the story and how you liked it. Once you have discussed your thoughts enough to know what you want to write, you can begin. If you don't know how to spell some of the words you want to use, ask your teacher to make a word bank for you, or look at your Jamestown Word Bank.

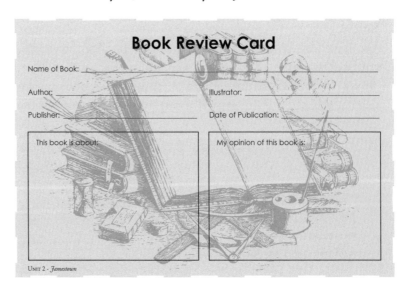

Book Review Card

Name of Book:

Author: Illustrator:

Publisher: Date of Publication:

This book is about: My opinion of this book is:

UNIT 2 - *Jamestown*

Next, write a few sentences to tell what the story was about. Since you only have a few sentences, you will have to choose the most important facts to tell.

Finally, write a few sentences to tell what you thought about the story. It would be good to tell whether you liked the book and then give some examples of what you did or did not like about it. Remember to use your Jamestown Word Bank to help you.

꙰ Create a book review card on the reader, *A Lion to Guard Us*.

꙰ Create a book review card on either the reader, *A Lion to Guard Us*, or the read-aloud, *Surviving Jamestown*.

꙰ Create a book review card on the read-aloud book, *Surviving Jamestown*.

G. Independent Reading

Choose something to read that you will enjoy. Find a quiet, comfortable place and read for the following length of time:

꙰ 20 minutes

꙰ 25 minutes

꙰ 30 minutes

Over time, it's fun to see how much you have read. Be sure to write down what you read today on the Reading Log in your Student Notebook.

G. See Independent Reading note in Part 1.

Lesson 6, Part 4

A. Copywork/Dictation   *Language Skills*

Look carefully at the following passage, and read it silently. Show your teacher any words you don't know, and practice saying them aloud. Now read the passage aloud, or ask your teacher to read it to you.

> We are grateful to those first settlers of Jamestown. Since they lived through such difficult times, the first permanent English settlement in America survived and was the beginning of a new country. As John Smith would say, "Huzzah!"

A. See Copywork/Dictation note in Part 1.

❧❧ Copy the above lines into your Student Notebook. When you are finished, compare your copy to the model (word by word) and make any needed corrections.

❧ Listen as your teacher dictates the above lines, and write them in your Student Notebook. When you are finished, compare your copy to the model and make any needed corrections.

❧ Finish copying the rest of Sam Collier's letter on pages 170 and 171 in *Surviving Jamestown*. When you are finished, compare your copy to the text and make any needed corrections.

B. Reader

Language Skills, Thinking Skills, History

Read the Historical Note on pages 116 and 117 in *A Lion to Guard Us*.

❧ Read one or two paragraphs in your read-aloud book, *Surviving Jamestown*.

❧ Read one or two pages from today's read-aloud assignment in *Surviving Jamestown*.

C. See Discussion note in Part 2.

C. Read-Aloud and Discussion

Language Skills, Thinking Skills

Listen carefully as your teacher reads page 177 through paragraph 7 on page 180 aloud from *Surviving Jamestown*.

Listen as your teacher reads the story and the following discussion question. Think about what you know from the story, and answer in your own words. Give any examples you can think of that help show your answer.

Discussion Question: As the number of settlers and settlements grew, John Smith was required to be in charge of more and more. Some of the settlers thought he was too hard on them. Others didn't like him for treating gentlemen like common workers. Do you think John Smith was a good leader? Why or why not?

D. The goal of vocabulary study is to build knowledge of words and their meanings in a natural manner. Part of that building process is review and connection to meaning. Again, understanding and the ability to use the word—not memorization—is the goal.

D. Word Study

Spelling, Phonics, Vocabulary

Gather together all the vocabulary cards you made for the last unit about Columbus. Practice reading the words and telling what you think they mean.

Make a stack of the words you remember, and another stack of words you need to review.

From the stack of words you remember, tell your teacher how you think each word relates to your study of Jamestown.

E. History

Language Skills

Listen to or read the story about William Shakespeare in *Profiles from History.* Complete the timeline activities and any other activities you would like to do.

F. Art

Tomorrow you will complete your read-aloud book, *Surviving Jamestown.* In preparation for the end of this unit, review the chapter titles of this book and look at the pictures in each chapter. Discuss the main events that occurred in each chapter. Choose one event out of this story that you think was interesting and draw a picture of it to go in your Student Notebook. Underneath the picture, tell what event you chose and why.

G. Independent Reading

Choose something to read that you will enjoy. Find a quiet, comfortable place and read for the following length of time:

G. See Independent Reading note in Part 1.

🐾🐾 20 minutes

🐾 25 minutes

🐾 30 minutes

Congratulations on completing six weeks of independent reading! Today's entry in your reading log will be the last one for this unit. Make sure you have included all the information needed on your log such as book titles, authors, and dates read.

Look over all that you have accomplished during your independent reading time. If you would like, share your reading log with others during your Unit Presentation tomorrow.

Lesson 6, Part 5

This part is set aside for completion of any work left undone from the lesson, and review of concepts and content. It is also a time to expand the work in the lesson by doing art, timeline activities, or games.

• On the large outline map of the world label all the places from the list in Lesson 6, Part 2, Section E, that have not yet been placed on your map.

• Listen carefully as your teacher reads pages 185 through 193 aloud from *Surviving Jamestown.* You may want to look through the

Most of the labeling has already been completed in the Student Notebook during this lesson. Instruct students to use the maps in their Student Notebooks as a reference. When they label the larger map, students will see the "big picture" and gain a broader understanding of their lessons.

Author's Note at the end of the book for further information on the Jamestown settlement.

• Listen as your teacher reviews the Steps for Thinking from the unit on Jamestown that you have just completed. Discuss how you can apply the Steps for Thinking to what you have learned.

• Make a Unit Presentation to your family telling about what you have learned in the unit you have just completed on Jamestown and the colony that was established there. Share your Student Notebook, the poems, and the artwork you have prepared for display. You may also choose to read or recite the poems you have written as well as "The Kingfisher" poem from the *Handbook of Nature Study.*

Use your Explorer page as a guideline to tell what you have learned about John Smith. Don't forget to speak clearly and stand still while speaking. After your presentation, don't forget to ask if anyone has questions.

• Play Jamestown Bingo or the Old World/New World game.

Congratulations on completing Unit 2 of *Paths of Exploration!*

Teachers can find a copy of these games in Appendix B. Instructions and answer keys for all games are located in Appendix A.

Lesson 1, Part 1

```
╔══════════════════════════════════════════╗
║            ∮ Steps for Thinking ∮          ║
║                                            ║
║  1. It takes strong motivation to cause    ║
║     someone to leave the place he          ║
║     considers his home. When someone       ║
║     does leave his home, it gives you      ║
║     insight into the strength of his       ║
║     convictions or the difficulty of       ║
║     his situation.                         ║
║                                            ║
║  2. There is a strong connection between   ║
║     the geography of the land and the      ║
║     lifestyle of the people.               ║
╚══════════════════════════════════════════╝
```

The **Steps for Thinking** section gives you the main ideas about the topics presented. Understanding these helps you to have productive discussions with your children so they, too, understand the bigger ideas. This forms more permanent learning, contrary to just learning facts, which tends to be temporary. These steps are useful prior to instruction, and they are also useful for review at the end of the week.

∾ *Materials* ∾

- *Squanto*
- *Stories of the Pilgrims*
- *Stories of the Pilgrims Answer Key*
- *Intermediate World Atlas*
- *Profiles from History*
- *North American Wildlife Guide*
- *Handbook of Nature Study*
- Access to King James version of the Bible, and one other translation
- Student Notebook
- Index cards and markers
- Scissors
- Materials for hands-on spelling such as dry erase board and markers, colored chalk, modeling clay, or water-based paint and paper
- Composition book
- Small plastic bag
- Old or "extra" family pictures
- Glue
- Colored pencils or crayons
- Large world outline map

Additional resources for Enrichment Activities are found in Part 5.

A. **Copywork/Dictation**   *Language Skills*

Life in England in 1600 was quite different from life in America today. People were ruled by kings and queens and did not have the freedom we hold so dear. King James ruled over how people in his kingdom could worship God.

🐾 Copy the above lines into your Student Notebook. When you are finished, compare your copy to the model (word by word) and make any needed corrections.

🐾 Listen as your teacher dictates the above lines, and write them in your Student Notebook. When you are finished, compare your copy to the model and make any needed corrections.

🐾 Copy, or write as your teacher dictates, paragraph 5 on page 9 ("It seemed . . .") in *Stories of the Pilgrims*. When you are finished, compare your copy to the text and make any needed corrections.

B. **Reader**   *Language Skills, Thinking Skills, History*
In your book, *Squanto,* read pages 5–9 aloud.

🐾 Read one or two paragraphs in your read-aloud book, *Stories of the Pilgrims.*

🐾 Read one or two pages from today's read-aloud assignment in *Stories of the Pilgrims.*

A. Copywork and dictation assignments go from an easier level (designated by 🐾) to harder levels (designated by 🐾 and 🐾). Take two days for the copywork if that is more comfortable for your child. Please adapt instructions to your child's individual needs. Your child should be **consistently successful** at one level before progressing to the next, **regardless of grade**.

C. Answers to Comprehension Questions are found in the *Stories of the Pilgrims Answer Key.*

D. In this unit you will create some new tools that will help focus on your child's individual spelling needs. Word Study for this unit will consist of three or four words from reading assignments each week. You and your child may want to choose three to five additional words to work on. If you decide to work on more words, choose them from words your child has read or spelled incorrectly. Do *not* work on more than eight to ten words each week.

Personal Dictionary: Help your child create a personal dictionary for help with writing. Use a composition book and label one or two pages with each letter of the alphabet. When your child is able to spell a word correctly by Part 4, have him write the word in his personal dictionary on the page with the correct beginning letter. Do not worry about alphabetizing or defining these words. The purpose is for your child to use this as a tool to help him when he wants to write. Remember, the focus should not be memorization only, but the ability to use his personal dictionary to write.

Letter Cards: Another tool will be the addition of Letter Cards to use for spelling practice. Use index cards to make your set of Letter Cards. Either you or your child can make the cards by cutting 4 × 6 index cards in half. Make 20 copies of each vowel letter (*a, e, i, o, u*) and 10 copies of all of the most frequently used consonant letters (*b, c, d, f, g, h, k, l, m, n, p, r, s, t, w*). Now make 5 copies of the less frequently used consonants (*j, q, v, x, y, z*). Put your letter cards in a small plastic bag.

C. Read-Aloud and Discussion
Language Skills, Thinking Skills

In *Stories of the Pilgrims,* listen as your teacher reads pages 1 through the top of page 10 aloud.

Listen as your teacher reads the Comprehension Questions on page 5 in *Stories of the Pilgrims.* Talk with your teacher about what you think the answers are.

D. Word Study
Spelling, Phonics, Vocabuary

Read these words from your study of the Pilgrims, or listen as your teacher reads them:

> Separatists
> King James
> Scrooby Inn

Now practice reading them silently. Use your Letter Cards to spell these words and any other words you and your teacher choose for this lesson.

Make a list of your word study words on the Pilgrim Word Bank sheet in your Student Notebook.

E. Geography
History, Science

The story of the Pilgrims begins in England, which is part of the British Isles. Part of understanding why people move from place to place is understanding where they have come from. The sacrifice that the Pilgrims made would not seem so great if you did not know that they loved their homes in England, and the only reason they could not stay there was because of the struggle they had with the laws of King James.

Look at Map P-1 of the British Isles and find England. Notice that it is a country that is surrounded by water. Water played an important role in the lives of the Pilgrims. Find the following bodies of water in and around England:

> Atlantic Ocean   Irish Sea
> North Sea   Thames River

Now label these bodies of water on the map in your Student Notebook.

Larger bodies of water such as oceans and seas have a name for the place where the land and the water meet. This place is called the **shore.** Use your finger to trace around the map of England, where the land meets the ocean and sea. Notice how long the shoreline is in England. There were long stretches of shore not far from the homes of the Pilgrims. This fact became important to them as they started to consider ways to leave their homeland.

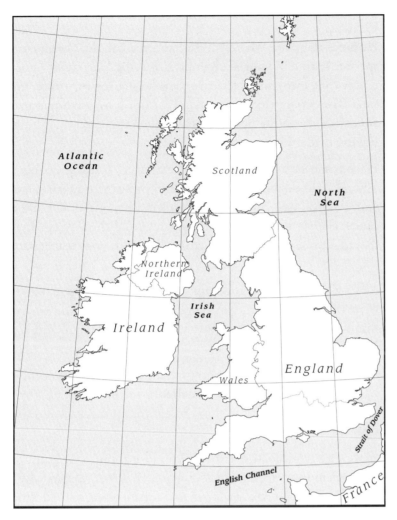

Map P-1

Two important, but smaller, bodies of water that are close to England are the English Channel and the Strait of Dover. A **channel** is a wide waterway that goes between an island and a larger body of land, and a **strait** is a narrow waterway that joins two larger bodies of water. Find these on the map of the British Isles. What island and body of land does the English Channel go between?[1] What two bodies of water does the Strait of Dover connect?[2]

Label this channel and strait on the map in your Student Notebook.

🐾 Look at the Physical Map for each continent in the *Intermediate World Atlas*. Try to find at least two other channels and two other straits. Write the names of the channels and straits that you find in your Student Notebook.

🐾 Look at the Physical Map for each continent in the *Intermediate World Atlas*. Try to find a channel and a strait on each continent's map. These types of waterways may not exist on every continent, but list those you find in your Student Notebook. Remember the definitions of these terms when you are looking at the maps.

E. Each word in bold letters is considered a vocabulary word. It is a word that may or may not be new to your child. You can write these vocabulary words on index cards and use them for occasional review, but not for memorizing. Give the child the meaning of the words if he doesn't remember. Try to use the new vocabulary words during conversation, and encourage your students to do the same.

Each time your student makes a vocabulary card for this unit, have him write a "P" (for Pilgrims) in the upper left corner. This will make it possible to review vocabulary by unit at the end of the year.

The small superscript numbers that appear after some of the questions in this unit refer to answers found in the answer key, located immediately after Part 5.

F. Writing   *Thinking Skills*

Home is the place where you live and the people who make it special. People in your read-aloud story (the Separatists) and in your reader (Squanto) chose to leave their homes for very different reasons. The Separatists were looking for freedom and Squanto wanted adventure. Both the Separatists and Squanto loved their homes, and leaving made them both sad.

Have you ever had to move to a new home? It was probably very difficult. Think about your home and things that make it special to you. For example, Squanto loved his mother and father and also his other relatives who lived nearby. He enjoyed the forests where he had played and hunted for many years. Talk with your teacher about the things you enjoy about your home.

Make a list of at least three things you love about your home and write them in your Student Notebook. Tell one reason why you think it would be hard to move to another place, and add it to your list.

Make a list of at least four things you love about your home and write them in your Student Notebook. Tell two reasons why you think it would be hard to move to another place, and add them to your list.

Make a list of at least five things you love about your home and write them in your Student Notebook. Tell two reasons why you think it would be hard to move to another place, and add them to your list. Talk with your teacher about any possible reasons for moving that might be exciting. Choose one and add it to your list.

G. Independent Reading

Choose something to read that you will enjoy. Find a quiet, comfortable place and read for the following length of time:

20 minutes

25 minutes

30 minutes

Over time, it's fun to see how much you have read. Be sure to write down what you read today on the Reading Log in your Student Notebook.

G. Reading fluency is developed through having frequent silent reading opportunities that continue for the length of time suggested here. Since a primary focus of this activity is to nurture your child's enjoyment of reading, help him to choose reading material that interests him and is at a level that allows him to read with understanding by himself. You can incorporate this activity into your school day whenever it is most convenient.

If the suggested length of time is too long for your child to continue reading by himself, start with an amount of time he can accomplish successfully and make the suggested time a goal.

Lesson 1, Part 2

A. Copywork/Dictation   *Language Skills*

> When men refused to attend the King's Church in England they could be sent to prison. Some people did not agree with the beliefs of the Church of England and separated themselves in order to worship freely. These people were called Separatists.

🐾 Copy the above lines into your Student Notebook. When you are finished, compare your copy to the model (word by word) and make any needed corrections.

🐾 Listen as your teacher dictates the above lines, and write them in your Student Notebook. When you are finished, compare your copy to the model and make any needed corrections.

🐾 Copy, or write as your teacher dictates, paragraph 1 on page 13 ("For a time . . .") in *Stories of the Pilgrims.* When you are finished, compare your copy to the text and make any needed corrections.

B. Reader   *Language Skills, Thinking Skills, History*

In your book, *Squanto,* read page 10 to the end of paragraph 1 on page 15 aloud.

🐾 Read one or two paragraphs in your read-aloud book, *Stories of the Pilgrims.*

🐾 Read one or two pages from today's read-aloud assignment in *Stories of the Pilgrims.*

C. Read-Aloud and Narration   *Language Skills, Thinking Skills*

Listen carefully as your teacher reads from top of page 10 through page 20 aloud from *Stories of the Pilgrims.*

To *narrate* means to retell. In your own words, tell what happened in your assigned passage below. Try to remember as many details as possible. Listen carefully as your teacher reads (or rereads) the part you are to retell.

🐾 Reread pages 9 and 10 of *Squanto.* Tell your teacher what Squanto's uncle said about the visitors.

🐾 Use the book and pictures to retell the chapter "A Ship from Far Away" to your teacher.

A. The dictation method enables your child to hear language and correctly write down what he hears. It involves building two different skills. First, the ability to listen and understand what is heard, and second, the ability to transfer what is heard into written language. This process takes time and practice, so begin as gradually as needed for successfully reaching the goal of getting the words the child hears on the paper correctly. 1) Read the whole passage, then reread one sentence at a time, giving your child time to write what he hears. 2) After he has finished, reread the passage again, allowing him to double check what he has written. 3) Then proceed to the step of comparing his writing to the model. As his skill builds, you can move more quickly through the steps, maintaining your child's level of success.

C. The skill of narration is gained over time. If your child has never retold a story, start with the assignment for the lower level, no matter what grade he is in. Work up from there, being careful to allow him to stay at the level of success for a while before going to a longer section.

🐾 Tell your teacher about the chapter entitled "Meeting in Secret" in *Stories of the Pilgrims.*

D. Word Study   *Spelling, Phonics, Vocabulary*

Look at the list of spelling words you wrote in your Student Notebook in Part 1. Read the words silently, or listen as your teacher reads them.

Now say each word and tell how many syllables, or word parts you hear in each word. Write the number of syllables you hear in each word next to the word.

Choose a way to practice your spelling words from the list below:

- Dry erase board and markers.
- Colored chalk and chalkboard *or* sidewalk.
- Modeling clay.
- Water-based paint and paper.
- Letter cards.

E. Each time your student makes an Animal I.D. card for this unit, have him write a "P" (for Pilgrim) in the upper left corner. This will make it possible to review the animals studied by unit at the end of the year.

E. Science

Hunting in the time of the Pilgrims was a primary way of obtaining food. Because of the many ponds, lakes, and rivers in the area, ducks were plentiful. Some of the ducks that are commonly found in England are also commonly found in North America. While not a primary source of food today, wild ducks are still enjoyed in Europe and North America as a vital part of nature.

The mallard is a very common duck. Look on page 90 in your *North American Wildlife Guide.* Draw or trace and color the male and female in your Student Notebook. Tell how big the mallard is, where it lives, and what it eats.[3]

The northern pintail, also found on page 90 in the *North America Wildlife Guide,* is a "dabbling" or "tip-up" eater like the mallard. That means they both tip their heads down to search for food on the bottom of the pond, causing their tails to stick up. Draw or trace and color the male and female northern pintail in your Student Notebook. Tell how big it is and where it lives.[4]

Make Animal I.D. cards like those you made in the Jamestown Unit for each of these birds.

The common goldeneye is also found in both Europe and North America. Draw or trace and color the male and female in your Student Notebook. Tell how big it is and where it lives.[5] Tell what unusual sound it makes.[6] Make Animal I.D. cards for the common goldeneye.

The green-winged teal can be smaller than the other birds, but its colors make it very noticeable. Draw or trace and color the male green-winged teal in your Student Notebook. Tell how big it is and where it lives.[7] Make Animal I.D. cards for the green-winged teal.

Do further research on the waterfowl (including ducks) that are found in England either at the library or on the Internet. With your parent's permission, a good place to do research is online at the Royal Society for the Protection of Birds, or www.rspb.org.uk. Tell your teacher what you found out.

F. Art

Yesterday you wrote about your home. By sharing the things you love about it, and what you would miss, you created a picture with words. Today you will add more meaning to your words by creating a collage of pictures or drawings that show what you love about your home. With your parent's permission, gather together photographs of anything or anyone that makes it special for you, such as holiday celebrations, birthdays, pets, relatives, or friends. Arrange these pictures around the words you wrote yesterday and glue them in place.

G. Independent Reading

Choose something to read that you will enjoy. Find a quiet, comfortable place and read for the following length of time:

- 20 minutes
- 25 minutes
- 30 minutes

Over time, it's fun to see how much you have read. Be sure to write down what you read today on the Reading Log in your Student Notebook.

G. See Independent Reading note in Part 1.

Lesson 1, Part 3

A. Copywork/Dictation　　　　　　　　　*Language Skills*

With your teacher's help, choose a passage from your reader or another book that you enjoy reading. Copy, or write as your teacher dictates, the passage you chose. When you are finished, compare your copy to the text and make any needed corrections. Follow the guidelines below for the minimum assignment:

🐾 At least 3 sentences

🐾 At least 4 sentences

🐾 At least 5 sentences

B. Reader　　　　　*Language Skills, Thinking Skills, History*

In your book, *Squanto,* read from paragraph 2 on page 15 through page 19 aloud.

🐾 Read one or two paragraphs in your read-aloud book, *Stories of the Pilgrims.*

🐾 Read one or two pages from today's read-aloud assignment in *Stories of the Pilgrims.*

C. Read-Aloud and Discussion　　　*Language Skills, Thinking Skills*

In *Stories of the Pilgrims,* listen as your teacher reads pages 21-30 aloud.

Listen as your teacher reads the Comprehension Questions on page 25 in *Stories of the Pilgrims.* Talk with your teacher about what you think the answers are.

C. Discussion is very important in developing your child's ability to organize his thoughts. This in turn builds the ability to think and write. The goal of the discussion questions is not just to find the answer to a particular question, but also to create a situation where thoughts about the question and its answer are shared and considered in a detailed way. Do not rush this activity, but encourage your student to share his or her ideas relating to the topic, and any additional ideas that may come to mind. You can also share your thoughts and questions as an example for your students.

Answers to discussion Comprehension Questions are found in the *Stories of the Pilgrims Answer Key.*

D. Word Study　　　　　*Spelling, Phonics, Vocabulary*

Tell your teacher what each spelling word means and how it relates to your Pilgrim study. In your Student Notebook, fill out a Pilgrim Word Bank entry for each of your words and include this information.

Practice your words by using one of the following:

- Dry erase board and markers.
- Colored chalk and chalkboard *or* sidewalk.
- Modeling clay.
- Water-based paint and paper.
- Letter cards.

E. Geography

History

At the time the Pilgrims' story began, King James required everyone to go to the same church. This was a result of many things that had happened in the country, and King James felt it was best for his people. The Pilgrims did not agree, and began to meet in their own churches in secret. Breaking King James' law was hard for the Pilgrims to do, but they felt they had to obey the laws of God as they understood them. Though they were very law-abiding people, they could not obey the laws about church because it would mean going against their **conscience,** or sense of right and wrong. It is because of this sense of conflict that the Pilgrims thought of leaving their beloved homes.

William Brewster was one of the **elders**, or leaders, of the Pilgrims. He owned and operated the Scrooby Inn, in the town of Scrooby, England. Find Scrooby on Map P-2. Notice that it is close to the town of Lincoln. Lincoln was near the childhood home of John Smith, explorer and leader of Jamestown. Find Lincoln on the map. Add these two towns to the map in your Student Notebook.

Map P-2

A **landmark** is a place that is well-known to people. There is a landmark near the town of Scrooby that is known to most people who love great stories. It is Sherwood Forest, the home of the character Robin Hood. In the book *The Adventures of Robin Hood,* the main character and his band of followers broke laws made by the ruler of England that went against their consciences. Talk with your parents about how to deal with rules that disagree with your conscience.

Find Sherwood Forest on the map. Add it to the map in your Student Notebook.

Find the cities of London and Plymouth. Both of these cities will be important to the events told about in your readers. Add them to your map. Plymouth is a **port,** which is a city that has a harbor. A **harbor** is a place of safety where ships come and go, loading and unloading cargo.

On Map P-2, look at the water around the city of Plymouth. You will see numbers there. These numbers tell the depths of the water in **fathoms.** A fathom is six feet. Which measurement shows the most shallow water?[8] Which measurement shows the deepest water?[9]

To figure out the depth in feet, multiply the number of fathoms by six. Figure out the depth of water in feet for each fathom measurement shown, and write it on your map.

Why is the depth of water around a harbor important?[10] Who would need this information in order to be safe?[11]

F. **Writing**

Many times you will be asked to answer a question with a complete sentence. This is not a difficult thing to do. The key is to use the words in the question as a word bank. Here is an example:

> Question – What was the name of the explorer who became the leader of Jamestown?

> Answer – The explorer who became the leader of Jamestown was John Smith.

As you can see, the beginning of the answer was taken from the question. The explorer's name is all that was added. All the words you need may not always be in the question, but the words you need to start your answer will be. Look at the next example:

> Question – Why do you think the Jamestown Colony had so many struggles?

Answer – I think the Jamestown Colony had so many struggles because the people were not prepared for such a hard life.

Using words from the question will help you make sure your answer is a complete thought. In this unit you will be answering questions contained in *Stories of the Pilgrims.* Remember to answer these questions with complete sentences. You may use the Pilgrim Word Bank you are creating as well as the words in the questions to help you with your answers.

F. Answers to *Stories of the Pilgrims* questions are in the *Stories of the Pilgrims Answer Key.*

❦❦ Read question 1 on page 17 in *Stories of the Pilgrims.* Now go back to the beginning of the chapter, "Meeting in Secret," and find the paragraph that tells about two strangers. Listen as your teacher rereads this paragraph, and then write the answer in your Student Notebook. Be sure to use a complete sentence.

❦ Read questions 1-3 on page 17 in *Stories of the Pilgrims.* Go to the beginning of the chapter, "Meeting in Secret," and find the paragraphs that relate to each question. **Skim,** or look at without reading all the words, through these paragraphs to find the information you need to answer each question with a complete sentence. Write the answers in your Student Notebook.

❦ Read questions 1-5 on page 17 in *Stories of the Pilgrims.* Go to the beginning of the chapter, "Meeting in Secret," and find the paragraphs that relate to each question. **Skim,** or look at without reading all the words, through these paragraphs to find the information you need to answer each question with a complete sentence. Write the answers in your Student Notebook.

G. Independent Reading

Choose something to read that you will enjoy. Find a quiet, comfortable place and read for the following length of time:

G. See Independent Reading note in Part I.

❦❦ 20 minutes

❦ 25 minutes

❦ 30 minutes

Over time, it's fun to see how much you have read. Be sure to write down what you read today on the Reading Log in your Student Notebook.

Lesson 1, Part 4

A. See Copywork/Dictation note in Part 1.

A. **Copywork/Dictation**　　　　*Language Skills*

> A group of Separatists met and worshiped at Scrooby Inn, owned by Elder William Brewster. After being treated badly again and again, the Separatists decided to leave England even though they loved their homes and way of life.

🐾 Copy the above lines into your Student Notebook. When you are finished, compare your copy to the model (word by word) and make any needed corrections.

🐾 Listen as your teacher dictates the above lines, and write them in your Student Notebook. When you are finished, compare your copy to the model and make any needed corrections.

🐾 Copy, or write as your teacher dictates, paragraph 3 on page 31 ("They peered . . .") in *Stories of the Pilgrims*. When you are finished, compare your copy to the text and make any needed corrections.

B. **Reader**　　　*Language Skills, Thinking Skills, History*
In your book, *Squanto,* read pages 20–24 aloud.

🐾 Read one or two paragraphs in your read-aloud book, *Stories of the Pilgrims.*

🐾 Read one or two pages from today's read-aloud assignment in *Stories of the Pilgrims.*

C. See Narration note in Part 2.

C. **Read-Aloud and Narration**　　*Language Skills, Thinking Skills*
Listen carefully as your teacher reads pages 31-41 aloud from *Stories of the Pilgrims.*

To *narrate* means to retell. In your own words, tell what happened in your assigned passage below. Try to remember as many details as possible. Listen carefully as your teacher reads (or rereads) the part you are to retell.

🐾 Reread page 16 of *Squanto.* Tell your teacher what happened to Squanto.

🐾 Use the book and pictures to retell the chapter "The Fire-Stick" to your teacher.

🐾 Tell your teacher about the chapter entitled "Away to Holland" in *Stories of the Pilgrims.*

D. Word Study

Spelling, Phonics, Vocabulary

Review the word study words you are working on in this lesson by reading them, spelling them aloud, and then checking to see if you were correct.

When you feel you are ready, spell them for your teacher. Once you have done that, and your teacher gives you permission, write your word study words in your personal dictionary.

Look through your personal dictionary and choose several words to spell aloud for your teacher.

E. Science

On the map of British Isles in your Student Notebook, you have labeled Sherwood Forest. This **forest,** or large area of trees growing close together, was used by royalty long ago as a place for hunting. Now it has been set aside as a park. Many different types of trees can be found there, but the most famous are the oak trees. There are many different types of oak trees in North America as well.

 Look at pages 638 through 640 in your *Handbook of Nature Study.* Read, or listen as your teacher reads, about oak trees. Ask your parent if there are any oak trees near where you live. So you can recognize the oak trees around you, look at pages 304–306 in the *North American Wildlife Guide.*

Listen as your teacher reads Lesson 176 in the *Handbook of Nature Study* on pages 641 and 642. Write your answers to questions 1-3 in your Student Notebook. Remember not to put anything in your mouth without your teacher's permission.

Read questions 1-6, 8 and 9 in Lesson 176 in the *Handbook of Nature Study,* and complete as many of them as possible. Write your answers in your Student Notebook. Remember not to put anything in your mouth without your teacher's permission.

F. Art

History, Thinking Skills

Look at the words you have added to your Pilgrim Word Bank during this lesson. Illustrations can help you remember what words mean and the way they are used. Use your reader or read-aloud book for ideas and draw a picture to illustrate each of these words. Your drawing can show what the word means or something that reminds you of the word, like a crown for King James. Use colored pencils or crayons to complete your illustrations.

G. See Independent Reading note in Part 1.

Most of the labeling has already been completed in the Student Notebook during this lesson. Instruct students to use the maps in their Student Notebooks as a reference. When they label the larger map, students will see the "big picture" and gain a broader understanding of their lessons.

To read different translations of the Bible online (including the King James version), visit www.biblegateway.com.

G. **Independent Reading**

Choose something to read that you will enjoy. Find a quiet, comfortable place and read for the following length of time:

✵ 20 minutes

✵ 25 minutes

✵ 30 minutes

Over time, it's fun to see how much you have read. Be sure to write down what you read today on the Reading Log in your Student Notebook.

Lesson 1, Part 5

This part is set aside for completion of any work left undone from the lesson, and review of concepts and content. It is also a time to expand the work in the lesson by doing art, timeline activities, or games.

• Review the Steps for Thinking from the beginning of this lesson.

• On the large outline map of the world label: North Sea; Irish Sea; Straits of Dover; Ireland; Northern Ireland; Scotland; Scrooby, England; and Plymouth, England.

• Review the spelling words for this lesson. In your Student Notebook, write a sentence using each word that tells how it is related to the unit. Do your best to write the spelling words correctly. After you have finished, check your sentences against the list in your Student Notebook and see how many spelling words you spelled correctly. (Don't count off for other words that are misspelled.) Remember your goal is to improve, not necessarily to get them all right immediately.

• Be sure to look at all the words in your Pilgrim dictionary and tell your teacher what they mean.

• Do the Pilgrim Word Search in your Student Notebook.

• King James is best remembered for commissioning the first English translation of the Bible. Talk with your parents about the difference between this translation of the Bible and other translations. What do you notice the most about the King James translation? If it is available to you, read a well-known scripture in this translation, such as Psalm 23. If possible, now read this passage in another version and compare the two.

Enrichment Activities

1. In this lesson, you read about Sherwood Forest, home of the legendary figure, Robin Hood. Read the book, *The Adventures of Robin Hood* by Howard Pyle, or with your parent's permission, watch one of the many video versions of this story. Tell what you like best about the story and any connections you see between the story of Robin Hood and the Pilgrims.

2. King James followed a very successful ruler in England who had recently passed away. Queen Elizabeth I ruled England from 1559 to 1603 and her rule was called the Golden Age. Learn about her and prepare a presentation to share what you learn.

Additional Resources

The Adventures of Robin Hood by Howard Pyle

Video versions of *Robin Hood*

www.sherwoodforest.org.uk – An online resource about the Sherwood Forest Park and Sherwood Forest Trust.

Books or videos about Queen Elizabeth

www.elizabethi.org – An online resource about Queen Elizabeth I.

Who's That Stepping on Plymouth Rock? by Jean Fritz

Use one or more of the Enrichment Activities if your child completes his assigned work and has the time or desire to learn more. These activities are flexible, so choose the one(s) that seem most interesting to your student. Allow him to work at a level that is appropriate for him, and remember that the learning process is more important than the product.

It is suggested that parents preview all videos.

Answers

1. England is the island and Europe is the larger body of land.

2. the English Channel and the North Sea

3. mallard: 16 – 24 inches, lives in shallow ponds and marshes, eats plants and animals at the bottom of the pond or marsh, grain.

4. northern pintail: 20 – 30 inches, lives in lakes, ponds, and marshes.

5. common goldeneye: 15 – 20 inches, lives in rivers, lakes, and bays.

6. They make a ringing sound when they fly.

7. green-winged teal: 23 – 26 inches, lives in shallow ponds, lakes, streams, and marshes.

8. four

9. 42

10. The larger a ship is, the deeper the water needs to be so it can travel safely in and out.

11. the captain or navigator

Lesson 2, Part 1

> ### ⸎ Steps for Thinking ⸎
>
> 1. The absence of an outward struggle does not always mean the presence of peace. If you are not acting in agreement with your conscience, you cannot be at peace.
>
> 2. You are influenced by many things around you. You must constantly evaluate how to respond to situations and ideas, based on your worldview.

The **Steps for Thinking** section gives you the main ideas about the topics presented. Understanding these helps you to have productive discussions with your children so they, too, understand the bigger ideas. This forms more permanent learning, contrary to just learning facts, which tends to be temporary. These steps are useful prior to instruction, and they are also useful for review at the end of the week.

𝒜. Copywork/Dictation   *Language Skills*

They had many troubles leaving England. On one try, the women and children were stranded when the ship's captain set sail without them. Eventually they all made it to Amsterdam, Holland, to avoid the bad treatment by King James.

🐾 Copy the above lines into your Student Notebook. When you are finished, compare your copy to the model (word by word) and make any needed corrections.

🐾 Listen as your teacher dictates the above lines, and write them in your Student Notebook. When you are finished, compare your copy to the model and make any needed corrections.

🐾 Copy, or write as your teacher dictates, paragraph 4 on page 42 ("What were . . .") in *Stories of the Pilgrims*. When you are finished, compare your copy to the text and make any needed corrections.

ℬ. Reader   *Language Skills, Thinking Skills, History*
In your book, *Squanto*, read pages 25–29 aloud.

🐾 Read one or two paragraphs in your read-aloud book, *Stories of the Pilgrims*.

🐾 Read one or two pages from today's read-aloud assignment in *Stories of the Pilgrims*.

⸎ Materials ⸎

- *Squanto*
- *Stories of the Pilgrims*
- *Stories of the Pilgrims* Answer Key
- *Intermediate World Atlas*
- *North American Wildlife Guide*
- *Eat Your Way Around the World*
- Materials for hands-on spelling: dry erase board and markers, colored chalk, modeling clay, water-based paint and paper, or Letter Cards
- Index cards/marker
- Student notebook
- Colored pencils or crayons
- Plain or tracing paper
- Access to Internet or Library
- Personal dictionary
- Large world outline map

Additional resources for Enrichment Activities are found in Part 5.

𝒜. Copywork and dictation assignments go from an easier level (designated by 🐾) to harder levels (designated by 🐾 and 🐾). Take two days for the copywork if that is more comfortable for your child. Please adapt instructions to your child's individual needs. Your child should be **consistently successful** at one level before progressing to the next, **regardless of grade**.

C. Answers to the discussion Comprehension Questions are found in the *Stories of the Pilgrims Answer Key.*

E. Each word in bold letters is considered a vocabulary word. It is a word that may or may not be new to your child. You can write these vocabulary words on index cards and use them for occasional review, but not for memorizing. Give the child the meaning of the words if he doesn't remember. Try to use the new vocabulary words during conversation, and encourage your students to do the same.

Each time your student makes a vocabulary card for this unit, have him write a "P" (for Pilgrims) in the upper left corner. This will make it possible to review vocabulary by unit at the end of the year.

C. **Read-Aloud and Discussion**   *Language Skills, Thinking Skills*

In *Stories of the Pilgrims,* listen as your teacher reads pages 42-52 aloud.

Listen as your teacher reads the Comprehension Questions on page 45 in *Stories of the Pilgrims.* Talk with your teacher about what you think the answers are.

D. **Word Study**   *Spelling, Phonics, Vocabulary*

Read these words from your study of the Pilgrims, or listen as your teacher reads them:

> Amsterdam
> Leiden, Holland
> Pewter dishes

Now practice reading them silently. Use your Letter Cards to spell these words and any other words you and your teacher choose for this lesson.

Make a list of your word study words in your Student Notebook. Ask your teacher to pick several words for you to practice spelling aloud.

E. **Geography**

The Separatists went to live in Amsterdam, which is the capital city of the Netherlands. This country has a shore along the sea, like England. But it is also different from England because the land is very low, so there is much more water.

Look at Map P-3 of the Netherlands. This country is made up of **provinces,** which are like states. North Holland and South Holland are two of those provinces, and make up an area known simply as Holland. This is the area you will learn about. Find these two provinces and label them on the map in your Student Notebook.

Since water is such an important part of life in Holland, find the following large bodies of water and label them on your map:

> North Sea   Ijsselmeer

Ijsselmeer is a large lake in Holland that used to be called the Southern Sea. A **dike,** or large wall, was built to keep out the saltwater. Over time, the salty water trapped inside the dike was pumped out, and fresh water from the Ijssel River flowed in. Eventually, it became a freshwater lake instead of a saltwater sea!

Several rivers flow across the Netherlands towards the North Sea. Find the following rivers and label them on your map:

> Rhine River   Waal River   Maas River   Ijssel River

Two cities in Holland were important to the visitors from England. Amsterdam was the first city the Pilgrims came to. They felt welcomed by the **Dutch**, which is what people who live in Holland are called. People who live in provinces other than North and South Holland are not considered Dutch. After leaving Amsterdam, the Pilgrims moved to a city named Leiden, where they lived for eleven years.

Label the cities of Amsterdam and Leiden on your map.

Holland is famous for its windmills, and they have an important purpose. Since there is so much water in the country, windmills pump extra water off of the land and back to the sea. As the arms of the windmill are blown by the wind and turn, it causes the pump to pump.

Look at the pictures of windmills on pages 34 and 39 in *Stories of the Pilgrims*. Sketch or trace a windmill in your Student Notebook and tell what it does.[1]

Read about the city of Venice, Italy. It is another city that is famous for its canals. Look for information at the library, or with your parent's permission, on the Internet.

Make a list of at least three things that are different in Venice from other cities you know about, because there is so much water.[2]

E. The small superscript numbers that appear after some of the questions in this unit refer to answers found in the answer key, located immediately after Part 5.

Map P-3

F. **Writing**   *History, Thinking Skills*

Read question 4 on page 30 in *Stories of the Pilgrims*. Now go back to page 29 of the chapter, "Away to Holland." Listen as your teacher rereads this page, and write the answer to question 4 in a complete

F. If your child has any trouble remembering how to answer questions in complete sentences, please go over the examples in Lesson 1, Part 3, Section F.

sentence. Write this answer in your Student Notebook. Remember to use your Pilgrim Word Bank to help you.

Read questions 1 and 2 on pages 29 and 30 in *Stories of the Pilgrims.* Go to the beginning of the chapter, "Away to Holland," and find the paragraphs that relate to each question. **Skim,** or look at without reading all the words, through these paragraphs to find the information you need to answer each question with a complete sentence. Write the answers in your Student Notebook. Remember to use your Pilgrim Word Bank to help you.

Read questions 1-4 on pages 29 and 30 in *Stories of the Pilgrims.* Go to the beginning of the chapter, "Away to Holland," and find the paragraphs that relate to each question. **Skim,** or look at without reading all the words, through these paragraphs to find the information you need to answer each question with a complete sentence. Write the answers in your Student Notebook. Remember to use your Pilgrim Word Bank to help you.

G. Reading fluency is developed through having frequent silent reading opportunities that continue for the length of time suggested here. Since a primary focus of this activity is to nurture your child's enjoyment of reading, help him to choose reading material that interests him and is at a level that allows him to read with understanding by himself. You can incorporate this activity into your school day whenever it is most convenient.

If the suggested length of time is too long for your child to continue reading by himself, start with an amount of time he can accomplish successfully and make the suggested time a goal.

G. Independent Reading

Choose something to read that you will enjoy. Find a quiet, comfortable place and read for the following length of time:

20 minutes

25 minutes

30 minutes

Over time, it's fun to see how much you have read. Be sure to write down what you read today on the Reading Log in your Student Notebook.

Lesson 2, Part 2

A. See Copywork/Dictation note in Part 1.

A. Copywork/Dictation   *Language Skills*

The Separatists who left their homes in England to find a new place to live were now called Pilgrims, or people who travel or wander from place to place. The Pilgrims moved to Leiden, Holland, where they lived for eleven years.

Copy the above lines into your Student Notebook. When you are finished, compare your copy to the model (word by word) and make any needed corrections.

🐾 Listen as your teacher dictates the above lines, and write them in your Student Notebook. When you are finished, compare your copy to the model and make any needed corrections.

🐾 Copy, or write as your teacher dictates, paragraph 2 on page 54 ("What a merry . . .") in *Stories of the Pilgrims*. When you are finished, compare your copy to the text and make any needed corrections.

B. Reader   *Language Skills, Thinking Skills, History*
In your book, *Squanto,* read pages 30–34 aloud.

🐾 Read one or two paragraphs in your read-aloud book, *Stories of the Pilgrims.*

🐾 Read one or two pages from today's read-aloud assignment in *Stories of the Pilgrims.*

C. Read-Aloud and Narration   *Language Skills, Thinking Skills*
Listen carefully as your teacher reads pages 53-62 aloud from *Stories of the Pilgrims.*

To *narrate* means to retell. In your own words, tell what happened in your assigned passage below. Try to remember as many details as possible. Listen carefully as your teacher reads (or rereads) the part you are to retell.

🌵🌵 Reread page 34 of *Squanto*. Tell your teacher what happened to Squanto when he first arrived in London.

🐾 Use the book and pictures to retell the chapter "Squanto and the Englishmen" to your teacher.

🐾 Tell your teacher about the chapter entitled "In Leiden" in *Stories of the Pilgrims.*

D. Word Study
Look at the list of spelling words you wrote in your Student Notebook in Part 1. Read the words silently, or listen as your teacher reads them.

Now say each word and tell how many syllables, or word parts you hear in each word. Write the number of syllables you hear in each word next to the word.

Choose a way to practice your spelling words from the list below:

- Dry erase board and markers
- Colored chalk and chalkboard *or* sidewalk
- Modeling clay
- Water-based paint and paper
- Letter Cards

C. The skill of narration is gained over time. If your child has never retold a story, start with the assignment for the lower level, no matter what grade he is in. Work up from there, being careful to allow him to stay at the level of success for a while before going to a longer section.

E. Science

Geography

Canals are very important in Holland. Canals are man-made waterways that are used for travel or carrying things. They are also used to bring water to fields and take extra water away. In Holland they were a big part of life everyday for the Separatists. Canal boats brought many of the things they needed, like fresh drinking water.

What do you think happened in the winter when it got so cold that the canals froze? During the Separatist's time, iceboats were used to carry things in the same way as the canal boats. Ice skating was also very popular for travel and for fun.

What is the climate like in Holland? Look at the Europe Physical Map in your *Intermediate World Atlas.* Find the Netherlands, which is colored the darkest green. Now look at the key. What level is the land?[3] This is the lowest level land can be.

Look at the Physical Map again. Are there any mountains nearby?[4] Mountains nearby would affect the climate.

Now look at the Europe Climate Map in your *Intermediate World Atlas.* Again, the Netherlands are the darkest green color. Look at the key. What is the climate like?[5] Do you remember what moderate means?[6]

The other factor to think about when you consider climate is how far away Holland is from the equator. Look at your globe and find the Netherlands. It is closer to the North Pole than it is to the Equator, so that would make the climate there colder than it is in America.

- Look at the Climate Map of Europe in the *Intermediate World Atlas.* Find two or three other countries that have the same climate as the Netherlands. You will need to look at the Europe Political Map to find out the names of the countries. Write their names in your Student Notebook.

- Look at the United States Climate Map in the *Intermediate World Atlas.* What places have the same climate as the Netherlands?[7] Look at the Climate Map of Europe. Is England's climate similar to the climate in the Netherlands?[8]

F. Art

You have been reading about the people of the Netherlands and the role they played in the Separatist's journey to freedom. There were many things that were memorable to the Pilgrims about their time in Holland. One of the things for which the people of Holland have always been famous is growing beautiful flowers such as tulips. Not only are these flowers pleasant to look at, they also represent a very large business. Flowers from Holland are sold all over the world.

🐾 Choose a flower to sketch in your Student Notebook. You may find several choices in a florist shop, in your yard, or in a park. If this is not possible, look through magazines or books for a picture of a flower to trace or draw. If you want, you can use the *North American Wildlife Guide.*

🐾 Choose several flowers to sketch in your Student Notebook. You may find several choices in a florist shop, in your yard, or in a park. If this is not possible, look through magazines or books for a picture of a flower to trace or draw. If you want, you can use the *North American Wildlife Guide.*

🐾 On the Internet or in your library, learn about the flowers produced in Holland. Include at least one of these flowers in your sketches.

G. **Independent Reading**
Choose something to read that you will enjoy. Find a quiet, comfortable place and read for the following length of time:

🐾 20 minutes

🐾 25 minutes

🐾 30 minutes

Over time, it's fun to see how much you have read. Be sure to write down what you read today on the Reading Log in your Student Notebook.

G. See Independent Reading note in Part 1.

Lesson 2, Part 3

A. **Copywork/Dictation**   *Language Skills*
With your teacher's help, choose a passage from your reader or another book that you enjoy reading. Copy, or write as your teacher dictates, the passage you chose. When you are finished, compare your copy to the text and make any needed corrections. Follow the guidelines below for the minimum assignment:

🐾 At least 3 sentences

🐾 At least 4 sentences

🐾 At least 5 sentences

A. See Copywork/Dictation note in Part 1.

B. **Reader** *Language Skills, Thinking Skills, History*

In your book, *Squanto,* read pages 35–39 aloud.

Read one or two paragraphs in your read-aloud book, *Stories of the Pilgrims.*

Read one or two pages from today's read-aloud assignment in *Stories of the Pilgrims.*

C. See Discussion note in Part 1.

Answers to discussion Comprehension Questions are found in the *Stories of the Pilgrims Answer Key.*

C. **Read-Aloud and Discussion** *Language Skills, Thinking Skills*

In *Stories of the Pilgrims,* listen as your teacher reads pages 63-73 aloud.

Listen as your teacher reads the Comprehension Questions on page 67 in *Stories of the Pilgrims.* Talk with your teacher about what you think the answers are.

D. **Word Study** *Spelling, Phonics, Vocabulary*

Tell your teacher what each spelling word means and how it relates to your Pilgrim study. In your Student Notebook, fill out a Pilgrim Word Bank entry for each of your words and include this information.

Practice your words by using one of the following:

- Dry erase board and markers
- Colored chalk and chalkboard *or* sidewalk
- Modeling clay
- Water-based paint and paper
- Letter Cards

E. **Geography**

Today you will once again practice finding things on a grid, and then telling the address of that thing. When you learn to use grids well, you will be able to use an address, or coordinate, to find places on a map.

Look at the grid on the next page. There are letters that are in a **vertical** (up and down) row, and there are numbers that go in a **horizontal** (across the top) row. When you find the address of an **intersection**, or place where the lines meet, you use the letters and numbers to tell where it is. Look at the blank grid on the next page. Find the following addresses with your finger:

D5	A2	G7	E4

Draw these objects onto the blank grid in your Student Notebook. Then tell the address where you drew each object.

heart	blue triangle	red circle
star	green square	orange smiley face

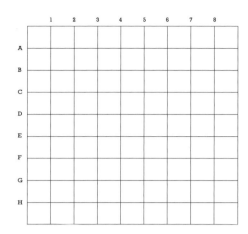

🐾 Think of three more objects to put on your grid and write their addresses.

Now look at the grid below that covers part of a map of the United States. Look at each state and find at least two intersections, or map addresses, that fall within each state:

Michigan	Virginia	Illinois	North Carolina
Tennessee	Pennsylvania	Wisconsin	

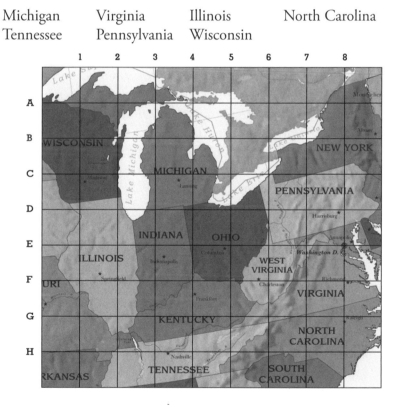

Grid Map A

🐾 Now look at the second blank grid map in your Student Notebook. Draw at least two bodies of water, such as lakes or rivers, that touch at least two intersections. Give your bodies of water a name, such as Lake Happy Camper, and write it on the grid map. Then give the grid coordinates for Lake Happy Camper below the grid. Now draw at least two bodies of water that touch at least three intersections. Give your bodies of water a name and list them below the grid map with the intersections they touch. You may add more if you like.

Look back at Grid Map A of the United States above. Give the name of one of the lakes and a coordinate that touches it, located near Wisconsin, Michigan, Ohio, Pennsylvania, or New York.

F. Writing
History, Thinking Skills

Ψ Read question 4 on page 73 in *Stories of the Pilgrims.* Now go back to paragraph 5 on page 72 in the chapter, "Preparing for the Journey." Listen as your teacher rereads this paragraph, and write the answer to question 4 in a complete sentence. Write this answer in your Student Notebook. Remember to use your Pilgrim Word Bank to help you.

Read questions 1 and 2 on page 73 in *Stories of the Pilgrims.* Go to the beginning of the chapter, "Preparing for the Journey," and find the paragraphs that relate to each question. **Skim,** or look at without reading all the words, through these paragraphs to find the information you need to answer each question with a complete sentence. Write the answers in your Student Notebook. Remember to use your Pilgrim Word Bank to help you.

Read questions 1-4 on page 73 in *Stories of the Pilgrims.* Go to the beginning of the chapter, "Preparing for the Journey," and find the paragraphs that relate to each question. **Skim,** or look at without reading all the words, through these paragraphs to find the information you need to answer each question with a complete sentence. Write the answers in your Student Notebook. Remember to use your Pilgrim Word Bank to help you.

G. See Independent Reading note in Part 1.

G. Independent Reading

Choose something to read that you will enjoy. Find a quiet, comfortable place and read for the following length of time:

Ψ 20 minutes

25 minutes

30 minutes

Over time, it's fun to see how much you have read. Be sure to write down what you read today on the Reading Log in your Student Notebook.

Lesson 2, Part 4

A. **Copywork/Dictation**   *Language Skills*   *A.* **See Copywork/Dictation note in** Part 1.

> They learned about a whole new way of life in Holland where waterways, or canals, served as transportation. They were fascinated by the iceboats that moved on skis across the frozen canals in winter. They saw earthen dikes that held back water, and windmills.

🐾 Copy the above lines into your Student Notebook. When you are finished, compare your copy to the model (word by word) and make any needed corrections.

🐾 Listen as your teacher dictates the above lines, and write them in your Student Notebook. When you are finished, compare your copy to the model and make any needed corrections.

🐾 Copy, or write as your teacher dictates, paragraph 2 on page 76 ("There on . . .") in *Stories of the Pilgrims*. When you are finished, compare your copy to the text and make any needed corrections.

B. **Reader**   *Language Skills, Thinking Skills, History*

In your book, *Squanto,* read page 40 to the end of paragraph 5 on page 43 aloud.

🐾 Read one or two paragraphs in your read-aloud book, *Stories of the Pilgrims*.

🐾 Read one or two pages from today's read-aloud assignment in *Stories of the Pilgrims*.

C. **Read-Aloud and Narration**   *Language Skills, Thinking Skills*   *C.* **See Narration note in Part 2.**

Listen carefully as your teacher reads pages 74-82 aloud from *Stories of the Pilgrims*.

To *narrate* means to retell. In your own words, tell what happened in your assigned passage below. Try to remember as many details as possible. Listen carefully as your teacher reads (or rereads) the part you are to retell.

🐾 Reread page 39 of *Squanto*. Tell about what Squanto did to try to get to sleep.

🐾 Use the book and pictures to retell the chapter "London" to your teacher.

🐾 Tell your teacher about the chapter entitled "Farewell to Holland" in *Stories of the Pilgrims*.

D. Word Study

Spelling, Phonics, Vocabulary

Review the spelling words you are working on in this lesson by reading them, spelling them aloud, and then checking to see if you were correct.

When you feel you are ready, spell them for your teacher. Once you have done that, and your teacher gives you permission, write your word study words in your personal dictionary.

Look through your personal dictionary and choose several words to spell aloud for your teacher.

E. Science

In a nation filled with water, wading birds are a part of the environment. At the time the Pilgrims lived in Holland, storks were a common sight on rooftops and were considered a sign of good luck. On the other hand, it was considered bad luck to harm a stork. The white stork is commonly found in Europe and is often two to five feet tall. When storks mate, both parents take care of the eggs.

There are many species of storks in Europe, but the only stork found in America is the wood stork. These birds used to be called the wood ibis.

Look in the *North American Wildlife Guide* on page 86. Draw or trace and color the wood stork in your Student Notebook. Write how large it is and where it lives?[9] Add one more interesting fact you learned about the wood stork.

Storks are part of the family of wading birds with long legs. Herons, ibises, and storks like to live in warmer climates.

Make Animal I.D. cards for the wood stork.

🐾 Another bird seen in Holland is the great egret, also called the great white egret. Look on page 85 in the *North American Wildlife Guide*. Trace or draw and color the great egret into your Student Notebook. Write down how large it is and where it lives.[10]

Make Animal I.D. cards for the great egret.

🐾 Look in the *North American Wildlife Guide* and find out if any herons, egrets, or ibises live near you. Choose two birds that live near you to include in your Student Notebook. If there are none of these types of birds near you, choose two of them that are interesting to you and include them. Draw or trace and color the birds, and then write how large they are, where they live, and what they eat. Add one interesting fact you learn about each bird. Make Animal I.D. cards for each bird you chose.

E. Each time your student makes an Animal I.D. card for this unit, have him write a "P" (for Pilgrims) in the upper left corner. This will make it possible to review the animals studied by unit.

F. Art

History, Thinking Skills

Look at the words you have added to your Pilgrim Word Bank during this lesson. Illustrations can help you remember what words mean and the way they are used. Use your reader or read-aloud book for ideas and draw a picture to illustrate each of these words. Your drawing can show what the word means or something that reminds you of the word, like a crown for King James. Use colored pencils or crayons to complete your illustrations.

G. Independent Reading

Choose something to read that you will enjoy. Find a quiet, comfortable place and read for the following length of time:

- 20 minutes

- 25 minutes

- 30 minutes

Over time, it's fun to see how much you have read. Be sure to write down what you read today on the Reading Log in your Student Notebook.

G. See Independent Reading note in Part 1.

Lesson 2, Part 5

This part is set aside for completion of any work left undone from the lesson, and review of concepts and content. It is also a time to expand the work in the lesson by doing art, timeline activities, or games.

- Review the Steps for Thinking from the beginning of this lesson.

- On the large outline map of the world label: Netherlands; Amsterdam, Netherlands.

- Review the spelling words for this lesson. In your Student Notebook, write a sentence using each word that tells how it is related to the unit. Do your best to write the spelling words correctly. After you have finished, check your sentences against the list in your Student Notebook and see how many spelling words you spelled correctly. (Don't count off for other words that are misspelled.) Remember your goal is to improve, not necessarily to get them all right immediately.

- You have been learning about the people of Holland and their customs. One of the most important ways to get to know people is to learn about the way they cook and eat their food, and the

Most of the labeling has already been completed in the Student Notebook during this lesson. Instruct students to use the maps in their Student Notebooks as a reference. When they label the larger map, students will see the "big picture" and gain a broader understanding of their lessons.

Teachers can find a copy of these games in Appendix B. Instructions and answer keys for all games are located in Appendix A.

Use one or more of the Enrichment Activities if your child completes his assigned work and has the time or desire to learn more. These activities are flexible, so choose the one(s) that seem most interesting to your student. Allow him to work at a level that is appropriate for him, and remember that the learning process is more important than the product.

traditions that surround it. Look in *Eat Your Way Around the World* and read the section on Holland. With your parent's permission, choose one or more of the recipes listed to make and eat.

• Play Columbus or Jamestown Bingo.

Enrichment Activities

1. Two famous Dutch artists are Rembrandt and Vermeer. Learn more about their paintings done in the 1600s, during the Dutch Golden Age. Look at examples of their work at the library or, with your parent's permission, on the Internet. Tell something you like about each artist's work.

2. Cheese is a famous export for Holland. Edam and Gouda are two types of cheese originally made in Holland and named after the cities where they were made. With your parent's permission, sample different types of cheese and decide which you like best. Learn about how cheese is made.

Additional Resources

Books or resources about Rembrandt and Vermeer.

Books or resources about Edam and Gouda cheeses.

Pilgrim Stories, revised and expanded by Elvajean Hall

Answers

1. pumps water from an area back to the sea or into a canal

2. Answers will vary.

3. 0–656 feet

4. no

5. moderate with mild, rainy summer

6. Moderate is not extremely cold or hot.

7. the coasts of Washington, Oregon, and California

8. yes

9. wood stork: 36–42 inches long; live in swamps, marshy meadows, shallow freshwater areas

10. white egret: 6-42 inches long; lives in wetlands

Lesson 3, Part 1

> ## ❧ Steps for Thinking ❧
>
> 1. Geography often determines where people decide to live.
> 2. The challenges that geography presents cause people to come up with creative answers to problems.

A. **Copywork/Dictation**   *Language Skills*

> The Pilgrims longed for life in England where they could live simple lives serving God. But they could not return and have the freedom to worship. They began to plan their move to the New World, where they could raise their families and serve God.

🐾 Copy the above lines into your Student Notebook. When you are finished, compare your copy to the model (word by word) and make any needed corrections.

🐾 Listen as your teacher dictates the above lines, and write them in your Student Notebook. When you are finished, compare your copy to the model and make any needed corrections.

🐾 Copy, or write as your teacher dictates, paragraph 3 on page 83 ("They loved . . .") in *Stories of the Pilgrims*. When you are finished, compare your copy to the text and make any needed corrections.

B. **Reader**   *Language Skills, Thinking Skills, History*

In your book, *Squanto,* read from paragraph 6 on page 43 through page 47 aloud.

🐾 Read one or two paragraphs in your read-aloud book, *Stories of the Pilgrims.*

🐾 Read one or two pages from today's read-aloud assignment in *Stories of the Pilgrims.*

The **Steps for Thinking** section gives you the main ideas about the topics presented. Understanding these helps you to have productive discussions with your children so they, too, understand the bigger ideas. This forms more permanent learning, contrary to just learning facts, which tends to be temporary. These steps are useful prior to instruction, and they are also useful for review at the end of the week.

❧ Materials ❧

- *Squanto*
- *Stories of the Pilgrims*
- *Stories of the Pilgrims* Answer Key
- *Eat Your Way Around the World*
- *North American Wildlife Guide*
- *Handbook of Nature Study*
- *Profiles from History*
- Student Notebook
- Index cards/marker
- Materials for hands-on spelling: dry erase board and markers, colored chalk, modeling clay, water-based paint and paper, or Letter Cards
- Plain or tracing paper
- Personal dictionary
- Construction paper
- Colored pencils or crayons
- Ruler
- Several ears of corn with husks
- Large world and U.S. outline maps

Additional resources for Enrichment Activities are found in Part 5.

A. Copywork and dictation assignments go from an easier level (designated by 🐾) to harder levels (designated by 🐾 and 🐾). Take two days for the copywork if that is more comfortable for your child. Please adapt instructions to your child's individual needs. Your child should be **consistently successful** at one level before progressing to the next, **regardless of grade**.

C. Discussion is very important in developing your child's ability to organize his thoughts. This in turn builds the ability to think and write. The goal of the discussion questions is not just to find the answer to a particular question, but also to create a situation where thoughts about the question and its answer are shared and considered in a detailed way. Do not rush this activity, but encourage your student to share his or her ideas relating to the topic, and any additional ideas that may come to mind. You can also share your thoughts and questions as an example for your students.

Answers to discussion Comprehension Questions are found in the *Stories of the Pilgrims Answer Key.*

C. **Read-Aloud and Discussion**   *Language Skills, Thinking Skills*

In *Stories of the Pilgrims,* listen as your teacher reads pages 83-91 aloud.

Listen as your teacher reads the Comprehension Questions on page 87 in *Stories of the Pilgrims.* Talk with your teacher about what you think the answers are.

D. **Word Study**   *Spelling, Phonics, Vocabulary*

Read these words from your study of the Pilgrims, or listen as your teacher reads them:

> *Mayflower*
> *Speedwell*
> Myles Standish
> Gideon

Now practice reading them silently. Use your Letter Cards to spell these words and any other words you and your teacher choose for this lesson.

Make a list of your word study words in your Student Notebook. Ask your teacher to pick several words for you to practice spelling aloud.

E. **Geography**   *History*

Squanto came to be someone very important to the survival of the Pilgrim colony. Many years before the Pilgrims arrived in the New World, he began a series of voyages that resulted in his traveling many thousands of miles. Squanto left his village in 1605 to travel to England. When he arrived in London he probably saw many of the sights the city is famous for, such as London Bridge and the River Thames.

Look at the World Map in your Student Notebook. Use a colored pencil and a ruler to draw a line from Plymouth, Massachusetts, to London, England. In the bottom left hand corner of your map, write "Voyage 1" and make a short line with the same colored pencil you used. Leave room for several more voyages underneath this one. You are making your own key for this map.

 After you draw the line to show Squanto's first voyage, measure it with a ruler. (It should be approximately 1¾ inches.) Line your ruler up with the Map Scale on the bottom of the map. Since one inch equals approximately 2,666 miles, write that number on a piece of scrap paper. To find out how many miles the remaining three fourths of an inch equals, you first need to figure out the distance represented by one fourth of an inch. You can find this distance by dividing 2,666 miles by 4. The answer is about 666. Now, simply add 666 three times, or multiply it times three. Then add the number you get to 2,666 on your scrap paper. This is the approximate number of miles that Squanto traveled when he went to England. Write this distance on the map key you are making, next to the colored line that represents Squanto's first voyage.[1]

☙ Squanto wanted to take the trip to England so he could learn more about the English people and their ways. Think of phrases that describe the two places where Squanto lived—his Indian village and London—and write them in your Student Notebook. Include things like where Squanto lived in each place, where he worked, the food he ate, and the people he saw. Talk with your teacher about how difficult you think these changes would have been for Squanto.

F. Writing

History, Thinking Skills

As you are learning, the Separatists left England in search of **freedom,** or the ability to choose what to think, do, or believe. The Separatists were willing to leave their homes to obtain freedom to worship God. Freedom is valuable to everyone.

Talk with your teacher about some of the ways freedom is important to you and your family. Below is the word **FREEDOM.** Copy it onto a piece of construction paper exactly as you see it below:

F
R
E
E
D
O
M

Now think of ways to describe what freedom means to you. Write a word or phrase that begins with each of the letters of this important word. This is called an acrostic poem. Here is an example:

Fragrant
Lovely to look at
Open in the morning
Wilts without water
Every mom's delight
Red roses

☙ Choose another word from your reading about the Separatists and create another acrostic poem on construction paper with that word.

F. Each word in bold letters is considered a vocabulary word. It is a word that may or may not be new to your child. You can write these vocabulary words on index cards and use them for occasional review, but not for memorizing. Give the child the meaning of the words if he doesn't remember. Try to use the new vocabulary words during conversation, and encourage your students to do the same.

Each time your student makes a vocabulary card for this unit, have him write a "P" (for Pilgrims) in the upper left corner. This will make it possible to review vocabulary by unit at the end of the year.

G. Reading fluency is developed through having frequent silent reading opportunities that continue for the length of time suggested here. Since a primary focus of this activity is to nurture your child's enjoyment of reading, help him to choose reading material that interests him and is at a level that allows him to read with understanding by himself. You can incorporate this activity into your school day whenever it is most convenient.

If the suggested length of time is too long for your child to continue reading by himself, start with an amount of time he can accomplish successfully and make the suggested time a goal.

A. The dictation method enables your child to hear language and correctly write down what he hears. It involves building two different skills. First, the ability to listen and understand what is heard, and second, the ability to transfer what is heard into written language. This process takes time and practice, so begin as gradually as needed for successfully reaching the goal of getting the words the child hears on the paper correctly. 1) Read the whole passage, then reread one sentence at a time, giving your child time to write what he hears. 2) After he has finished, reread the passage again, allowing him to double check what he has written. 3) Then proceed to the step of comparing his writing to the model. As his skill builds, you can move more quickly through the steps, maintaining your child's level of success.

G. Independent Reading

Choose something to read that you will enjoy. Find a quiet, comfortable place and read for the following length of time:

❧❧ 20 minutes

❧ 25 minutes

❧ 30 minutes

Over time, it's fun to see how much you have read. Be sure to write down what you read today on the Reading Log in your Student Notebook.

Lesson 3, Part 2

A. Copywork/Dictation   *Language Skills*

> The Pilgrims began preparations for the long journey into a new land where they would start fresh building a community. Among the supplies they would bring were white linen, spinning wheels, and pewter dishes that were not easily broken.

❧❧ Copy the above lines into your Student Notebook. When you are finished, compare your copy to the model (word by word) and make any needed corrections.

❧ Listen as your teacher dictates the above lines, and write them in your Student Notebook. When you are finished, compare your copy to the model and make any needed corrections.

❧ Copy, or write as your teacher dictates, paragraph 5 on page 92 ("But Mistress . . .") in *Stories of the Pilgrims*. When you are finished, compare your copy to the text and make any needed corrections.

B. Reader   *Language Skills, Thinking Skills, History*

In your book, *Squanto,* read pages 48–53 aloud.

❧ Read one or two paragraphs in your read-aloud book, *Stories of the Pilgrims*.

❧ Read one or two pages from today's read-aloud assignment in *Stories of the Pilgrims*.

C. Read-Aloud and Narration

Language Skills, Thinking Skills

Listen carefully as your teacher reads pages 92-101 aloud from *Stories of the Pilgrims.*

To *narrate* means to retell. In your own words, tell what happened in your assigned passage below. Try to remember as many details as possible. Listen carefully as your teacher reads (or rereads) the part you are to retell.

❦ Reread pages 49 and 50 of *Squanto.* Tell your teacher what Squanto wanted to do and how it worked out.

❦ Use the book and pictures to retell the chapter "The Indian Show" to your teacher.

❦ Tell your teacher about the chapter entitled "A Wild Land" in *Stories of the Pilgrims.*

D. Word Study

Spelling, Phonics, Vocabulary

Look at the list of spelling words you wrote in your Student Notebook in Part 1. Read the words silently, or listen as your teacher reads them.

Now say each word and tell how many syllables, or word parts, you hear in each word. Write the number of syllables you hear in each word next to the word.

Choose a way to practice your spelling words from the list below:

- Dry erase board and markers
- Colored chalk and chalkboard *or* sidewalk
- Modeling clay
- Water-based paint and paper
- Letter Cards

E. Science

Many of the animals you read about in the stories of the explorers are considered protected today. In the early 1600's, these animals were still important sources of food and could make the difference between eating or starving, especially in the winter months. Though many of these animals are still hunted, it is not the thing that most people nowadays think of when they happen to see a deer or rabbit.

C. The skill of narration is gained over time. If your child has never retold a story, start with the assignment for the lower level, no matter what grade he is in. Work up from there, being careful to allow him to stay at the level of success for a while before going to a longer section.

E. Each time your student makes an Animal I.D. card for this unit, have him write a "P" in the upper left corner. This will make it possible to review the animals by unit at the end of the year.

Look at the white-tailed deer on page 67 in the *North American Wildlife Guide.* Draw or trace and color both the male and female deer into your Student Notebook. Tell how large a deer usually is, where it lives, and what it eats.[2] Write one additional fact you learned about deer. Do you have deer where you live? Have you ever seen one in the wild?

Make Animal I.D. cards for the white-tailed deer.

Another animal that is common in the area where the Pilgrims lived is the eastern cottontail rabbit. Look at page 57 in the *North American Wildlife Guide.* Draw or trace and color this rabbit into your Student Notebook. Tell how large it is, and where it lives.[3] Write one additional fact you learned about the eastern cottontail.

Make Animal I.D. cards for the eastern cottontail rabbit.

Both deer and rabbits are mammals. Do you remember what a mammal is? If not, talk with your teacher or look at your vocabulary cards or in a dictionary for the definition. Review the different types of animals, and then play the Animal I.D. game. Include all the cards you have made so far.

🐾 How is a hare different from a rabbit? Read about the snowshoe hare on page 57 in the *North American Wildlife Guide.* After reading the description, compare it to the eastern cottontail rabbit. You may also look in other reference materials or a dictionary if needed. Write two or three sentences telling the differences between a hare and a rabbit.

Make Animal I.D. cards for the hare.

F. **Art**

Yesterday you created at least one acrostic poem. You used words to paint a picture. Today you will add color, designs, or pictures that emphasize the words you have already placed on the construction paper. Your goal is to give the words more meaning with your illustrations.

Talk with your teacher about the materials available to you such as markers, colored pencils, crayons, or paint. With her permission, choose what will best highlight your thoughts. Your copy of this poem will be part of your Unit Presentation at the end of this unit, so remember to do your best.

🐾 Prepare all the poems you created to be part of the Unit Presentation at the end of this unit by following the directions above.

G. Independent Reading

Choose something to read that you will enjoy. Find a quiet, comfortable place and read for the following length of time:

- 20 minutes

- 25 minutes

- 30 minutes

Be sure to write down what you read today on the Reading Log in your Student Notebook.

G. See Independent Reading note in Part 1.

Lesson 3, Part 3

A. Copywork/Dictation   *Language Skills*

With your teacher's help, choose a passage from your reader or another book that you enjoy reading. Copy, or write as your teacher dictates, the passage you chose. When you are finished, compare your copy to the text and make any needed corrections. Follow the guidelines below for the minimum assignment:

- At least 3 sentences

- At least 4 sentences

- At least 5 sentences

A. See Copywork/Dictation note in Part 1.

B. Reader   *Language Skills, Thinking Skills, History*

In your book, *Squanto,* read pages 54–57 aloud.

- Read one or two paragraphs in your read-aloud book, *Stories of the Pilgrims.*

- Read one or two pages from today's read-aloud assignment in *Stories of the Pilgrims.*

C. Read-Aloud and Discussion   *Language Skills, Thinking Skills*

In *Stories of the Pilgrims,* listen as your teacher reads pages 102-115 aloud.

Listen as your teacher reads the Comprehension Questions on page 105 in *Stories of the Pilgrims.* Talk with your teacher about what you think the answers are.

C. See Discussion note in Part 1.

Answers to discussion Comprehension Questions are found in the *Stories of the Pilgrims Answer Key.*

D. Word Study   *Spelling, Phonics, Vocabulary*

Tell your teacher what each spelling word means and how it relates to your Pilgrim study. In your Student Notebook, fill out a Pilgrim Word Bank entry for each of your words and include this information.

Practice your words by using by using one of the following:

- Dry erase board and markers
- Colored chalk and chalkboard *or* sidewalk
- Modeling clay
- Water-based paint and paper
- Letter Cards

E. Geography   *Drawing*

You have learned how to find objects on a grid by using the letters and numbers to guide you. Now, continue to improve your skill by using the grid parts to draw a picture. Remember, when using a grid to find an object or a place, start with the letters on the side and then find the number at the top. The place where the letter-line and number-line meet is called an intersection, just like when two roads cross, making a shape that looks like a plus sign (+).

Look carefully at Grid Map D below. Use your finger to trace slowly around the outline of the dog. Pay attention when your finger crosses one of the grid lines. Try to find a place where the drawing crosses the grid at, or very close to, an intersection. Now, copy the dog onto the blank grid in your Student Notebook. Try to make each square of the blank grid look like the square on Grid Map D that has the same address.

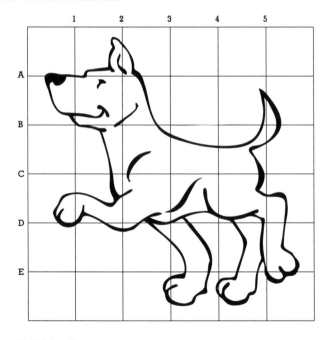

Grid Map D

🐾 With your teacher's permission use a ruler and a pencil to draw a grid over a simple picture you have printed or chosen from a magazine. The squares should be one inch boxes, so start measuring at the bottom of the page. Make a mark at each inch marker. Now do the same with the top and both sides. Lay the ruler so that it connects the inch mark on one side with the opposite inch mark. Now draw a line connecting the two. As you continue to do this, you are creating a grid. Look at the blank grid in your Student Notebook. Find the point you see most easily in your picture and start your drawing with that box. Continue until you have copied the picture onto the blank grid.

F. Writing   *History, Thinking Skills*

🐾🐾 Read question 4 on page 115 in *Stories of the Pilgrims*. Now go back to the last two paragraphs on page 114 and the top of page 115 in the chapter, "Plymouth Bay." Listen as your teacher rereads this section, and write the answer to question 4 in a complete sentence. Write this answer in your Student Notebook.

🐾 Read questions 1 and 2 on page 115 in *Stories of the Pilgrims*. Go to the beginning of the chapter, "Plymouth Bay," and find the paragraphs that relate to each question. **Skim,** or look at without reading all the words, through these paragraphs to find the information you need to answer each question with a complete sentence. Write the answers in your Student Notebook.

🐾 Read questions 1-4 on page 115 in *Stories of the Pilgrims*. Go to the beginning of the chapter, "Plymouth Bay," and find the paragraphs that relate to each question. **Skim,** or look at without reading all the words, through these paragraphs to find the information you need to answer each question with a complete sentence. Write the answers in your Student Notebook.

G. Independent Reading

Choose something to read that you will enjoy. Find a quiet, comfortable place and read for the following length of time:

🐾🐾 20 minutes

🐾 25 minutes

🐾 30 minutes

Over time, it's fun to see how much you have read. Be sure to write down what you read today on the Reading Log in your Student Notebook.

G. See Independent Reading note in Part 1.

Lesson 3, Part 4

A. See Copywork/Dictation note in Part 1.

A. **Copywork/Dictation**   *Language Skills*

> Dried peas and fruits were also part of the supplies they took. From milk they churned butter and prepared cheese. They preserved meat by salting it. Barrels of meal and sacks of beans were also filled for food until they could harvest their first crops.

🐾 Copy the above lines into your Student Notebook. When you are finished, compare your copy to the model (word by word) and make any needed corrections.

🐾 Listen as your teacher dictates the above lines, and write them in your Student Notebook. When you are finished, compare your copy to the model and make any needed corrections.

🐾 Copy, or write as your teacher dictates, paragraph 1 on page 117 ("It was Christmas . . .") in *Stories of the Pilgrims*. When you are finished, compare your copy to the text and make any needed corrections.

B. **Reader**   *Language Skills, Thinking Skills, History*

In your book, *Squanto,* read page 58 through the end of paragraph 1 on page 64 aloud.

🐾 Read one or two paragraphs in your read-aloud book, *Stories of the Pilgrims*.

🐾 Read one or two pages from today's read-aloud assignment in *Stories of the Pilgrims*.

C. See Narration note in Part 2.

C. **Read-Aloud and Narration**   *Language Skills, Thinking Skills*

Listen carefully as your teacher reads pages 116-126 aloud from *Stories of the Pilgrims*.

To *narrate* means to retell. In your own words, tell what happened in your assigned passage below. Try to remember as many details as possible. Listen carefully as your teacher reads (or rereads) the part you are to retell.

🐾 Reread pages 58 and 60 of *Squanto*. Tell what happened to Squanto.

🐾 Use the book and pictures to retell the chapter "Captain John Smith" to your teacher.

🐾 Tell your teacher about the chapter entitled "The First Winter in Plymouth" in *Stories of the Pilgrims*.

D. Word Study   *Spelling, Phonics, Vocabulary*

Review the spelling words you are working on in this lesson by reading them, spelling them aloud, and then checking to see if you were correct.

When you feel you are ready, spell them for your teacher. Once you have done that, and your teacher gives you permission, write your word study words in your personal dictionary.

Look through your personal dictionary and choose several words to spell aloud for your teacher.

E. Science   *History*

When the Pilgrims first arrived in Plymouth, it was already winter and food was a valuable thing. During a scouting party, the Pilgrims were fortunate to find ten bushels of Indian Corn that had been stored. They decided that they would pay the Indians back for the corn, but they took it since they needed it.

On pages 598–601 in the *Handbook of Nature Study* read, or listen as your teacher reads, about corn. If you have access to a corn plant, you can do the activities described in #1–7. If you do not have access to a corn plant, read the questions anyway and discuss the questions and vocabulary with your teacher.

Now listen as your teacher reads questions 9–14. Use several ears of corn, which you can usually get at a grocery store or market. Each child should have at least one ear, in its natural form with the husk in place. Complete the activities or questions for numbers 9–14.[4] Talk with your teacher about what foods you can make with corn, and make a list of at least three in your Student Notebook.

🐾 Sketch and color the ear of corn in several conditions: with the husk on, with the husk off, and broken in half. With your parent's permission and help, make the recipe for corn on the cob found in *Eat Your Way Around the World* in the United States section.

F. Art   *History, Thinking Skills*

Look at the words you have added to your Pilgrim Word Bank during this lesson. Illustrations can help you remember what words mean and the way they are used. Use your reader or read-aloud book for ideas and draw a picture to illustrate each of these words. Your drawing can show what the word means or something that reminds you of the word, like a crown for King James. Use colored pencils or crayons to complete your illustrations.

G. See Independent Reading note in Part 1.

G. **Independent Reading**

Choose something to read that you will enjoy. Find a quiet, comfortable place and read for the following length of time:

🌱 20 minutes

🐾 25 minutes

🐾 30 minutes

Over time, it's fun to see how much you have read. Be sure to write down what you read today on the Reading Log in your *Student Notebook*.

───❦───

Lesson 3, Part 5

This part is set aside for completion of any work left undone from the lesson, and review of concepts and content. It is also a time to expand the work in the lesson by doing art, timeline activities, or games.

• Review the Steps for Thinking from the beginning of this lesson.

Most of the labeling has already been completed in the Student Notebook during this lesson. Instruct students to use the maps in their Student Notebooks as a reference. When they label the larger map, students will see the "big picture" and gain a broader understanding of their lessons.

• On the large outline map of the world label: Plymouth, Massachusetts, and mark Squanto's voyage from Plymouth, Massachusetts, to London in red. Use Arrows to show direction. On the large outline map of the U.S. label Plymouth, Massachusetts.

• Review the spelling words for this lesson. In your Student Notebook, write a sentence using each word that tells how it is related to the unit. Do your best to write the spelling words correctly. After you have finished, check your sentences against the list in your Student Notebook and see how many spelling words you spelled correctly. (Don't count off for other words that are misspelled.) Remember your goal is to improve, not necessarily to get them all right immediately.

Teachers can find a copy of this game in Appendix B. Instructions and answer keys for all games are located in Appendix A.

• Complete the Pilgrim Word Scramble located in your Student Notebook.

• Listen to or read the story about William Bradford in *Profiles from History.* Complete the timeline activities and any other activities you would like to do.

Enrichment Activities

1. The type of provisions, or food, that could be taken on a ship's voyage was the kind that would not spoil easily. Dried fruit was one such food. With your parent's permission, taste different types of dried fruits and decide which you like best. Learn about how to dry fruits.

2. The Pilgrims felt strongly that the Sabbath should be observed as a special day of rest and devotion to worship. Discuss the meaning of the Sabbath with your parents and find out what their views are. How are your family's views similar to or different from the views of the Pilgrims?

Additional Resources

Fruits

Equipment to dry fruit

Of Plimoth Plantation by William Bradford

Use one or more of the Enrichment Activities if your child completes his assigned work and has the time or desire to learn more. These activities are flexible, so choose the one(s) that seem most interesting to your student. Allow him to work at a level that is appropriate for him, and remember that the learning process is more important than the product.

Answers

1. 4,662 miles.

2. deer: 4-6 feet long; live in forests and swamps; eats green plants in the summer; corn, nuts, acorns in fall; buds and twigs in winter

3. eastern cottontail rabbit: 13-16 inches long; lives in bushy areas, forests, swamps

4. Answers can be found on pages 598 – 602 of the *Handbook of Nature Study*.

Lesson 4, Part 1

> ### § Steps for Thinking §
>
> 1. The Pilgrims found an Indian leader of character named Massasoit whom they could trust. Because the Pilgrims and Massasoit kept their word, there was peace with his tribe. Being true to your word is a key to peace with your neighbors.
>
> 2. Everyone experiences difficulties at some time. Helping a neighbor in need is a good thing to do and a way to prepare for the future.

The **Steps for Thinking** section gives you the main ideas about the topics presented. Understanding these helps you to have productive discussions with your children so they, too, understand the bigger ideas. This forms more permanent learning, contrary to just learning facts, which tends to be temporary. These steps are useful prior to instruction, and they are also useful for review at the end of the week.

A. Copywork/Dictation
Language Skills

> After some careful thought, they loaded their belongings on two ships: the *Speedwell* and the *Mayflower*. When the *Speedwell* proved unfit, the supplies and people were all loaded onto the *Mayflower*. Some people decided to stay behind, fearing the problems were a sign of trouble to come.

ᴪᴪ Copy the above lines into your Student Notebook. When you are finished, compare your copy to the model (word by word) and make any needed corrections.

ꚛ Listen as your teacher dictates the above lines, and write them in your Student Notebook. When you are finished, compare your copy to the model and make any needed corrections.

ꚛ Copy, or write as your teacher dictates, paragraph 4 on page 131 ("When Samoset . . .") in *Stories of the Pilgrims*. When you are finished, compare your copy to the text and make any needed corrections.

B. Reader
Language Skills, Thinking Skills, History

In your book, *Squanto*, read from paragraph 2 on page 64 through page 67 aloud.

ꚛ Read one or two paragraphs in your read-aloud book, *Stories of the Pilgrims*.

⁓*Materials*⁓

- *Squanto*
- *Stories of the Pilgrim*
- *Stories of the Pilgrims* Answer Key
- *United States History Atlas*
- *North American Wildlife Guide*
- *Intermediate World Atlas*
- *Profiles from History*
- *Student Notebook*
- Materials for hands-on spelling: dry erase board and markers, colored chalk, modeling clay, water-based paint and paper, or Letter Cards
- Index cards/marker
- Colored pencils or crayons
- Personal dictionary
- Ruler
- Construction paper
- Plain or tracing paper
- Animal I.D. cards
- Vocabulary cards
- Shallow box or lid
- Large U.S. outline map

Additional resources for Enrichment Activities are found in Part 5.

A. Copywork and dictation assignments go from an easier level (designated by ᴪᴪ) to harder levels (designated by ꚛ and ꚛ). Take two days for the copywork if that is more comfortable for your child. Please adapt instructions to your child's individual needs. Your child should be **consistently successful** at one level before progressing to the next, **regardless of grade**.

🐾 Read one or two pages from today's read-aloud assignment in *Stories of the Pilgrims*.

C. **Read-Aloud and Discussion**   *Language Skills, Thinking Skills*

In *Stories of the Pilgrims*, listen as your teacher reads pages 127-136 aloud.

Listen to your teacher reads the Comprehension Questions on page 132 in *Stories of the Pilgrims*. Talk with your teacher about what you think the answers are.

D. **Word Study**   *Spelling, Phonics, Vocabulary*

Read these words from your study of the Pilgrims, or listen as your teacher reads them:

> Pilgrims
>
> Cape Cod Bay
>
> prayer
>
> Plymouth

Now practice reading them silently. Use your Letter Cards to spell these words and any other words you and your teacher choose for this lesson.

Make a list of your word study words in your Student Notebook. Ask your teacher to pick several words for you to practice spelling aloud.

E. **Geography**

The accomplishments of the Pilgrims seem much greater when you consider the difficulty of life onboard the *Mayflower* during their long journey, and the hardships they faced when they finally arrived in the New World.

The *Mayflower* was not a large ship by today's standards. It was only 90 feet long and weighed 180 tons. A **ton** is 2,000 pounds. It crossed the Atlantic Ocean and encountered rough storms and winds strong enough to push it off course to the north of its original destination, which was Virginia. As the *Mayflower* approached Massachusetts in November of 1620, the weary Pilgrims looked forward to setting foot in the New World.

Look at Map P-4 of of eastern Massachusetts. Find the Atlantic Ocean. Now find Provincetown. It was in this harbor, or shelter, that the Pilgrims first dropped anchor. Next, they sailed across Cape Cod Bay to reach Plymouth. This is the place they chose for their settlement. Later this state would be named Massachusetts, with a capital city of Boston.

C. Discussion is very important in developing your child's ability to organize his thoughts. This in turn builds the ability to think and write. The goal of the discussion questions is not just to find the answer to a particular question, but also to create a situation where thoughts about the question and its answer are shared and considered in a detailed way. Do not rush this activity, but encourage your student to share his or her ideas relating to the topic, and any additional ideas that may come to mind. You can also share your thoughts and questions as an example for your students.

Answers to the Comprehension Questions are found in the *Stories of the Pilgrims Answer Key*.

E. Each word in bold letters is considered a vocabulary word. It is a word that may or may not be new to your child. You can write these vocabulary words on index cards and use them for occasional review, but not for memorizing. Give the child the meaning of the words if he doesn't remember. Try to use the new vocabulary words during conversation, and encourage your students to do the same.

Each time your student makes a vocabulary card for this unit, have him write a "P" (for Pilgrims) in the upper left corner. This will make it possible to review vocabulary by unit at the end of the year.

Map P-4

On the outline map of Massachusetts in your Student Notebook, label the following bodies of water:

         Atlantic Ocean   Cape Cod Bay

Now label the following places on land:

         Massachusetts   Plymouth   Boston

🐾 Add Massachusetts Bay and Provincetown to your map of Massachusetts.

🐾 Look at the United States Political Map in your *Intermediate World Atlas*. Use a ruler to measure the approximate distance between Cape Cod Bay (near Boston) and Chesapeake Bay (near Virginia). (approximately 2 ½ inches) To find out how far off course the *Mayflower* was blown, put your ruler on the Map Scale. How many miles does one inch equal?[1] The distance between the two bays is 2½ times 200 miles, or 200 plus 200 plus 100 (½ of 200). How far were they blown off course?[2]

𝓕. Art

The weather in fall and winter is different depending on where you live. Plants that live in your area may be green and growing if you

ℰ. The small superscript numbers that appear after some of the questions in this unit refer to answers found in the answer key, located immediately after Part 5.

live in a warmer climate, or leaves may change color and fall off the trees if you live a colder climate.

Today, make a collage of the things you can find outside at your house. A collage is a picture or design made by arranging and gluing a variety of objects to a piece of paper or other backing.

With your parent's permission, gather leaves, twigs, nuts, or other things you find outside in the fall and arrange them on a piece of construction paper that is a fall color. Remember not to use any leaves or flowers unless you know they are safe. Ask your parent before touching any unknown plant. When you are happy with the arrangement of your fall items, glue them down.

Another way to make a collage that may be easier is to use a shallow box or lid as the base. Glue construction paper that is a fall color inside, and then glue the items on top of the paper. You may give your collage a title if you would like.

G. Reading fluency is developed through having frequent silent reading opportunities that continue for the length of time suggested here. Since a primary focus of this activity is to nurture your child's enjoyment of reading, help him to choose reading material that interests him and is at a level that allows him to read with understanding by himself. You can incorporate this activity into your school day whenever it is most convenient.

If the suggested length of time is too long for your child to continue reading by himself, start with an amount of time he can accomplish successfully and make the suggested time a goal.

G. **Independent Reading**

Choose something to read that you will enjoy. Find a quiet, comfortable place and read for the following length of time:

❧ 20 minutes

❧ 25 minutes

❧ 30 minutes

Over time, it's fun to see how much you have read. Be sure to write down what you read today on the Reading Log in your Student Notebook.

Lesson 4, Part 2

A. See Copywork/Dictation note in Part 1.

A. **Copywork/Dictation**　　　　　　　*Language Skills*

Finally on September 16, 1620, the *Mayflower* set sail from Plymouth, England, with 101 men, women, and children on board. Not all were Pilgrims. Captain Christopher Jones' crew and others they called Strangers also left on this journey. Myles Standish, with his trusty sword Gideon, was hired to help protect the new colony.

❧❧ Copy the above lines into your Student Notebook. When you are finished, compare your copy to the model (word by word) and make any needed corrections.

❧ Listen as your teacher dictates the above lines, and write them in your Student Notebook. When you are finished, compare your copy to the model and make any needed corrections.

❧ Copy, or write as your teacher dictates, paragraph 2 on page 139 ("Tomorrow, . . ") in *Stories of the Pilgrims*. When you are finished, compare your copy to the text and make any needed corrections.

B. Reader   *Language Skills, Thinking Skills, History*

In your book, *Squanto,* read page 68 through paragraph 1 on page 72 aloud.

❧ Read one or two paragraphs in your read-aloud book, *Stories of the Pilgrims.*

❧ Read one or two pages from today's read-aloud assignment in *Stories of the Pilgrims.*

C. Read-Aloud and Narration   *Language Skills, Thinking Skills*

Listen carefully as your teacher reads pages 137-145 aloud from *Stories of the Pilgrims.*

To *narrate* means to retell. In your own words, tell what happened in your assigned passage below. Try to remember as many details as possible. Listen carefully as your teacher reads (or rereads) the part you are to retell.

❧❧ Reread pages 66 and 67 of *Squanto.* Tell about Squanto's problems and what is about to happen to him.

❧ Use the book and pictures to retell the chapter "Captain Hunt" to your teacher.

❧ Tell your teacher about the chapter entitled "Back to England?" in *Stories of the Pilgrims.*

D. Word Study   *Spelling, Phonics, Vocabulary*

Look at the list of spelling words you wrote in your Student Notebook in Part 1. Read the words silently, or listen as your teacher reads them.

Now say each word and tell how many syllables, or word parts, you hear in each word. Write the number of syllables you hear in each word next to the word.

Choose a way to practice your spelling words from the list below:

- Dry erase board and markers
- Colored chalk and chalkboard *or* sidewalk

C. The skill of narration is gained over time. If your child has never retold a story, start with the assignment for the lower level, no matter what grade he is in. Work up from there, being careful to allow him to stay at the level of success for a while before going to a longer section.

• Modeling clay
• Water-based paint and paper
• Letter Cards

E. Each time your student makes an Animal I.D. card for this unit, have him write a "P" (for Pilgrim) in the upper left corner. This will make it possible to review the animals studied by unit at the end of the year.

E. Science

So far in this curriculum you have learned about the following categories of animals:

reptiles	mammals	birds
fish	invertebrates	

Take out your Animal I.D. cards, and the vocabulary cards for the above words that you made during the Jamestown Unit. Review the qualities of each of the categories above. Now look at the list of animals below. You have already learned about most of them. If you haven't already, make two Animal I.D. cards for each animal. Write the animal's name at the top of the card, and be sure to include any important information you have learned about it. If you want, you may also draw a picture of the animal. Write the category of the animal on the bottom. All of these animals can be found in the *North American Wildlife Guide*.

Mallard Duck	Northern Pintail
Common Goldeneye	Green-winged Teal
Wood Stork	Great Egret
White-tailed Deer	Eastern Cottontail rabbit

Now you are ready to play the Animal I.D. game. Shuffle the cards and deal 5 cards face down to each player. Put the remainder of the cards in a stack, face down. There must be at least two players to play. Now play a "Go Fish" type of game, where you ask the other person for a certain animal. If he or she doesn't have it, draw a card. Your goal is to match animal pairs. When you get a pair, put it down during your turn. When all the cards are gone, or someone matches all his cards, the game is over. The one with the most pairs wins.

F. Writing   *Thinking Skills*

Sometimes when you read sentences, you have to be a detective. Detectives look for clues to learn the truth. Read this sentence: *My brother has green skin.* Do you think this sentence is true? No, it is not true, this sentence is false. When you are reading a sentence to decide if it is true or false, remember that *all* the parts of the sentence have to be true to make the whole sentence true. Look at this example:

I am reading this sentence, and my brother has green skin.

The first part is true because you really were reading the sentence. But the second part is false because your brother does not have green skin. So altogether, would you consider this sentence true or false?[3]

In your story you have been learning about the Pilgrims' arrival in America. Read the following sentence and decide if it is true or false:

The Pilgrims arrived in America on the *Speedwell.*

The sentence is false because the Pilgrims arrived in America on the *Mayflower.* Even though the beginning of the sentence (the Pilgrims did arrive in America) is true, the remainder of the sentence is **false**, or not true.

Look carefully at the sentences in your Student Notebook. Read them silently or listen as your teacher reads them aloud.

Talk with your teacher about each sentence and decide whether it is true or false. You may look at the chapter entitled "Squanto" in *Stories of the Pilgrims* if you have any questions. Then write a "T" (for true) or an "F" (for false) on the short line in front of each sentence.[4]

☙ Scan the chapter entitled "Squanto" in *Stories of the Pilgrims*, and find the words or phrases that make each false statement true. Write the words or phrases that you find on the line following the false sentence that they correct.

☙ Scan the chapter entitled "Squanto" in *Stories of the Pilgrims*, and find the words or phases that correct each false statement. Reword the false sentences to make them true, and write them on the lines in your Student Notebook.

G. **Independent Reading**
Choose something to read that you will enjoy. Find a quiet, comfortable place and read for the following length of time:

☙ 20 minutes

☙ 25 minutes

☙ 30 minutes

Over time, it's fun to see how much you have read. Be sure to write down what you read today on the Reading Log in your Student Notebook.

G. See Independent Reading note in Part 1.

———— ❧ ————

Lesson 4, Part 3

A. **Copywork/Dictation**   *Language Skills*
With your teacher's help, choose a passage from your reader or another book that you enjoy reading. Copy, or write as your teacher dictates, the passage you chose. When you are finished, compare

A. See Copywork/Dictation note in Part 1.

your copy to the text and make any needed corrections. Follow the guidelines below for the minimum assignment:

❦❦ At least 3 sentences

❦ At least 4 sentences

❦ At least 5 sentences

B. Reader   *Language Skills, Thinking Skills, History*

In your book, *Squanto,* read from paragraph 2 on page 72 through page 75 aloud.

❦ Read one or two paragraphs in your read-aloud book, *Stories of the Pilgrims.*

❦ Read one or two pages from today's read-aloud assignment in *Stories of the Pilgrims.*

C. See Discussion note in Part 1.

Answers to discussion Comprehension Questions are found in the *Stories of the Pilgrims Answer Key.*

C. Read-Aloud and Discussion

In *Stories of the Pilgrims,* listen as your teacher reads pages 146-154 aloud. Do not read the poem, "Thanksgiving," at this time. Listen as your teacher reads the Comprehension Questions on page 150 in *Stories of the Pilgrims.* Talk with your teacher about what you think the answers are.

D. Word Study   *Spelling, Phonics, Vocabulary*

Tell your teacher what each spelling word means and how it relates to your Pilgrim study. In your Student Notebook, fill out a Pilgrim Word Bank entry for each of your words and include this information.

Practice your words by using by using one of the following:

- Dry erase board and markers
- Colored chalk and chalkboard *or* sidewalk
- Modeling clay
- Water-based paint and paper
- Letter Cards

E. Geography   *History, Thinking Skills*

As the *Mayflower* sat anchored in Provincetown Harbor, the men who had come from England realized that they had a problem. Since they had not arrived in Virginia where a colony with a government had already been established, they would have to create their own **government,** or group of people who make laws and rules to live by. Since the London Company, who sent them, had not set up a government for this place, it was left up to the people aboard the Mayflower to decide what type of government they would have.

The Mayflower Compact is the agreement the men on the ship came up with. It was agreed to and is considered to be the basis for the Constitution of the United States that would later be written. This agreement was different than other governments because it allowed the people to rule themselves. This is called **self-government.**

Agreements among people, such as the Mayflower Compact, helped determine the boundaries of colonies, and eventually countries. Political maps show the borders between states and countries that have been set by governments.

Look at the map of the French, Spanish, and English Settlements to 1776 in the *United States History Atlas.* This shows the way the land in America was divided by agreements between people at that time.

Now look at the map of the Louisiana Purchase and Western Exploration, 1804–1807, also found in the *United States History Atlas.* Compare the two maps and talk with your teacher about what changed.

🐾 The borders of countries also change through the processes of war. Look through the *United States History Atlas.* Find at least one map that shows changes in the borders of a state or country due to war.

F. Writing

In past lessons you have learned how important letters were to people during the time of exploring and establishing colonies. A letter may have taken months to get to someone, and months for a response to come back. Not everyone could read and write, so the ability to send and receive letters was even more special.

In the Jamestown Unit you learned the basics of letter writing. Review this lesson (Jamestown, Lesson 4, Part 1) and identify the parts of a letter and where they go.

At this point in the read-aloud book, *Stories of the Pilgrims,* the Pilgrims have endured many hardships. Some encouraging things have also happened. **Encouragement,** or the support that inspires a person to keep going, was very important to the Pilgrims at this time.

Choose a character from the Pilgrim story and write them a letter of encouragement. Include whatever you think would help them keep going. Since we know the outcome of all their hard work and sacrifice, you could include that in your letter as well. If you have ever struggled with something and had to keep going, you could tell them about that as well. You can write or type this letter. With your teacher's permission you can dictate a rough draft to her and then recopy it. Remember to use your Pilgrim Word Bank to help you.

🐾 Do you know of someone who needs encouragement? With your teacher's permission, write him or her a brief letter or make a card.

Encourage this person to keep going and let him know how much you appreciate him.

🐾 Do you know of anyone who lives near you who would be encouraged by a visit from you? Talk with your teacher about someone you could visit with, and what you might say or do for that person. Some options may be someone you know at church, a neighbor, or someone who is sick or disabled. If you are able to visit this person, write a brief **summary,** or a short description with only the main points, of what happened. You may want to include pictures or drawings with your summary.

G. See Independent Reading note in Part 1.

G. Independent Reading

Choose something to read that you will enjoy. Find a quiet, comfortable place and read for the following length of time:

🐾 20 minutes

🐾 25 minutes

🐾 30 minutes

Over time, it's fun to see how much you have read. Be sure to write down what you read today on the Reading Log in the back of your notebook.

Lesson 4, Part 4

A. See Copywork/Dictation note in Part 1.

A. Copywork/Dictation
Language Skills

> After 65 days of traveling across the Atlantic Ocean, the Pilgrims finally arrived, but not in Virginia where they would have had to submit to the government of England. Winds had blown them off course and they dropped anchor in Provincetown Harbor on November 21, 1620.

🐾 Copy the above lines into your Student Notebook. When you are finished, compare your copy to the model (word by word) and make any needed corrections.

🐾 Listen as your teacher dictates the above lines, and write them in your Student Notebook. When you are finished, compare your copy to the model and make any needed corrections.

🐾 Copy, or write as your teacher dictates, paragraph 6 on page 156 ("But at last . . .") in *Stories of the Pilgrims.* When you are finished, compare your copy to the text and make any needed corrections.

B. Reader   *Language Skills, Thinking Skills, History*

In your book, *Squanto,* read pages 76–79 aloud.

🐾 Read one or two paragraphs in your read-aloud book, *Stories of the Pilgrims.*

🐾 Read one or two pages from today's read-aloud assignment in *Stories of the Pilgrims.*

C. Read-Aloud and Narration   *Language Skills, Thinking Skills*

Listen carefully as your teacher reads pages 155-162 aloud from *Stories of the Pilgrims.*

To *narrate* means to retell. In your own words, tell what happened in your assigned passage below. Try to remember as many details as possible. Listen carefully as your teacher reads (or rereads) the part you are to retell.

🐾 Reread pages 74 and 75 of *Squanto.* Tell what happened to Squanto at the slave market.

🐾 Use the book and pictures to retell the chapter "In the Dark" to your teacher.

🐾 Tell your teacher about the chapter entitled "Tit for Tat" in *Stories of the Pilgrims.*

C. See Narration note in Part 2.

D. Word Study   *Spelling, Phonics, Vocabulary*

Review the spelling words you are working on in this lesson by reading them, spelling them aloud, and then checking to see if you were correct.

When you feel you are ready, spell them for your teacher. Once you have done that, and your teacher gives you permission, write your spelling words in your personal dictionary.

Look through your personal dictionary and choose several words to spell aloud for your teacher.

E. Science

Squirrels are a common sight in many areas of America. Though they are common, they are very interesting and demonstrate the ability to live within different settings, such as the country or the city. Squirrels lived in the area that the Pilgrims settled and probably were a source of food when it was scarce. Again, our attitude today towards wildlife is mostly that it should be protected, not hunted, since other sources of food are readily available.

E. Each time your student makes an Animal I.D. card for this unit, have him write a "P" (for Pilgrim) in the upper left corner. This will make it possible to review the animals studied by unit at the end of the year.

Read, or listen as your teacher reads, from paragraph 3 on page 233 to page 236 in the *Handbook of Nature Study*. Together with your teacher, observe squirrels wherever they are available to you. Make a sketch of any squirrel you see. What kind of animals do you think they are?[5]

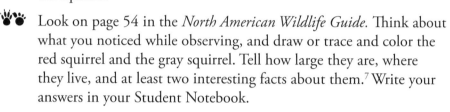

After observation, answer questions 1-7 on page 236 in the *Handbook of Nature Study*. Write your answers in your Student Notebook.[6]

Make Animal I.D. cards for the squirrel.

Look on page 54 in the *North American Wildlife Guide*. Think about what you noticed while observing, and draw or trace and color the red squirrel and the gray squirrel. Tell how large they are, where they live, and at least two interesting facts about them.[7] Write your answers in your Student Notebook.

Make Animal I.D. cards for the red squirrel and the gray squirrel.

Look at the questions about squirrels on page 237 in the *Handbook of Nature Study*. Use information from your reading, observation, or other resource material to answer questions 8-12.

F. Art
History, Thinking Skills

Look at the words you have added to your Pilgrim Word Bank during this lesson. Illustrations can help you remember what words mean and the way they are used. Use your reader or read-aloud book for ideas and draw a picture to illustrate each of these words. Your drawing can show what the word means or something that reminds you of the word, like a crown for King James. Use colored pencils or crayons to complete your illustrations.

G. See Independent Reading note in Part I.

G. Independent Reading

Choose something to read that you will enjoy. Find a quiet, comfortable place and read for the following length of time:

20 minutes

25 minutes

30 minutes

Over time, it's fun to see how much you have read. Be sure to write down what you read today on the Reading Log in your Student Notebook.

Lesson 4, Part 5

This part is set aside for completion of any work left undone from the lesson, and review of concepts and content. It is also a time to expand the work in the lesson by doing art, timeline activities, or games.

- Review the Steps for Thinking from the beginning of this lesson.

- On the large outline map of the U.S. label: Boston, Massachusetts; and Cape Cod Bay.

- Review the spelling words for this lesson. In your Student Notebook, write a sentence using each word that tells how it is related to the unit. Do your best to write the spelling words correctly. After you have finished, check your sentences against the list in your Student Notebook and see how many spelling words you spelled correctly. (Don't count off for other words that are misspelled.) Remember your goal is to improve, not necessarily to get them all right immediately.

- Do the Pilgrim Crossword in your Student Notebook.

- Listen to or read the story about Squanto in *Profiles from History*. Complete the timeline activities and any other activities you would like to do.

Enrichment Activities

1. At the library or, with your parent's permission, on the Internet research one or more of the following tribes: the Wampanoag tribe, the Abenaki tribe, and/or the Narragansett tribe. Then fill out a Native American Profile sheet, found on your Student Resources CD, for the tribes you choose to find out more about. Add the profile sheet(s) to your Native American Notebook.

2. Many people enjoy the sports of hunting and fishing. With your parent's permission, do research on the Internet or at the library about what types of hunting or fishing are done in your area.

3. Many hymns, or songs of praise to God, have been written about thankfulness. Talk with your parent about songs you may already know that express gratefulness. Try to learn at least one new hymn on this topic.

Additional Resources

Magazines

Hymnals

Most of the labeling has already been completed in the Student Notebook during this lesson. Instruct students to use the maps in their Student Notebooks as a reference. When they label the larger map, students will see the "big picture" and gain a broader understanding of their lessons.

Teachers can find a copy of this game in Appendix B. Instructions and answer keys for all games are located in Appendix A.

Use one or more of the Enrichment Activities if your child completes his assigned work and has the time or desire to learn more. These activities are flexible, so choose the one(s) that seem most interesting to your student. Allow him to work at a level that is appropriate for him, and remember that the learning process is more important than the product.

This year your child has many opportunities to research and learn about different Native American tribes as Enrichment Activities, and to make a Native American Notebook with the information he finds. Place the finished profiles in a separate binder or add them to your child's Student Notebook. Teachers can find a copy of this profile sheet in Appendix B.

Color the Classics has created resources for homeschoolers combining music and art. They offer an item on "Hymn Writers," and can be accessed at www.colortheclassics.com.

N.C. Wyeth's *Pilgrims,* text by Robert San Souci

Answers

1. One inch is approximately 200 miles.

2. 500 miles

3. false

4. Answers for all levels of this Student Notebook assignment are located in Appendix A on page 320.

5. mammals

6. Answers found in text student has read.

7. red squirrel: 7 ½ - 8 ½ inches long; lives in northern and mountain forests; gray squirrel: 8–11 inches long; lives in forests, parks, suburbs

Lesson 5, Part 1

> ### ❦ Steps for Thinking ❦
>
> 1. When a government considers the input of its people, the people are more willing to work together.
>
> 2. People from different backgrounds can work together when their agreements are based on common beliefs about what is important.

The **Steps for Thinking** section gives you the main ideas about the topics presented. Understanding these helps you to have productive discussions with your children so they, too, understand the bigger ideas. This forms more permanent learning, contrary to just learning facts, which tends to be temporary. These steps are useful prior to instruction, and they are also useful for review at the end of the week.

❧ Materials ❧

- *Squanto*
- *Stories of the Pilgrim*
- *Stories of the Pilgrims* Answer Key
- *Intermediate World Atlas*
- *North American Wildlife Guide*
- *Handbook of Nature Study*
- Personal dictionary
- Colored pencils or crayons
- Materials for hands-on spelling: dry erase board and markers; colored chalk; modeling clay; water-based paint and paper, or Letter Cards
- Student Notebook
- Index cards/marker
- Vocabulary cards
- Globe
- Large world outline map

Additional resources for Enrichment Activities are found in Part 5.

A. Copywork/Dictation   *Language Skills*

Since there was no established law, they agreed to govern themselves, and nearly everyone signed the Mayflower Compact. This became the basis for the Constitution of the United States of America. They elected John Carver as their governor. This was the first election of the people, by the people.

🐾 Copy the above lines into your Student Notebook. When you are finished, compare your copy to the model (word by word) and make any needed corrections.

🐾 Listen as your teacher dictates the above lines, and write them in your Student Notebook. When you are finished, compare your copy to the model and make any needed corrections.

🐾 Copy, or write as your teacher dictates, the last paragraph on page 167 ("Of course, . .") in *Stories of the Pilgrims*. When you are finished, compare your copy to the text and make any needed corrections.

A. Copywork and dictation assignments go from an easier level (designated by 🐾) to harder levels (designated by 🐾 and 🐾). Take two days for the copywork if that is more comfortable for your child. Please adapt instructions to your child's individual needs. Your child should be **consistently successful** at one level before progressing to the next, **regardless of grade**.

B. Reader   *Language Skills, Thinking Skills, History*

In your book, *Squanto*, read pages 80–83 aloud.

🐾 Read one or two paragraphs in your read-aloud book, *Stories of the Pilgrims*.

🐾 Read one or two pages from today's read-aloud assignment in *Stories of the Pilgrims*.

C. Discussion is very important in developing your child's ability to organize his thoughts. This in turn builds the ability to think and write. The goal of the discussion questions is not just to find the answer to a particular question, but also to create a situation where thoughts about the question and its answer are shared and considered in a detailed way. Do not rush this activity, but encourage your student to share his or her ideas relating to the topic, and any additional ideas that may come to mind. You can also share your thoughts and questions as an example for your students.

Answers to the Comprehension Questions are found in the *Stories of the Pilgrims Answer Key.*

C. Read-Aloud and Discussion   *Language Skills, Thinking Skills*

In *Stories of the Pilgrims,* listen as your teacher reads pages 163-174 aloud.

Listen as your teacher reads the Comprehension Questions on page 168 in *Stories of the Pilgrims.* Talk with your teacher about what you think the answers are.

D. Word Study   *Spelling, Phonics, Vocabulary*

Read these words from your study of the Pilgrims, or listen as your teacher reads them:

> Massasoit
> John Carver
> Samoset

Now practice reading them silently. Use your Letter Cards to spell these words and any other words you and your teacher choose for this lesson.

Make a list of your word study words in your Student Notebook. Ask your teacher to pick several words for you to practice spelling aloud.

E. Geography

You have already learned about some of the markings on a globe. Look at your globe and find the Equator. Put your finger on the Equator and move it up towards the North Pole. The next lines you come to on the globe are called **latitude**. The farther you go toward the North Pole, the farther north the latitude is! This part of Earth, above the equator, is called the Northern Hemisphere. Return to the Equator and start moving your finger down, toward the South Pole. The closer you get to the South Pole, the farther south the latitude is. This part of the earth is called the Southern Hemisphere.

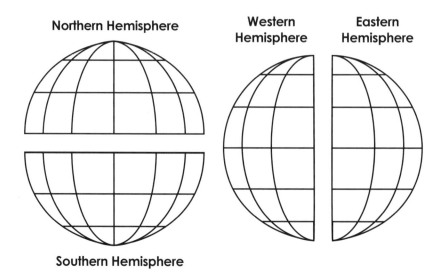

Northern Hemisphere   **Western Hemisphere**   **Eastern Hemisphere**

Southern Hemisphere

Now you are going to learn about the lines that tell you how far you have moved to the east or west. Look at your globe. Like the Equator, there is another imaginary line that runs around the globe, called the **Prime Meridian**. This line runs through the North and South Poles and like the Equator, it divides the globe into two hemispheres.

Put your finger on the Prime Meridian. You can locate it by first finding England on your globe because the Prime Meridian runs through England. Now look at the North Pole. See how the Prime Meridian seems to run through it? The same is true of the South Pole. The Prime Meridian and the other lines like it that run through the North and South Poles, are used to measure longitude.

Move your finger towards America from the Prime Meridian in England. Just like the Pilgrims, you are moving to the west. The lines you cross, running up and down as you move towards America, are lines of **longitude**. Since you moved west from the Prime Meridian, you are in the Western Hemisphere. Move your finger to the east from England. Now you are looking at the Eastern Hemisphere.

Longitude and latitude are the lines drawn on maps and globes that create a grid, and they can help you find any place in the world. Just like your grid activities, you can locate a place by finding the intersections of the lines.

🐾 Find the Prime Meridian again on your globe. In your Student Notebook, make a list of at least four countries that it runs through.

🐾 Find the Prime Meridian again on your globe. In your Student Notebook, make a list of at least five countries and three bodies of water that it runs through.

🐾 Look at the World Political Map in your *Intermediate World Atlas*. The Prime Meridian runs up and down through the center of the map, where the two pages meet. The blue grid lines are the lines of Longitude (if they meet at the Poles) and Latitude (if they move north or south from the Equator). At the top and sides of your map are letters and numbers that tell the grid sections on the map. Turn to the section called "How to Use the Atlas." Together with your teacher, read the part called "Map Grids."

Much of the United States can be found in squares D5, D6, and D7. Find these squares on the map.

Look at Greenland on the World Political Map. Make a list of the squares that cover Greenland.[1]

E. The small superscript numbers that appear after some of the questions in this unit refer to answers found in the answer key, located immediately after Part 5.

F. Oral Presentation

History

Poetry is a way of telling a story with words that paint pictures. Look at pages 151 in *Stories of the Pilgrims.* Listen as your teacher reads the poem "Thanksgiving," by Amelia E. Barr. Talk with your teacher about what the poem describes. As she reads the poem a second time, repeat each sentence after her. Try to use the same rhythm and emphasis on words that she uses. Once you feel comfortable with pronouncing each word, practice reading this poem aloud. You may want to include a reading of this poem at your Unit Presentation.

Illustrations give words more meaning. Choose at least two images in this poem to illustrate. Include your illustrations with any presentation of this poem.

The poem "Thanksgiving" can be presented in several different ways. You can read the lines after your teacher, read the lines independently, or memorize the lines. Choose which method you would like to use to present this poem during your Unit Presentation.

G. Reading fluency is developed through having frequent silent reading opportunities that continue for the length of time suggested here. Since a primary focus of this activity is to nurture your child's enjoyment of reading, help him to choose reading material that interests him and is at a level that allows him to read with understanding by himself. You can incorporate this activity into your school day whenever it is most convenient.

If the suggested length of time is too long for your child to continue reading by himself, start with an amount of time he can accomplish successfully and make the suggested time a goal.

G. Independent Reading

Choose something to read that you will enjoy. Find a quiet, comfortable place and read for the following length of time:

20 minutes

25 minutes

30 minutes

Over time, it's fun to see how much you have read. Be sure to write down what you read today on the Reading Log in your Student Notebook.

Lesson 5, Part 2

A. Copywork/Dictation

Language Skills

Some of the men rowed ashore to find a good place to settle. Their first act on dry land was to pray and thank God for their safe arrival. The *Mayflower* later sailed across Cape Cod Bay and anchored in Plymouth Harbor. The Pilgrims made this their new home on December 26, 1620.

🐾 Copy the above lines into your Student Notebook. When you are finished, compare your copy to the model (word by word) and make any needed corrections.

🐾 Listen as your teacher dictates the above lines, and write them in your Student Notebook. When you are finished, compare your copy to the model and make any needed corrections.

🐾 Copy, or write as your teacher dictates, paragraph 1 on page 176 ("Once an . . .") in *Stories of the Pilgrims*. When you are finished, compare your copy to the text and make any needed corrections.

B. **Reader**   *Language Skills, Thinking Skills, History*

In your book, *Squanto,* read page 84 through paragraph 1 on page 88 aloud.

🐾 Read one or two paragraphs in your read-aloud book, *Stories of the Pilgrims*.

🐾 Read one or two pages from today's read-aloud assignment in *Stories of the Pilgrims*.

C. **Read-Aloud and Narration**   *Language Skills, Thinking Skills*

Listen carefully as your teacher reads pages 175-181 aloud from *Stories of the Pilgrims*.

To *narrate* means to retell. In your own words, tell what happened in your assigned passage below. Try to remember as many details as possible. Listen carefully as your teacher reads (or rereads) the part you are to retell.

🐾 Reread pages 80 and 81 of *Squanto*. Tell why Squanto was at this house looking for help.

🐾 Use the book and pictures to retell the chapter "The Slave Market" to your teacher.

🐾 Tell your teacher about the chapter entitled "The Indians and the Lanterns" in *Stories of the Pilgrims*.

D. **Word Study**   *Spelling, Phonics, Vocabulary*

Look at the list of spelling words you wrote in your Student Notebook in Part 1. Read the words silently, or listen as your teacher reads them.

Now say each word and tell how many syllables, or word parts you hear in each word. Write the number of syllables you hear in each word next to the word.

A. The dictation method enables your child to hear language and correctly write down what he hears. It involves building two different skills. First, the ability to listen and understand what is heard, and second, the ability to transfer what is heard into written language. This process takes time and practice, so begin as gradually as needed for successfully reaching the goal of getting the words the child hears on the paper correctly. 1) Read the whole passage, then reread one sentence at a time, giving your child time to write what he hears. 2) After he has finished, reread the passage again, allowing him to double check what he has written. 3) Then proceed to the step of comparing his writing to the model. As his skill builds, you can move more quickly through the steps, maintaining your child's level of success.

C. The skill of narration is gained over time. If your child has never retold a story, start with the assignment for the lower level, no matter what grade he is in. Work up from there, being careful to allow him to stay at the level of success for a while before going to a longer section.

Choose a way to practice your spelling words from the list below:

- Dry erase board and markers
- Colored chalk and chalkboard *or* sidewalk
- Modeling clay
- Water-based paint and paper
- Letter Cards

E. Geography/Science   *Language Skills, Thinking Skills*

Gather together all the vocabulary cards you have made for this unit. Practice reading the words and telling what you think they mean.

Make a stack of the words you remember, and another stack of words you need to review.

From the stack of words you remember, tell your teacher how you think each word relates to our unit studies.

F. Writing

Think about what you have learned about William Bradford. Look at the Explorer page in your Student Notebook. Read over the questions and discuss your answers with your teacher. When you feel you know how to best answer each question, write your answers in the spaces provided. Remember to use your Pilgrim Word Bank to help you.

You will share what you have learned about the Pilgrims with your family at the end of this unit. You may want to use these questions as a guide for part of your Unit Presentation. Make sure you include your answers in your presentation.

G. See Independent Reading note in Part 1.

G. Independent Reading

Choose something to read that you will enjoy. Find a quiet, comfortable place and read for the following length of time:

❧❧ 20 minutes

❧ 25 minutes

❧ 30 minutes

Over time, it's fun to see how much you have read. Be sure to write down what you read today on the Reading Log in your Student Notebook.

Lesson 5, Part 3

A. **Copywork/Dictation**   *Language Skills*

With your teacher's help, choose a passage from your reader or another book that you enjoy reading. Copy, or write as your teacher dictates, the passage you chose. When you are finished, compare your copy to the text and make any needed corrections. Follow the guidelines below for the minimum assignment:

ΨΨ At least 3 sentences

🐾 At least 4 sentences

🐾 At least 5 sentences

A. See Copywork/Dictation note in Part 1.

B. **Reader**   *Language Skills, Thinking Skills, History*

ΨΨ In your book, *Squanto*, read from paragraph 2 on page 88 through page 92 aloud.

🐾 Read one or two paragraphs in your read-aloud book, *Stories of the Pilgrims.*

🐾 Read one or two pages from today's read-aloud assignment in *Stories of the Pilgrims.*

C. **Read-Aloud and Discussion**   *Language Skills, Thinking Skills*

In *Stories of the Pilgrims,* listen as your teacher reads pages 183-192 aloud.

Discuss the events you have just listened to from the chapter entitled "Two Little Captives." Share your feelings about what has happened to Isaac and Joseph.

C. See Discussion note in Part 1.

D. **Word Study**   *Spelling, Phonics, Vocabulary*

Tell your teacher what each spelling word means and how it relates to your Pilgrim study. In your Student Notebook, fill out a Pilgrim Word Bank entry for each of your words and include this information.

Practice your words by using by using one of the following:

- Dry erase board and markers
- Colored chalk and chalkboard *or* sidewalk
- Modeling clay
- Water-based paint and paper
- Letter Cards

E. **Geography**

As you remember, Squanto eventually became someone very important to the survival of the Pilgrim colony. He first left his village in 1605 to travel to England. This was the first of many voyages that resulted in his traveling thousands of miles.

Look at the World Map in your Student Notebook that you began labeling in Lesson 3, Part 1. Use your ruler, and a different colored pencil than you used to mark Squanto's first voyage, to draw a line from London, England, to Plymouth, Massachusetts. In the bottom left hand corner of your map, write "Voyage 2," and make a short line with the same colored pencil you used. Leave room for several more voyages underneath this one. You are making your own key for this map.

Follow the above instructions for Squanto's remaining voyages. Be sure to use a diffferent color to mark each of the following:

Voyage 3 – Plymouth, Massachusetts, to Malaga, Spain

Voyage 4 – Malaga, Spain, to London, England

Voyage 5 – London, England, to Plymouth, Massachusetts

After you have drawn lines to show Squanto's voyages, measure the lincs with a ruler. Line your ruler up with the Map Scale on the bottom of the map. One inch equals approximately 2,666 miles, so one-fourth of an inch equals approximately 666 miles. Multiply this number by the number of ¼ inches to find the distance of Squanto's voyages. Write the total distance of each voyage in your Student Notebook.[2]

Add the mileage of each of the five voyages together to find out how many miles Squanto traveled altogether.[3]

Squanto's life was full of surprises. It is easy to believe that he never dreamed that he would travel so far. Some of the reasons for his voyages were happy, and some were sad. After his first voyage, all of his travels involved trying to get back to his home. Look at the reasons for each voyage listed below:

Voyage 2 – Squanto returned to Plymouth, Massachusetts, with John Smith.

Voyage 3 – Squanto was taken captive by Captain Hunt.

Voyage 4 – Brothers at a monastery in Spain freed Squanto and helped him return to London.

Voyage 5 – Squanto returned to Plymouth with Captain Dermer.

In your Student Notebook, summarize how you think Squanto felt about each voyage.

F. Art

Thinking Skills, History

In the next lesson you will complete your read-aloud book, *Stories of the Pilgrims*. In preparation for the end of this unit, review the chapter titles of this book and look at the pictures in each chapter. Discuss the main events that occurred in the story. Choose one event out of this story that you think was the most interesting so far and draw a picture of that event to go in your Student Notebook. Underneath the picture, tell what event you chose and why.

G. Independent Reading

Choose something to read that you will enjoy. Find a quiet, comfortable place and read for the following length of time:

- 20 minutes
- 25 minutes
- 30 minutes

Be sure to write down what you read today on the Reading Log in your Student Notebook.

G. See Independent Reading note in Part 1.

Lesson 5, Part 4

A. Copywork/Dictation

Language Skills

The first winter was a hard one and many became sick and died. In spring, the Pilgrims were surprised when an Indian came into the village and greeted them in English! His name was Samoset. A lasting friendship between the Pilgrims and the Indians began this day.

A. See Copywork/Dictation note in Part 1.

- Copy the above lines into your Student Notebook. When you are finished, compare your copy to the model (word by word) and make any needed corrections.

- Listen as your teacher dictates the above lines, and write them in your Student Notebook. When you are finished, compare your copy to the model and make any needed corrections.

- Copy, or write as your teacher dictates, paragraph 2 on page 193 ("The women , . .") in *Stories of the Pilgrims*. When you are finished, compare your copy to the text and make any needed corrections.

B. Reader   *Language Skills, Thinking Skills, History*

In your book, *Squanto,* read page 93 through paragraph 1 on page 97 aloud.

🐾 Read one or two paragraphs in your read-aloud book, *Stories of the Pilgrims.*

🐾 Read one or two pages from today's read-aloud assignment in *Stories of the Pilgrims.*

C. See Narration note in Part 2.

C. Read-Aloud and Narration   *Language Skills, Thinking Skills*

Listen carefully as your teacher reads pages 193-202 aloud from *Stories of the Pilgrims.*

To *narrate* means to retell. In your own words, tell what happened in your assigned passage below. Try to remember as many details as possible. Listen carefully as your teacher reads (or rereads) the part you are to retell.

🐾🐾 Reread page 84 of *Squanto.* Tell about Squanto's friends. Does he still want to go home?

🐾 Use the book and pictures to retell the chapter "Christmas Eve" to your teacher.

🐾 Tell your teacher about the 2nd half of the chapter entitled "Two Little Captives" in *Stories of the Pilgrims.*

D. Word Study   *Spelling, Phonics, Vocabulary*

Review the spelling words you are working on in this lesson by reading them, spelling them aloud, and then checking to see if you were correct.

When you feel you are ready, spell them for your teacher. Once you have done that, and your teacher gives you permission, write your spelling words in your personal dictionary.

Look through your personal dictionary and choose several words to spell aloud for your teacher.

E. Geography

You have read and learned much about the Pilgrims during this unit. Now listen to your teacher read "A Pilgrim Story," which is in Appendix A. This is a summary of the events that occurred from the time the Separatists first met in secret until the Plymouth colony was well established and had survived much.

Find the Pilgrim Bingo game boards on your Student Resources CD, and read each one with your teacher. Arrange the game boards in front of you on a table, and listen as your teacher reads the summary story a second time. When you hear a word or fact read aloud that you see on a Bingo game board, raise your hand. Follow the directions in Appendix A and play Pilgrim Bingo.

F. Art
History, Thinking Skills

Look at the words you have added to your Pilgrim Word Bank during this lesson. Illustrations can help you remember what words mean and the way they are used. Use your reader or read-aloud book for ideas and draw a picture to illustrate each of these words. Your drawing can show what the word means or something that reminds you of the word, like a crown for King James. Use colored pencils or crayons to complete your illustrations.

G. Independent Reading

Choose something to read that you will enjoy. Find a quiet, comfortable place and read for the following length of time:

ǂǂ 20 minutes

✾ 25 minutes

✾ 30 minutes

Be sure to write down what you read today on the Reading Log in your Student Notebook.

G. See Independent Reading note in Part 1.

Lesson 5, Part 5

This part is set aside for completion of any work left undone from the lesson, and review of concepts and content. It is also a time to expand the work in the lesson by doing art, timeline activities, or games.

• Review the Steps for Thinking from the beginning of this lesson.

• On the large outline map of the world label: Equator; Prime Meridian; mark Squanto's voyage from Plymouth, Massachusetts, to Malaga, Spain; from Malaga, Spain, to London; from London back to Plymouth, Massachusetts, in purple. Use arrows to show direction.

• Review the spelling words for this lesson. In your Student Notebook, write a sentence using each word that tells how it is related to the unit. Do your best to write the spelling words correctly. After you have finished, check your sentences against the list in your Student Notebook and see how many spelling words you spelled correctly. (Don't count off for other words that are misspelled.) Remember your goal is to improve, not necessarily to get them all right immediately.

Most of the labeling has already been completed in the Student Notebook during this lesson. Instruct students to use the maps in their Student Notebooks as a reference. When they label the larger map, students will see the "big picture" and gain a broader understanding of their lessons.

Teachers can find a copy of this game in Appendix B. Instructions and answer keys for all games are located in Appendix A.

Use one or more of the Enrichment Activities if your child completes his assigned work and has the time or desire to learn more. These activities are flexible, so choose the one(s) that seem most interesting to your student. Allow him to work at a level that is appropriate for him, and remember that the learning process is more important than the product.

This year your child has many opportunities to research and learn about different Native American tribes as Enrichment Activities, and to make a Native American Notebook with the information he finds. Make a copy of the Native American Profile sheet, found in Appendix B, for each tribe your child studies. Then, place the finished profiles in a separate binder or add them to your child's student notebook.

- Play the Pilgrim Bingo game found on your Student Resources CD.

- You have learned about many animals, but the animal most people know best lives in their homes. With your teacher's help, look in the *Handbook of Nature Study* to find information about your pet. The common pets included are dogs, cats, birds, horses, goats, fish, and reptiles. Make a sketch of your pet and color it. Now look for at least three facts you did not know about your pet and make a list of them on the back of your sketch.

  If you do not have a pet, choose the animal from the *Handbook of Nature Study* that you like the best and follow the directions above. Additional pictures of most of these animals can be found in the *North American Wildlife Guide*.

Enrichment Activities

1. Samoset and Squanto were very valuable to the Pilgrims because they were able to translate the Indian language into English. How different do you think it would be to work with and understand someone whose language you do not speak? If you don't understand a person's language, what else might be hard to understand about him?

2. Look at page 5 in your *United States History Atlas*, and choose one or more Native American tribes that lived in the Northeastern part of the United States at the time of the Pilgrims. Then, at the library or, with your parent's permission, on the Internet research the tribes you have chosen. Fill out a Native American Profile sheet for each one to go in your Native American Notebook.

3. You have learned about many different types of animals: birds, fish, invertebrates, mammals, and reptiles. After doing some research on the animals in your area, make a guide about the animals found around your home. It could just be a guide to the pets in your neighborhood, or could include wild animals in your area. Draw or sketch each animal and include what it looks like, where it lives, and any interesting facts about it.

Additional Resources

Wycliffe Bible Translators (www.wycliffe.org)

North American Wildlife Guide

Handbook of Nature Study

The Pilgrims of Plimoth by Marcia Sewall

Answers

1. A8, A9, A10, A11, B9, B10, B11

2. Voyage two – approximately 4,662 miles; Voyage three – approximately 4,662 miles; Voyage four – approximately 1,998 miles; Voyage five – approximately 4,662 miles

3. 20, 646

Lesson 6, Part 1

A. **Copywork/Dictation**   *Language Skills*

> Samoset later brought another Indian named Squanto, who could speak English well. Squanto became a good friend to the Pilgrims. He taught them to plant Indian Corn and acted as an interpreter. Edward Winslow learned the Indian language from Squanto and taught him how to read the Bible.

🐾 Copy the above lines into your Student Notebook. When you are finished, compare your copy to the model (word by word) and make any needed corrections.

✋ Listen as your teacher dictates the above lines, and write them in your Student Notebook. When you are finished, compare your copy to the model and make any needed corrections.

🐾 Copy, or write as your teacher dictates, paragraph 3 on page 210 ("But the words . . .") in *Stories of the Pilgrims*. When you are finished, compare your copy to the text and make any needed corrections.

B. **Reader**   *Language Skills, Thinking Skills, History*

In your book, *Squanto,* read from paragraph 2 on page 97 through page 101 aloud.

✋ Read one or two paragraphs in your read-aloud book, *Stories of the Pilgrims.*

🐾 Read one or two pages from today's read-aloud assignment in *Stories of the Pilgrims.*

C. **Read-Aloud and Discussion**   *Language Skills, Thinking Skills*

In *Stories of the Pilgrims*, listen as your teacher reads pages 203-211 aloud.

Listen to your teacher read the Comprehension Questions on page 211 in *Stories of the Pilgrims.* Talk with your teacher about what you think the answers are.

D. **Word Study**   *Spelling, Phonics, Vocabulary*

Read these words from your study of the Pilgrims, or listen as your teacher reads them:

～Materials～

- *Squanto*
- *Stories of the Pilgrim*
- *Stories of the Pilgrims* Answer Key
- *Intermediate World Atlas*
- *North American Wildlife Guide*
- *Handbook of Nature Study*
- *Profiles from History*
- *Eat Your Way Around the World*
- Personal dictionary
- Colored pencils or crayons
- Materials for hands-on spelling: dry erase board and markers; colored chalk; modeling clay; water-based paint and paper, or Letter Cards
- Student Notebook
- Index cards/marker
- Vocabulary cards
- Construction paper
- Globe
- Animal I.D. cards
- Pumpkin
- Ingredients for Pumpkin recipe

Additional resources for Enrichment Activities are found in Part 5.

A. Copywork and dictation assignments are meant to go from an easier level (designated by 🐾) to harder levels (designated by ✋ and 🐾). Copywork can be accomplished over two days if that is more comfortable for your child. Please adapt instructions to your child's individual needs. Your child should be **consistently successful** at one level before progressing to the next, **regardless of grade**.

C. Discussion is very important in developing your child's ability to organize his thoughts. This in turn builds the ability to think and write. The goal of the discussion questions is not just to find the answer to a particular question, but also to create a situation where thoughts about the question and its answer are shared and considered in a detailed way. Do not rush this activity, but encourage your student to share his or her ideas relating to the topic, and any additional ideas that may come to mind. You can also share your thoughts and questions as an example for your students.

William Bradford
Squanto
Indian Corn

Now practice reading them silently. Use your Letter Cards to spell these words and any other words you and your teacher choose for this lesson.

Make a list of your word study words in your Student Notebook. Ask your teacher to pick several words for you to practice spelling aloud.

E. Science

In Lesson 4, Part 2 you reviewed the following categories of animals. You added the names of more animals you have studied to your set of Animal I.D. cards, as well as the category that each animal fits into:

| reptiles | mammals | birds |
| fish | invertebrates | |

Look at the vocabulary card you made for each of the categories above, and review the qualities of each. Make sure you can tell your teacher what animals in each category are like. If you haven't already, make two cards for each of the animals listed below. Remember to write the name of the animal on the top of the card. You may also draw a picture of the animal on the card and include important information. Write the category of the animal on the bottom.

red squirrel   gray squirrel

Now you are ready to play the Animal I.D. game. Shuffle the cards and deal 5 cards face down to each player. Put the remainder of the cards in a stack, face down. There must be at least two players to play. Now play a "Go Fish" type of game, where you ask the other person for a certain animal. If he or she doesn't have it, draw a card. Your goal is to match animal pairs. When you get a pair, put it down during your turn. When all the cards are gone, or someone matches all his cards, the game is over. The one with the most pairs wins.

F. Writing   *Thinking Skills*

At this point in the *Stories of the Pilgrims,* you have heard that the Pilgrims felt they had much to be thankful for. Though they had endured many hardships and lost many who were dear to them, still they had survived and built a home in a place of freedom.

Make a list of the things you think the Pilgrims were thankful for. Now add some things that you are thankful for to this list. Below is the word **THANKFUL.** Copy it onto a piece of construction paper exactly as you see it below:

E. Each time your student makes an Animal I.D. card for this unit, have him write a "P" (for Pilgrim) in the upper left corner. This will make it possible to review the animals studied by unit at the end of the year.

T
H
A
N
K
F
U
L

Use the list you made above and choose a word or phrase that begins with each of the letters of this important word. This is called an acrostic poem. If you have any trouble with this activity, review the example in Lesson 3, Part 1, Section F.

🐾 Choose a second word from your reading about the Pilgrims and create another acrostic poem on construction paper with that word.

G. Independent Reading

Choose something to read that you will enjoy. Find a quiet, comfortable place and read for the following length of time:

🐾 20 minutes

🐾 25 minutes

🐾 30 minutes

Be sure to write down what you read today on the Reading Log in your Student Notebook.

G. Reading fluency is developed through having frequent silent reading opportunities that continue for the length of time suggested here. Since a primary focus of this activity is to nurture your child's enjoyment of reading, help him to choose reading material that interests him and is at a level that allows him to read with understanding by himself. You can incorporate this activity into your school day whenever it is most convenient.

If the suggested length of time is too long for your child to continue reading by himself, start with an amount of time he can accomplish successfully and make the suggested time a goal.

———※———

Lesson 6, Part 2

A. Copywork/Dictation   *Language Skills*

After the first harvest the Pilgrims celebrated with games, activities, and food. They invited their Indian friends to celebrate God's blessing on the harvest. The Pilgrims celebrated Thanksgiving every year after the harvest, and for many years the Indians joined them on this special day.

A. See Copywork/Dictation note in Part 1.

🐾 Copy the above lines into your Student Notebook. When you are finished, compare your copy to the model (word by word) and make any needed corrections.

🐾 Listen as your teacher dictates the above lines, and write them in your Student Notebook. When you are finished, compare your copy to the model and make any needed corrections.

🐾 Copy, or write as your teacher dictates, paragraph 2 on page 212 ("It was . . .") in *Stories of the Pilgrims*. When you are finished, compare your copy to the text and make any needed corrections.

B. Reader   *Language Skills, Thinking Skills, History*
In your book, *Squanto*, read pages 102–105 aloud.

🐾 Read one or two paragraphs in your read-aloud book, *Stories of the Pilgrims*.

🐾 Read one or two pages from today's read-aloud assignment in *Stories of the Pilgrims*.

C. Read-Aloud and Narration   *Language Skills, Thinking Skills*
Listen carefully as your teacher reads pages 212-216 aloud from *Stories of the Pilgrims*.

To *narrate* means to retell. In your own words, tell what happened in your assigned passage below. Try to remember as many details as possible. Listen carefully as your teacher reads (or rereads) the part you are to retell.

🌵🌵 Reread page 92 of *Squanto*. Tell why Squanto is sad.

🐾 Use the book and pictures to retell the chapter "John Slanie's House" to your teacher.

🐾 Tell your teacher about the chapter entitled "Two Brass Kettles" in *Stories of the Pilgrims*.

D. Word Study   *Spelling, Phonics, Vocabulary*
Look at the list of spelling words you wrote in your Student Notebook in Part 1. Read the words silently, or listen as your teacher reads them.

Now say each word and tell how many syllables, or word parts you hear in each word. Write the number of syllables you hear in each word next to the word.

Choose a way to practice your spelling words from the list below:

- Dry erase board and markers
- Colored chalk and chalkboard *or* sidewalk
- Modeling clay
- Water-based paint and paper
- Letter Cards

C. The skill of narration is gained over time. If your child has never retold a story, start with the assignment for the lower level, no matter what grade he is in. Work up from there, being careful to allow him to stay at the level of success for a while before going to a longer section.

E. Geography

You have been introduced to many places on the map since the beginning of these units. Use your globe or a map to point out to your teacher all the places you have learned about, as well as things on the map or globe, such as the compass rose or a key. Tell your teacher what you remember about each place or thing.

You may want to play a game where one person picks a place and the other person tries to tell what it is and how it relates to the Columbus, Jamestown, or Pilgrims units. Players should only choose places covered in these units. Or you can choose a place off the list below and find it.

> **Oceans:** Atlantic, Pacific, Indian, Arctic, and Antarctic (or Southern)
>
> **Seas:** Mediterranean, Caribbean, North, Irish
>
> **Bays and Rivers:** Chesapeake Bay, James River, Thames River, English Channel, Strait of Dover, Maas River, Rijn River, Ijssel River, Waal River, Plymouth Bay, Cape Cod Bay
>
> **Continents:** North America, South America, Africa, Asia, Europe
>
> **Countries:** Spain, Portugal, England, Italy, Cuba, America, Dominican Republic, Jamaica, Puerto Rico, Netherlands
>
> **States:** Virginia, Massachusetts
>
> **Islands:** Bermuda Islands, West Indies, Canary Islands
>
> **Map Markers:** Equator, Northern Hemisphere, Southern Hemisphere, North Pole, South Pole, Latitude, Longitude

You may want to add any other country or place that you learned about. Look at all the places you have explored!

F. Art

Yesterday you created at least one acrostic poem. You used words to paint a picture. Today you will add color, designs, or pictures that emphasize the words you have already placed on the construction paper. Your goal is to give the words more meaning with your illustrations.

Talk with your teacher about the materials available to you such as markers, colored pencils, crayons, or paint. With her permission, choose what will best highlight your thoughts. Your copy of this poem will be part of your Unit Presentation at the end of this unit, so remember to do your best.

🐾 Prepare all the poems you created to be part of the Unit Presentation at the end of this unit by following the directions above.

Independent Reading note in

G. Independent Reading

Choose something to read that you will enjoy. Find a quiet, comfortable place and read for the following length of time:

🐾 20 minutes

🐾 25 minutes

🐾 30 minutes

Over time, it's fun to see how much you have read. Be sure to write down what you read today on the Reading Log in your Student Notebook.

Lesson 6, Part 3

A. See Copywork/Dictation note in Part 1.

A. Copywork/Dictation   *Language Skills*

With your teacher's help, choose a passage from your reader or another book that you enjoy reading. Copy, or write as your teacher dictates, the passage you chose. When you are finished, compare your copy to the text and make any needed corrections. Follow the guidelines below for the minimum assignment:

🐾 At least 3 sentences

🐾 At least 4 sentences

🐾 At least 5 sentences

B. Reader   *Language Skills, Thinking Skills, History*

In your book, *Squanto*, read pages 106–108 aloud.

🐾 Read one or two paragraphs in your read-aloud book, *Stories of the Pilgrims*.

🐾 Read one or two pages from today's read-aloud assignment in *Stories of the Pilgrims*.

C. See Discussion note in Part 1.

Answers to discussion Comprehension Questions are found in the *Stories of the Pilgrims Answer Key*.

C. Read-Aloud and Discussion   *Language Skills, Thinking Skills*

In *Stories of the Pilgrims*, listen as your teacher reads pages 217-221 aloud.

Listen to your teacher reads the Comprehension Questions on page 219 in *Stories of the Pilgrims*. Talk with your teacher about what you think the answers are.

D. Word Study

Spelling, Phonics, Vocabulary

Tell your teacher what each spelling word means and how it relates to your Pilgrim study. In your Student Notebook, fill out a Pilgrim Word Bank entry for each of your words and include this information.

Practice your words by using one of the following:

- Dry erase board and markers
- Colored chalk and chalkboard *or* sidewalk
- Modeling clay
- Water-based paint and paper
- Letter Cards

E. Science

At the end of this unit, you will be using pumpkin to prepare food for your Pilgrim Unit Presentation. This is one of the foods that was typically a part of the harvest celebration. Over the years, pumpkins have come to symbolize a successful harvest and Thanksgiving.

Listen as your teacher reads about the pumpkin on pages 611–615 in the *Handbook of Nature Study*. Now, answer questions 1-5 on page 616. These questions are best answered with the use of a real pumpkin.

Include a sketch of a pumpkin in your Student Notebook.

F. Writing

Now that you have almost completed your reader and the read-aloud book, make a book review card. The purpose of a book review card is to give a brief description of what you read or heard, and then to tell what you thought of the book. It should not include as much information as a book report. The goal is to give someone who has not read the book enough information to decide whether or not they might like to read it. In a sense, it is like an advertisement for a book. Give enough information to let someone know the good points about the book, while not retelling the story.

How to Create a Book Review Card:

Your book review can be written on a large index card or on the page provided in your Student Notebook. Include the following information on your card:

- name of the book

- author of the book (person who wrote the book)

- illustrator of the book (person who drew the pictures)

- name of the company who published the book

- date the book was published

Most of this information can be found on the title page of the book.

Rehearse, or practice telling, what you will say about the story and how you liked it. Once you have discussed your thoughts enough to know what you want to write, you can begin. If you don't know how to spell some of the words you want to use, ask your teacher to make a word bank for you, or look at your Pilgrim Word Bank.

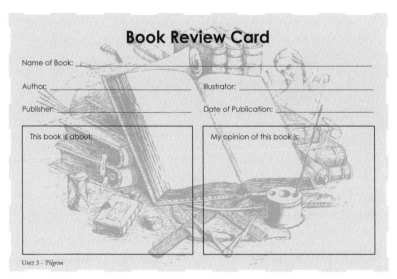

Next, write a few sentences to tell what the story was about. Since you only have a few sentences, you will have to choose the most important facts to tell.

Finally, write a few sentences to tell what you thought about the story. It would be good to tell whether you liked the book and then give some examples of what you did or did not like about it. Remember to use your Pilgrim Word Bank to help you.

🐾🐾 Create a book review card on the reader, *Squanto.*

🐾 Create a book review card on either the reader, *Squanto* or the read-aloud, *Stories of the Pilgrims.*

🐾 Create a book review card on the read-aloud book, *Stories of the Pilgrims.*

G. See Independent Reading note in Part 1.

G. **Independent Reading**

Choose something to read that you will enjoy. Find a quiet, comfortable place and read for the following length of time:

🐾🐾 20 minutes

🐾 25 minutes

🐾 30 minutes

Be sure to write down what you read today on the Reading Log in your Student Notebook.

Lesson 6, Part 4

A. **Copywork/Dictation**   *Language Skills*

> Governor Carver died the first year, and William Bradford became the new governor. He served for over 30 years and kept a diary of their experiences. The Pilgrims laid a foundation for something dear to every American. They willingly gave all to gain the right to freedom.

❧❧ Copy the above lines into your Student Notebook. When you are finished, compare your copy to the model (word by word) and make any needed corrections.

❧ Listen as your teacher dictates the above lines, and write them in your Student Notebook. When you are finished, compare your copy to the model and make any needed corrections.

❧ Copy, or write as your teacher dictates, the last paragraph on page 223 ("At the sound . . .") in *Stories of the Pilgrims*. When you are finished, compare your copy to the text and make any needed corrections.

B. **Reader**   *Language Skills, Thinking Skills, History*
In your book, *Squanto*, read pages 109–112 aloud.

❧ Read one or two paragraphs in your read-aloud book, *Stories of the Pilgrims*.

❧ Read one or two pages from today's read-aloud assignment in *Stories of the Pilgrims*.

C. **Read-Aloud and Narration**   *Language Skills, Thinking Skills*
Listen carefully as your teacher reads pages 222-228 aloud from *Stories of the Pilgrims*.

To *narrate* means to retell. In your own words, tell what happened in your assigned passage below. Try to remember as many details as possible. Listen carefully as your teacher reads (or rereads) the part you are to retell.

❧❧ Reread pages 104 and 105 of *Squanto*. Tell what Squanto helped to do and the decision he made.

❧ Use the book and pictures to retell the chapter "Home" to your teacher.

❧ Tell your teacher about the chapter entitled "Holidays and Holy Days" in *Stories of the Pilgrims*.

A. See Copywork/Dictation Part 1.

C. See Narration note in Part 2.

D. Word Study   *Spelling, Phonics, Vocabulary*

Review all of the word study words you are working on in this lesson by reading them, spelling them aloud, and then checking to see if you were correct. When you feel you are ready, spell them for your teacher. Once you have done that, and your teacher gives you permission, write your spelling words in your personal dictionary.

You have now completed all the assigned word study words for the Pilgrim Unit. Review the spelling of any words from the Pilgrim Unit that you have not already added to your personal dictionary in past weeks. Without looking, spell these aloud for your teacher. Once spelled correctly, add them to your personal dictionary.

E. History

Listen to or read the information about Galileo in *Profiles from History*. Complete the timeline activities and any other activities you would like to do.

F. Art   *History, Thinking Skills*

Look at the words you have added to your Pilgrim Word Bank during this lesson. Illustrations can help you remember what words mean and the way they are used. Use your reader or read-aloud book for ideas and draw a picture to illustrate each of these words. Your drawing can show what the word means or something that reminds you of the word, like a crown for King James. Use colored pencils or crayons to complete your illustrations.

G. See Independent Reading note in Part 1.

G. Independent Reading

Choose something to read that you will enjoy. Find a quiet, comfortable place and read for the following length of time:

ᐱᐱ 20 minutes

🐾 25 minutes

🐾 30 minutes

Congratulations on completing six weeks of independent reading! Today's entry in your reading log will be the last one for this unit. Make sure you have included all the information needed on your log such as book titles, authors, and dates read.

Look over all that you have accomplished during your independent reading time. If you would like, share your reading log with others during your Unit Presentation tomorrow.

Lesson 6, Part 5

This part is set aside for completion of any work left undone from the lesson, and review of concepts and content. It is also a time to expand the work in the lesson by doing art, timeline activities, or games.

- Listen as your teacher reviews the Steps for Thinking from this unit about the Pilgrims that you have completed. Discuss how you can apply the Steps for Thinking to what you have learned.

- Prepare a dish made with pumpkin for your Unit Presentation. Your family may have a favorite recipe, or you can use the Pumpkin Soup recipe on page 95 in *Eat Your Way Around the World*.

- Make a Unit Presentation to your family telling about what you have learned in the unit you have just completed about the Pilgrims. Share your Student Notebook and the poems you have prepared for display. You may also choose to read or recite the poems you have written as well as the poem "Thanksgiving" from *Stories of the Pilgrims*.

- Use your Explorer page as a guideline to tell what you have learned about William Bradford. Don't forget to speak clearly and stand still while speaking. After your presentation, don't forget to ask if anyone has questions.

- Play Pilgrim Bingo.

Teachers can find a copy of this game in Appendix B. Instructions and answer keys for all games are located in Appendix A.

Congratulations on completing Unit 3 of *Paths of Exploration!*

Paths of Exploration

- Appendix -

Appendix A

COLUMBUS UNIT – Lesson 1 At A Glance

A. Copywork/Dictation				*Christopher Columbus*
	Part 1	□ "A Journey of Adventure," Stanza 1		□ Paragraph 4, page 4
	Part 2	□ "A Journey of Adventure," Stanza 2		□ Paragraph 2, page 8
	Part 3	□ "A Journey of Adventure," Stanza 3		□ Paragraph 2, page 12
	Part 4	□ "A Journey of Adventure," Stanza 4		□ Paragraph 3, page 20
B. Reader		*Meet Christopher Columbus*	*Christopher Columbus*	*Christopher Columbus*
	Part 1	□ Pages 1, 2	□ 1–2 paragraphs	□ 1–2 pages
	Part 2	□ Pages 3, 4	□ 1–2 paragraphs	□ 1–2 pages
	Part 3	□ Pages 5–7	□ 1–2 paragraphs	□ 1–2 pages
	Part 4	□ Pages 8–10	□ 1–2 paragraphs	□ 1–2 pages
C. Read Aloud		*Christopher Columbus*		
	Part 1	□ Pages 1–6	□ Discussion	
	Part 2	□ Pages 6–10	□ Narration	
	Part 3	□ Pages 11–15	□ Discussion	
	Part 4	□ Pages 16–22	□ Narration	
D. Word Study				
	Part 1	□ *igh* words □ Practice □ Silly sentence	□ List, *un* words	□ Map exercise □ Definition, *port* □ Port cities
	Part 2	□ List, descriptive words	□ Word ending, *ed* □ Synonym, *strange*	□ List of places
	Part 3	□ Syllables □ List □ Discussion	□ List, *re* words	□ List, descriptive words
	Part 4	□ Syllables □ List □ Word practice	□ List of events □ Sequencing	□ Narration □ List of events
E. Geography/Science				
	Part 1	□ Compass skills □ Globe skills, poles	□ Additional compass skills	
	Part 2	□ Imaginary trip		
	Part 3	□ Globe familiarization □ Discussion		
	Part 4	□ Mental map □ Drawing	□ Mapmaking □ Drawing	□ Additional mapmaking □ Drawing
F. Writing/Drawing				
	Part 1	□ List, Columbus □ List, student □ Compare	□ Write lists □ Compare	□ Venn diagram
	Part 2	□ Rug design		
	Part 3	□ Capitalization	□ Journal entry	□ 2 explanatory sentences
	Part 4	□ Drawing □ Discussion □ Sentence skills	□ Picture cut and paste	□ Sequencing □ Descriptive sentences
G. Independent Reading		□ 20 minutes daily □ □ □	□ 25 minutes daily □ □ □ □	□ 30 minutes daily □ □ □
Review	Part 5	□ Steps for Thinking review □ Map activity	□ Spelling review □ Art lesson	□ Columbus Word Search

Materials: *Meet Christopher Columbus* by James T. de Kay; *Christopher Columbus* by Bennie Rhodes; *Intermediate World Atlas* from Rand McNally; *Eat Your Way Around the World* by Jamie Aramini — Thesaurus, Birthday Pictures, Student Notebook, Yellow highlighter or Crayon, Globe, Index card or Paper, Crayons or Colored pencils, Magazines, Newspapers, Paste, Graph paper, Dictionary, Large world outline map

Columbus Unit – Lesson 2 At A Glance

Subject	Part	Track 1	Track 2	Track 3 — *Christopher Columbus*
A. Copywork/Dictation		*"A Journey of Adventure," Stanza 5*		
	Part 1	□ Columbus Story, #1		□ Paragraph 3, page 24
	Part 2	□ Columbus Story, #2		□ Paragraph 4, page 24
	Part 3	□ Columbus Story, #3		□ Last para, page 25–3rd sentence, page 27
	Part 4			□ Paragraph 2, page 27
B. Reader		*Meet Christopher Columbus*	*Christopher Columbus*	*Christopher Columbus*
	Part 1	□ Pages 11, 12	□ 1–2 paragraphs	□ 1–2 pages
	Part 2	□ Pages 13, 14	□ 1–2 paragraphs	□ 1–2 pages
	Part 3	□ Pages 15–17	□ 1–2 paragraphs	□ 1–2 pages
	Part 4	□ Pages 18–20	□ 1–2 paragraphs	□ 1–2 pages
C. Read Aloud		*Christopher Columbus*		
	Part 1	□ Pages 23–28	□ Discussion	
	Part 2	□ Pages 29–33	□ Narration	
	Part 3	□ Pages 34–38	□ Discussion	
	Part 4	□ Pages 39–44	□ Narration	
D. Word Study				
	Part 1	□ Rhyming words □ More words	□ Imaginary trip □ Sentence skills	□ Comparison and contrast □ Definitions
	Part 2	□ *ex* words □ Practice	□ List, *ing* words □ Root words □ Rule	□ Research, Prince Henry □ Questions
	Part 3	□ Practice □ Word clues	□ List, *ing* words □ Definition □ Descriptive sentences	□ List, languages □ Discussion
	Part 4	□ Sentence skills □ Paragraph	□ Main idea	□ Discussion, Marco Polo and Columbus
E. Geography/Science				
	Part 1	□ Mapmaking □ Drawing	□ Mental map	□ Directions
	Part 2	□ List, explorer qualities □ Discussion	□ Discussion	□ Discussion
	Part 3	□ Drawing □ Descriptive words	□ Collecting info □ Recording info □ Drawing	□ Additional collecting & recording □ Drawing
	Part 4	□ Globe skills, oceans □ Experiment, salt □ Examine crystals □ Questions 1–4	□ Discussion, questions 5–7	□ Questions 5–7
F. Writing/Drawing				
	Part 1	□ Oral presentation preparation		
	Part 2	□ Timed observation □ List □ Drawing		
	Part 3	□ Discussion, worldview □ 3 Reasons	□ 3 Interviews □ Discussion	□ Discussion □ Interviews
	Part 4	□ Globe skills, oceans □ Labeling □ Coloring	□ Ranking, oceans	□ Research, nearest ocean □ List
G. Independent Reading		20 minutes daily □ □ □ □	25 minutes daily □ □ □	30 minutes daily □ □ □
Review	Part 5	□ Steps for Thinking review □ Map activity	□ Spelling review □ Marco Polo profile	□ Timeline □ Columbus Word Search

Materials

Meet Christopher Columbus   *Christopher Columbus*
Intermediate World Atlas
Profiles from History by Ashley (Strayer) Wiggers
Handbook of Nature Study by Anna Botsford Comstock

Student Notebook, Crayons or Colored pencils, Watch or Timing device, Dictionary, Highlighter, Index cards/marker, globe, Napkin or paper towel, Spices (at least 4), Library or Internet access, Supplies for experiment: cup, saucer, small square of paper, salt, water, hand lens, Large world outline map

Columbus Unit – Lesson 3 At A Glance

Section	Part	Level 1	Level 2	Level 3 (Christopher Columbus)
A. Copywork/Dictation	Part 1	□ Columbus Story, #4		□ Paragraph 4, page 45
	Part 2	□ Columbus Story, #5		□ Paragraph 7, page 51
	Part 3	□ Columbus Story, #6		□ Paragraph 1, page 57
	Part 4	□ Columbus Story, #7		□ Paragraph 5, page 65
B. Reader		*Meet Christopher Columbus*	*Christopher Columbus*	*Christopher Columbus*
	Part 1	□ Pages 27, 28	□ 1–2 paragraphs	□ 1–2 pages
	Part 2	□ Pages 29–31	□ 1–2 paragraphs	□ 1–2 pages
	Part 3	□ Pages 32–34	□ 1–2 paragraphs	□ 1–2 pages
	Part 4	□ Pages 35–37	□ 1–2 paragraphs	□ 1–2 pages
C. Read Aloud		*Christopher Columbus*		
	Part 1	□ Pages 45-50	□ Discussion	
	Part 2	□ Pages 51-55	□ Narration	
	Part 3	□ Pages 56-61	□ Discussion	
	Part 4	□ Pages 62-69	□ Narration	
D. Word Study	Part 1	□ Antonyms	□ List	□ Drawing □ Describing words
	Part 2	□ Past tense	□ List	□ List □ Categorize
	Part 3	□ Who Am I?	□ Additional clues	□ Concentration game
	Part 4	□ List □ Dictionary exercise	□ Dictionary skills	□ Additional dictionary skills
E. Geography/Science	Part 1	□ Ship's parts □ 4 Decks □ 6 below deck	□ Definitions	□ Research □ 2 Reasons
	Part 2	□ Globe skills □ Map skills □ Coloring	□ Labeling	
	Part 3	□ Winds □ Globe skills □ Discussion	□ Labeling	□ Chart □ Labeling
	Part 4	□ Discussion	□ Examples	□ Research □ Drawing □ Captioning □ Discussion
F. Writing/Drawing	Part 1	□ Drawing/Tracing □ Labeling	□ Discussion	□ Travel brochure
	Part 2	□ Research □ Drawing		□ Research □ Discussion
	Part 3	□ Cloud observation □ Drawing/coloring □ Labeling	□ Definitions □ Discussion	□ Drawing/tracing □ Describing words □ Coloring □ Categorizing
	Part 4	□ Ships' parts review	□ Picture clues □ Discussion □ Ranking	
G. Independent Reading		20 minutes daily □ □ □	25 minutes daily □ □ □	30 minutes daily □ □ □
Review	Part 5	□ Steps for Thinking review □ Map activity	□ Spelling review	□ Ocean and Continent Concentration □ Art activity □ Antonym activity
Materials		*Meet Christopher Columbus* United States History Atlas Handbook of Nature Study	*Christopher Columbus*	Crayons or Colored pencils, Dictionary, Student Notebook, Index cards/marker, Globe, Library or Internet access, RealEarth®GlobeMap,™ Large world outline map

COLUMBUS UNIT – *Lesson 4 At A Glance*

A. COPYWORK/DICTATION	Part 1	☐ Columbus Story, #8		*Christopher Columbus* ☐ Paragraph 2, page 72
	Part 2	☐ Columbus Story, #9		☐ Paragraph 2, page 79
	Part 3	☐ Columbus Story, #10		☐ Paragraph 9, page 83
	Part 4	☐ Columbus Story, #11		☐ Paragraph 5, page 91
B. READER		*Meet Christopher Columbus*	*Christopher Columbus*	*Christopher Columbus*
	Part 1	☐ Pages 38, 39	☐ 1–2 paragraphs	☐ 1–2 pages
	Part 2	☐ Pages 40–42	☐ 1–2 paragraphs	☐ 1–2 pages
	Part 3	☐ Pages 43–46	☐ 1–2 paragraphs	☐ 1–2 pages
	Part 4	☐ Pages 47–49	☐ 1–2 paragraphs	☐ 1–2 pages
C. READ ALOUD		*Christopher Columbus*		
	Part 1	☐ Pages 70–75	☐ Discussion	
	Part 2	☐ Pages 76–81	☐ Narration	
	Part 3	☐ Pages 82–86	☐ Discussion	
	Part 4	☐ Pages 86–91	☐ Narration	
D. WORD STUDY	Part 1	☐ *kn* words ☐ Definitions ☐ Silly sentence	☐ List from dictionary, *kn* words	☐ Definitions, *kn* words
	Part 2	☐ Review, *kn* ☐ Definitions	☐ *gh* Words ☐ Rhyming words	☐ Dictionary exercise ☐ List, *gh* words
	Part 3	☐ List, capitalized words ☐ Categorize	☐ Sentence skills	☐ Add words to categories
	Part 4	☐ Antonyms ☐ Antonyms in reader	☐ Antonyms in dictation	☐ Antonyms in copywork
E. GEOGRAPHY/SCIENCE	Part 1	☐ Collect and analyze information	☐ List, Sun facts	☐ Questions 1–8 ☐ Activity 9 ☐ Activity 13 ☐ Record information from activities
	Part 2	☐ Climate map exercises ☐ Comparing information	☐ List, comparing climates	☐ Descriptive paragraph, comparing climates
	Part 3	☐ Poetry reading ☐ Inner planets ☐ 1 Fact, each planet ☐ Label	☐ 2 Facts, each planet	☐ Planet chart
	Part 4	☐ Address ☐ Map skills	☐ Population chart ☐ Research	☐ Research ☐ Comparison and contrast
F. WRITING/DRAWING	Part 1	☐ Shading lesson		
	Part 2	☐ Comparison and contrast ☐ Predicting		
	Part 3	☐ Sun experiment ☐ Discussion		
	Part 4	☐ Drawing/tracing ☐ Titles ☐ Describing words ☐ Comparison and contrast ☐ Antonym exercise	☐ 2 Descriptive sentences	☐ 3 Descriptive sentences ☐ Main idea sentence
G. INDEPENDENT READING		☐ 20 minutes daily ☐ ☐ ☐	☐ 25 minutes daily ☐ ☐ ☐	☐ 30 minutes daily ☐ ☐ ☐
REVIEW	Part 5	☐ Steps for Thinking review ☐ Map activity	☐ Spelling review ☐ Gutenberg profile	☐ Columbus Bingo
MATERIALS		*Meet Christopher Columbus* *Handbook of Nature Study* *Intermediate World Atlas*	*Christopher Columbus* *Profiles from History*	Student Notebook, Dictionary, Highlighter, Television, Newspaper or Internet access, Dark construction paper, Common household items (pen, key, spoon, etc.), Crayons or colored pencils, City map, Almanac, Large world and U.S. outline maps

COLUMBUS UNIT – *Lesson 5 At A Glance*

A. Copywork/Dictation	Part 1	□ Columbus Story, #12		□ Paragraph 4, page 96, *Christopher Columbus*
	Part 2	□ Columbus Story, #13		□ Paragraph 8, page 98, *Christopher Columbus*
	Part 3	□ Columbus Story, #14		□ Paragraph 3, page 104, *Christopher Columbus*
	Part 4	□ Columbus Story, #15		□ Paragraph 3, page 109, *Christopher Columbus*
B. Reader	Part 1	□ *Meet Christopher Columbus*, pages 50-52	□ 1-2 paragraphs from *Christopher Columbus*	□ 1-2 pages from *Christopher Columbus*
	Part 2	□ *Meet Christopher Columbus*, pages 53-55	□ 1-2 paragraphs from *Christopher Columbus*	□ 1-2 pages from *Christopher Columbus*
	Part 3	□ *Meet Christopher Columbus*, pages 56-59	□ 1-2 paragraphs from *Christopher Columbus*	□ 1-2 pages from *Christopher Columbus*
	Part 4	□ *Meet Christopher Columbus*, pages 60-62	□ 1-2 paragraphs from *Christopher Columbus*	□ 1-2 pages from *Christopher Columbus*
C. Read Aloud	Part 1	□ *Christopher Columbus*, pages 92-97	□ Discussion	□ Discussion
	Part 2	□ *Christopher Columbus*, pages 98-102	□ Narration	□ Narration
	Part 3	□ *Christopher Columbus*, pages 103-107	□ Discussion	
	Part 4	□ *Christopher Columbus*, pages 108-113	□ Narration	
D. Word Study	Part 1	□ *g* Words □ Categorize	□ Definition, *gale* □ Categorize	□ *g* Words □ Categorize □ Definition, *gawk*
	Part 2	□ *g* Words □ Categorize	□ Word ending	□ *g* Words □ Categorize □ Definition, *gaiety*
	Part 3	□ *g* Words □ Categorize	□ Discussion	□ *g* Words □ Categorize □ Definition, *kedging*
	Part 4	□ *g* Words □ Categorize	□ Definition, *glory*	□ *g* Words □ Categorize □ Definition, *thriving*
E. Geography/Science	Part 1	□ Labeling, Haiti □ Coloring □ Map key	□ Additional labeling, Haiti	□ Discussion □ Research
	Part 2	□ Sun diagram □ Star observation	□ Star map □ Describing words	□ Research
	Part 3	□ Labeling, Dom. Rep. □ Coloring □ Map key	□ Additional labeling, Dominican Rep.	□ Flamingo □ Additional labeling
	Part 4	□ Star observation □ Star mapmaking	□ Questions 1-7	□ Questions 8-12
F. Writing/Drawing	Part 1	□ Discussion □ Flying fish □ Drawing/tracing	□ Brown pelican	□ Bottle-nosed dolphin
	Part 2	□ Myths □ Star mapmaking □ Storytelling		
	Part 3	□ Remora fish	□ Laughing gull	□ Loggerhead turtle
	Part 4	□ Poetry writing – cinquain	□ Additional cinquains	
G. Independent Reading		20 minutes daily □ □ □	25 minutes daily □ □ □	30 minutes daily □ □ □
Review	Part 5	□ Steps for Thinking review □ Map activity	□ Spelling review □ Columbus Crossword	□ Ship model
Materials		*Meet Christopher Columbus* *Christopher Columbus* *Handbook of Nature Study* *North American Wildlife Guide* from Reader's Digest	Index cards/marker, Student Notebook, Dictionary, Black construction paper, White crayon or pencil, Crayons or colored pencils, Library or Internet access, Large world outline map	

Columbus Unit – Lesson 6 At A Glance

A. Copywork/Dictation	Part 1	□ Columbus Story, #16		● *Christopher Columbus*
				□ Paragraph 4, page 116
	Part 2	□ Part 1, Letter to King Ferdinand		□ Part 1, Letter to King Ferdinand
	Part 3	□ Part 2, Letter to King Ferdinand		□ Part 2, Letter to King Ferdinand
	Part 4	□ Part 3, Letter to King Ferdinand		□ Part 3, Letter to King Ferdinand
B. Reader		*Meet Christopher Columbus*	*Christopher Columbus*	● *Christopher Columbus*
	Part 1	□ Pages 63, 64	□ 1–2 paragraphs	□ 1–2 pages
	Part 2	□ Pages 65–67	□ 1–2 paragraphs	□ 1–2 pages
	Part 3	□ Pages 68, 69	□ 1–2 paragraphs	□ 1–2 pages
	Part 4	□ Pages 70–72	□ 1–2 paragraphs	□ 1–2 pages
C. Read Aloud		*Christopher Columbus*		
	Part 1	□ Pages 114–118	□ Discussion	
	Part 2	□ Pages 120–124	□ Narration	
	Part 3	□ Pages 125–130	□ Discussion	
	Part 4	□ Pages 131–137	□ Narration	
D. Word Study	Part 1	□ Vocabulary review □ Relate words to topics		
	Part 2	□ Vocabulary review □ Relate words to topics		
	Part 3	□ Poetry reading □ Definitions □ Presentation preparation		
	Part 4	□ Charades		
E. Geography/Science	Part 1	□ Moon observation		
	Part 2	□ Map and globe review		
	Part 3	□ Review □ Relate topics to unit		□ List of inaccuracies
	Part 4	□ Michelangelo profile		
F. Writing/Drawing	Part 1	□ Recording moon observations □ Phases	□ 2 Descriptive sentences	□ 3 Descriptive sentences
	Part 2	□ Explorer page, Columbus		
	Part 3	□ Identifying main events □ Drawing		
	Part 4	□ Book review		
G. Independent Reading		20 minutes daily □ □ □	25 minutes daily □ □ □	30 minutes daily □ □ □
Review	Part 5	□ Steps for Thinking review □ Unit presentation	*Christopher Columbus* □ Columbus Bingo	□ Ocean and Continent Concentration
Materials		*Meet Christopher Columbus* *Intermediate World Atlas*/Globe *Handbook of Nature Study*	*Christopher Columbus* *Profiles from History*	Student Notebook, 4×6 Index cards/marker, Vocabulary cards, Crayons or colored pencils

JAMESTOWN UNIT – Lesson 1 At A Glance

A. Copywork/Dictation	Part 1	Jamestown Story, #1		Paragraph 7, page 2-top of page 4, *Surviving Jamestown*
	Part 2	Jamestown Story, #2		Paragraph 3, page 12, *Surviving Jamestown*
	Part 3	Jamestown Story, #3		Paragraph 1, page 15, *Surviving Jamestown*
	Part 4	Jamestown Story, #4		Paragraph 5, page 21, *Surviving Jamestown*
		A Lion to Guard Us	*A Lion to Guard Us*	
B. Reader	Part 1	*A Lion to Guard Us*, Chapter 1	1–2 paragraphs from *Surviving Jamestown*	1–2 pages from *Surviving Jamestown*
	Part 2	*A Lion to Guard Us*, Chapter 2	1–2 paragraphs from *Surviving Jamestown*	1–2 pages from *Surviving Jamestown*
	Part 3	*A Lion to Guard Us*, Chapter 3	1–2 paragraphs from *Surviving Jamestown*	1–2 pages from *Surviving Jamestown*
	Part 4	*A Lion to Guard Us*, Chapter 4	1–2 paragraphs from *Surviving Jamestown*	1–2 pages from *Surviving Jamestown*
C. Read Aloud	Part 1	*Surviving Jamestown*, Preface–page 7	Narration	
	Part 2	*Surviving Jamestown*, pages 7–14	Discussion	
	Part 3	*Surviving Jamestown*, pages 15–21	Narration	
	Part 4	*Surviving Jamestown*, pages 21–27	Discussion	
D. Word Study	Part 1	Apostrophe list ☐ Contractions	Contraction exercise	Contraction or "belonging" list
	Part 2	Word Bank (categorizing)	*age* words	Categorizing
	Part 3	Categorizing		Additional categorizing ☐ Contractions
	Part 4	Proper nouns ☐ List people		Additional listing
E. Geography/Science	Part 1	Map exercises	Additional map exercises	Capital cities, strait
	Part 2	Climate map ☐ Ocean symbol ☐ Mountain symbol ☐ Latitude symbol	Temperature research	Map comparison
	Part 3	Map exercises	Additional map exercises	Borders, capitals
	Part 4	Climate map ☐ Questions	Climate research	Physical comparisons
F. Writing/Drawing	Part 1	Storytelling	Story writing	Captioning, story writing
	Part 2	Illustration	Labeling	Captioning
	Part 3	Storytelling	Tales	Identifying fiction
	Part 4	Illustrations	Labeling	Captioning
G. Independent Reading		20 minutes daily ☐ ☐ ☐	25 minutes daily ☐ ☐ ☐	30 minutes daily ☐ ☐ ☐
Review	Part 5	Steps for Thinking review ☐ Map activity	Spelling review ☐ John Smith profile	Timeline ☐ Art activity
Materials		*A Lion to Guard Us* by Clyde Robert Bulla; *Surviving Jamestown* by Gail Karwoski; *Profiles from History*; *Intermediate World Atlas*		Student Notebook, Access to Folk Tales, Tracing Paper, Tape, Globe, Scissors, Glue, Index cards/marker, Crayons or colored pencils, Newspaper or Internet access, Large U.S. outline map

JAMESTOWN UNIT – *Lesson 2 At A Glance*

A. Copywork/Dictation	Part 1	☐ Jamestown Story, #5		☐ Paragraph 2, page 28, *Surviving Jamestown*
	Part 2	☐ Jamestown Story, #6		☐ Paragraph 3, page 37, *Surviving Jamestown*
	Part 3	☐ Jamestown Story, #7		☐ Paragraph 4, page 44, *Surviving Jamestown*
	Part 4	☐ Jamestown Story, #8		☐ Paragraph 2, page 50, *Surviving Jamestown*
B. Reader		*A Lion to Guard Us*		
	Part 1	☐ *A Lion to Guard Us*, Chapter 5	☐ 1–2 paragraphs from *Surviving Jamestown*	☐ 1–2 pages from *Surviving Jamestown*
	Part 2	☐ *A Lion to Guard Us*, Chapter 6	☐ 1–2 paragraphs from *Surviving Jamestown*	☐ 1–2 pages from *Surviving Jamestown*
	Part 3	☐ *A Lion to Guard Us*, Chapter 7	☐ 1–2 paragraphs from *Surviving Jamestown*	☐ 1–2 pages from *Surviving Jamestown*
	Part 4	☐ *A Lion to Guard Us*, Chapter 8	☐ 1–2 paragraphs from *Surviving Jamestown*	☐ 1–2 pages from *Surviving Jamestown*
C. Read Aloud	Part 1	☐ *Surviving Jamestown*, pages 28–34	☐ Narration	
	Part 2	☐ *Surviving Jamestown*, pages 34–41	☐ Discussion	
	Part 3	☐ *Surviving Jamestown*, pages 42–47	☐ Narration	
	Part 4	☐ *Surviving Jamestown*, pages 48–54	☐ Discussion	
D. Word Study	Part 1	☐ 4 words to spell	☐ 5 words to spell	☐ Blends ☐ 10 words to spell
	Part 2	☐ Word endings	☐ Word endings	☐ Word endings ☐ Identifying true statements
	Part 3	☐ Word endings	☐ Word endings	☐ ian Words
	Part 4	☐ Charades	☐ Charades	☐ Charades ☐ Dictionary skills
E. Geography/Science	Part 1	☐ Map exercises	☐ Rivers, continents	☐ Rivers, countries
	Part 2	☐ River otter ☐ Mute swan		☐ Stickleback ☐ Mudminnow
	Part 3	☐ Discussion		☐ Research
	Part 4	☐ Landmarks		☐ Landmark research
F. Writing/Drawing	Part 1	☐ Character descriptions ☐ Thinking writing		☐ Character Portraits
	Part 2	☐ Nature sketching #1 ☐ Nature sketching #2		☐ Nature sketching #1 ☐ Descriptive words ☐ Nature sketching #2
	Part 3	☐ List ☐ 1 Sentence, 3 things	☐ 2 Sentences, 3 things	☐ 2 Paragraphs
	Part 4	☐ Drawing ☐ Discussion	☐ Discussion	☐ Drawing ☐ Discussion
G. Independent Reading		20 minutes daily ☐ ☐ ☐ ☐	25 minutes daily ☐ ☐ ☐ ☐	30 minutes daily ☐ ☐ ☐ ☐
Review	Part 5	☐ Steps for Thinking review ☐ Map activity	☐ Spelling review	☐ Old World/New World Game ☐ British Customs and Cooking
Materials		*A Lion to Guard Us* *Surviving Jamestown* *Intermediate World Atlas* *North American Wildlife Guide* *Eat Your Way Around the World*		Student Notebook, Globe, Plain or tracing paper, Crayons or colored pencils, Watch or timing device, Construction paper, Newspaper, library, or Internet access, Dictionary, Index cards/marker, Ingredients for English tea time recipes, Large world outline map

JAMESTOWN UNIT – Lesson 3 At A Glance

A. Copywork/Dictation				*Surviving Jamestown*
	Part 1	☐ Jamestown Story, #9		☐ Paragraph 2, page 54
	Part 2	☐ Jamestown Story, #10		☐ Paragraphs 5–6, page 66
	Part 3	☐ Jamestown Story, #11		☐ Paragraph 7, page 75
	Part 4	☐ Jamestown Story, #12		☐ Paragraph 5, page 78
B. Reader		*A Lion to Guard Us*	*Surviving Jamestown*	*Surviving Jamestown*
	Part 1	☐ Chapter 9	☐ 1–2 paragraphs	☐ 1–2 pages
	Part 2	☐ Chapter 10	☐ 1–2 paragraphs	☐ 1–2 pages
	Part 3	☐ Chapter 11	☐ 1–2 paragraphs	☐ 1–2 pages
	Part 4	☐ Chapter 12	☐ 1–2 paragraphs	☐ 1–2 pages
C. Read Aloud		*Surviving Jamestown*		
	Part 1	☐ Pages 55–62	☐ Discussion	
	Part 2	☐ Pages 63–70	☐ Narration	
	Part 3	☐ Pages 71–77	☐ Discussion	
	Part 4	☐ Pages 77–84	☐ Narration	
D. Word Study				
	Part 1	☐ *ou* Words	☐ Additional *ou* words	☐ *ou* words
	Part 2	☐ Practice	☐ Finding *ou* words	☐ Rhyming words
	Part 3	☐ Word clues		☐ Additional word clues
	Part 4	☐ List		
E. Geography/Science				
	Part 1	☐ Shore crab ☐ Eastern oyster	☐ Atlantic surf clam	☐ Blue crab
	Part 2	☐ Map exercises ☐ List ☐ Discussion		
	Part 3	☐ Discussion ☐ Alligator ☐ Map exercises	☐ Loggerhead turtle	
	Part 4	☐ Animal cards		
F. Writing/Drawing				
	Part 1	☐ Drawing/tracing		☐ Tracing ☐ Labeling
	Part 2	☐ Discussion ☐ List #1 ☐ List #2		☐ Discussion ☐ List
	Part 3	☐ Drawing/coloring		☐ Drawing/coloring
	Part 4	☐ Describing words		
G. Independent Reading		20 minutes daily ☐ ☐ ☐ ☐	25 minutes daily ☐ ☐ ☐ ☐	30 minutes daily ☐ ☐ ☐ ☐
Review	Part 5	☐ Steps for Thinking review ☐ Map activity	☐ Spelling review ☐ Leonardo da Vinci profile	☐ Timeline ☐ Jamestown Word Search
Materials		*A Lion to Guard Us* *North American Wildlife Guide* *Eat Your Way Around the World*	*Surviving Jamestown* *Intermediate World Atlas* *Profiles from History*	Crayons or colored pencils, Index cards/marker, Plain or tracing paper, Student Notebook, Large world outline map

Jamestown Unit – Lesson 4 At A Glance

A. Copywork/Dictation

Surviving Jamestown

Part			*Surviving Jamestown*
Part 1	☐ Jamestown Story, #13		☐ Paragraph 2, page 86
Part 2	☐ Jamestown Story, #14		☐ Paragraphs 2–4, page 97,
Part 3	☐ Jamestown Story, #15		☐ Paragraph 2, page 103
Part 4	☐ Jamestown Story, #16		☐ Paragraph 4, page 111

B. Reader

Part	*A Lion to Guard Us*	*Surviving Jamestown*	*Surviving Jamestown*
Part 1	☐ Chapter 13	☐ 1–2 paragraphs	☐ 1–2 pages
Part 2	☐ Chapter 14	☐ 1–2 paragraphs	☐ 1–2 pages
Part 3	☐ Chapter 15	☐ 1–2 paragraphs	☐ 1–2 pages
Part 4	☐ Chapter 16	☐ 1–2 paragraphs	☐ 1–2 pages

C. Read Aloud

Surviving Jamestown

Part 1	☐ Pages 85–91	☐ Discussion
Part 2	☐ Pages 91–97	☐ Narration
Part 3	☐ Pages 88–105	☐ Discussion
Part 4	☐ Pages 106–114	☐ Narration

D. Word Study

Part 1	☐ Suffix	☐ Opposites	☐ List
Part 2	☐ Jamestown Word Bank		
Part 3	☐ Suffix ☐ List (5 words)	☐ List (8 words)	☐ Spelling practice
Part 4	☐ *ly* Words ☐ Word Bank		☐ *ly* words

E. Geography/Science

Part 1	☐ Red mulberry ☐ Wild strawberry	☐ Strawberry recipe	
Part 2	☐ Grid activity		
Part 3	☐ Peppermint ☐ Sassafras	☐ Discussion	
Part 4	☐ Map scale		☐ Additional map scales

F. Writing/Drawing

Part 1	☐ Letter Writing	
Part 2	☐ Pet Sketch ☐ Labeling	
Part 3	☐ Envelopes	☐ 2nd letter and envelope
Part 4	☐ Research ☐ Drawing	

G. Independent Reading

20 minutes daily ☐ ☐ ☐ ☐	25 minutes daily ☐ ☐ ☐	30 minutes daily ☐ ☐ ☐ ☐

Review

Part 5	☐ Steps for Thinking review ☐ Map activity	☐ Spelling review ☐ Pocahontas profile	☐ Timeline ☐ Jamestown Bingo

Materials

A Lion to Guard Us
Surviving Jamestown
North American Wildlife Guide
Profiles History

Student Notebook, Crayons or colored pencils, Stationery and envelope (if desired), Plain or tracing paper, Ingredients for strawberry dish, Ruler, Dictionary, Large world and U.S. outline map

Jamestown Unit – Lesson 5 At A Glance

Section	Part	ꙭꙭ ꗧꗧ	ꗧ / ꙭꙭ ꗧꗧ	ꗧꗧ Surviving Jamestown
A. Copywork/Dictation		ꙭꙭ ꗧꗧ		ꗧꗧ Surviving Jamestown
	Part 1	☐ Jamestown Story, #17		☐ Paragraphs 1-4, page 119
	Part 2	☐ Jamestown Story, #18		☐ Paragraph 4, page 130
	Part 3	☐ Jamestown Story, #19		☐ Paragraph 4, page 133
	Part 4	☐ Jamestown Story, #20		☐ Paragraph 3, page 142
B. Reader		ꙭꙭ ꗧꗧ A Lion to Guard Us	ꗧ Surviving Jamestown	ꗧꗧ Surviving Jamestown
	Part 1	☐ Chapter 17	☐ 1-2 paragraphs	☐ 1-2 pages
	Part 2	☐ Chapter 18	☐ 1-2 paragraphs	☐ 1-2 pages
	Part 3	☐ Chapter 19	☐ 1-2 paragraphs	☐ 1-2 pages
	Part 4	☐ Chapter 20	☐ 1-2 paragraphs	☐ 1-2 pages
C. Read Aloud		ꙭꙭ ꗧꗧ Surviving Jamestown	ꙭꙭ ꗧꗧ	ꗧꗧ
	Part 1	☐ Pages 115-119, 122, 123	☐ Discussion	
	Part 2	☐ Pages 124-130	☐ Narration	
	Part 3	☐ Pages 130-138	☐ Discussion	
	Part 4	☐ Pages 139-149	☐ Narration	
D. Word Study		ꙭꙭ ꗧꗧ		ꗧꗧ
	Part 1	☐ a words ☐ Categorizing		
	Part 2	☐ Practice	☐ Add 6 Words	☐ Add 10 words
	Part 3	☐ Spelling Review Cards		
	Part 4	☐ Practice ☐ Go Fish game		
E. Geography/Science		ꙭꙭ ꗧꗧ		ꗧꗧ
	Part 1	☐ Belted Kingfisher ☐ Canada goose		☐ Research
	Part 2	☐ Map scales		
	Part 3	☐ Belted Kingfisher ☐ Discuss questions 1-7		
	Part 4	☐ Color flags		
F. Writing/Drawing		ꙭꙭ ꗧꗧ		ꗧꗧ
	Part 1	☐ Poetry reading ☐ Bird watching ☐ Sketching ☐ Poetry writing		☐ Write questions 1-7
	Part 2	☐ Map designs		
	Part 3	☐ Letter writing		
	Part 4	☐ Character Portrait		☐ Additional Character Portrait
G. Independent Reading		ꙭꙭ	ꗧ	ꗧꗧ
		20 minutes daily ☐ ☐ ☐ ☐	25 minutes daily ☐	30 minutes daily ☐ ☐ ☐
Review	Part 5	☐ Steps for Thinking review ☐ Map activity	☐ Spelling review ☐ Jamestown Crossword	

Materials: *A Lion to Guard Us, North American Wildlife Guide, Handbook of Nature Study, Surviving Jamestown, Profiles from History, Intermediate World Atlas,* Student Notebook, Plain or tracing paper, Index cards/marker, Crayons or colored pencils, Ruler, Tape, glue, or stapler; ꗧ Internet access (home or library), One or more of the following: dry erase board/markers, colored chalk, water-based paint, modeling clay, Large world outline map

Jamestown Unit – Lesson 6 At A Glance

A. Copywork/Dictation	Part 1	❑ Jamestown Story, #21	*Surviving Jamestown*	❑ Paragraph 7, pages 150,151
	Part 2	❑ Jamestown Story, #22		❑ Paragraph 1, page 165
	Part 3	❑ Jamestown Story, #23		❑ Letter, page 170
	Part 4	❑ Jamestown Story, #24		❑ Letter, pages 170–171
B. Reader	Part 1	*A Lion to Guard Us* ❑ Chapter 21	*Surviving Jamestown*	❑ 1–2 pages
	Part 2	❑ Chapter 22		❑ 1–2 pages
	Part 3	❑ Chapter 23		❑ 1–2 pages
	Part 4	❑ Pages 116, 117		❑ 1–2 pages
C. Read Aloud	Part 1	*Surviving Jamestown* ❑ Pages 150–156	❑ 1–2 paragraphs	❑ Narration
	Part 2	❑ Pages 156–165	❑ 1–2 paragraphs	❑ Discussion
	Part 3	❑ Pages 166–176	❑ 1–2 paragraphs	❑ Narration
	Part 4	❑ Pages 177–180	❑ 1–2 paragraphs	❑ Discussion
D. Word Study	Part 1	❑ Vocabulary review		
	Part 2	❑ Practice	❑ Go Fish game	
	Part 3	❑ Review	❑ Practice	
	Part 4	❑ Vocabulary review		
E. Geography/Science	Part 1	❑ Animal I.D. game		
	Part 2	❑ Map/globe review		
	Part 3	❑ Bodies of water review	❑ Topic relationships	
	Part 4	❑ Shakespeare profile	❑ Timeline	
F. Writing/Drawing	Part 1	❑ Explorer page, John Smith		
	Part 2	❑ Poetry preparation		
	Part 3	❑ Book review		
	Part 4	❑ Review	❑ Illustration	
G. Independent Reading		20 minutes daily ❑ ❑ ❑ ❑	25 minutes daily ❑ ❑ ❑ ❑	30 minutes daily ❑ ❑ ❑ ❑
Review	Part 5	❑ *Surviving Jamestown*, pages 185–193	❑ Steps for Thinking review ❑ Map activity	❑ Unit presentation ❑ Jamestown Bingo or Old World/New World

Materials:

A Lion to Guard Us
Surviving Jamestown
Profiles from History
Intermediate World Atlas

Student Notebook, Globe, Paste, Page Protector, Long *a* cards, Animal classification cards, Index cards/marker, Construction paper, Scissors. Vocabulary cards: Columbus Unit, Jamestown Unit; One or two of the following: colored chalk, markers, clay, water-based paint, typewriter, Large world outline map

Pilgrim Unit – *Lesson 1 At A Glance*

A. Copywork/Dictation

Part		*Stories of the Pilgrims*
Part 1	☐ The Pilgrim Story, #1	☐ Paragraph 5, page 9
Part 2	☐ The Pilgrim Story, #2	☐ Paragraph 1, page 13
Part 3	☐ Student's Choice, 3 sentences · ☐ Student's Choice, 4 sentences	☐ Student's Choice, 5 sentences
Part 4	☐ The Pilgrim Story, #3	☐ Paragraphs 3, page 31

B. Reader

Part	*Squanto*	*Stories of the Pilgrims*	*Stories of the Pilgrims*
Part 1	☐ Pages 5–9	☐ 1–2 paragraphs	☐ 1–2 pages
Part 2	☐ Pages 10–15	☐ 1–2 paragraphs	☐ 1–2 pages
Part 3	☐ Pages 15–19	☐ 1–2 paragraphs	☐ 1–2 pages
Part 4	☐ Pages 20–24	☐ 1–2 paragraphs	☐ 1–2 pages

C. Read Aloud — *Stories of the Pilgrims*

Part 1	☐ Pages 1 through top of page 10	☐ Discussion
Part 2	☐ Top of page 10 through page 20	☐ Narration
Part 3	☐ Pages 21-30	☐ Discussion
Part 4	☐ Pages 31-41	☐ Narration

D. Word Study

Part 1	☐ Add words to list	☐ Practice	☐ List
Part 2	☐ Syllable exercise	☐ Practice	
Part 3	☐ Meanings	☐ Word Bank	☐ Practice
Part 4	☐ Review	☐ Personal dictionary	☐ Pick and spell

E. Geography/Science

Part 1	☐ Map exercises	☐ *Intermediate World Atlas* exercise	☐ 2nd *Intermediate World Atlas* exercise
Part 2	☐ Mallard · ☐ Pintail	☐ Goldeneye	☐ Green-winged teal · ☐ Waterfowl research
Part 3	☐ Map Exercises · ☐ Discussion	☐ Cities	☐ Fathoms
Part 4	☐ Oak trees · ☐ Questions 1–3		☐ Questions 1–6, 8, 9

F. Writing/Drawing

Part 1	☐ Discussion	☐ List
Part 2	☐ Collage	
Part 3	☐ Complete sentences	
Part 4	☐ Illustrations	

G. Independent Reading

20 minutes daily ☐ ☐ ☐ ☐	25 minutes daily ☐ ☐ ☐	30 minutes daily ☐ ☐ ☐

Review

Part 5: ☐ Steps for Thinking review · ☐ Map activity · ☐ Spelling review · ☐ Discussion · ☐ Pilgrim dictionary · ☐ Word Search

Materials

Stories of the Pilgrims by Margaret Pumphrey
Squanto by Clyde Robert Bulla
North American Wildlife Guide
Handbook of Nature Study
Profiles From History
Intermediate World Atlas

Stories of the Pilgrims Answer Key, Student Notebook, Index cards/marker, Scissors, Materials for hands-on spelling: dry erase board and markers; colored chalk; modeling clay; or water-based paint and paper, Composition book, Small plastic bag, Old or "extra" family pictures, Glue, Colored pencils or crayons, Access to King James version of the Bible, and one other translation, Large world outline map

Pilgrim Unit – Lesson 2 At A Glance

A. COPYWORK/DICTATION		ΨΨ 🐾	🐾	🐾🐾 *Stories of the Pilgrims*
	Part 1	☐ The Pilgrim Story, #4		☐ Paragraph 4, page 42
	Part 2	☐ The Pilgrim Story, #5		☐ Paragraphs 2, page 54
	Part 3	☐ Student's Choice, 3 sentences (Ψ)	☐ Student's Choice, 4 sentences	☐ Student's Choice, 5 sentences
	Part 4	☐ The Pilgrim Story, #6		☐ Paragraph 2, page 76
B. READER		ΨΨ 🐾🐾 *Squanto*	🐾 *Stories of the Pilgrims*	🐾🐾 *Stories of the Pilgrims*
	Part 1	☐ Pages 25–29	☐ 1–2 paragraphs	☐ 1–2 pages
	Part 2	☐ Pages 30–34	☐ 1–2 paragraphs	☐ 1–2 pages
	Part 3	☐ Pages 35–39	☐ 1–2 paragraphs	☐ 1–2 pages
	Part 4	☐ Pages 40–43	☐ 1–2 paragraphs	☐ 1–2 pages
C. READ ALOUD		ΨΨ 🐾🐾 *Stories of the Pilgrims*	🐾🐾	
	Part 1	☐ Pages 42–52	☐ Discussion	
	Part 2	☐ Pages 53–62	☐ Narration	
	Part 3	☐ Pages 63–73	☐ Discussion	
	Part 4	☐ Pages 74–82	☐ Narration	
D. WORD STUDY		ΨΨ 🐾	ΨΨ 🐾🐾	
	Part 1	☐ Add words to list	☐ Practice	☐ List
	Part 2	☐ Syllable exercise	☐ Practice	☐ Practice
	Part 3	☐ Meanings	☐ Word bank	☐ Practice
	Part 4	☐ Review	☐ Personal dictionary	☐ Pick and spell
E. GEOGRAPHY/SCIENCE		ΨΨ	🐾	🐾
	Part 1	☐ Map exercises	☐ Windmills	☐ Venice, Italy comparison
	Part 2	☐ Climate exercises	☐ Climate comparisons	☐ Additional climate comparisons
	Part 3	☐ Grid activity		
	Part 4	☐ Wood stork	☐ Great Egret	☐ Two additional birds
F. WRITING/DRAWING		ΨΨ	🐾	🐾
	Part 1	☐ Comprehension question 5	☐ Comprehension questions 1, 2	☐ Comprehension questions 1–5
	Part 2	☐ Sketch	☐ Sketch	☐ Sketch
	Part 3	☐ Comprehension question 5	☐ Comprehension questions 1, 2	☐ Comprehension questions 1–5
	Part 4	☐ Illustrations	☐ Illustrations	☐ Illustrations
G. INDEPENDENT READING		ΨΨ 20 minutes daily ☐ ☐ ☐	🐾 25 minutes daily ☐ ☐ ☐	🐾 30 minutes daily ☐ ☐ ☐
REVIEW	Part 5	☐ Steps for Thinking review ☐ Map activity *(Squanto)*	☐ Spelling review ☐ Dutch Cooking	☐ Columbus or Jamestown Bingo
MATERIALS		*Stories of the Pilgrims* *North American Wildlife Guide* *Intermediate World Atlas* *Eat Your Way Around the World*		*Stories of the Pilgrims* Answer Key, Student Notebook, Index cards/marker, Materials for hands-on spelling: dry erase board and markers; colored chalk; modeling clay; water-based paint and paper, or Letter cards, Index cards/marker, Colored pencils or crayons, Plain or tracing paper, Access to Internet or library, Personal dictionary, Large world outline map

Pilgrim Unit – Lesson 3 At A Glance

A. Copywork/Dictation	Part 1	The Pilgrim Story, #7		*Stories of the Pilgrims* — Paragraph 3, page 83
	Part 2	The Pilgrim Story, #8		Paragraphs 5, page 92
	Part 3	Student's Choice, 3 sentences (🐾)	Student's Choice, 4 sentences	Student's Choice, 5 sentences
	Part 4	The Pilgrim Story, #9		Paragraph 1, page 117
B. Reader		*Squanto*	*Stories of the Pilgrims*	*Stories of the Pilgrims*
	Part 1	Pages 43–47	1–2 paragraphs	1–2 pages
	Part 2	Pages 48–53	1–2 paragraphs	1–2 pages
	Part 3	Pages 54–57	1–2 paragraphs	1–2 pages
	Part 4	Pages 58–64	1–2 paragraphs	1–2 pages
C. Read Aloud		*Stories of the Pilgrims*		
	Part 1	Pages 83–91	Discussion	
	Part 2	Pages 92–101	Narration	
	Part 3	Pages 102–115	Discussion	
	Part 4	Pages 116–126	Narration	
D. Word Study	Part 1	Add words to list	Practice	List
	Part 2	Syllable exercise	Practice	Practice
	Part 3	Meanings	Word bank	Practice
	Part 4	Review	Personal dictionary	Pick and spell
E. Geography/Science	Part 1	Voyage exercise	Map scales	Descriptive words · Comparisons
	Part 2	White-tailed deer / Discussion · Eastern cottontail / Animal I.D. game		Snowshoe hare
	Part 3	Grid exercise		Additional grid
	Part 4	Activities 1–7 · Activities 9–14		Sketch & color
F. Writing/Drawing	Part 1	Acrostic poem		2nd Acrostic poem
	Part 2	Illustration		
	Part 3	Question 4 (🐾)	Questions 1, 2	Questions 1 – 4
	Part 4	Illustration		
G. Independent Reading		20 minutes daily	25 minutes daily	30 minutes daily
Review	Part 5	Steps for Thinking review · Map activity	Spelling review · William Bradford profile	Timeline · Pilgrim Scramble

Materials:
Stories of the Pilgrims, *North American Wildlife Guide*, *Eat Your Way Around the World*, *Handbook of Nature Study* | *Squanto*, *Profiles from History* | Student Notebook, Index cards/marker, Materials for hands-on spelling: dry erase board and markers; colored chalk; modeling clay; water-based paint and paper, or Letter cards, Plain or tracing paper, *Stories of the Pilgrims* Answer Key, Personal dictionary, Construction paper, Colored pencils or crayons, Ruler, Several ears of corn with husks, Large world and U.S. outline map

PILGRIM UNIT – Lesson 4 At A Glance

				Stories of the Pilgrims
A. Copywork/Dictation	Part 1	□ The Pilgrim Story, #10		□ Paragraph 4, page 131
	Part 2	□ The Pilgrim Story, #11		□ Paragraphs 2, page 139
	Part 3	□ Student's Choice, 3 sentences (🐾)	□ Student's Choice, 4 sentences	□ Student's Choice, 5 sentences
	Part 4	□ The Pilgrim Story, #12		□ Paragraph 6, page 156
		Squanto	*Stories of the Pilgrims*	*Stories of the Pilgrims*
B. Reader	Part 1	□ Pages 64-67	□ 1–2 paragraphs	□ 1–2 pages
	Part 2	□ Pages 68-72	□ 1–2 paragraphs	□ 1–2 pages
	Part 3	□ Pages 72-75	□ 1–2 paragraphs	□ 1–2 pages
	Part 4	□ Pages 76-79	□ 1–2 paragraphs	□ 1–2 pages
		Stories of the Pilgrims		
C. Read Aloud	Part 1	□ Pages 127-136	□ Discussion	
	Part 2	□ Pages 137-145	□ Narration	
	Part 3	□ Pages 146-154	□ Discussion	
	Part 4	□ Pages 155-162	□ Narration	
D. Word Study	Part 1	□ Add words to list	□ Practice	□ List
	Part 2	□ Syllable exercise	□ Practice	
	Part 3	□ Meanings	□ Word Bank	□ Practice
	Part 4	□ Review	□ Personal dictionary	□ Pick and spell
E. Geography/Science	Part 1	□ Map exercises	□ Additional map exercises	□ Map scales
	Part 2	□ Review □ Animal I.D. game		
	Part 3	□ Map comparison □ Discussion		□ Borders
	Part 4	□ Squirrels □ Sketch □ Questions 1–7	□ Red squirrel □ Gray squirrel	□ Questions 8–12
F. Writing/Drawing	Part 1	□ Collage		
	Part 2	□ Comprehension discussion □ True false statements	□ Complete sentences	□ Rewording sentences
	Part 3	□ Letter writing, imaginary	□ Letter writing, real	□ Visit
	Part 4	□ Illustrations		
G. Independent Reading		20 minutes daily □ □ □ □	25 minutes daily □ □ □ □	30 minutes daily □ □ □ □
Review	Part 5	□ Steps for Thinking review □ Map activity	□ Spelling review □ Squanto profile	□ Timeline □ Pilgrim Crossword

Materials: *Stories of the Pilgrims* / *Intermediate World Atlas* / *Profiles from History* / *North American Wildlife Guide* | *Squanto* / *U. S. History Atlas* | Student Notebook, Materials for hands-on spelling; dry erase board and markers; colored chalk; modeling clay; water-based paint and paper, or Letter cards, *Stories of the Pilgrims* Answer Key, Index cards/marker, Colored pencils or crayons, Personal dictionary, Ruler, Construction paper, Plain or tracing paper, Shallow box or lid, Large U.S. outline map

Pilgrim Unit – Lesson 5 *At A Glance*

A. Copywork/Dictation		*Squanto*		*Stories of the Pilgrims*	
	Part 1	☐ The Pilgrim Story, #12			☐ Last paragraph on page 167
	Part 2	☐ The Pilgrim Story, #13			☐ Paragraph 1, page 176
	Part 3	☐ Student's Choice, 3 sentences		☐ Student's choice, 4 sentences	☐ Student's Choice, 5 sentences
	Part 4	☐ The Pilgrim Story, #14			☐ Paragraph 2, page 193
B. Reader		*Squanto*		*Stories of the Pilgrims*	*Stories of the Pilgrims*
	Part 1	☐ Pages 80–83		☐ 1–2 paragraphs	☐ 1–2 pages
	Part 2	☐ Pages 84–88		☐ 1–2 paragraphs	☐ 1–2 pages
	Part 3	☐ Pages 88–92		☐ 1–2 paragraphs	☐ 1–2 pages
	Part 4	☐ Pages 93–97		☐ 1–2 paragraphs	☐ 1–2 pages
C. Read Aloud		*Stories of the Pilgrims*			
	Part 1	☐ Pages 163–174		☐ Discussion	
	Part 2	☐ Pages 175–181		☐ Narration	
	Part 3	☐ Pages 183–192		☐ Discussion	
	Part 4	☐ Pages 193–202		☐ Narration	
D. Word Study					
	Part 1	☐ Add words to list	☐ Practice		☐ List
	Part 2	☐ Syllable exercise	☐ Practice		☐ Practice
	Part 3	☐ Meanings	☐ Word Bank		☐ Practice
	Part 4	☐ Review	☐ Review with Bingo cards	☐ Personal dictionary	☐ Pick and spell
E. Geography/Science					
	Part 1	☐ Globe exercises	☐ Additional globe exercises		☐ Map grids
	Part 2	☐ Vocabulary review			
	Part 3	☐ Voyages	☐ Map Scales		☐ Voyage reflections
	Part 4	☐ Pilgrim narrative			
F. Writing/Drawing					
	Part 1	☐ Oral presentation ☐ Oral preparation		☐ Illustrations	
	Part 2	☐ Explorer page, Bradford			
	Part 3	☐ Discussion	☐ Drawing		
	Part 4	☐ Illustrations			
G. Independent Reading		20 minutes daily ☐ ☐ ☐	25 minutes daily ☐	30 minutes daily ☐ ☐ ☐	
Review	Part 5	☐ Steps for Thinking review ☐ Map activity	☐ Spelling review ☐ Pilgrim Bingo	☐ Pet sketch	

Materials

Stories of the Pilgrims, *Intermediate World Atlas*, *North American Wildlife Guide*, *Squanto*, *HB of Nature Study*. Personal dictionary; Colored pencils or crayons; Materials for hands-on spelling: dry erase board and markers; colored chalk; modeling clay; water-based paint and paper, or Letter cards. *Stories of the Pilgrims* Answer Key, Student Notebook, Index cards/marker, Vocabulary cards, Globe, Large world outline map

PILGRIM UNIT – *Lesson 6 At A Glance*

A. Copywork/Dictation		🐾🐾	🐾	🐾 *Stories of the Pilgrims*
	Part 1	☐ The Pilgrim Story, #16		☐ Paragraph 3, page 210
	Part 2	☐ The Pilgrim Story, #17		☐ Paragraph 2, page 212,
	Part 3	☐ Student's Choice, 3 sentences (🐾)	☐ Student's Choice, 4 sentences	☐ Student's Choice, 5 sentences
	Part 4	☐ The Pilgrim Story, #18		☐ Last paragraph on page 223
B. Reader		🐾🐾 🐾🐾 *Squanto*	🐾🐾 *Stories of the Pilgrims*	🐾🐾 *Stories of the Pilgrims*
	Part 1	☐ Pages 97–101	☐ 1–2 paragraphs	☐ 1–2 pages
	Part 2	☐ Pages 102–105	☐ 1–2 paragraphs	☐ 1–2 pages
	Part 3	☐ Pages 106–108	☐ 1–2 paragraphs	☐ 1–2 pages
	Part 4	☐ Pages 109–112	☐ 1–2 paragraphs	☐ 1–2 pages
C. Read Aloud		🐾🐾 🐾🐾 *Stories of the Pilgrims*	🐾🐾	
	Part 1	☐ Pages 200–209	☐ Discussion	
	Part 2	☐ Pages 210–219	☐ Narration	
	Part 3	☐ Pages 220–231	☐ Discussion	
	Part 4	☐ Pages 232–244	☐ Narration	
D. Word Study		🐾🐾 🐾🐾	🐾🐾 🐾🐾	
	Part 1	☐ Add words to list	☐ Practice	☐ List
	Part 2	☐ Syllable Exercise	☐ Practice	☐ Practice
	Part 3	☐ Meanings	☐ Word Bank	☐ Practice
	Part 4	☐ Review	☐ Personal dictionary	☐ Pick and spell
E. Geography/Science		🐾🐾 🐾🐾	🐾🐾 🐾🐾	
	Part 1	☐ Review	☐ Animal I.D. game	
	Part 2	☐ Globe/map review		
	Part 3	☐ Pumpkin	☐ Questions 1–5	☐ Sketch
	Part 4	☐ Galileo profile	☐ Timeline	
F. Writing/Drawing		🐾🐾 🐾🐾		
	Part 1	☐ Acrostic poem		
	Part 2	☐ Illustration		
	Part 3	☐ Book review		
	Part 4	☐ Illustrations		
G. Independent Reading		🐾🐾 20 minutes daily ☐ ☐ ☐	🐾 25 minutes daily ☐	🐾 30 minutes daily ☐ ☐ ☐
Review	Part 5	☐ Steps for Thinking review ☐ Pumpkin recipe	☐ Pumpkin recipe ☐ Unit presentation	☐ Pilgrim Bingo
Materials		*Stories of the Pilgrims* Intermediate World Atlas *Profiles from History* Eat Your Way Around the World	*Squanto* Handbook of Nature Study North American Wildlife Guide	Personal dictionary, Animal I.D. cards, Materials for hands-on spelling: dry erase board and markers; colored chalk; modeling clay; water-based paint and paper, or Letter cards, Ingredients for Pumpkin recipe, *Stories of the Pilgrims* Answer Key, Student Notebook, Index cards/marker, Vocabulary cards, Construction paper, Colored pencils or crayons, Globe, Pumpkin

Language Skills

Skills & Topics	✸	✸	✸
Antonyms	•	•	•
Compound Words	•	•	•
Decoding	•	•	•
Describing Words	•	•	•
Dictionary Skills	•	•	•
Journal Skills	•	•	•
Oral Presentation	•		
Past Tense	•	•	•
Penmanship	•		•
Poetry Reading	•	•	•
Prefixes	•	•	•
Proper Nouns	•	•	•
Reading for Enjoyment	•	•	•
Reading with Understanding	•	•	•
Root Words	•	•	•
Rhyming Words	•	•	•
Spelling Strategies	•	•	•
Suffixes	•	•	•
Syllables	•	•	•
Synonyms	•	•	•
Vocabulary	•	•	

Writing

Skills & Topics	✸	✸	✸
Brochure Writing			•
Descriptive Writing	•	•	•
Expository Writing			•
Narrative Writing	•	•	•
Paragraph Writing	•	•	•
Poetry Writing – Cinquains	•	•	•
Reflective Writing	•	•	•
Sentence Skills	•	•	•

Thinking Skills

Skills & Topics	✸	✸	✸
Analyzing Information	•	•	•
Categorizing	•	•	•
Cause & Effect	•	•	•
Comparison & Contrast	•	•	•
Comprehension	•	•	•
Context Clues	•	•	•
Discussion	•	•	•
Evaluating Information	•	•	•
Identifying Main Idea	•	•	•
Identifying Facts	•	•	•
Interviewing	•	•	•
Investigating	•	•	•
Labeling	•	•	•
Listening Skills	•	•	•
List Making	•	•	•
Narration	•	•	•
Observation Skills	•	•	•
Organization	•	•	•
Predicting	•	•	•
Picture Clues	•	•	•
Recording Information	•	•	•
Research/Reference Skills	•	•	•
Sequencing	•	•	•
Summarizing	•	•	•
Supporting Ideas	•	•	•
Synthesizing Information	•	•	•
Thinking Skills	•		•
Understanding Worldviews	•		
Venn Diagram			•

Art

Skills & Topics	✸	✸	✸
Captioning	•	•	•
Drawing	•	•	•
Illustrating	•	•	•
Interpreting Illustrations	•	•	•
Tracing/Coloring	•	•	•

Geography/Science/History

Skills & Topics	✸	✸	✸
Atlas Skills	•	•	•
Bays			•
Boundaries			•
Intermediate Compass Directions	•		
Chart Reading	•		
Collecting Information	•		•
Constellations			•
Diagrams	•	•	•
Globe Skills	•	•	•
Identifying Historical Figures	•	•	•
Mapmaking with Details		•	•
Map Skills		•	•
Observation Skills	•		
Star Map		•	•
Timeline		•	•
Climate	•	•	
Continents	•	•	•
Gulfs	•	•	
Islands	•	•	•
Lakes	•	•	•
Lunar Phases	•		•
Mid-Eastern Culture	•		•
Moon	•	•	•
Mountains	•	•	•
Myths	•	•	•
Navigation	•	•	•
Oceans	•	•	•
Printing Press	•	•	•
Rivers	•	•	•
Sailing Ships	•	•	•
Salt	•	•	•
Seas	•	•	•
Solar System	•	•	•
Stars	•	•	•
Sun	•	•	•
Weather	•	•	•
Winds	•	•	•
Worldviews	•	•	•
Wildlife Study:			
Flying Fish	•	•	•
Brown Pelican	•	•	•
Remora Fish	•	•	•
Bottle-nose Dolphin	•	•	•
Laughing Gull	•	•	•
Flamingo			•
Loggerhead Turtle			•
Historical Figures:			
Christopher Columbus	•	•	•
Johannes Gutenberg	•	•	•
Marco Polo	•	•	•
Michelangelo	•	•	•

Jamestown Unit

	Skills & Topics	✦	✦	✦
LANGUAGE SKILLS	Adverbs	•	•	•
	Apostrophes	•	•	•
	Blends			•
	Contractions	•	•	•
	Decoding	•	•	•
	Descriptive Words	•	•	•
	Descriptive Sentences		•	•
	Dictionary Skills		•	•
	Oral Presentation	•	•	•
	Penmanship	•	•	•
	Poetry Reading	•	•	•
	Possessives	•	•	•
	Proper Nouns	•	•	•
	Reading for Enjoyment	•	•	•
	Reading with Understanding	•	•	•
	Rhyming Words	•	•	•
	Spelling Strategies	•	•	•
	Storytelling	•	•	•
	Suffixes	•	•	•
	Vocabulary	•	•	•
	Word Study		•	
WRITING	Book Review	•	•	•
	Character Profiling	•	•	•
	Letter Writing	•	•	•
	Paragraphs			
	Poetry Writing	•	•	•
	Rough Drafts	•	•	•
	Sentence Skills	•	•	•
	"Thinking Writing"	•	•	•
	Word Banks	•	•	•
THINKING SKILLS	Analyzing Information	•	•	•
	Categorizing	•	•	
	Cause & Effect	•	•	
	Comparison & Contrast	•	•	•
	Comprehension	•	•	
	Context Clues	•	•	
	Discussion	•	•	
	Evaluating Information	•	•	
	Identifying Facts	•	•	
	Investigating	•	•	
	Labeling	•	•	
	List Making	•	•	
	Listening Skills	•	•	
	Narration	•	•	
	Non-verbal Communication	•	•	
	Observation Skills	•	•	
	Organization	•	•	
	Picture Clues	•	•	
	Predicting	•	•	
	Recording Information	•	•	•
	Research/Reference Skills	•	•	
	Sequencing	•	•	•
	Synthesizing Information	•	•	•

	Skills & Topics	✦	✦	✦
ART	Captioning	•	•	•
	Coloring	•	•	•
	Drawing	•	•	•
	Illustration	•	•	•
	Sketching	•	•	•
	Tracing	•	•	•
GEOGRAPHY/SCIENCE/HISTORY	Bays			•
	Bermuda			•
	Birds			•
	Borders			•
	British Food			•
	Capital Cities			•
	Channels			•
	Chart Reading	•		•
	Chesapeake Bay	•	•	•
	Climate	•		•
	Cold-Blooded	•		•
	Collecting Information	•		•
	Content Maps			•
	Cultural Customs	•		•
	Fish	•		•
	Globe Skills	•		•
	Invertebrates	•		•
	James River	•		•
	Jamestown	•		•
	Landmarks	•		•
	Latitude	•		•
	London	•		•
	Mammals	•		•
	Map Scales	•		•
	Map Skills	•		•
	Mollusks	•		•
	Physical Maps	•		•
	Plants:			
	Peppermint	•		•
	Red Mulberry	•		•
	Sassafras	•		•
	Wild Strawberry	•		•
	Political Maps	•		•
	Pollution	•		•
	Reptiles	•		•
	Rivers	•		•
	River Sources	•		•
	Straits			•
	Tales			•
	Tidal Marsh			•
	Timeline			•
	Tributaries			•
	United Kingdom			•
	Virginia			•
	Warm-Blooded			•
	Water Cycle	•	•	•
	West Indies	•		•

JAMESTOWN UNIT CON'T

	Skills & Topics	🐾	✋	🐾
GEOGRAPHY/SCIENCE/HISTORY	**Wildlife Study:**			
	River Otter	•	•	•
	Stickleback	•	•	•
	Mudminnow	•	•	•
	Shore Crab	•	•	•
	Eastern Oyster	•	•	•
	Alligators	•	•	•
	Mute Swan	•	•	•
	Belted Kingfisher	•	•	•
	Canada Goose	•	•	•
	Atlantic Surf Clam		•	•
	Historical Figures:			
	Leonardo da Vinci	•	•	•
	Pocahontas	•	•	•
	William Shakespeare	•	•	•
	John Smith	•	•	•

PILGRIM UNIT

	Skills & Topics	🐾	✋	🐾
LANGUAGE SKILLS	Answering Strategies	•	•	•
	Cloze Reading Skills	•	•	•
	Decoding	•	•	•
	Identifying Complete Sentences	•	•	•
	Oral Presentation	•	•	•
	Penmanship	•	•	•
	Personal Dictionary	•	•	•
	Poetry Reading	•	•	•
	Reading for Enjoyment	•	•	•
	Reading with Understanding	•	•	•
	Spelling Strategies	•	•	•
	Summaries	•	•	•
	Syllables	•	•	•
	Vocabulary	•	•	•
	Word Study	•	•	•
WRITING	Book Review	•	•	•
	Character Profiling	•	•	•
	Letter Writing	•	•	•
	Poetry Writing - Acrostic	•	•	•
	Rough Drafts	•	•	•
	Sentence Skills	•	•	•
	Word Banks	•	•	•

	Skills & Topics	🐾	✋	🐾
THINKING SKILLS	Analyzing Information	•	•	•
	Categorizing	•	•	•
	Cause & Effect	•	•	•
	Comparison & Contrast	•	•	•
	Comprehension	•	•	•
	Context Clues	•	•	•
	Discussion	•	•	•
	Evaluating Information	•	•	•
	Identifying Facts	•	•	•
	Investigating	•	•	•
	Labeling	•	•	•
	List Making	•	•	•
	Listening Skills	•	•	•
	Matching	•	•	•
	Narration	•	•	•
	Observation Skills	•	•	•
	Organization	•	•	•
	Picture Clues	•	•	•
	Predicting	•	•	•
	Recording Information	•	•	•
	Research/Reference Skills	•	•	•
	Sequencing	•	•	•
	Symbols	•	•	•
	Synthesizing Information		•	•
	True/False Statements	•	•	•

PILGRIM UNIT CON'T

Skills & Topics	🌿	🐾	🐾
ART			
Collages	•	•	•
Coloring	•	•	•
Design	•	•	•
Drawing	•	•	•
Illustration	•	•	•
Sketching	•	•	•
Tracing	•	•	•
GEOGRAPHY/SCIENCE/HISTORY			
Birds	•	•	•
Borders/Boundaries	•	•	•
Canals	•	•	•
Capital Cities	•	•	•
Channels	•	•	•
Chart Reading	•	•	•
Climate	•	•	•
Collecting Information	•	•	•
Cultural Customs	•	•	•
Dutch Food	•	•	•
England	•	•	•
Fathoms		•	•
Fish	•	•	•
Globe Skills	•	•	•
Grids:			
Maps	•	•	•
Pictures	•	•	•
Harbors		•	•
Ijsselmeer	•	•	•
Invertebrates	•	•	•
Landmarks	•	•	•
Latitude	•	•	•
Longitude	•	•	•
Mammals	•	•	•
Map Scales	•	•	•
Map Skills	•	•	•
Massachusetts	•	•	•
Mayflower	•	•	•
Mayflower Compact	•	•	•

Skills & Topics	🌿	🐾	🐾
GEOGRAPHY/SCIENCE/HISTORY			
Netherlands	•	•	•
Physical Maps	•	•	•
Pilgrims	•	•	•
Plants:			
Oak Trees	•	•	•
Corn	•	•	•
Pumpkins	•	•	•
Political Maps	•	•	•
Ports	•	•	•
Prime Meridian	•	•	•
Reptiles	•	•	•
Self Government	•	•	•
Separatists	•	•	•
Sherwood Forest	•	•	•
Straits	•	•	•
Timeline	•	•	•
Thanksgiving	•	•	•
Windmills	•	•	•
Wildlife Study:			
Mallard Duck	•	•	•
Northern Pintail	•	•	•
Wood Stork/Ibis	•	•	•
White-tailed Deer	•		•
Eastern Cottontail Rabbit	•	•	
Red and Gray Squirrels	•	•	
Great Egreg		•	
Common Goldeneye		•	
Green-winged Teal			
Snowshoe Hare			
Historical Figures:			
William Bradford	•	•	•
John Carver	•	•	•
Galileo	•	•	•
King James	•	•	•
Massasoit	•	•	•
Samoset	•	•	•
Myles Standish	•	•	•
Squanto	•	•	•

A Journey of Adventure

The walls of the mightiest fortress,
The wake of a ship on the sea,
Charts lead to the busiest seaports,
Trails light up the paths of the free.

To the east or the west where the compass rose points,
A bazaar of strange foods we shall see.
To the north or the south as the map shows the signs,
We'll follow the road's decree.

A journal they write gives us faraway sight;
The fame of their travels leads on.
From Cathay to Venice to points on the way,
The steps of the Polos are drawn.

Come join the explorers and travel the globe.
You can add to the maps that they make
Of the stars, or the towns or the new sights you see,
With the bright thoughts your travels awake.

The vagabonds joins you to share all the joys,
That seeking and finding can be.
Just open your atlas and unlock the door,
With the ease of geography's key.

Art Lesson: Nature

"Nature is the art of God." – Dante

Nature studies can be a wonderful form of learning, especially for the young artist. We greatly encourage you to take your pencils and pad and go outdoors to study what God has created. There are many interesting and delightful things to observe: rock formations, insects, flowers, trees, birds, and clouds. Nature studies encourage us to draw from life. Going outside can open our eyes to light and the way it forms things with brilliant array of colors. God's studio, the outdoors, can be much more rewarding than simply drawing at your desk or in the comfort of your own home.

As an art student, learn to draw the things which are around you. Nature studies are perfect for this: a branch with a few leaves, some pebbles, a distant tree, a running brook, weeds, thistles, and so on. The Orientals are noted for the simple studies they did from nature: one flower, a branch and a song bird, or a sunset.

There are several things you may want to take along when you go outside:
1. A hat to protect you from the sun.
2. Clips to hold your paper down when it is windy.
3. A comfortable chair.
4. Your art supplies.

Feed My Sheep by Barry Stebbing, pg. 164, used by permission.

Art Lesson: Shading

The quickest way to make something look three dimensional is to apply shading, shadow, and texture.

The purpose of shading is to make the object dark on one side and light on the other, with the easiest gradient as possible.

1. Draw a cylinder in the space provided in your Student Notebook.
2. Pick the direction the light is coming from.
3. Shade the cylinder.

Try several techniques to determine which one you like best. Some techniques may work better for you on one kind of picture than another, so get familiar with all of them.

Figure 2 shows several shading techniques on the same cylinder.

#1 is pointillism, the use of dots or points, the more dots, the darker the shading.

#2 is cross hatching, the more cross hatch the darker the shade.

#3 is just straight lines, the more lines the darker.

#4 is contour lines. These follow the shape. The lines are made longest first, and then shorter and shorter lines are added between each line.

#5 is shading made by a pile of pencil lead (graphite) places on the paper and spread out with a smudge stick or forefinger.

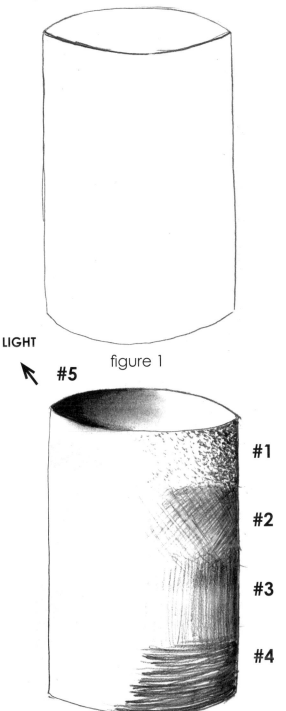

LIGHT

#5

figure 1

#1

#2

#3

#4

figure 2

A large part of being an artist is developing observation skills. Take your drawings and really look at them. Turn them upside down and look carefully. Turn them over on the back and look through the paper, by holding it up to a light. What do you see? Are all the vertical lines really vertical? Get a straight edge and lay it along a supposed straight line. Is it straight? Next time as you begin drawing, remember what you observed and make corrections before you darken your lines.

This sphere (figure 4) was shaded with a combination of techniques. Draw several basic shapes in your student notebook, and shade them using various techniques. Try doing cylinders, cones, and spheres.

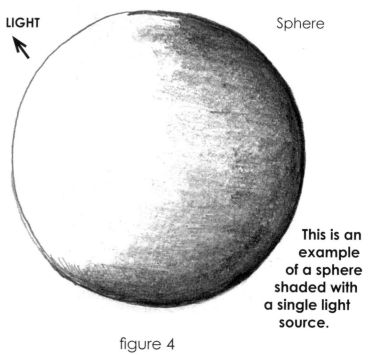

LIGHT

Sphere

This is an example of a sphere shaded with a single light source.

figure 4

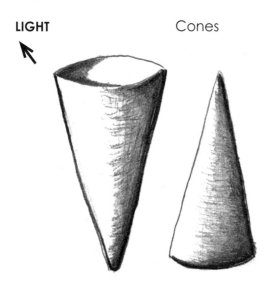

LIGHT

Cones

figure 3

So far we have been doing objects with curved surfaces. When you shade things with flat sides such as cubes, you shade each side the same tone, like the ones below. This is because the side is not curved. Each side should have a slightly different shade, depending on the light source.

Notice the example of incorrect shading in figure 6 below. The cube's sides look rounded. This is because the use of a gradient makes the flat sides curve. I would not say, "Never shade like this." Someday you may want a metallic look, which is what the cube below looks like. But in general, to make a cube look "right," keep each side flat by the use of uniform shading as explained earlier. In your Student Notebook, practice shading cubes.

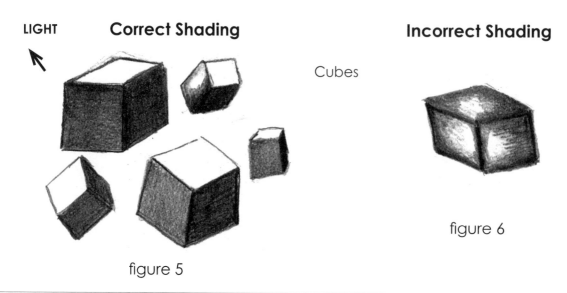

LIGHT

Correct Shading

Incorrect Shading

Cubes

figure 6

figure 5

As a part of this lesson find some real objects that represent basic shapes. Cylinder shapes, for example, are hair spray cans, flashlight batteries, soup cans, paper towel rolls, bananas, carrots, and telescopes. Sphere shapes are marbles, balls, green peas, frog eggs, oranges, and apples. Get several examples and draw them from different angles. Be careful to draw what you see, not what you think you see. A good artist is a good observer.

Shade each object as you see it. If it does not have a definite light source, move it to a light source. For the time being, don't try to imagine the shading, set it up so that it has shading.

These three apples are drawn from three different angles.

Remember to draw what you see, not what you <u>think</u> you see.

Paper Towels

Remember this is an exercise in shading. You need to draw from <u>REAL</u> objects, not from any pictures. Not even from these great examples!

Artists have always drawn from real things. Until the 1830s, there were no photographs to draw from. When Leonardo da Vinci painted the *Mona Lisa,* he had her sitting in front of him. He did not dream up her smile!

Master Drawing by Sharon Jeffus: Lesson I used by permission.

POPULATION: CONTINENTS		
Continent	**Population**	**Area**
Africa	866,300,000	11,700,000 sq mi
Antarctica	1000 (none permanent)	5,400,000
Asia	3,800.000.000	17,300,000 sq mi
Europe	729,300,000	3,800,000 sq mi
North America	505, 800.000	9,500,000 sq mi
Oceania	32,170,000	3,300,000 sq mi
South America	366,600,000	6.900,000 sq mi

POPULATION: COUNTRIES		
Country	**Population**	**Area**
Australia	19,825,000	2,969,910 sq mi
Belize	270,000	8867 sq mi
Canada	32,360,000	3,855,103 sq mi
China	1,298,720,000	3,690,045 sq mi
Egypt	75,420,000	386,662 sq mi
Germany	82,415,000	137,847 sq mi
India	1,057,415,000	1,222,510 sq mi
Italy	58,030,000	116,342 sq mi
Japan	127,285,000	145,850 sq mi
Kenya	31,840,000	224,961 sq mi
New Zealand	3,975,000	104,454 sq mi
United States	291,680,000	3,794,083 sq mi

POPULATION: CANADIAN PROVINCES AND TERRITORIES		
Province or Territory	Population	Area
Alberta	3,413,500	661,848 km²
British Columbia	4,310,452	925,186 km²
Manitoba	1,177,765	647,797 km²
New Brunswick	749,168	72 908 km²
Newfoundland and Labrador	509,677	373,872 km²
Nova Scotia	934,405	53,338 km²
Ontario	12,686,952	917,741 km²
Prince Edward Island	38,519	5,660 km²
Quebec	7,651,531	1,183,128 km²
Saskatchewan	985,386	591,670 km²
Northwest Territories	41,861	1,346,106 km²
Nunavut	30,850	1,936,113 km²
Yukon	31,229	474,391 km²

Milk Carton Model Sailing Ship

A Sea Breeze:

Did you know that there is wind that blows off the ocean called a sea breeze? The land absorbs heat faster than the water in the ocean. As the air above the land becomes warmer, it rises. The cool air over the sea moves inland and brings a delightful sea breeze. Make the following boat and put it in a stream or puddle outside when the wind is blowing.

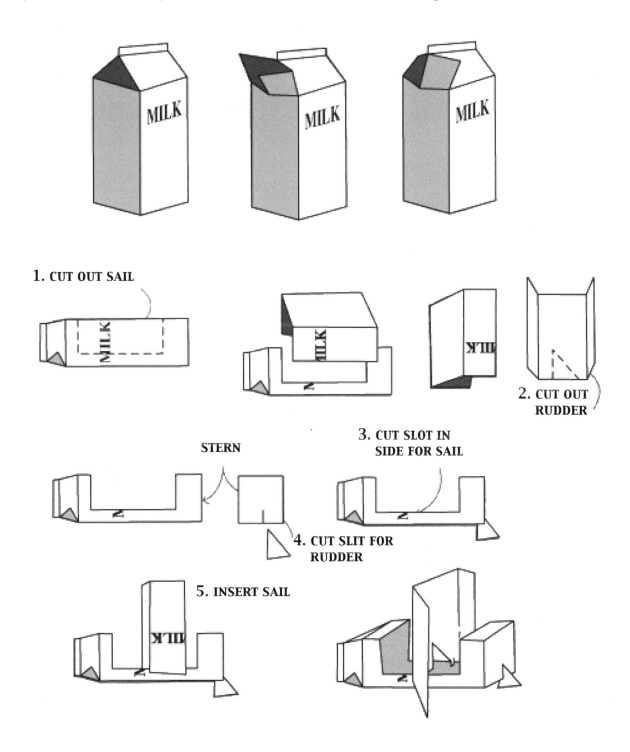

Science Through Art by Sharon Jeffus, used by permission.

Houses of Parliament

Tower of London

Tower Bridge

Westminster Abbey

Buckingham Palace

St. Paul's Cathedral

Whitehall

Old London Bridge

✎—*A Pilgrim Story*—✎

Life in England in 1600 was quite different from life in America today. People were ruled by kings and queens and did not have the freedom we hold so dear. King James ruled over how people in his kingdom could worship God. When men refused to attend the King's Church in England they could be sent to prison. Some people did not agree with the beliefs of the Church of England and separated themselves in order to worship freely. These people were called Separatists. A group of Separatists met and worshiped at Scrooby Inn, owned by Elder William Brewster.

After being treated badly again and again, the Separatists decided to leave England even though they loved their homes and way of life. They had many troubles leaving England. On one try, the women and children were stranded when the ship's captain set sail without them. Eventually they all made it to Amsterdam, Holland, to avoid the bad treatment by King James. The Separatists who left their homes in England to find a new place to live were now called Pilgrims, or people who travel or wander from place to place.

The Pilgrims moved to Leiden, Holland, where they lived for eleven years. They learned about a whole new way of life in Holland where waterways, or canals, served as transportation. They were fascinated by the iceboats that moved on skis across the frozen canals in winter. They saw earthen dikes that held back water, and windmills. The Pilgrims longed for life in England where they could live simple lives serving God. But they could not return and have the freedom to worship.

They began to plan their move to the New World, where they could raise their families and serve God. The Pilgrims began preparations for the long journey into a new land where they would start fresh building a community. Among the supplies they would bring were white linen, spinning wheels, and pewter dishes that were not easily broken. Dried peas and fruits were also part of the supplies they took. From milk they churned butter and prepared cheese. They preserved meat by salting it. Barrels of meal and sacks of beans were also filled for food until they could harvest their first crops. After some careful thought, they loaded their belongings on two ships: the *Speedwell* and the *Mayflower*. When the *Speedwell* proved unfit, the supplies and people were all loaded onto the *Mayflower*. Some people decided to stay behind, fearing the problems were a sign of trouble to come.

Finally on September 16, 1620, the *Mayflower* set sail from Plymouth, England, with 101 men, women, and children on board. Not all were Pilgrims. Captain Christopher Jones' crew and others they called Strangers also left on this journey. Myles

❧ *A Pilgrim Story* ❧

Standish, with his trusty sword Gideon, was hired to help protect the new colony. After 65 days of traveling across the Atlantic Ocean the Pilgrims finally arrived, but not in Virginia where they would have had to submit to the government of England. Winds had blown them off course and they dropped anchor in Provincetown Harbor on November 21, 1620.

Since there was no established law they agreed to govern themselves, and nearly everyone signed the Mayflower Compact. This became the basis for the Constitution of the United States of America. They elected John Carver as their governor. This was the first election of the people, by the people. Some of the men rowed ashore to find a good place to settle.

Their first act on dry land was to pray and thank God for their safe arrival. The *Mayflower* later sailed across Cape Cod Bay and anchored in Plymouth Harbor. The Pilgrims made this their new home on December 26, 1620.

The first winter was a hard one and many became sick and died. In spring the Pilgrims were surprised when an Indian came into the village and greeted them in English! His name was Samoset. A lasting friendship between the Pilgrims and the Indians began this day. Samoset later brought another Indian named Squanto, who could speak English well. Squanto became a good friend to the Pilgrims. He taught them to plant Indian Corn and acted as an interpreter. Edward Winslow learned the Indian language from Squanto and taught him how to read the Bible.

After the first harvest the Pilgrims celebrated with games, activities, and food. They invited their Indian friends to celebrate God's blessing on the harvest. The Pilgrims celebrated Thanksgiving every year after the harvest, and for many years the Indians joined them on this special day. Governor Carver died the first year, and William Bradford became the new governor. He served for over 30 years and kept a diary of their experiences. The Pilgrims laid a foundation for something dear to every American. They willingly gave all to gain the right to freedom.

ᴼ⎯*Game Instructions*⎯ᴼ

Word Search

Circle or highlight the words from the list provided. Mark off each word as you find them.

Word Scramble

Unscramble the words and write them on the line provided. The words are from the unit Word Bank.

Crosswords

Use the clues provided and write the answers in the correct place across or down.

Animal I.D.

Deal five cards to each player, place remaining cards face down, and play like Go Fish. Each player asks the other for a certain animal. If he or she doesn't have it, draw a card. When a pair is matched, put it down during the turn and go again. When no match is made the turn is over. When no cards are left or a player matches all of his or her cards, the game is over. The player with the most cards wins.

Ocean and Continent Concentration (Columbus Lesson 3, Part 5)

Using the game cards provided, place all cards face down in several rows. The first player turns up two cards. If these cards match, the player removes them and turns up two more cards. Each time the cards match, the player takes another turn. If the cards do not match, turn them back down for the next player. When no cards are left, the game is over. The player with the most cards wins.

Bingo (Columbus and Jamestown Lesson 4, Part 5)

Give each player at least one Bingo game board and a number of tokens such as buttons, pennies, or dried beans. Listen as someone reads the Bingo clues. Place tokens in the squares that provide the correct answers to the clues. The first player to place tokens on all boxes in a row across, down, or diagonal says, "Bingo!" and wins that round. Play as many rounds as you wish.

Columbus Charades (Columbus Lesson 6, Part 4)

Using the Columbus Charades cards provided in the Appendix, act out the event listed on the card. Before you begin each charade, tell whether Columbus was a boy (gesture to show the height of a small child), a young man (make a muscle with each arm to show a young, strong man), or an explorer (hold hand up to forehead as if you are looking out to sea.) Other players guess what is on your card from your actions. Take turns acting and guessing until all cards are played.

Word Study Charades (Jamestown Lesson 2, Part 4)

Write each of the charade words on a separate slip of paper. You may use the vacabulary index cards students have made. Let students draw one and act it out.

Old World/New World Opposites (Jamestown Lesson 2, Part 5)

This game consists of two sets of game cards. One set of cards tells about something that would happen in the Old World. The second set tells about something that would happen in the New World. Match the Old World fact with its opposite New World fact. Play like Concentration or Go Fish.

Pilgrim Bingo (Pilgrim Lesson 5, Part 4)

Give each player at least one Bingo game board and a number of tokens such as buttons, candy corn, or dried beans. Listen as someone reads the Pilgrim Story. Then select and read Bingo clues at random. Place tokens in the squares that provide the correct answers to the clues. The first player to place tokens on all boxes in a row across, down, or diagonal says, "Bingo!" and wins that round. Play as many rounds as you wish.

Word Search - Lesson 1, Part 5

C	S	O	S	N	Y	A	A	X	M	I	N
H	A	C	N	R	B	O	V	F	A	A	E
R	N	E	N	I	C	V	O	E	R	M	W
I	T	A	O	S	O	V	Y	R	C	E	W
S	A	N	S	A	L	V	A	D	O	R	O
T	M	S	A	B	U	S	G	I	P	I	R
O	A	E	F	E	M	A	E	N	O	C	L
P	R	A	E	L	B	I	N	A	L	A	D
H	I	A	L	L	U	L	O	N	O	R	P
E	A	W	I	A	S	O	A	D	N	A	I
R	E	X	P	L	O	R	E	R	I	V	N
P	S	P	A	I	N	S	R	E	N	E	T
A	D	M	I	R	A	L	A	F	A	L	A

Crossword - Lesson 5, Part 5

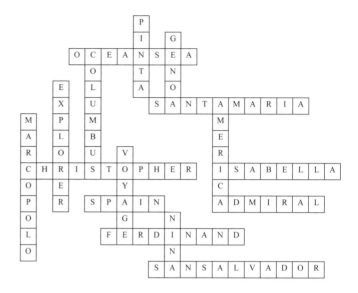

Word Scramble - Lesson 2, Part 5

1. Columbus
2. Nina
3. America
4. Pinta
5. Ferdinand
6. sailors
7. Isabella
8. Genoa
9. San Salvador
10. explorer
11. Marco Polo
12. voyage
13. Christopher
14. Spain
15. Ocean Sea
16. Admiral
17. Santa Maria
18. caravel
19. New World
20. Felipa

Old World/New World - Lesson 2, Part 5

OW: Land is passed down only from family member to family member.

NW: Anyone can own land.

OW: Gentlemen did no work.

NW: Gentlemen had to do work.

OW: The land was very crowded.

NW: There was much land open to settle.

OW: There were many skilled workers.

NW: There were few skilled workers.

OW: Everyone had to attend one church.

NW: People were free to worship God as they pleased.

OW: Leaders were born to their positions.

NW: Leaders could come from among the people.

OW: Little danger of being attacked where you lived.

NW: Great danger of being attacked where you lived.

OW: There was always food available.

NW: There was often no food available.

Word Search - Lesson 3, Part 5

Crossword - Lesson 5, Part 5

Word Search - Lesson 1, Part 5

```
P  L  Y  M  O  U  T  H  M  A  N  O  E  D  I  G  S
Q  Y  S  Y  V  O  T  N  A  U  Q  S  N  Q  R  R  T
C  S  E  L  T  S  H  E  Y  O  S  A  E  G  N  I  W
N  E  H  E  P  J  E  F  E  L  O  R  T  O  M  E  E
L  A  S  S  E  S  N  L  L  I  W  R  S  A  O  C  C
Y  G  I  S  O  E  B  R  O  O  R  E  A  D  P  L  A
E  S  D  T  M  D  A  H  W  T  Y  S  R  N  G  I  P
A  S  R  A  A  W  N  S  E  A  S  E  N  A  E  S  E
T  M  E  N  S  E  P  A  R  A  T  I  S  T  S  Y  C
I  I  T  D  D  L  O  P  M  S  Y  T  S  L  I  A  O
A  R  W  I  L  L  I  A  M  B  R  A  D  F  O  R  D
A  G  E  S  E  A  W  A  O  A  R  Y  I  E  E  D  B
D  L  P  H  L  E  J  O  H  N  C  A  R  V  E  R  A
M  I  D  R  M  N  R  O  C  N  A  I  D  N  I  W  Y
A  P  F  R  L  C  H  A  Y  N  P  S  M  A  P  N  R
E  M  I  O  S  E  M  A  J  G  N  I  K  E  P  P  D
```

Crossword - Lesson 4, Part 5

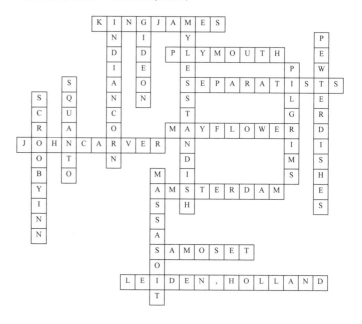

Word Scramble - Lesson 3, Part 5

1. Separatists
2. John Carver
3. Amsterdam
4. Indian corn
5. Squanto
6. pewter dishes
7. King James
8. Massasoit
9. Speedwell
10. Plymouth
11. William Bradford
12. Leiden Holland
13. Myles Standish
14. Mayflower
15. Cape Cod Bay
16. Scrooby Inn
17. Pilgrims
18. Gideon
19. Samoset
20. prayer

True or False Statements - Lesson 4, Part 2 F

All levels	Level 🐾🐾
1. F	willow twigs
2. T	
3. F	speak
4. F	fishes
5. T	
6. F.	every

Appendix B

Reading Log

_____
unit

_____
student name

Pages	Title	Author	Date

⌐Explorer⌐

_____
name

Explored for _____

Purpose of exploration _____

_____

People who helped this explorer _____

_____

Main accomplishment _____

_____

Hardships encountered _____

_____

What enabled him to persevere _____

_____

Best remembered for _____

_____

In what way I am like this explorer _____

_____

_____

In what way I am unlike this explorer _____

_____

_____

In what way I'd want to be like this explorer _____

_____

_____

_____

❧ *Character Portrait* ❧

_____
(name)

_____
(book title)

What this person looks like: _____

_____

_____

_____

What kind of person he or she is: _____

_____

_____

_____

_____

Two things this person did in the story

1. _____

_____

2. _____

_____

Do you like this character?   yes _____   no _____

Why or why not? _____

_____

_____

_____

_____

ᴼᴼ— Native American Profile —ᴼᴼ

Name of Tribe: _____

Where did they live? _____

What was their main source of food?

_____

What kind of dwellings did they live in?

_____

Use a colored pencil to shade areas
where they lived

Were they warlike or peaceful towards settlers?

_____

Does this tribe still exist today? _____

What explorer that you've studied came into

contact with this tribe?

Draw a picture of one of their houses

_____

Briefly tell about the kind of relationship they had: _____

_____

Are there any members of this tribe who are famous in History? If so, who?

_____

What is the most interesting thing you learned about this tribe?

_____

_____

Draw a picture that describes some part of this tribe's life

~ *Columbus Word Search* ~

```
U E D D O W O E A R A I E X E
A E E L I R I R R P W C A X A
A A N R I E A V E A I A P R E
A A A O M A R C O P O L O E O
S L A W N I I L I Y O D E U D
A L L W E R A R E R A F I F R
I M A E I A A A E V E G S R R
L O W N B M R R L R A M E C P
O C N I A A T A D M I R A L E
R E H P O T S I R H C S A S S
S A P R O N N I A P S A L C S
O N P I A A O N E G R L R L V
E S R S N S U B M U L O C S S
S E F D I T M S I R A I G A H
E A A N N E A R R A A B V C A
```

Admiral	explorer	Marco Polo	sailors
America	Felipa	New World	San Salvador
caravel	Ferdinand	Nina	Santa Maria
Christopher	Genoa	Ocean Sea	Spain
Columbus	Isabella	Pinta	voyage

∝ *Columbus Word Scramble* ∝

Admiral	explorer	Marco Polo	sailors
America	Felipa	New World	San Salvador
caravel	Ferdinand	Nina	Santa Maria
Christopher	Genoa	Ocean Sea	Spain
Columbus	Isabella	Pinta	voyage

Unscramble these words and write them correctly on the line.

1. bslumCuo _____

2. aniN _____

3. mriAcea _____

4. tinPa _____

5. dadinneFr _____

6. roissla _____

7. eslalsbla _____

8. oeaGn _____

9. vnaoaraSSld _____

10. pexroelr _____

11. colaMProo _____

12. aeygov _____

13. hitsrphCoe _____

14. aniSp _____

15. eeOncaaS _____

16. iAldmra _____

17. tiaaMSnara _____

18. laaverc _____

19. lodwerWN _____

20. apeliF _____

- Concentration Game -

- Concentration Game -

- Concentration Game -

- Concentration Game -

- Concentration Game -

- Concentration Game -

- Concentration Game -

- Concentration Game -

- Concentration Game -

- Concentration Game -

- Concentration Game -

- Concentration Game -

Atlantic Ocean	Pacific Ocean	Indian Ocean
Atlantic Ocean	Pacific Ocean	Indian Ocean
Arctic Ocean	Antarctic Ocean	North America
Arctic Ocean	Antarctic Ocean	North America

 - Concentration Game -

 - Concentration Game -

 - Concentration Game -

 - Concentration Game -

 - Concentration Game -

 - Concentration Game -

 - Concentration Game -

 - Concentration Game -

 - Concentration Game -

 - Concentration Game -

 - Concentration Game -

 - Concentration Game -

Europe	Africa	Australia
Europe	Africa	Australia
Asia	Antarctica	South America
Asia	Antarctica	South America

The explorer who opened the New World for others

Columbus

The ship on which Columbus sailed back to Spain

Nina

The ship whose captain was Martin Pinzon

Pinta

The name of the continents discovered in the New World

America

The king of Spain

Ferdinand

The queen of Spain

Isabella

Name meaning Christ-bearer

Christopher

Columbus' largest ship

Santa Maria

The first land Columbus found

San Salvador

Someone who seeks out new lands

explorer

Famous explorer known for his travels in China

Marco Polo

A long trip taken at sea

Voyage

The birthplace of Columbus **Genoa**	The country that sent Columbus to explore **Spain**	The name of the Atlantic Ocean in 1492 **Ocean Sea**
A high-ranking officer in a Navy **Admiral**	Those who work on ships **sailors**	A strong sailing ship that could be easily steered **caravel**
Brother of Columbus **Barolomeo**	Wife of Columbus **Felipa**	One who made maps for sailors and explorers **mapmaker**
A captain of one of Columbus' ships **Pinzon**	Son of Columbus **Diego**	Area first colonized by European explorers **New World**

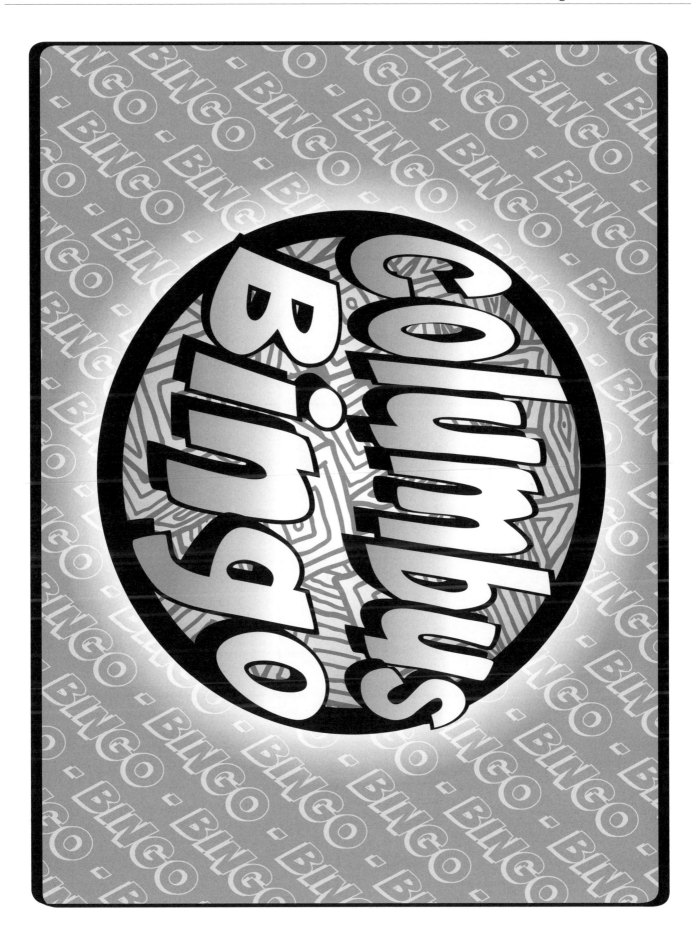

Columbus Bingo

Felipa	Ocean Sea	Marco Polo	Isabella	Columbus
Diego	Admiral	voyage	Christopher	Nina
Pinzon	sailors		Santa Maria	Pinta
Barolomeo	caravel	Genoa	San Salvador	America
New World	mapmaker	Spain	explorer	Ferdinand

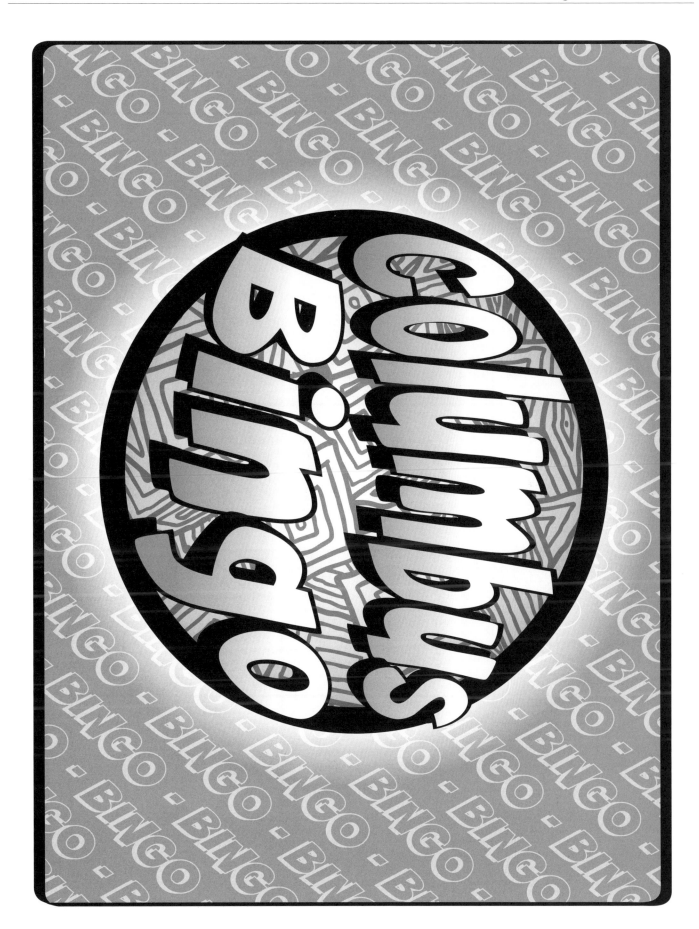

Columbus Bingo

explorer	Felipa	Pinta	Genoa	Barolomeo
Santa Maria	caravel	Columbus	Marco Polo	Diego
Isabella	Admiral		San Salvador	mapmaker
America	Spain	New World	Christopher	sailors
Nina	voyage	Pinzon	Ferdinand	Ocean Sea

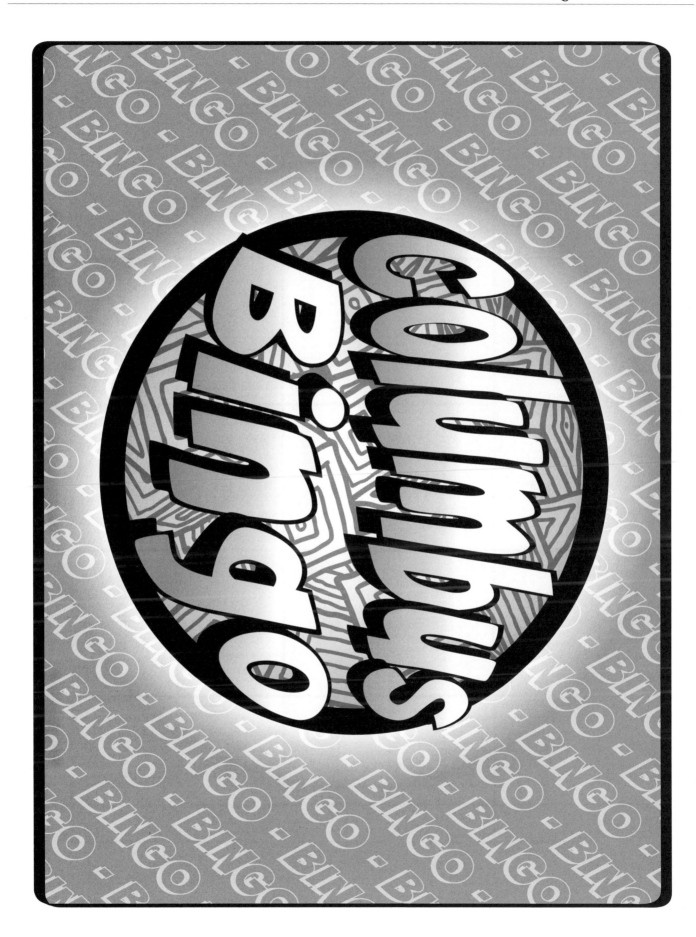

Columbus Bingo

Pinta	Isabella	San Salvador	voyage	Ocean Sea
caravel	Diego	New World	Nina	Ferdinand
Santa Maria	Marco Polo		Spain	sailors
Felipa	Barolomeo	Columbus	America	Christopher
explorer	Genoa	Admiral	mapmaker	Pinzon

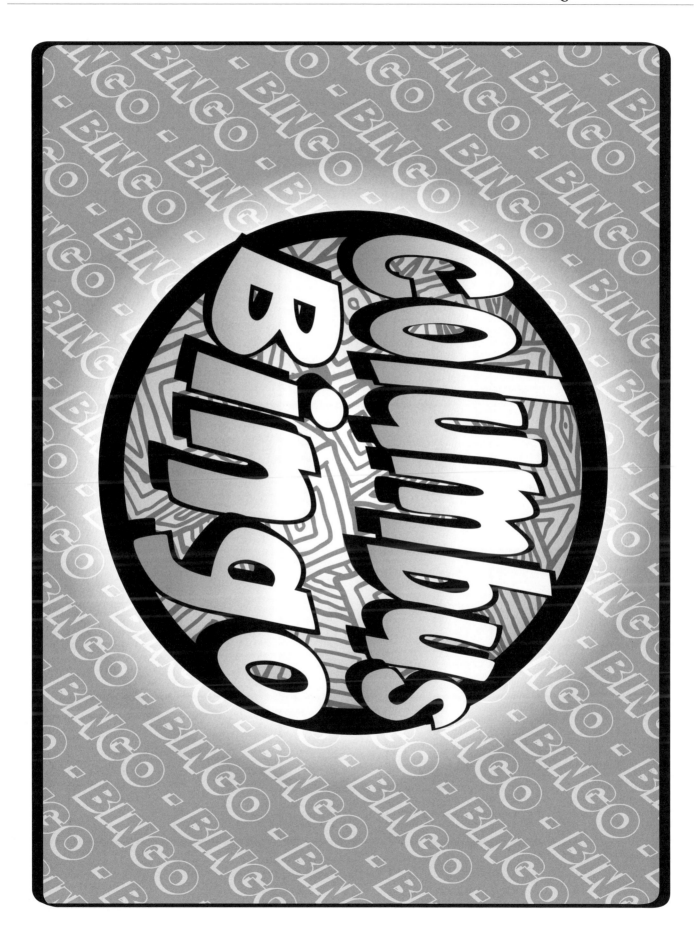

Columbus Bingo

Genoa	Columbus	Spain	Pinta	sailors
Nina	Ocean Sea	America	caravel	Christopher
Admiral	Ferdinand		Santa Maria	Diego
Isabella	mapmaker	San Salvador	Pinzon	Marco Polo
Felipa	explorer	Barolomeo	voyage	New World

ɔ~ *Columbus Crossword* ~ɕ

Across

3. The name of the Atlantic Ocean in 1492
6. Columbus' largest ship
10. Name meaning Christ-bearer
11. The queen of Spain
12. The country that sent Columbus to explore
13. A high-ranking officer in a Navy
15. The king of Spain
16. The first land Columbus found

Down

1. The ship whose captain was Martin Pinzon
2. The birthplace of Columbus
4. The explorer who opened the New World for others
5. Someone who seeks out new lands
7. The name of the continents discovered in the New World
8. Famous explorer known for his travels in China
9. A long trip taken at sea
14. The ship on which Columbus sailed back to Spain

Boy

Columbus helps card (comb) wool as a boy in his father's shop.

Explorer

Columbus claims the New World for the King and Queen of Spain.

Boy

Columbus watches ships in the port and dreams of sailing on ships.

Young man

Pirates attack his ship and he fights with them and is wounded by a sword.

Young man

Columbus becomes a bookseller and mapmaker.

Explorer

Columbus goes to see the King and Queen as the hero of the New World.

Explorer

Columbus is put into shackles (chains on his hands and feet) by the new leaders of Hispaniola.

Explorer

While Columbus sleeps, the *Santa Maria* hits the rocks and is shipwrecked.

- Opposites Game -

- Opposites Game -

- Opposites Game -

- Opposites Game -

- Opposites Game -

- Opposites Game -

- Opposites Game -

- Opposites Game -

- Opposites Game -

- Opposites Game -

- Opposites Game -

- Opposites Game -

Anyone can own land.	Gentlemen had to do work.	The land was very crowded.
Land is passed down only from family member to family member.	Gentlemen did no work.	There was much land open to settle.
There were many skilled workers.	Everyone had to attend one church.	Leaders were born to their positions.
There were few skilled workers.	People were free to worship God as they pleased.	Leaders could come from among the people.

- Opposites Game -

- Opposites Game -

- Opposites Game -

- Opposites Game -

- Opposites Game -

- Opposites Game -

- Opposites Game -

- Opposites Game -

- Opposites Game -

- Opposites Game -

- Opposites Game -

- Opposites Game -

There was little danger of being attacked where you lived.	There was always food available.	
There was great danger of being attacked where you lived.	There was often no food available.	

ᴥ— Jamestown Word Search —ᴥ

```
E  Y  R  E  V  O  C  S  I  D  O  K  N  G  B  J
A  N  A  P  D  I  R  G  E  N  T  L  E  M  E  N
S  O  I  B  I  N  A  E  F  L  O  R  N  H  O  J
P  O  N  S  E  A  A  D  V  E  N  T  U  R  E  S
A  S  I  C  M  K  N  L  D  I  Y  N  T  D  J  A
T  H  G  O  I  H  A  E  G  A  R  H  V  A  P  R
G  S  R  M  T  A  E  E  A  N  A  S  M  I  O  C
O  N  I  M  G  R  C  W  P  M  E  E  E  T  W  M
D  E  V  O  N  C  O  E  E  A  S  O  N  M  H  W
S  P  O  N  I  W  C  R  A  T  S  N  I  G  A  D
P  O  R  E  V  H  I  H  O  B  I  E  E  A  T  J
E  R  E  R  R  C  T  W  V  M  I  G  H  P  A  A
E  U  G  S  A  T  N  O  H  A  C  O  P  C  N  N
D  E  M  A  T  S  A  M  C  O  L  L  I  E  R  E
B  O  U  D  S  S  L  D  H  E  N  A  E  E  H  R
I  A  E  S  I  H  T  I  M  S  N  H  O  J  H  L
I  E  V  T  O  B  A  C  C  O  D  J  O  B  R  N
```

Atlantic Ocean	Europe	John Rolfe	Sam Collier
Chesapeake Bay	gentlemen	John Smith	Sea Adventure
commoners	Godspeed	North America	starving time
Discovery	James River	Pocahontas	tobacco
England	Jamestown	Powhatan	Virginia

Husband of Pocahontas	Crop raised in Virginia	Page to John Smith
John Rolfe	tobacco	Sam Collier

Bay near Jamestown	Ocean crossed by the Jamestown colonists	Those not born to noblemen
Chesapeake Bay	Atlantic Ocean	commoners

Island where the Sea Adventure was shipwrecked	Fort built by the Jamestown colonists	Largest of three ships that brought colonists to Jamestown
Bermuda	James Fort	*Susan Constant*

Ship bound for Jamestown that was shipwrecked	The business that sent colonists to Jamestown	Men born to noblemen
Sea Adventure	Virginia Company	gentlemen

Soldier leader of Jamestown colony John Smith	First permanent settlement in America Jamestown	Indian girl who helped colonists Pocahontas
Powerful chief of nearby Indian tribes Powhatan	Ship that went back and forth to England *Godspeed*	Time when almost all of the colony died starving time
Name of colony where Jamestown was built Virginia	Ship that stayed in Jamestown *Discovery*	Continent where Jamestown was built North America
Continent colonists came from Europe	Home country of colonists England	River near the Jamestown colony James River

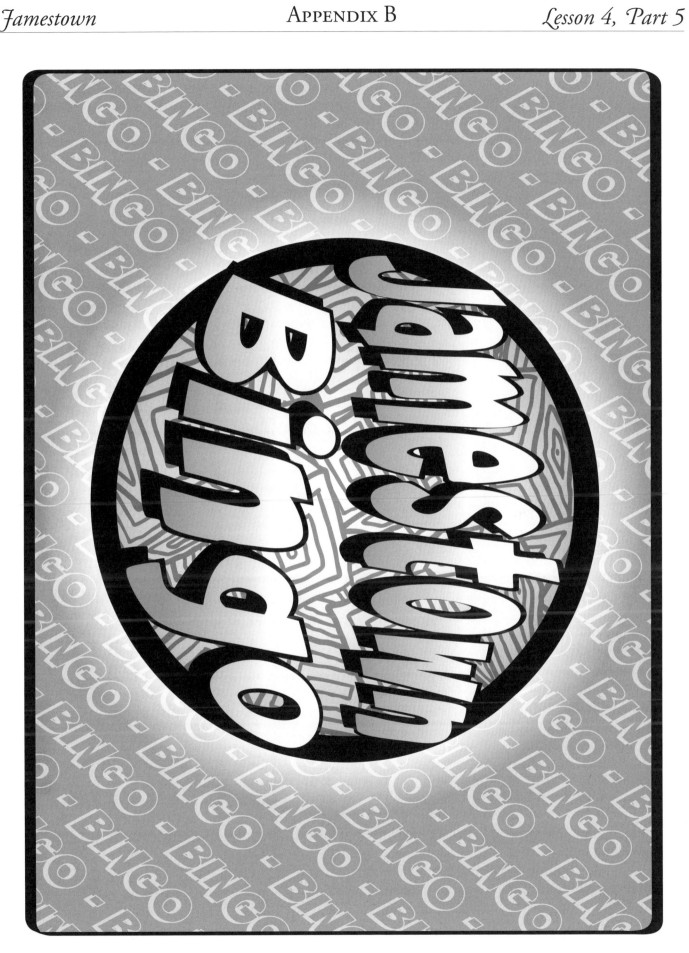

Jamestown Bingo

Atlantic Ocean	Virginia Company	gentlemen	commoners	James Fort
Sam Collier	Chesapeake Bay	Susan Constant	Sea Adventure	Bermuda
England	James River		John Rolfe	tobacco
starving time	Virginia	Discovery	North America	Europe
John Smith	Jamestown	Pocahontas	Powhatan	Godspeed

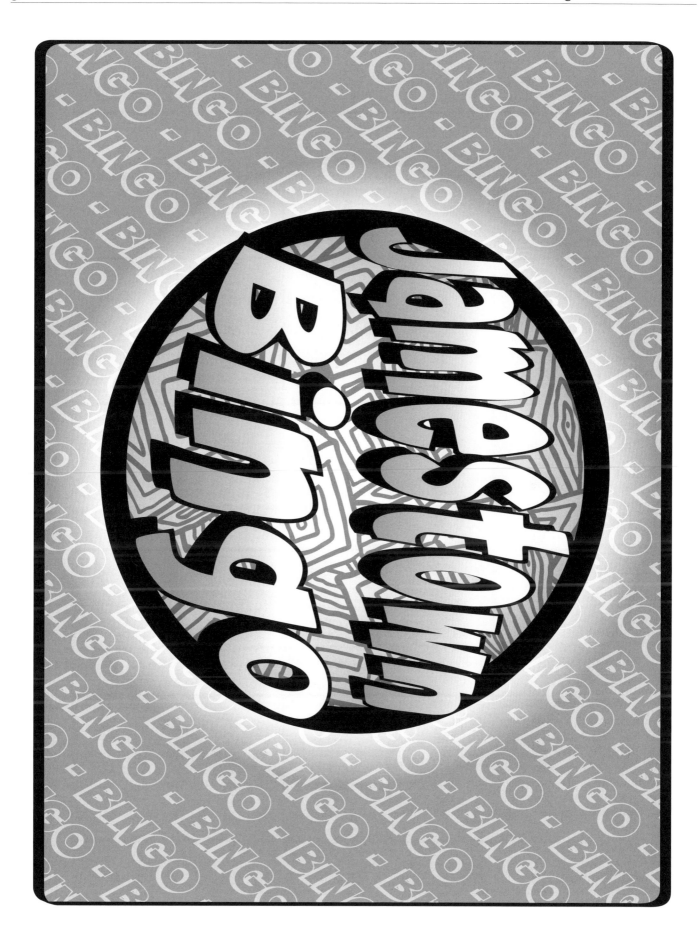

Jamestown Bingo

commoners	starving time	Susan Constant	Jamestown	tobacco
Europe	James Fort	Godspeed	Chesapeake Bay	John Smith
Atlantic Ocean	North America		Powhatan	Sam Collier
James River	Bermuda	Discovery	gentlemen	Pocahontas
John Rolfe	England	Sea Adventure	Virginia	Virginia Company

Jamestown Bingo

Europe	Atlantic Ocean	Pocahontas	John Rolfe	commoners
Discovery	Sea Adventure	John Smith	England	Virginia Company
starving time	Chesapeake Bay		North America	Bermuda
Powhatan	tobacco	James Fort	Virginia	Susan Constant
Jamestown	James River	gentlemen	Godspeed	Sam Collier

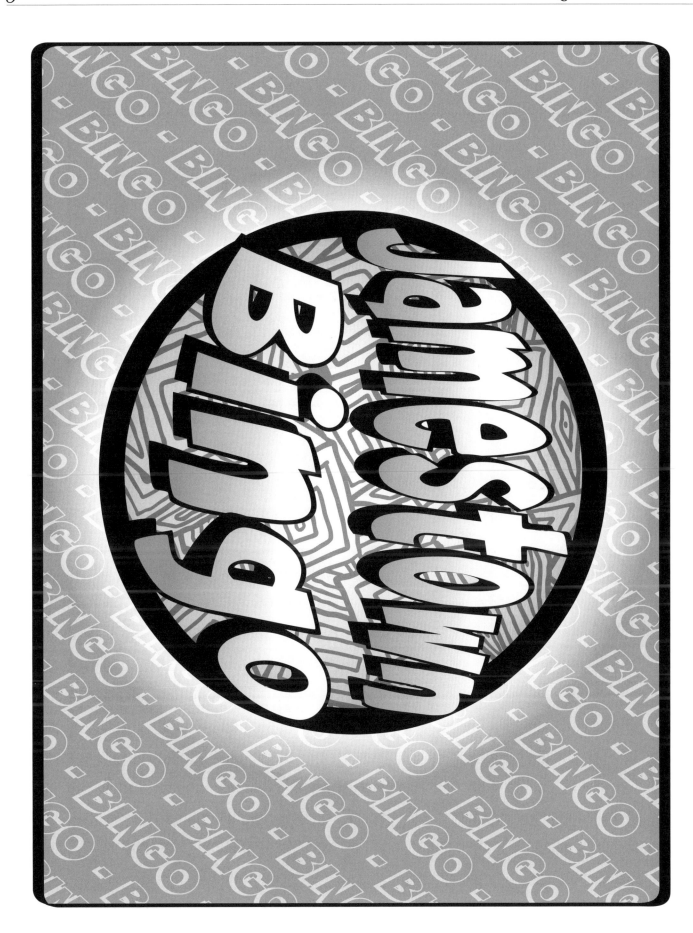

Jamestown Bingo

Sam Collier	Godspeed	Susan Constant	Virginia	gentlemen
James River	Jamestown	tobacco	Powhatan	Bermuda
North America	James Fort		John Smith	Chesapeake Bay
starving time	Virginia Company	England	commoners	John Rolfe
Pocahontas	Sea Adventure	Discovery	Atlantic Ocean	Europe

~ *Jamestown Crossword* ~

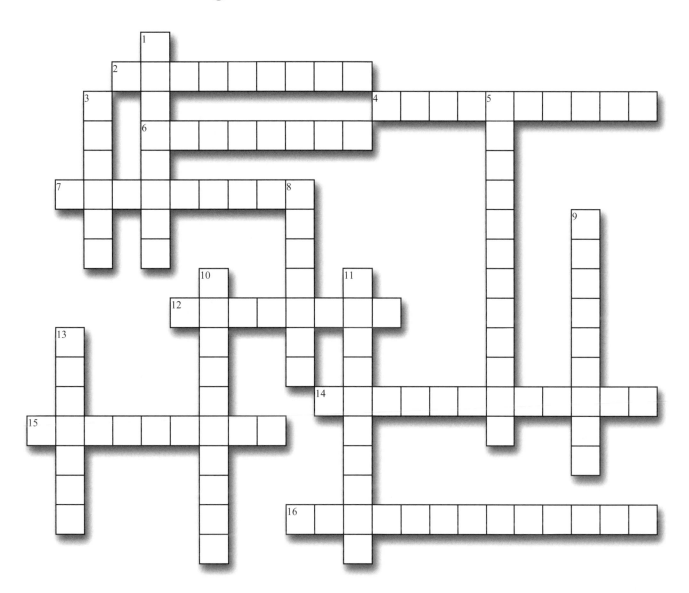

Across

2. Ship that stayed in Jamestown
4. River near the Jamestown colony
6. Ship that went back and forth to England
7. Husband of Pocahontas
12. Powerful chief of nearby Indian tribes
14. Continent where Jamestown was built
15. First permanent settlement in America
16. The bay near Jamestown

Down

1. Name of colony where Jamestown was built
3. Continent colonists came from
5. Time when almost all the colony died
8. Home country of colonists
9. Soldier leader of Jamestown colony
10. Indian girl who helped colonists
11. Page to John Smith
13. Crop raised in Virginia

⁓ *Pilgrim Word Search* ⁓

```
P  L  Y  M  O  U  T  H  M  A  N  O  E  D  I  G  S
Q  Y  S  Y  V  O  T  N  A  U  Q  S  N  Q  R  R  T
C  S  E  L  T  S  H  E  Y  O  S  A  E  G  N  I  W
N  E  H  E  E  P  J  E  F  E  L  O  R  T  O  M  E
L  A  S  S  S  E  S  N  L  L  I  W  R  S  A  O  C
Y  G  I  S  O  E  B  R  O  O  R  E  A  D  P  L  A
E  S  D  T  M  D  A  H  W  T  Y  S  R  N  G  I  P
A  S  R  A  A  W  N  S  E  A  S  E  N  A  E  S  E
T  M  E  N  S  E  P  A  R  A  T  I  S  T  S  Y  C
I  I  T  D  D  L  O  P  M  S  Y  T  S  L  I  A  O
A  R  W  I  L  L  I  A  M  B  R  A  D  F  O  R  D
A  G  E  S  E  A  W  A  O  A  R  Y  I  E  E  D  B
D  L  P  H  L  E  J  O  H  N  C  A  R  V  E  R  A
M  I  D  R  M  N  R  O  C  N  A  I  D  N  I  W  Y
A  P  F  R  L  C  H  A  Y  N  P  S  M  A  P  N  R
E  M  I  O  S  E  M  A  J  G  N  I  K  E  P  P  D
```

Amsterdam	King James	pewter dishes	Scrooby Inn
Cape Cod Bay	Leiden Holland	Pilgrims	Separatists
Gideon	Massasoit	Plymouth	Speedwell
Indian corn	Mayflower	prayer	Squanto
John Carver	Myles Standish	Samoset	William Bradford

❦ *Pilgrim Word Scramble* ❦

Amsterdam	King James	pewter dishes	Scrooby Inn
Cape Cod Bay	Leiden Holland	Pilgrims	Separatists
Gideon	Massasoit	Plymouth	Speedwell
Indian corn	Mayflower	prayer	Squanto
John Carver	Myles Standish	Samoset	William Bradford

Unscramble these words and write them correctly on the line.

1. aaprsteStis _____

2. gsnaJeiKm _____

3. notuaSq _____

4. rmsadteAm _____

5. utyhlPmo _____

6. sshlaeiSytndM _____

7. oidenG _____

8. isatoMsas _____

9. nveaoChrJr _____

10. oalinorncd _____

11. slmiirgP _____

12. etosamS _____

13. nonocybrlS _____

14. ddeoiaenHlLln _____

15. wyaoelMfr _____

16. iseehtwdpre _____

17. raiimdlflBoaWrd _____

18. yaaeoBdCCp _____

19. yperra _____

20. woleeelps _____

∽ *Pilgrim Crossword* ∾

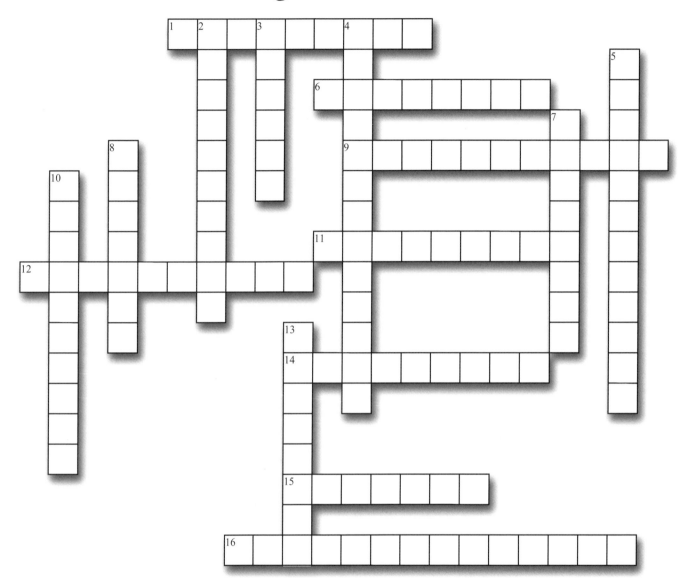

Across

1. The King who treated the Separatists badly
6. Place where the Pilgrims settled
9. Name given to people who separated from the Church of England to worship according to their beliefs
11. The ship that carried the Pilgrims to the New World
12. First governor of Plymouth Colony
14. Town the Separatists first moved to when fleeing England
15. The first Indian who spoke to the Pilgrims in broken English
16. The second town in Holland where the Separatists lived

Down

2. Crop Squanto taught the Pilgrims to plant
3. The name of Myles Standish's sword
4. Soldier hired to help protect the colony
5. Dishes chosen because they would not break
7. What the Separatists were called after they left their homes in search of a new home
8. Indian friend of the Pilgrims who acted as interpreter
10. The Inn where the Separatists met to worship in England
13. Indian Chief who made a treaty with Governor Carver

Name given to people who separated from the Church of England to worship according to their beliefs

Separatists

The King who treated the Separatists badly

King James

Indian friend of the Pilgrims who acted as interpreter

Squanto

Town the Separatists first moved to when fleeing England

Amsterdam

Place where the Pilgrims settled

Plymouth

Soldier hired to help protect the colony

Myles Standish

The name of Myles Standish's sword

Gideon

Indian Chief who made a treaty with Governor Carver

Massasoit

First governor of Plymouth Colony

John Carver

Crop Squanto taught the Pilgrims to plant

Indian corn

What the Separatists were called after they left their homes in search of a new home

Pilgrims

The first Indian who spoke to the Pilgrims in broken English

Samoset

The Inn where the Separatists met to worship in England

Scrooby Inn

The second town in Holland where the Separatists lived

Leiden, Holland

The ship which carried the Pilgrims to the New World

Mayflower

Dishes chosen because they would not break

Pewter dishes

Governor of Plymouth Colony for over 30 years

William Bradford

Bay the Mayflower sailed across to drop anchor in Plymouth Harbor

Cape Cod Bay

First thing done on land

Prayer

Ship that set sail with the *Mayflower* but had to turn back

Speedwell

Elder who owned the Scrooby Inn

William Brewster

What the Separatists left England in search of

Freedom

Captain of the *Mayflower*

Christopher Jones

Used to preserve meat

Salt

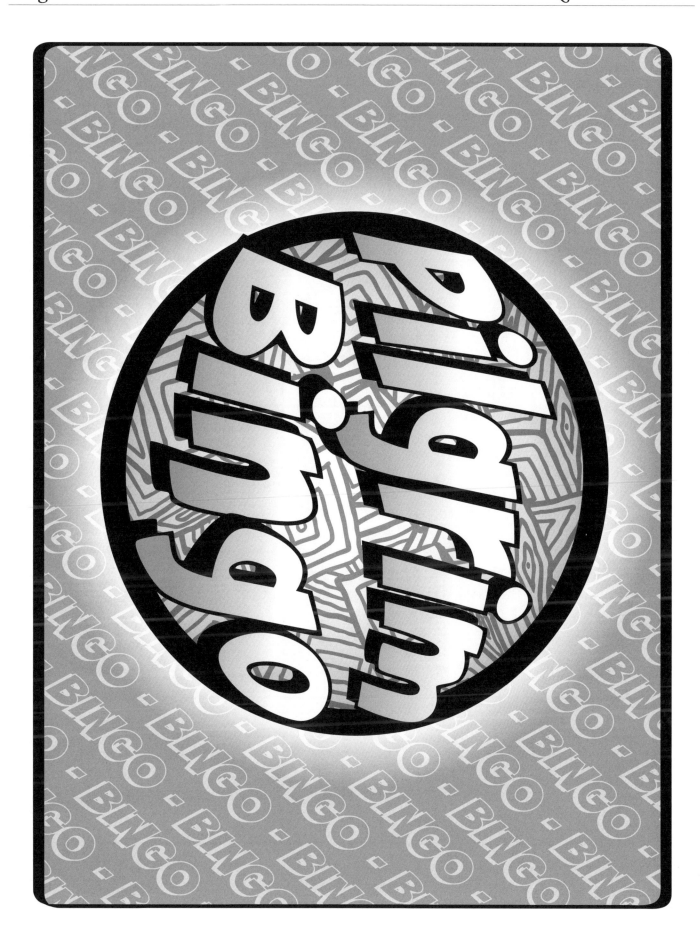

Pilgrim Bingo

Christopher Jones	Plymouth	King James	Mayflower	Massasoit
Myles Standish	Leiden, Holland	Salt	Amsterdam	Scrooby Inn
Cape Cod Bay	Separatists		William Brewster	William Bradford
Indian corn	Speedwell	pewter dishes	Prayer	Freedom
Squanto	John Carver	Samoset	Pilgrims	Gideon

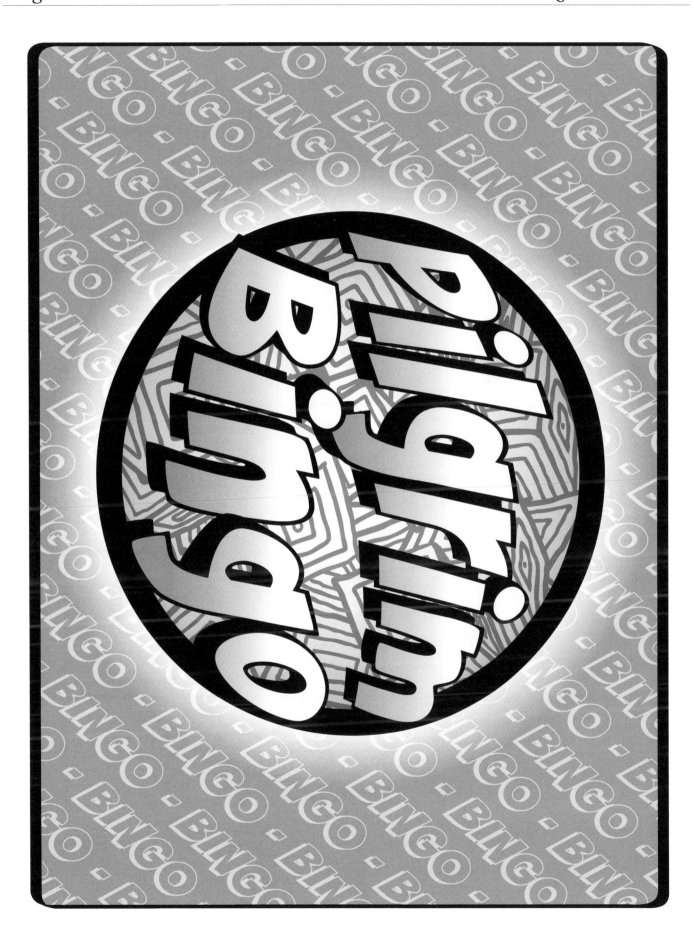

Pilgrim Bingo

Gideon	John Carver	King James	William Brewster	Separatists
Pilgrims	Speedwell	Cape Cod Bay	Amsterdam	Christopher Jones
Plymouth	Scrooby Inn		pewter dishes	Massasoit
Mayflower	Squanto	Samoset	Indian corn	Salt
Prayer	Freedom	Myles Standish	Leiden, Holland	William Bradford

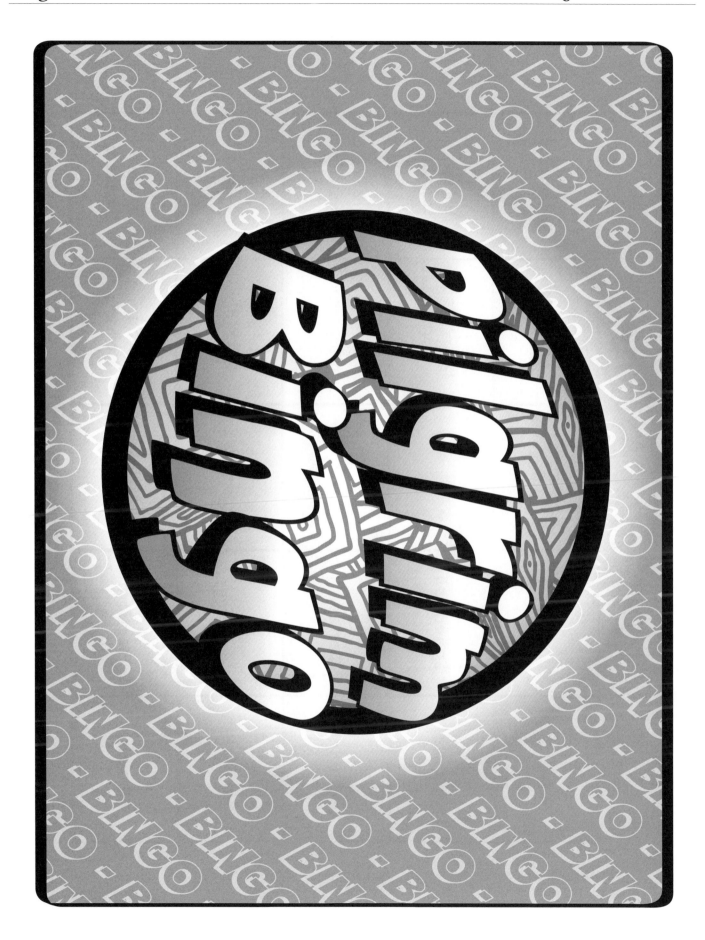

Pilgrim Bingo

Amsterdam	Separatists	Christopher Jones	Salt	Squanto
William Bradford	Cape Cod Bay	Mayflower	Speedwell	pewter dishes
Indian corn	Pilgrims		Samoset	King James
Freedom	Leiden, Holland	Gideon	John Carver	Scrooby Inn
Myles Standish	William Brewster	Prayer	Plymouth	Massasoit

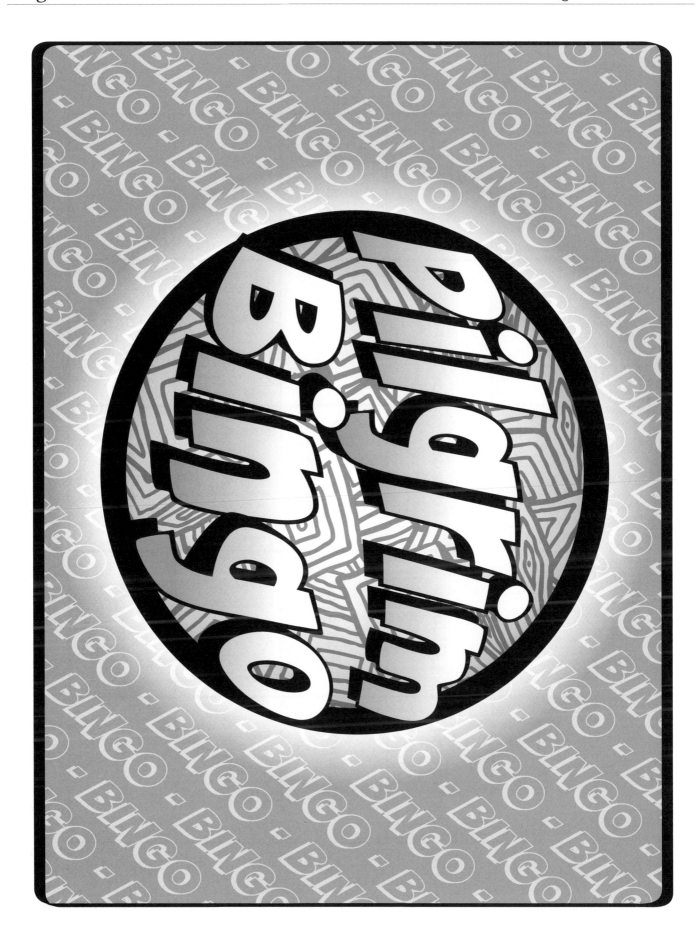

Pilgrim Bingo

Speedwell	Mayflower	Pilgrims	Myles Standish	Separatists
William Brewster	pewter dishes	Samoset	Gideon	King James
Freedom	William Bradford		Massasoit	Squanto
Christopher Jones	Cape Cod Bay	Scrooby Inn	John Carver	Amsterdam
Salt	Prayer	Leiden, Holland	Indian corn	Plymouth

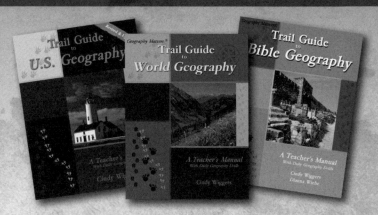

Trail Guide to Geography Series -
by Cindy Wiggers

Three books in the *Trail Guide to ...Geography* series include U.S., World, and Bible geography. Each book provides clear directions and assignment choices to encourage self-directed learning as students create their own personal geography notebooks. Daily atlas drills, mapping activities, and various weekly assignment choices address learning styles in a way that has kids asking for more! Use each book over several years by choosing more difficult activities as students grow older.

Trail Guide features:

• Weekly lesson plans – for 36 weeks
• 5-minute daily atlas drills (2 questions/day, four days/week)
• 3 levels of difficulty – all ages participate together
• Weekly mapping assignments
• A variety of weekly research and hands-on activity choices

Student Notebooks are available on CD-ROM

Trail Guide Levels
The *Trail Guide* Levels are just a guide. Select a level according to student ability, and match level with the appropriate atlas or student notebook.

• Primary: grades 2– 4
• Intermediate: grades 5–7
• Secondary: grades 8–12

All 3 levels in each book!

Note: Primary is ideal for independent 4th graders. Second and third graders will need plenty of guidance. If your oldest is 2nd–3rd grade range, please consider *Galloping the Globe* or *Cantering the Country* first.

Trail Guide to U.S. Geography
Grades 2 - 12

"The *Trail Guide to U.S. Geography* provides lots of guidance while allowing for (and encouraging) flexibility and this is just the balance most homeschool moms need! The manual is easy to navigate and I am very impressed with how thoroughly material is covered. This resource is destined to be a favorite with homeschool families for years to come!"
–Cindy Prechtel, homeschoolingfromtheheart.com
Paperback, 144 pages, $18.95

Trail Guide to World Geography
Grades 2 - 12

"We have the *Trail Guide to World Geography* and **love** it!! We are using it again this year just for the questions... I will never sell this guide!! I am looking forward to doing the U.S. one next year."
–Shannon, OK
Paperback, 128 pages, $18.95

Trail Guide to Bible Geography
Grades 2 - 12

"Here is another winner from Geography Matters! *Trail Guide to Bible Geography* is multi-faceted, user-friendly, and suited to a wide range of ages and abilities."
–Jean Hall, Eclectic Homeschool Association
Paperback, 128 pages, $18.95

Galloping the Globe
Grades K- 4
by Loreé Pettit and Dari Mullins

"If you've got kindergarten through fourth grade students, and are looking for unit study material for geography, hold on to your hat and get ready for *Galloping the Globe!* Loreé Pettit and Dari Mullins have written this great resource to introduce children to the continents and some of their countries. This book is designed to be completed in one to three years, depending on how much time you spend on each topic. And for each continent, there are suggestions and topics galore."
–Leslie Wyatt, www.homeschoolenrichment.com

Organized by continent, incorporates student notebooking, and covers these topics:

• Basic Geography	• History and Biographies	• Literature	• Science
• Bible	• Activities	• Internet Sources	• Language Arts

Paperback, 236 pages, $24.95

Cantering the Country
Grades 1–5
by Loreé Pettit and Dari Mullins

Saddle up your horses and strap on your thinking caps. Learning geography is an adventure. From the authors who brought you *Galloping the Globe,* you'll love its U.S. counterpart, *Cantering the Country.* This unit study teaches a wide range of academic and spiritual disciplines using the geography of the U.S. as a starting point. With this course, you won't have to put aside one subject to make time for another. They're all connected! This comprehensive unit study takes up to three years to complete and includes all subjects except math and spelling. Incorporates student notebooking and covers these topics:

• U.S. Geography	• Character	• Science	• Language Arts
• Activities	• Literature	• Civics	• History and Biographies
• Internet Sources	• Bible		

In addition to the 250+ page book, you will receive a CD-ROM packed full of reproducible outline maps and activities. Dust off your atlas and get ready to explore America! Paperback, 254 pages, $39.95

The Ultimate Geography and Timeline Guide

by Maggie Hogan and Cindy Wiggers

Grades K - 12

Learn how to construct timelines, establish student notebooks, teach geography through literature, and integrate science with activities on volcanoes, archaeology, and other subjects. Use the complete multi-level geography course for middle and high school students. Includes timeline figures, reproducible outline maps, and many more reproducible pages. Use for all students kindergarden through high school. Paperback, 353 pages, $34.95

- 18 Reproducible Outline Maps
- Teaching Tips
- Planning Charts
- Over 150 Reproducible Pages
- Over 300 Timeline Figures
- Lesson Plans
- Scope and Sequence
- Flash Cards
- Games

Mark-It Timeline of History

There's hardly no better way to keep history in perspective than creating a timeline in tandem with your history studies. This poster is just the tool to do so. Write or draw images of events as they are studied, or attach timeline figures to aid student understanding and comprehension of the topic at hand. 23" x 34". Laminated, $10.95, Paper (folded), $5.95

Timeline Figures on CD-ROM

Kids love the look of their timelines when they add color and variety. Students can draw on their timeline, write events and dates, and add timeline figures. We've created two different sets of color timeline figures that are ready to print from any computer. There are over 350 figures in each set plus templates to create your own. Our figures are appealing in style, simple to use, and include color-coding and icons to aid memory. Available with biblical events and general world events.

Historical Timeline Figures CD-ROM

Includes **bonus** "Who Am I?" game cards. Select from 2 sets of figures, one with borders and one without - both included on this disk. Figures from c. 3800 b.c. - 2001, CD-ROM (Mac & Windows Compatible), $24.95

Bible Timeline Figures CD-ROM

Includes figures for all major Bible events and characters, plus a bonus section of story-line figures that encourage youngsters to retell Bible stories in their own words. CD-ROM (Mac & Windows Compatible), $24.95

Adventures of Munford

by Jamie Aramini, illustrated by Bob Drost

Join Munford the water molecule on his adventures through time and experience real historical events through his eyes. Titles available at the time of this printing (with more to come) include: *Munford Meets Lewis and Clark, Munford at the Klondike Gold Rush, Munford at the Birth of Independence*. For kids of all ages, reading level: grades 3 and up. Paperback, 170 pages, $8.95

Eat Your Way Through the USA

by Loreé Pettit

Taste your way around the U.S.A. without leaving your own dining room table! Each state has its unique geographical features, culinary specialities, and agricultural products. These influence both the ingredients that go into a recipe and the way food is prepared. Compliment your geography lesson and tantalize your tastebuds at the same time with this outstanding cookbook.

This cookbook includes a full meal of easy to follow recipes from each state. Recipes are easy to follow. Though they aren't written at a child's level, it's easy to include your students in the preparation of these dishes. Cooking together provides life skills and is a source of bonding and pride. More than just a cookbook, it is a taste buds-on approach to geography. Spiral bound, 118 pages, $14.95

Eat Your Way Around the World

by Jamie Aramini

Get out the sombrero for your Mexican fiesta! Chinese egg rolls... corn pancakes from Venezuela...fried plantains from Nigeria. All this, and more, is yours when you take your family on a whirlwind tour of over thirty countries in this unique international cookbook. Includes a full meal of recipes from each country. Recipes are easy to follow, and ingredients are readily available. Jam-packed with delicious dinners, divine drinks, and delectable desserts, this book is sure to please.

The entire family will be fascinated with tidbits of culture provided for each country including: Etiquette hints, Food Profiles, and Culture a la Carté. For more zest, add an activity and violà, create a memorable learning experience that will last for years to come. Some activities include: Food Journal, Passport, and World Travel Night. Spiral bound, 120 pages, $14.95

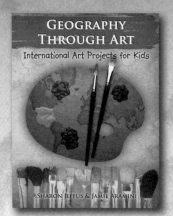

Geography Through Art
by Sharon Jeffus and Jamie Aramini

Geography Through Art is the ultimate book of international art projects. Join your children on an artistic journey to more than twenty-five countries spanning six continents (includes over a dozen United States projects). Previously published by Visual Manna as *Teaching Geography Through Art*, Geography Matters has added a number of enhancements and practical changes to this fascinating art book. Use this book as an exciting way to supplement any study of geography, history, or social studies. You'll find yourself reaching for this indispensable guide again and again to delight and engage students in learning about geography through the culture and art of peoples around the world. Paperback, 190 pages, $19.95

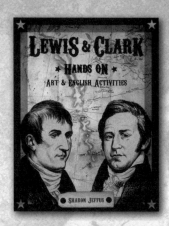

Lewis & Clark - Hands On
Art and English Activities

by Sharon Jeffus

Follow the experiences of Meriwether Lewis and William Clark with hands on art and writing projects associated with journal entries made during the Corps of Discovery Expedition. Ideal for adding interest to any Lewis and Clark study or to teach drawing and journaling. Includes profiles of American artists, step by step drawing instructions, actual journal entries, and background information about this famous adventure. Paperback, 80 pages, $12.95

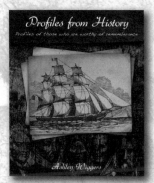

Profiles from History
by Ashley (Strayer) Wiggers

When studying history, a human connection is the most important connection that we can make. In *Profiles from History*, your student will not only learn about twenty famous people – but also why each one is worthy of remembrance. Everyone knows that Benjamin Franklin was a great inventor, but how many realize he was also a great man? He valued helping people more than making money or becoming famous. He refused to patent his popular Franklin stove, so more families could keep their homes warm during the cold, winter months. *Profiles from History* tells stories like this one, stories of greatness and inspiration. Each profile includes fun activities such as crosswords, word search, & timeline usage. Paperback, $14.95

- Reproducible Outline Maps -

Reproducible outline maps have a myriad of uses in the home, school, and office. Uncle Josh's quality digital maps provide opportunities for creative learning at all ages. His maps feature rivers and grid lines where possible, and countries are shown in context with their surroundings. (No map of Germany "floating" in the center of the page, here!) When students use outline maps and see the places they are studying in context they gain a deeper understanding of the subject at hand.

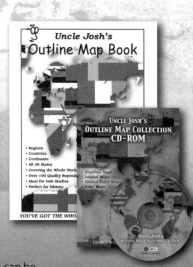

Uncle Josh's Outline Map Book

Take advantage of those spontaneous teaching moments when you have this set of outline maps handy. They are:

- Over 100 reproducible maps
- 15 world regions
- Continents with and without borders
- 25 countries
- Each of the 50 United States
- 8 U.S. regions

Useful for all grades and topics, this is by far one of the best book of reproducible outline maps you'll find. Paperback, 128 pages, $19.95

Uncle Josh's Outline Map Collection CD-ROM

In addition to all maps in *Uncle Josh's Outline Map Book* the CD-Rom includes color, shaded-relief, and labeled maps. Over 260 printable maps plus bonus activities. CD-ROM (Mac & Windows), $26.95

- Large-scale Maps -

Large-scale maps are great for detail labeling and for family or classroom use. Laminated Mark-It maps can be reused for a variety of lessons. Quality digital map art is used for each of the fifteen map titles published and laminated by Geography Matters. Choose from large scale continents, regions, United States, and world maps. US and World available in both outline version and with state, country, and capitals labeled. Ask about our ever expanding library of full, color shaded-relief maps. Paper and laminated, each title available separately or in discounted sets.

Trail Guide to Learning Series
Paths of Exploration
A Complete Curriculum
by Debbie Strayer and Linda Fowler

Volume 1   Volume 2

Optional Resources

Student Notebook Pages
Printing the student notebook pages from the Student Resources CD-ROM included in the curriculum is easy enough, but many folks requested we have them already printed and ready-to-use. Each set includes all notebook pages for that level and volume, three hole-punched for placing in a 3-ring binder. (The games on the CD are not included but are available separately below.)

Volume 1, third grade $32.00
Volume 2, third grade $32.00
Volume 1, fourth grade $32.00
Volume 2, fourth grade $32.00
Volume 1, fifth grade $32.00
Volume 2, fifth grade $32.00

Games
Although these games are in the textbook and Student Notebook Resources CD, this package saves you the time and preparation of printing or cutting out of the book. Includes instructions, game boards, and game cards used in both volumes of *Paths of Exploration*. Printed on cardstock for durability, 48 cards, 8.5 x 11, $12.95.

Optional Support Materials Available on CD-ROM

Assessments
Coupled with daily observations and interactive discussions and games this disk provides ample material upon which to base an accurate evaluation of student progress. Answer keys included, $24.95.

Light for the Trail Bible Study Supplement
Optional Bible study curriculum that coincides with the six units in *Paths of Exploration*. Easy-to-use guide provides daily assignments and helps students make the most important connection of all - the one between their faith and their view of the world around them, $12.95.

Required Resources

Volume 1
Meet Christopher Columbus, by James T. de Kay $4.99
Christopher Columbus, by Bennie Rhodes $7.99
Stories of the Pilgrims, by Margaret Pumphrey (2nd Ed., Christian Liberty Press) .. $8.95
Stories of the Pilgrims Answer Key $2.00
Squanto, Friend to the Pilgrims, by Clyde Robert Bulla $5.99
A Lion to Guard Us, by Clyde Robert Bulla $4.99
Surviving Jamestown, by Gail Karwoski $8.95
Profiles from History, by Ashley Strayer Wiggers $14.95
Handbook of Nature Study, by Anna Comstock $26.00
North American Wildlife Guide, published by Reader's Digest $29.95
Eat Your Way Around the World, by Jamie Aramini $14.95
Intermediate World Atlas, published by Rand Mc Nally $6.95
5" RealEarth® GlobeMap™ $3.95
*Large-Scale U.S. & World Outline Maps by Geography Matters $4.95

* denotes books used throughout the year in both Volumes 1 and 2

Volume 2
Daniel Boone, Frontiersman, by Janet and Geoff Benge $8.99
Daniel Boone, Young Hunter & Tracker, by Augusta Stevenson $5.99
Munford Meets Lewis and Clark, by Jamie Aramini $7.99
Seaman, by Gail Karwoski $8.95
Trouble for Lucy, by Carla Stevens $5.95
Johnny Appleseed, by David Collins $7.99
1911 Boy Scout Handbook, by Gail Karwoski $10.95
United States History Atlas, by Gail Karwoski $10.50
Lewis & Clark Hands On, by Sharon Jeffus (©2009) $12.95
Going West! a Kaleidoscope Kids book $12.95

Check the website or call for complete package specials.

www.geomatters.com/learning_series   •   800-426-4650

Geography Matters

- Order Form -

Title	Price	Qty	Total
1911 Boy Scout Handbook	10.95		
5" RealEarth® GlobeMap™	3.95		
A Lion to Guard Us	4.99		
Christopher Columbus	7.99		
Daniel Boone, Frontiersman	8.99		
Daniel Boone, Young Hunter & Tracker	5.99		
Eat Your Way Around the World	14.95		
Going West!	12.95		
Handbook of Nature Study	26.00		
Intermediate World Atlas	6.95		
Johnny Appleseed	7.99		
Large-Scale USA & World Outline Map	4.95		
Lewis & Clark Hands On	12.95		
Meet Christopher Columbus	4.99		
Munford Meets Lewis and Clark	8.95		
North American Wildlife Guide	29.95		
Profiles from History	16.95		
Seaman	8.95		

Title	Price	Qty	Total
Squanto, Friend to the Pilgrims	5.99		
Stories of the Pilgrims	8.95		
Stories of the Pilgrims Answer Key	2.00		
Surviving Jamestown	8.95		
Trouble for Lucy	5.95		
United States History Atlas	10.50		
3rd Grade Student Notebook Volume 1	32.00		
3rd Grade Student Notebook Volume 2	32.00		
4th Grade Student Notebook Volume 1	32.00		
4th Grade Student Notebook Volume 2	32.00		
5th Grade Student Notebook Volume 1	32.00		
5th Grade Student Notebook Volume 2	32.00		
Paths of Exploration: Assessments	24.95		
Paths of Exploration: Light for the Trail	12.95		
Paths of Exploration: Game Cards	12.95		

Subtotal _____

S & H (12% of Subtotal $6 min) _____

Tax: KY residents add 6% _____

Total _____

Mail Order With Payment to:

Geography Matters
P.O. Box 92
Nancy, KY 42544

Ship To:

_____
Name

_____
Address

_____
City/State/Zip

_____
Phone

_____
Email

Payment Info:

Visa ❑   MasterCard ❑   Discover ❑   Check ❑
Payment Type (Check One)

—   —   —

Card Number

/
Expiration Date   Security Code #

_____
Signature

All prices and availability are subject to change. Call or check online for current information.

800-426-4650   **orders@geomatters.com**   **www.geomatters.com**

About the Authors

Debbie Strayer

Debbie Strayer earned her bacherlor's and master's degrees in education and has many years of experience as an educator, consultant, and student evaluator. She is the former editor and co-founder of *Homeschooling Today* magazine, the author of *Gaining Confidence to Teach*, the editor of *The Homeschool Answer Book* by her mentor, Dr. Ruth Beechick, and co-author of the *Learning Language Arts Through Literature* series.

Debbie feels that her most important accomplishments are that she has been the wife of Greg Strayer for over 30 years, the mother of homeschool graduates Nate and Ashley, and a homeschooling parent for 16 years. She speaks and writes about homeschooling topics with humor, honesty, and encouragement.

Linda Fowler

Linda received a BA degree in Visual Communications from the University of South Florida, where she also met her husband, Colclough. She subsequently spent 17 years homeschooling their four children, from 1st through 12th grades, and developing an unshakeable appreciation for the power of encouragement. The Fowlers reside in Tampa, Florida.